# Shakespeare *on Film*

*Jack J. Jorgens*

# Shakespeare *on Film*

INDIANA UNIVERSITY PRESS

*Bloomington & London*

Library of Congress Cataloging in Publication Data
Jorgens, Jack J   1943–
Shakespeare on film.
Includes bibliographical references and index.
1. Shakespeare, William, 1564–1616—Film adaptations.   2. Moving
picture plays—History and criticism.   1. Title.
PR3093.J6   791.43'7   76–12365
ISBN 0–253–35196–0   1 2 3 4 5 81 80 79 78 77

*For / Elise, Catherine, & Elisabeth*

# Contents

PREFACE / *ix*

ACKNOWLEDGMENTS / *xii*

1 Realizing Shakespeare on Film     *1*

2 Max Reinhardt and William Dieterle's
    *A Midsummer Night's Dream*     *36*

3 Peter Hall's *A Midsummer Night's Dream*     *51*

4 Franco Zeffirelli's *Taming of the Shrew*     *66*

5 Franco Zeffirelli's *Romeo and Juliet*     *79*

6 Joseph Mankiewicz's *Julius Caesar*     *92*

7 Orson Welles's *Chimes at Midnight (Falstaff)*     *106*

8 Laurence Olivier's *Henry V*     *122*

9 Laurence Olivier's *Richard III*     *136*

10 Defining *Macbeth:* George Schaefer, Orson Welles,
    Akira Kurosawa     *148*

11 Roman Polanski's *Macbeth*     *161*

12 Orson Welles's *Othello*     *175*

13 Stuart Burge and John Dexter's *Othello*     *191*

14 Laurence Olivier's *Hamlet*     *218*

15 Grigori Kozintsev's *Hamlet*     *207*

16 *King Lear:* Peter Brook and Grigori Kozintsev     *235*

APPENDIX: Credits and Outlines of the Major Films / *252*

NOTES / *312*

INDEX / *332*

# *Preface*

THIS BOOK IS A MARRIAGE OF TWO PERSONAL LOVES DIS-
guised as professional interests: Shakespeare and film. My aims are to
illuminate Shakespeare's plays by looking at various visions and re-
visions, translations and adaptations of them, and to help us understand
and properly value cinematic works which have not received the critical
attention they deserve. This is an interpretative work, not a history of
Shakespeare films. (That enterprise has been begun by Robert Hamilton
Ball in his thoroughly documented chronological survey *Shakespeare
on Silent Film*.) Without apology, it focusses upon what is good or interesting in these films. We do not go to the concert hall to listen for
errors, bronchial spectators, or the sound of traffic outside, and we
should not come to Shakespeare films to demand impossible perfections
and "definitive" interpretations or to be clever at what is done badly.
If the word did not conjure up visions of mindless adulation, I would
call this study an "appreciation."

Many have written of the *problems* of rendering Shakespeare on film,
but few of the *possibilities*. After examining some of the prides and
prejudices, assumptions and categories which have made it difficult for
students of literature, theatre, and the cinema to think well about plays
on film, chapter 1 illustrates from a wide range of Shakespeare films
some of the many cinematic (which includes "theatrical") means of
expressing Shakespeare's characters, settings, themes, structures, and
verbal and dramatic styles. In addition to providing students of literature
with some background in the complex vocabulary of film (a good

introduction to film, such as Louis Gianetti's *Understanding Movies*, would make useful supplementary reading), it argues for a distinction between the merely "filmic" and the "cinematic," for a more sophisticated view of "imagery," and for the idea of "significant style," which together constitute a plea for a more sophisticated view of plays on film and for pedagogical uses of them which go far beyond "audio-visual aids."

Despite the swelling list of publications on Shakespeare on film, there are still very few detailed analyses of even the major Shakespeare films. Chapters 2 through 16 therefore provide explorations of *A Midsummer Night's Dream* by Max Reinhardt and William Dieterle and by Peter Hall; *The Taming of the Shrew* and *Romeo and Juliet* by Franco Zeffirelli; *Julius Caesar* by Joseph Mankiewicz; *Chimes at Midnight* (*Falstaff*) by Orson Welles; *Henry V* and *Richard III* by Laurence Olivier; *Macbeth* by George Schaefer (interesting for comparison but hardly a major film), by Welles, by Akira Kurosawa (*Throne of Blood*), and by Roman Polanski; *Othello* by Welles and by Stuart Burge and John Dexter; *Hamlet* by Olivier and by Grigori Kozintsev; and *King Lear* by Peter Brook and by Kozintsev. The order follows the categories of comedy, history, and tragedy and seeks further to link the works of single filmmakers like Zeffirelli and Olivier or to provide vivid contrasts of style and interpretation.

I have not attempted to say everything there is to say about each film, nor have I adhered to a party line. Rather, I have tried to deal with each film in a way that will do justice to its strengths. The source of insight and power in Burge and Dexter's *Othello*, for instance, lies in the actors' performances rather than in the camera work. For Mankiewicz's *Julius Caesar* we shall look both at its strong performances and at unpublished portions of the script in order to consider important differences between the original conception and the finished film. Kozintsev's *Hamlet* is approached as a cinepoem, a masterful weaving together of themes and techniques, words and images. In Zeffirelli's *Shrew* we shall consider the importance of the festive opening in defining the meaning of the action; in Welles's *Macbeth*, *Othello*, and *Chimes*, the importance of setting to Shakespeare's characters and themes; in Olivier's *Henry V* the shifts in mode and style and the director's shaping of the text, and in *Richard III* the recurring pattern of aborted or perverted ritual. In Brook's *King Lear* and Olivier's *Hamlet* we shall place the films against the critical views which influenced but by no means explain them, and in Reinhardt and Dieterle's *Dream* against the play's stage history.

Rather than use publicity stills for illustrations, I have sacrificed some quality and used frame blow-ups (not, unfortunately, always from wide-screen prints). This permitted me to choose the right moment, and to suggest interpretative points which could not be argued as precisely in the text. To allow me to concentrate on analysis rather than description, to freshen fading memories and permit detailed thought about the relations of the films to the original scripts, I have provided an appendix containing detailed descriptive outlines of the major films. Each film scene is preceded by the number of the corresponding play scene so that one may see the overall shaping at a glance. A full bibliography proved to be unwieldy and will be provided separately as part of *Shakespeare on Stage and Screen: An Annotated Bibliography* to be published by Indiana University Press. In the meantime, the notes will serve as a guide to the more important reviews and scholarship.

Writing a book is a humbling experience. I have had to leave out some interesting minor films. I have found it exceedingly difficult to deal with verbal performance, film music, and a number of other important elements of the Shakespeare film. I have used one still where I really wanted ten. Nevertheless, it is a beginning. I believe these essays at least underscore the tremendous variety of Shakespeare films, offer some fresh insights into the more important adaptations, and suggest critical contexts which bring these and other plays on film to life. If they have done that much, they will have served their purpose.

# ACKNOWLEDGMENTS

One acquires scholarly debts almost as rapidly as financial ones in the study of Shakespeare films. I hope I have not failed to make clear in the footnotes how much I have learned from the writings of fellow critics, even when disagreeing with them. But even my more specific debts are many. Thanks are extended to the helpful staffs of the branch of the New York Public Library at Lincoln Center, the Folger Shakespeare Library, the Harvard Theatre Collection, and the British Film Institute, to the Department of English and the Research Council of the University of Massachusetts at Amherst for released time and summer grants, and to various enlightened distributors who permitted me access to the films—Peppercorn-Wormser, Rank, Contemporary Films, United Artists, Walter Reade, Janus, Audio-Brandon/Macmillan, and Films Incorporated. Illustrations from Kozintsev's *King Lear* have been provided through the courtesy of the Rosa Madell Film Library. Excerpts from the script of Joseph Mankiewicz's *Julius Caesar* (© 1953, Loew's Incorporated) are gratefully acknowledged. Thanks are also given to the editors of *Literature/Film Quarterly*, *Shakespeare Newsletter*, and the collection *Focus on Orson Welles* (Prentice Hall) for permission to include materials which first appeared in their pages.

Among individuals, I thank several fine Shakespeare teachers, Owen Jenkins, George Soule, Edward Quinn, and Leonard F. Dean, many students who mulled over the subject with me at the University of Massachusetts and at Clark University, and Ron Gottesman, who encouraged the book. It was a great help to have colleagues like Kenneth Rothwell, Lillian Wilds, Michael Mullin, and others at the MLA Shakespeare on Film Seminar to exchange ideas with, and to have friends who were willing to act as unofficial tutors in film or to wade through preliminary drafts—Charles Eidsvik, John Harrington, Austin Quigley, and Herb Weil. Many thanks to Jules Trammel, who extracted images from very difficult negatives. I had hoped to boast that my wife Elise did not share in the drudgery of typing, proofing, and indexing, but in this and in other ways she was always there when I needed her most.

xii

# Shakespeare *on Film*

# Realizing Shakespeare on Film

FIRST CAME SCORES OF SILENT SHAKESPEARE FILMS, ONE- AND two-reelers struggling to render great poetic drama in dumb show.[1] Mercifully, most of them are lost, for those which survive are for the most part inadequate performances of Shakespeare and pale examples of film art. Sound arrived, and with it came Hollywood's first attempts: Sam Taylor's *Taming of the Shrew* (1929), with a bravura performance by Douglas Fairbanks; Max Reinhardt and William Dieterle's sparkling, extravagant blend of ballet, farce, Mendelssohn, and visual splendor, *A Midsummer Night's Dream* (1935); and Irving Thalberg and George Cukor's pallid, cautious *Romeo and Juliet* (1936), starring far from youthful Leslie Howard and Norma Shearer. Our scene then shifts to England with Paul Czinner's charming, decorative, overly mild *As You Like It* (1936), with a young velvet-voiced, curly-haired Olivier as Orlando and coy Elizabeth Bergner as Rosalind; then came Olivier's stylistically layered, glorious hymn to England, *Henry V* (1945), followed by a lyrical, subjective *Hamlet* (1948), with a fluid camera, dreamlike castle, oedipally crippled blonde Prince, and playing-card court.

Next in this strange eventful history comes the full flowering, international in scope, involving fine directors and actors, and ranging widely in interpretation and style: Orson Welles's primitive, expressionist *Macbeth* (1948) and his fragmented, modernist *Othello* (1952); Joseph Mankiewicz and John Houseman's stark, powerful *Julius Caesar* (1953); Renato Castellani's beautiful but indifferently acted *Romeo and Juliet*

(1954), which proved color and tragedy are not incompatible; and Olivier's jewel of a *Richard III* (1955), with its bold addresses to the camera and its delightful supporting performances of characters through whom Richard sweeps like a scythe. From Russia in the same year came Sergei Yutkevich's operatic, Verdiesque *Othello* and Yan Fried's painterly, mellow *Twelfth Night*. In 1957 from Japan came Akira Kurosawa's fine samurai *Macbeth, Throne of Blood*, which shows a warrior trapped between a labyrinthine wood and a cool, geometrical fortress.

The next decade saw, in addition to scores of TV productions and student and educational films, George Schaefer's *Macbeth* (1960), with Maurice Evans and Judith Anderson, Franz Wirth's *Hamlet* (1960), with Maximilian Schell, Grigori Kozintsev's two great epic films, *Hamlet* (1964) and *King Lear* (1970), Franco Zeffirelli's boisterous, colorful, and enormously popular *Taming of the Shrew* (1966), with Richard Burton and Elizabeth Taylor, and his *Romeo and Juliet* (1968). We saw film records of stage performances: Stuart Burge and John Dexter's *Othello* (1965), with Olivier; Frank Dunlop's *Winter's Tale* (1966), with Laurence Harvey; and Tony Richardson's claustrophobic *Hamlet* (1969), with Nicoll Williamson. And, bringing us closer to the present, in addition to rather uninspired films of *Julius Caesar* (1969) and *Antony and Cleopatra* (1972) by Stuart Burge and Charlton Heston respectively, and some really interesting TV productions such as Joseph Papp's roaring twenties *Much Ado About Nothing* and the Royal Shakespeare Company's *Antony and Cleopatra*, we have seen more ambitious undertakings: Peter Hall's avant-garde flavored *Midsummer Night's Dream* (1968), Welles's wintery, tragic *Chimes at Midnight* (*Falstaff*) (1966), Peter Brook's dark, brutal *King Lear* (1970), and Roman Polanski's bloody, cynical *Macbeth* (1971).[2]

It is an impressive list, and it will continue to grow. Students of Shakespeare may tremble with fear, anticipating a wave of homogenized mindless, commercially oriented wide-screen, star-ridden spectacles. They may shrink at bland, trendy, studio-bound TV versions restructured for station breaks and denuded of their poetry to suit the medium's supposed allergy to length, rhetoric, and lyricism.[3] Or they may look on the bright side, noting that sensitive cameras and microphones and multiple prints allow us to see and hear performances better and more often, that large budgets make possible better casts and quests for perfection seldom found in live theatre. They may take heart since films perhaps "offer the best possibility of rediscovering Shakespeare's popularity, in the best sense of that word.[4] In a more utopian mood, possibly "the psychic energy created by a superb movie version of a classic play is greater (quantitatively and qualitatively) than can usually be achieved by modern stage versions of the plays."[5]

Whatever their views, it is certain that millions of people each year will experience Shakespeare on the screen, and it will become increasingly impossible for teachers and critics to ignore these productions, as all too many have done up until now. We are more than due for a fresh look at the problems and the possibilities of realizing good plays on the screen. We need to reexamine the prides and prejudices which have driven critics and theorists of literature, theatre, and film to paint themselves into opposite corners of the same room. And we need sensitive, detailed analyses of individual adaptations which are truly interdisciplinary in their approach.

Students of Shakespeare's plays as literature, for example, might consider that the plays were conceived and written for performance, that the script is not the work, but the *score* for the work. In our very proper concern for character, structure, theme, and style, can we afford to ignore how

a play reveals itself in rehearsal: verbal ambiguities, emphases, hesitation; the forcefulness of a silent figure; the dispersal of an audience's interest, or the relaxation of tension, due to the time taken for a song, or for a corpse to be laid in the ground; a sharpness or irrelevancy in the writing which tends toward humor.[6]

As difficult as it is to deal with a play filtered through the sensibilities of directors, actors, and designers (so difficult that scholars have left the task largely to reviewers), we cannot rest easy with a view of the plays which gives complete emphasis to the word and denies the essentially collaborative nature of the drama. We cannot merely fall back on the authority of Aristotle, who said of tragedy: "the Spectacle, though an attraction, is the least artistic of all the parts, and has least to do with the art of poetry."[7]

Like live performances, a film can help us focus not only on what is said, but on how, why, and to whom, it is said. It can help to expand the term *imagery* to include much more than verbal imagery, since "the poetic image in a play is set in a context not of words alone, but of words, dramatic situation, interplay of character, stage-effect, and is also placed in a time-sequence."[8] James Agee struck the proper balance in arguing that Shakespeare was both great poet and great playwright.

> If Shakespeare had been no more gifted with words than, say, I am, the depth and liveliness of his interest in people and predicaments, and his incredible hardness, practicality, and resource as a craftsman and maker of moods, rhythms, and points, could still have made him almost his actual equal as a playwright.[9]

If criticism can ever hope to encompass Shakespeare's art, it must do so by recognizing that a play is not a thing, but a complex process incorporating the verbal and the nonverbal. Very different incarnations of a work on stage or screen may be equally "true" and help to spring us loose from a singleness of vision so that we can see other possibilities, other dimensions.

Students of Shakespeare's plays as theatre would do well to contemplate the many similarities between theatre and film, two greedy art forms constantly devouring their neighbors: fiction, poetry, dance, music, painting, sculpture, architecture. Despite some fundamental differences, the expressive languages of these arts are very much alike. James Clay and Daniel Krempel show rare wisdom among theatre critics in arguing that drama on film cannot be ignored.

> As directors and designers who have worked in both media can testify, though the required techniques may vary radically, many of the artistic problems are identical in principle. This is particularly true in the area of main concern, the interpretation of dramatic meaning. In fact it is possible to speak of interpretative ideas which would apply equally well whether the production were being conceived for the camera or a live audience.[10]

Should Susan Sontag, Stanley Kauffmann, John Simon, and a few others be so rare among writers who move easily between theatre and film? In both arts, the problems are the same: how to write with precision about performance as interpretation, the shaping of conflict, integration of verbal and visual bits of information, superimposed patterns, shifting levels of stylization and gradations of emphasis; how to read the complex ideas and emotions embedded in textures, colors, rhythms, movements, and sounds as well as in words. One suspects that the divisions between students of the stage and students of the cinema are due much more to habit, narrowly defined academic disciplines, fear, ignorance, and the timidity of people on both sides who prefer to remain among the established citizens of their rival republics of art where the streets are paved, the theoretical plumbing in, and the critical appliances work, than to essential differences between media/art forms.[11]

Students of Shakespeare films as films perhaps have the longest list of prejudices and false assumptions to overcome, despite the efforts of André Bazin, John Howard Lawson, Robert Gessner, Susan Sontag, and others.[12] It is time to ask whether the term *theatrical* ought to be used in film criticism as a synonym for the static, fake, or overblown. We ought to ask whether film history should be viewed as a narrow escape from the clammy clutches of the theatre—a steady progress from an outmoded art form—and whether it is really accurate to define screen naturalism "in terms of the medium's divorcement from the theatre."[13] Perhaps we should set aside the theory underlying much of the scorn of "canned theatre" and "talky movies"—we might call it the subtractive theory of film—according to which one arrives at the essence of an art by taking from it everything it shares with the other arts. (Peer Gynt peeled the onion until nothing was left.)

In light of many fine modern films, not merely Shakespeare films, the axioms of early critics and theorists ring false. "The film derives its principal strength from the realism of the photographic medium," we are told.[14] "Films cling to the surfaces of things. They seem to be the more cinematic, the less they focus directly on inward life, ideology, and spiritual concerns."[15] "The film being a presentational medium (except for its use of dialogue), cannot have direct access to the power of discursive forms" since it is "perceptual," not "conceptual."[16]

It is less narrow, and more accurate, however, to assume that "realism in the cinema is just one way of looking at life, one style among several."[17] Given the film artist's control over the sounds and images on the screen, his shaping, selecting, and ordering in front of and behind the camera, his control in the editing and the mixing, is it not clear that, like the painter in Henry James's "The Real Thing," he has "an innate preference for the represented object over the real one"?[18] The screenwriter Wolf Rilla is correct. Defining film in terms of film conventions—"realistic surfaces, emphasis on motion, dominance of the visual over the verbal, and unobtrusive, logical exposition and continuity—"is taking film at its most obvious and simplistic, and is therefore in a curious sense misleading."

There is no such thing as "the movies," no one essential quality common to all movies. . . . Some things, to be sure, come more easily to them than others—action, comedy, and spectacle more easily than analysis, tragedy, and verbal theme. Nevertheless, the argument that good cinema can be produced by doing only what comes naturally with the camera makes a neat deduction but a poor observation. As the Modern novel illustrates—in its case a descriptive, temporal genre gets sharply wrenched in order to render an essential, atemporal reality—the most exciting artistic achievements may be generated from a tension between the medium and a view of things unnatural for it.[19]

Shakespeare films are interesting as films because they stretch the capabilities and challenge the inhibitions of the art. They suggest that "symptomatic dialogue" is not the only effective kind, that "verbal poetry is an essential aspect of cinematic expression, and . . . the present lack of poetry in film impoverishes and depletes the art."[20] They provide actors with complex, challenging roles of the kind that, according to their own testimony, they seldom get in other films. The best of these films suggest that it is possible to have good film acting, which is not only "behaving" but "behaving plus interpretation."[21] By undermining established notions of what is "intrinsically filmic" (do we talk about what is "intrinsically literary"?), Shakespeare films help us to see the truly liberating implications of Bazin's assertion that

there is a hundred times more cinema, and better cinema at that, in one fixed shot in [Wyler's] *The Little Foxes* or [Welles's] *Macbeth* than in all the natural settings, in all the geographical exoticism, in all the shots of the reverse side of the set, by means of which up to now the screen has ingeniously attempted to make us forget the stage. Far from being a sign of decadence, the mastering of the theatrical repertoire by the cinema is on the contrary a proof of maturity. In short, to adapt is no longer to betray but to respect.[22]

In order to fully understand and appreciate good Shakespeare films, we need the vocabularies of all three disciplines—literature, theatre, and film. We need the flexibility of a literary critic like John Russell Brown who is willing to transcend the boundaries of his discipline when they threaten to inhibit understanding, the breadth and freshness of vision of Susan Sontag as she sweeps the cobwebs from thought about theatre and film, and the broad background and lack of snobbery of Eisenstein in *Film Form* and *The Film Sense*. We need the

6

optimism to assume that the difficulty modern audiences have in under-standing articulate, condensed expression on the screen has much more to do with lack of education and thousands of hours of aural and visual pablum on the screen than to "the nature of the medium." And we require the patience to study films as we do books and live per-formances. The result, I believe, will be that we will discover that film is no enemy to Shakespeare, and Shakespeare no enemy to film.

## MODES AND STYLES

Critics often sort out Shakespeare films by measuring their relative distance from the language and conventions of the theatre.[23] The theatrical mode uses film as a transparent medium which "can encapsulate any of the performing arts and render it in a film tran-scription."[24] It has the look and feel of a performance worked out for

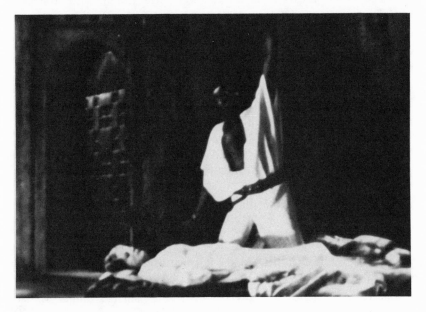

Theatrical (Burge-Dexter *Othello*)

a static theatrical space and a live audience. Lengthy takes in medium or long shot stress the durational quality of time, and, the frame acting as a kind of portable proscenium arch, meaning is generated largely through the words and gestures of the actors. Style in this mode de-

7

rives primarily from the style of the performances, which are usually of a distinctly theatrical cast—more demonstrative, articulate, and continuous than actors are usually permitted in films. But it also derives from the manner of staging, varying from "Elizabethan" in parts of Olivier's *Henry V*, to ninteeth century proscenium in Burge and Dexter's *Othello*, to modern thrust stage in Dunlop's *Winter's Tale*, to Wirth's constructionist/modernist *Hamlet*, to Gielgud's "rehearsal" *Hamlet* on a Broadway stage stripped of scenery, to the cavernous dark spaces of Richardson's Roundhouse *Hamlet*.

The great strength of the theatrical mode is that because the performance is conceived in terms of the theatre the text need not be heavily cut or rearranged. Shakespeare's tremendous range of verbal and dramatic styles from stark naturalism to metatheatrical playfulness need not be narrowed in the name of film convention and decorum. (It is the blatant *theatricality* of Olivier's *Hamlet* which permits him to instruct the players from off-camera in the simultaneous roles of film director, Prince of Denmark, and surrogate for Shakespeare, and allows us to enjoy the irony that the performances in "The Murder of Gonzago" prove they weren't listening.) Its great weaknesses are that superficially it seems to be cheap and easy to capture the essence of a theatrical performance on film (in fact it is very time-consuming and difficult, for like anything else a great performance must be powerfully *seen* to be effective on film). On the screen as on the stage,

> the Deadly Theatre takes easily to Shakespeare. We see his plays done by good actors in what seems like the proper way—they look lively and colourful, there is music and everyone is all dressed up, just as they are supposed to be in the best classical theatres. Yet secretly we find it excruciatingly boring—and in our hearts we either blame Shakespeare, or theatre as such, or even ourselves.[25]

Most films in the theatrical mode fail because they were never good theatre in the first place.

The realistic mode takes advantage of "the camera's unique ability to show us *things*—great, sweeping landscapes or the corner of a friar's cell, a teeming market-place or the intimacy of a boudoir, all in the flash of a moment."[26] This is the most popular kind of Shakespeare film, not merely because filmmakers are most familiar with it and mass audiences enjoy the spectacle of historical recreations, but because everyone senses that at bottom Shakespeare is a realist. If realism in film implies something more than a visual style or authentic costumes and settings, it seems to many that this playwright—who filled his Globe with duels, battles, shipwrecks, tortures, assassinations, storms, coronations, trials, suicides, feasts, and funerals, who juxtaposed the ugly with the sublime, the base with the noble, everyday with holiday, who ruthlessly explored both the need for and the dangers of centralized power, the conflicts of young and old, the rocking of order and tradition by frightening, invigorating forces of change—virtually demands screen realism. The kind may be left up to the filmmaker. It may be Zeffirelli's decorative, spectacular, orchestrally accompanied variety, which is a descendant of the elaborate productions of the nineteenth century, or the harsh documentary style of Brook's *Lear*, or a mixed style, as in Polanski's gory, twilight *Macbeth*, the fortress and tangled forest of Kurosawa's *Throne of Blood*, or the silences and wintery empty spaces of Welles's *Chimes at Midnight*.

Realist (Zeffirelli *Taming of the Shrew*)

One weakness of this mode is that since for many "the poetic drama does not thrive on photographic realism . . . [which] has the effect of making the poetry sound unnatural and self-conscious,"[27] Shakespeare's poetic and rhetorical patterning, overtly formal structures, and

9

emblematic scenes and objects must be disguised or cut. A playwright who juxtaposes several levels of illusion and creates highly subjective dramatic worlds often finds realist collaborators who can deal with but one level of illusion and do not always succeed in avoiding a neutral and unaffecting objectivity. Realistic settings are seldom suffused with emotions and ideas, with poetry, biography, and ideology as well as history. Their outer eloquence is not always matched by inner truth.

The second major weakness is that in shifting the emphasis from the actors to actors-in-a-setting, one risks loss of focus. In response to the declared quest for "authenticity" in Cukor and Thalberg's *Romeo and Juliet*, John Fuegi quite properly asks, "does the wealth of physical detail (the life of a great epoch) illuminate the story or does it weigh the story down under a mass of intrusive detail? Does Shakespeare in his 'pursuit of reality' actually seek to 'present life in all its fullness'?"[28] Details must be given the proper emphasis, be powerful and significant yet also subordinated to an overall design, lest they obscure what is important.

The filmic mode is the mode of the film poet, whose works bear the same relation to the surfaces of reality that poems do to ordinary conversation. A filmic rendering of Shakespeare, says Kozintsev,

> shifts the stress from the aural to the visual. The problem is not one of finding means to speak the verse in front of the camera, in realistic circumstances ranging from long-shot to close-up. The aural has to be made visual. The poetic texture itself has to be transformed into a visual poetry, into the dynamic organization of film imagery.[29]

Like the realist, the film poet uses many nontheatrical techniques—a great variety of angles and distances, camera movement. He substitutes for the classical style of playing *on* the lines, the modern style of playing *between* the lines.[30] But unlike the other modes, there is emphasis on the *artifice* of film, on the expressive possibilities of distorting the surfaces of reality. In Olivier's *Henry V* we find "the frank admixture of the real (e.g., horses and the sea) and the unreal (painted backdrops, frank acknowledgment of the presence of an audience, stylized gesture, overtly symbolic settings)." His films "avoid a simple equation of film and realism, . . . hover magnificently, as André Bazin has also observed, between 'things' and 'art,' the very area in which the plays themselves have their life and being."[31] In Welles's films we find strong graphic compositions; in Reinhardt and Dieterle's *Dream*, fluid, lyrical

Filmic (Welles *Othello*)

movements set to Mendelssohn's music; in Hall's *Dream*, abstract patterns of light and jump cuts. Each work uses antirealist techniques to express important aspects of the plays.

The great strength of the filmic mode is that it takes advantage of the film's power to tell a story "by overcoming the forms of the outer world, namely space, time, and causality, and by adjusting the events to the forms of the inner world, namely attention, memory, imagination, and emotion."[32] It acknowledges the importance of everything that is not literal in Shakespeare's plays by exploring through sounds and images what Stanislavsky called "subtext,"

> the manifest, the inwardly felt expression of a human being in a part which flows uninterruptedly beneath the words of the text, giving them life and a basis for existing . . . a web of innumerable varied inner patterns inside a play and a part . . . all sorts of figments of the imagination, inner movements, objects of attention, smaller and greater truths and a belief in them, adaptations, adjustments and other similar elements.[33]

Peter Brook has written,

> if you could extract the mental impression made by the Shakespearean strategy of images, you would get a piece of pop collage. . . .

The background that Shakespeare can conjure in one line evaporates in the next and new images take over. . . . The nonlocalized stage means that every single thing under the sun is possible, not only quick changes of location: a man can turn into twins, change sex, be his past, his present, his future, be a comic version of himself, and be none of them, *all at the same time*.[34]

To the extent that this is so, despite the dangers of dazzling technique for its own sake, wooden performances, and decimated texts, the filmic mode is truest to the effect of Shakespeare's dramatic verse.

Parallel but by no means congruent with the theatrical, realist, and filmic modes are three means of treatment which describe a film's relative distance from the original text—presentation, interpretation, and adaptation.[35] In a presentation, the artist attempts to convey the original with as little alteration and distortion as possible. At its worst, presentation represents a fatal misunderstanding of the collaborative nature of dramatic art and a failure of intelligence, feeling, and imagination. Here the artist substitutes for the living work a blend of stale, unemphatic run-through and unconsciously retailed cliches. He only manages to prove that it is possible for actors to speak every word of a Shakespeare play before an audience and be completely untrue to its spirit. On film, one thinks of the opening court scene in Hall's *Dream*, the scene in England between Malcolm and MacDuff in Welles's *Macbeth*, and scores of studio TV productions and pedagogical "Scenes from the Bard."

At its best, presentation is what John Russell Brown has called "free Shakespeare,"[36] where the work is allowed its archaic words, thoughts, and conventions, raw juxtapositions of formalism and realism, full length, contradictions, and welter of possible meanings. In tone and emphasis, the performance attempts to preserve the balances and tensions of the original while in an open, improvisatory, exploratory way seeking to rediscover its fluid, chaotic Elizabethan essence. Above all, good presentation avoids explaining, experiencing, and digesting the work for the audience—it is a realization of the play, not a set of footnotes to it or a critical essay upon it. Examples: the closet scene in Richardson's *Hamlet;* Brutus's and Cassius's quarrel in Mankiewicz's *Julius Caesar;* the King's wooing of Katherine in *Henry V;* and "Pyramus and Thisby" in Hall's *Dream.*

Interpretation entails shaping and performing a play according to a definite "view" of it. Proponents of interpretative directing note that "interpretation is inevitable. . . . The actor's figure, the way he enters the stage, the color of his hair, etc., everything perceived by the audience is interpretation whether it is so intended or not."[37] They argue that it is a fiction (though fictions may be useful) that theatre artists render a work without altering it, that performers, audiences, and critics can somehow escape the influence of the French Revolution, the Industrial Revolution, Freud, Darwin, Marx, and mass media. They ask whether it is desirable or even possible for a single performance of a dramatic work to realize *all* its possibilities. At its worst, interpretation in performance is like "modernizing" a noble work of architecture in Second-Rate Contemporary, or bringing "progress" to a lush tropical island. At its best, it involves imaginative collaborative creation, revelatory and powerful emphases which so enrich and illuminate the play that they challenge the stern admonition by Susan Sontag: "to interpret is to impoverish."[38]

Reductive interpretations on film are all too easily illustrated: Olivier's cutting of Henry's vicious threats before the gates of Harfleur, Reinhardt's excision of Titania's long description of death, disease, and disorder in his *Dream*, and Czinner's heavy censoring of Touchstone's earthy humor and Jaques's cynicism in his *As You Like It*. One thinks of speeches uprooted from their contexts and used as "explanatory" prologues (the Prince's "vicious mole of nature" speech in Olivier's *Hamlet*, and fawning Rosencrantz's proclamation to Claudius that "the cess of majesty/Dies not alone, but like a gulf doth draw/What's near with it" in Wirth's *Hamlet*), eccentric performances by actors, melodramatic scores, and bathetic interpolated scenes. Yet there is truth in Boris Pasternak's advice to Kozintsev, which locates the Shakespearean essence not in the poetry but in the characters and action:

> I always regard half of the text of any play, of even the most immortal and classic work of genius, as a diffused remark that the author wrote in order to acquaint the actors as thoroughly as possible with the heart of the action to be played. As soon as a theatre has penetrated his artistic intention, and mastered it, one can and should sacrifice the most vivid and profound lines (not to mention the pale and indifferent ones), provided that the actors have achieved an equally talented performance of an acted, mimed, silent, or laconic equivalent to these lines. . . .[39]

In *Hamlet* Kozintsev repeatedly demonstrates how a collaborator can be true to the original by altering it. When he divides Claudius's opening speech among a rough soldier reading it perfunctorily and threateningly to the peasants outside, smooth courtiers who mutter snatches of it to one another in several foreign languages, and finally Claudius himself to his councillors, he underscores the King's mixture of crass power, flamboyance, and sophisticated statesmanship. By removing the "words, words, words" between the wounding of Hamlet and "the rest is silence," he underscores Hamlet's transcendence of the mundane order, which is at least one of the major truths told in Shakespeare's conclusion. And on a larger scale, both Olivier's *Hamlet*, which incorporates the Freud/Jones oedipal interpretation, and Brook's *Lear*, which was shaped by Jan Kott's existential view, are true enough to important dimensions of the original and powerful enough in their own right to be valued alongside good presentations of the same works.

Frequently the interpretative process of conceptualizing, shaping, and reimaging shades off into adaptation in which, just as Plutarch and Holinshed served Shakespeare, Shakespeare's plays serve as source material for new but still related works of art. More than any other period since the Restoration, this is the period of Shakespeare recast in new forms: musicals, ballets, operas, political satires, avant-garde collages, animated films, dramatic films, plays, and everything else imaginable.[40] Many of these are so distant from the scope and intent of the originals, or so slight, that they do not merit critical attention. A few, however, which borrow elements directly from Shakespeare, alter others, and add still others, being as Welles put it "variations on his themes,"[41] are of very high quality indeed.

There are three critical frameworks which seem useful in dealing with such works as Kurosawa's *Throne of Blood* and Welles's *Chimes at Midnight:* source study, the study of translation, and comparative literature. In source study one peers over the shoulder of the artist and watches the way he works with his raw materials. The earlier work clarifies, enriches, and provides a lever for discussion of the later. We study a translation (and in a sense *all* Shakespeare films are translations) as a creative attempt to recast and reimage a work conceived in a different language and for a different culture. Any but the most mindless literal translation is part literal rendering, part figurative leap, and part record of the translator's own responses. ("Don't translate what I wrote," said Ezra Pound, "translate what I meant to write."[42]) Using a comparative approach, we place two works side by side so that they may mutually illuminate each other. Shared patterns, relations to tradition, and unique qualities stand out because of their treatments of similar situations, themes, characters, styles, and structures. With regard to Shakespeare films, it is accurate to say that the true test is "not whether the filmmaker has respected his model, but whether he has respected his own vision."[43] It is necessary to add further, however, that because the artist has chosen to work with Shakespeare and knows his audience will come to his new work with knowledge of the earlier one, there must be important points of contact between Shakespeare's vision and his own, some resonance when the two works are juxtaposed, lest adaptation become travesty.

Used sensibly, these categories are, as Algernon says in *The Importance of Being Earnest*, "quite as true as any observation in civilized life ought to be." But having gathered what honey we could from these abstract flowers, we should pause and consider their limitations. First, they are useful chiefly as descriptive and not as evaluative terms. "There can no more be a set of rules for principles for filming Shakespeare than there can be a set of rules or principles for staging him."[44] Reading through the criticism of Shakespeare films, one gets the uneasy feeling that a game has evolved in which works are automatically praised or blamed because they have been made in a particular style or mode. Critics crucify Welles's films for being atrocious presentations or overrate them because they are ostentatiously filmic. They contemptuously dismiss Burge and Dexter's *Othello* as "anti-cinematic" or praise it for being free of "film gimmicks." They rate Castellani's *Romeo and Juliet* above Olivier's *Hamlet* because it creates a more believable world. Zeffirelli is now despised for treating Shakespeare like a hack scriptwriter, now hailed for avoiding a dry, respectfully dull academic style. But granting that there will always be differences in taste and that we must not forego the obligation to judge, it still seems wise to avoid elevating our particular sensitivities to the status of universal laws. We ought to remain open to as many different kinds of excellence in Shakespeare films as possible.

Second, like many divisions favored by critics and theorists, these three conceal much more than they reveal, perpetuating as they do the largely artificial division between the disciplines of literature, theatre, and film. Good Shakespeare films often move fluidly between modes and styles, merge several simultaneously, so that it is not possible to make simple judgments.

Third, and most important, these categories do not penetrate very deeply into the process of re-creating Shakespeare on film, into the interrelations of style and meaning which lie at the heart of these visions and re-visions. For this we require different terms and a different approach.

## Shakespeare and Cinematic Expression: Words and Images

The remarkable density of Shakespeare's plays results from a blend of strong "horizontal" movements (good plots, developing characters) with powerful "vertical" moments (resonant images, penetrating meditations, complex poetic patterns).[45] Part of the filmmaker's task is to preserve the balance of the two. The first is relatively easy, for strong narrative movement has always been important in conventional films. The second is a complex and delicate matter, for Shakespeare's poetic images function in many ways. If they were simply word-painting intended to fill in the scenery which the Elizabethan stage lacked, the interpreter could deal with them like descriptive passages in novels. But Shakespearean images function in all sorts of ways: as embodiments of ideas and conflicts (the flash of light in *Romeo and Juliet*, animals in *King Lear*), as symbols for things unseen (disease in *Hamlet*), as renderings of emotional states (darkness and choking in *Macbeth*). Images may sum up the essence of the action (a body on the rack in *King Lear*), may bind together themes ("sun" and "son" in *Hamlet*, "crown" in *Richard III*), and may reflect character (Othello's images of glorious war, exotic places, sweeping landscapes; Iago's images of rutting animals, poison, webs, snares). Furthermore, the poetic images do not function independently of the theatrical images. They are all part of the same pattern. The shocking scene of the blinding of Gloucester and Kent's defiant "see better Lear" merge. When we say that Shakespeare, like a good filmmaker, *thought* in images, we mean not merely verbal images, but movements ("The weird sisters, hand in hand . . . Thus do go about, about"; Lady Macbeth walking in her sleep), gestures (Titania embracing Bottom the ass), and objects (a throne, a bed, a handkerchief).

It is often argued that "the literary greatness of Shakespeare's dialogue, and to an equivalent degree that of the dialogue of all the masters of dramatic literature from the Elizabethans to Shaw, is the obstacle to its success as film dialogue."[46] We are told that "the photographic images and the language inevitably neutralize each other."[47] But on the contrary, many Shakespeare films successfully imitate or find analogies for his unions of the verbal and the visual. The richest moments in these films often derive from the expressive possibilities of shifting relations between words and images. In rare instances, for example, the visual image may *be* the words when, as at the beginning of Olivier's *Hamlet,* the director wishes us to focus solely on the abstract meaning of a speech. When a director wishes the words to function alone, he may throw the images on the screen out of focus (Brook's *King Lear*), or make them so uninteresting that they "disappear" (Lysander's speech on "the course of true love" in Hall's *Dream*). The camera may play over the actor who registers, disguises, or plays against the ideas and emotions in the lines—the speeches being spoken openly (Olivier's stirring appeals to his men in *Henry V*) or rendered voice-over, emphasizing the isolation and disturbed nature of the hero (Welles's *Macbeth*). Then too the camera may show the impact of the words on other characters: Hamlet's face as the Player describes Pyrrus's sword sticking in the air, Claudius's response as Hamlet sardonically describes the progress of a king through the guts of a beggar.

Frequently the visual image will both show the speaker and in some way embody the form or content of the lines. A verbal figure may become visual. Oxymoron may leap to life in a shot of angry Capulet and Tybalt in the foreground and a pair of dancing lovers in the background. Hamlet's repetition "except my life, except my life, except my life" may be underlined by two sharply pointed arches and repeating arcades.[48] Helena's contrasting pair of lines "things base and vile, holding no quantity, / Love can transpose to form and dignity" may be wittily echoed when she appears from behind a bush, plucks off a leaf, turns her back, plucks another leaf, and disappears once more. Often there is some attempt at direct illustration as when Macbeth's bloody hand is stretched out by a wide-angle lens as he asks "will all great Neptune's ocean wash this blood clean from my hand?", Othello speaks farewell to his occupation on a hillside filled with the tents of his troops, or Macbeth remarks "so foul and fair a day I have not seen" as he and Banquo watch refugees flee Duncan's wars on the muddy road below.

The visual image may exclude the speaker and even more directly work to embody the lines, making the character a voice-over commentator. In Schaefer's *Macbeth* we dissolve from the tyrant vowing to make his bloody thoughts deeds to hanging bodies and a burning village. In Brook's *King Lear* we watch hunted Edgar and his blind father set out across a bleak wasteland littered with dead horses as Gloucester speaks chorically: "as flies to wanton boys are we to the gods—they kill us for their sport." In Olivier's *Henry V* the camera pans away from sad Burgundy to illustrate in painterly tableaux the havoc wreaked on France by the war. The illustrations need not always be so realistic or so literal, however. In moments of extreme disturbance, directors have often permitted themselves a great deal of freedom in seeking a Shakespearean effect with cinematic means, as in the striking clay idol in Welles's *Macbeth*, the eerie blue green willow swirling in the wind at Desdemona's death in Yutkevitch's *Othello*, blurred shots of drowned rats in Brook's *Lear*, heaps of skulls and bones in *Throne of Blood*, and a white mask streaming with blood in Calpurnia's dream in David Bradley's student film of *Julius Caesar*.

To avoid redundancy, the lines themselves may be cut, the visuals replacing or expanding upon them. Like other techniques, this is not always successful. Not only is the link between character and imagery broken, but the effect is often very different. When Zeffirelli substituted a rather pedestrian shot of an early morning Italian countryside for the Friar's lines,

> The grey-eyed morn smiles on frowning night,
> Check-ring the eastern clouds with streaks of light;
> And flecked darkness like a drunkard reels
> From forth day's path and Titan's burning wheels,

he captured one essential point—the Friar's optimism—but the personifications and ornamentation are given up for no appreciable gain. The visuals must be *powerfully* visual as well as significant. In Schaefer's *Macbeth* Birnam wood coming to Dunsinane regrettably resembles bargain day at a Christmas tree lot. In Kurosawa's film it becomes a superb poetic hallucinatory moment as swaying, disembodied branches move in slow motion through the fog to ominous music. Shakespeare films achieve power not only by portraying the action, the battles, say, in *Henry V* and in *Chimes at Midnight*, and illustrating the lines directly. Free renderings are also sometimes very effective. In Kozintsev's *King Lear*, "Albany's closing quatrain ('The weight of this sad time'), for instance, is conveyed simply in an image of a shattered Edgar, walking into the camera, leaving behind him the devastations of the battlefield where the Fool sits piping a crazy dirge."[49]

A filmmaker can be quite literal, direct, and realistic in rendering a Shakespearean theme and still be very effective. In his gory film of a gory play, Polanski suggests through images all of the meanings of "blood" in *Macbeth:* heredity, kinship, lust, guilt, cleansing sacrifice (including the ritual link between blood and wine), and the hunter's thirst for the lifeblood of his prey. But at times a freer translation is in order, as in Reinhardt and Dieterle's *Dream*, where the central conflict is expressed in terms of the natural polarity of monochromatic film: night (Satan, evil, the grotesque) versus moonlight (lyricism, good, angelic beauty). And at other times, the image may not illustrate or reinforce the lines at all, but may heighten their effect through contrast. As Falstaff eulogizes sack, Hal drops his cup and joins the soldiers leaving the battlefield, and becomes smaller and smaller. In one film Mercutio dies howling "a plague on both your houses" by the well which gives Verona life-giving water, in another, on the cathedral steps where, the Friar and his values being impotent to prevent disaster, the bodies of the young lovers later lie in state.

Part of the interest in seeing several different films of the same play is in seeing what choices the artist has made in "imaging" Shakespeare on the screen. J. Blumenthal has argued, for instance, that unlike Macbeth, "Hamlet would be untranslatable because of the verbality of his experience."[50] But this is to assume that verbal experience is foreign to good cinema, and that the only acceptable translation is a direct one. Hamlet's soliloquy, "To be or not to be," has been rendered in many ways. It has been done humorously by Fred Mogubgub in a short film called "Enter Hamlet," where with brightly colored cartoon figures he provides a separate image for each word: "Whether [man and nude woman under umbrella in bloody rain] 'tis [voice comes out of a well] nobler [man lashed to train tracks, train coming] in [bearded prisoner in cell] the [pianist plinking 'the' on piano and echoed by conductor and audience] mind [shout from skyscraper causing shouter to fall]," and so on. In more serious efforts, Olivier has spoken to elaborate music as he stares dizzily down at the sea from the walls of Elsinore; Schell, with eyes shut, his face framed by stairs; Smoktunovsky, as he wanders among boulders at the meeting of Denmark and the sea; and Williamson, as he lies indolent in a hammock. John Howard Lawson has suggested still another rendering:

> Since it is manifestly impossible to translate the verbal metaphors into visual terms, a film version of the soliloquy must find contrasting images which take advantage of the contradiction between sight and sound to interpret the poetry, emphasize its philosophy or underline its irony. The voice might be heard while Hamlet is engaged in the dull round of court activities, comparing the cloud castles of his thought to the painful routine at Elsinore. The moral intensity of his thought might be contrasted to the depravity of the royal household. There might be another contrast between the words and the slimy waters of a moat, with shadows and shapes and monstrous insects moving across the rippling reflection of the hero's face. Visual images would in some way comment on the changing rhythm of the speech. In the short passage quoted, the flow is broken abruptly by the two monosyllables, "end them." There would be a sudden shift of visual emphasis, and possibly a discordant clash of sound, on these words.[51]

Macbeth's immortal speech of despair, "Tomorrow, and tomorrow, and tomorrow," has also been realized visually in many different ways. Schaefer shows a graying, weary man leaning against a huge stone wall and speaking aloud, Polanski a man "thinking" in a monotone as he walks down emblematic stairs and looks without emotion on his wife's contorted corpse. Kurosawa cut the speech altogether, choosing to show Washizu's despair in less articulate ways (he stares into space, shouts "Fool!", grimaces and moves violently), while Welles has Macbeth look down at swirling, chaotic fog which eventually fills the frame —a perfect symbol of the horror and formlessness of his vision of life. If we are concerned with the art of filming Shakespeare and not merely with the craft of photographing actors, we must be sensitive to such varied and often complex relations between words and images.

## Shakespeare and Nonverbal Expression

There is nothing more *un*-Shakespearean than a film which relies solely on the poetry for its power, unity, and meaning. The words are always important, for on film, as on stage, the actors are like musicians performing a verbal score—badly in the case of Reinhardt and Dieterle's *Dream*, superbly in the case of Hall's. Part of the interpretation will always rely upon the actors' readings—shifts in rhythm and emphasis, pitch and volume—as they mold their parts, build and release tension over the whole arc of the role. A simple pause can force us to anticipate, adjust, reconsider. An unexpected inflection can hint at a flow of emotions and ideas which reveal the meaning of their lines. The very quality of the voice—Marianne Faithfull's worldly, sophisticated Ophelia versus Jean Simmons's timid, innocent one; Burton's virile, authoritative Hamlet, Olivier's sighing, melancholy Prince, and Williamson's nasty, snarling nasal one—shapes our response to the character and hence to the play. We can never spend too much time and effort listening to the words—their patterns and meaning.

But in films, as in live performances, there is so much more. Plays "mean" in hundreds of nonverbal ways not often stressed in criticism or the classroom. We perceive the words in the context of gestures, costumes, groupings, and movements. The meaning of the action is colored by its setting and the object involved in it. On the screen, the way lines, shapes, colors, and textures are arranged affects our response, as do music and nonverbal sounds, montage, and the structuring of the action beat by beat, scene by scene. These things communicate "the psychological, physical or sociological realities that lie behind, and not infrequently enrich or deny, the more conscious interchanges of speech."[52] Much of the freedom, the creativity allowed collaborators with an "open" playwright like Shakespeare lies precisely in this fleshing out and orchestration of the nuances of the language and dramatic action.

Shakespeare thought in terms of eloquent gestures as well as eloquent speeches: Macbeth shattering a festive banquet with shrieks and a drawn sword, Othello putting out the light, Lear kneeling mockingly before Regan for raiment and food and later in earnest before Cordelia for forgiveness, Romeo tossing off the poison as a toast to his love. But a sensitive director will always complement these with other gestures which illuminate a dramatic moment, reveal the meaning of the words, define relationships, or establish a contrast or parallel.[53] Olivier as Richard III locates the point at which his controlled energy becomes uncontrolled when, in an unnecessarily emphatic demonstration of what is to be done to the young Princes in the Tower, he nearly smothers the man who is to do it. In Richardson's *Hamlet* a passionate kiss between Laertes and Ophelia shows how the disease of incest has spread

"Put out the light . . ." (Welles *Othello*)

outward in the court from the King and Queen. In Bradley's *Julius Caesar* a close-up of flowers being trampled on the marble steps foreshadows the general destruction to follow. Even where Shakespeare has provided the gesture, the actor must articulate it: one Othello stares at the handkerchief in disbelief, another is tortured by its softness and sweet smell, still another tears it in his teeth like a wild animal.

Costume, an extension of the actor's body, is really another form of gesture. It communicates not only sex, age, social class, occupation, nationality, season of the year, and occasion, but subjective qualities—moods, tastes, values. Costumes speak to an audience through line, shape, color, and texture. Often Shakespeare gives some direction—Hamlet's suit of mourning, Osric's foppish hat, Malvolio's yellow stockings—but again much is left to the performing artists. Welles makes great comic capital out of the incongruous sight of Falstaff drifting across the battlefield like a huge armored blimp. It is not only his movement but his flowing robes that set Othello apart from the Venetians. Changes in character are often signalled by shifts in dress—Juliet or Ophelia appearing in mourning, Hamlet in a travelling robe, Lear in rags, the young Athenian lovers in the *Dream* in muddy, torn parodies of the civilized, freshly laundered apparel of the opening.

The effect of the forest on civilized dress (Hall *Midsummer
Night's Dream*)

Bergman once said "our work in films begins with the human face."[54]
Despite the complaints of insensitive viewers about the boredom of
"talking faces," in many of the best Shakespeare films it is the expres-
siveness of those faces, controlled from within by the actors and from
without by makeup and lighting artists, that generates much of their
power: the ferocious mask-face of Washizu in *Throne of Blood*, the
obscene grins of Polanski's witches, the immobile brutal faces of Goneril, Regan, and Cornwall in Brook's *Lear*. Recall too the fresh, innocent faces in Zeffirelli's *Romeo and Juliet*, Joe E. Brown's deadpan
Flute, Mickey Rooney's Pan-like Puck, Welles's Father Christmas Falstaff, and various incarnations of Gertrude's beauty gone to seed. Quite
apart from casting and facial expression, faces are photographed in a
great variety of ways: from the front, the rear, or in profile, distorted
by reflections and shadows, masked by bars, veils, flames, armor, and
"beetle brows." Faces are rouged and powdered, glisten with sweat,
are dirty or bloodied. They appear upside down, sway back and forth,
are fragmented by the edges of the frame, and all of these things affect
the meaning of the dramatic moment.

Spatial arrangements and relationships, on stage and on film, are

Emotion in faces: Starveling and Quince mourn "poor bully Bottom" (Hall *Midsummer Night's Dream*)

metaphoric. To be spatially in between is to be caught in conflict— Gertrude between Claudius and Hamlet, Romeo between Mercutio and Tybalt, Desdemona between Othello and Brabantio. As Othello and Desdemona become estranged in Welles's film, the distances between them become huge. Movements away from one character and toward another often announce a shift in allegiance, as when the lords hastily abandon Hastings when they realize Richard intends to kill him. Rapid regroupings signal confusion, as in the mob in *Julius Caesar* or the lovers in *Dream* who do a kind of dance in which they constantly change partners. Film is capable of capturing larger movements, like the fine assassination scene in Mankiewicz's *Julius Caesar*, where after swimming from blow to blow and wiping the blood from his eyes, Caesar staggers down steps toward Brutus only to receive the fatal thrust. Film far surpasses the stage in portraying the charge and countercharge of battle scenes.

Despite the capacity of theatergoers to "zoom in" on a detail, however, film also has more power to make small movements and relationships huge and important. On film, a glance or the nervous flutter of a fan may be as striking as a forty-foot leap. Motion in films is also com-

Emotion in setting and composition: Desdemona after being accused (Welles *Othello*)

plicated by the fact that the camera can move and the focal length of the lens can change, placing the characters, setting, objects, and camera in an intricate dance. Distance, perspective, and relationships can change with the fluidity and subtlety of a line of verse. Static theatrical space becomes dynamic. The rhetoric may be very strong, as when the camera races along with charging troops, wanders the halls of Elsinore, or rushes toward Hamlet as he spies the ghost in Kozintsev's film. Or it may be "invisible" as we move with an actor, including or excluding elements of setting, light, or color, shifting tempo to comment quietly on the action.

As in poetry and fiction, rooms, buildings, streets, and landscapes may be saturated with ideas, associations, and emotions in film. Realist or expressionist, settings may reinforce or counterpoint with action, character, themes, and verbal styles. The pastoral scene behind Orsino as he sighs out his melancholy to Viola underscores the distinctly forced, literary quality of his love in Fried's Russian *Twelfth Night*. The innocence of the young children playing outside the cathedral in Castellani's film contrasts with Juliet's new seriousness and maturity as she seeks the Friar.

Sometimes the worlds of Shakespeare's plays are single—Denmark in many films is a political, psychological, and philosophical prison, puzzling, unknowable, sinister. Brook's Lear inhabits a world of unrelieved darkness and primitiveness which may conflict with Shakespeare's renaissance language and court but which unquestionably contributes to the intensity of the work.[55] Castellani's *Romeo and Juliet* takes place in a beautiful but stifling Verona, emblematic of an old civilization built on rivalry and materialism which imprisons and eventually destroys innocence and love.[56] The exterior of Macbeth's castle in Welles's film suggests Faustian aspiration, but inside it is a solipsistic world of dizzying heights, jagged rocks, moonscapes, gnarled dead trees, fog, and Rorschach-test floors from which there is no escape. Sometimes the plays have two worlds and the films elaborate the conflicts between the two: the kingdom of Falstaff versus the kingdom of Henry IV; the daylight world of Theseus and the nocturnal world of Oberon; Venice and Cyprus. In his lush color imitation of Welles's *Othello*, Yutkevitch created a film which, from the splendid shots of the ghost ship under the titles to Othello's death on the ramparts of Cyprus, is saturated with images of the sea, demonstrating that a motif can work as powerfully in setting as it can in poetry.

A king no longer a king (Kozintsev *King Lear*) Rosa Madell Film Library

In Shakespeare's plays, props often carry great symbolic weight, but once again it is up to his collaborators to articulate and complement what is indicated explicitly in the text. In Welles's *Macbeth*, the awkward, oversized, horned crown blends the Satanic theme with the poetic theme of ill-fitting clothes. In Schaefer's film there are two crowns: a crown of thorns mockingly given Macbeth by the prophetic witches, and the jewelled symbol of the power which Macbeth cannot keep from passing on to Banquo's sons. In Polanski's version, the crown is part of a circular motif which runs through the entire film, from the circle inscribed in the sand by the witches, to the iron collar around Cawdor's neck, to the huge shield at Macbeth's coronation, and the ring to which the baited bear is chained. In Brook's *Lear*, the throne is a coffinlike stone enclosure which isolates the King, makes his voice boom out at his subjects, and prefigures death. In Kozintsev's film, it is a huge chair which dwarfs the wispy, white-haired King, who sits on its edge like a child.

Occasionally such effects are obtrusive and unsubtle: Duncan riding through a herd of sheep as he goes to be sacrificed at Macbeth's castle, Othello wandering distracted among picturesque classical ruins which are an emblem of his own ruined grandeur. Often, however, they enrich our understanding. In Wirth's *Hamlet*, Polonius's monocle reveals both his pretentiousness and his figurative blindness. The flaring flame as Lady Macbeth burns Macbeth's letter reflects her inner fire in Schaefer's film, and the skull-like oil lamp on the table as Antony, Octavius, and Lepidus determine which of their enemies must die underscores the grisly nature of their work in Bradley's *Julius Caesar*.

Consider the various uses of the bed in Shakespeare films. In Olivier's *Hamlet* it is a rather abstract symbol, overstuffed, decorated with labial curtains, helping to emphasize the Oedipal nature of Hamlet's conflict. Richardson's film shows the bed as a "nasty sty" where overweight Claudius and pallid Gertrude drink blood-red wine and feast with their dogs on greasy chicken and fruit. In films of *Macbeth*, beds connote sterility, brutality, perversion, in *Othello* altars for sacrifice, symbols for love covered with shadows or fragmented by the frame. While in Zeffirelli's *Shrew* the bed is a playful battleground, in *Romeo and Juliet* it is associated with the funeral bier. Not only do words and acts speak in Shakespeare films. *Things* speak.

From one perspective, the camera selects and records things in front of the lens, the most important variables being the apparent distance

The bed as symbol
(Olivier *Hamlet*)
(Kurosawa *Throne of Blood*)
(Welles *Othello*)

from the subject (are we involved or detached? do we see individual details or the larger pattern?) and the angle of view. From another perspective, film is a graphic art in which the artist composes images with light and shadow, color and texture, shape and line, within a rectangle. Within shots we "read" a hundred different variables which work on us more or less simultaneously and often carry conflicting messages. Welles makes us *see* the sound of the trumpets in *Othello* by creating a harmony of diagonal lines and bell-shaped mouths. When Richard III's shadow fills the frame or a lense distorts his face as he moves near the camera, we *see* his egotism and warped personality. The formal beauty of the shot in which Washizu kneels beside a rack of arrows before going to kill his lord in *Throne of Blood* suits the cool ironic tone of the film and contrasts vividly with the scene in which he is slain violently with arrows. In *Macbeth*,

> Welles uses silhouettes throughout the entire film. Characters and objects are very frequently shown with the source of light behind them, as if they had passed over to a realm beyond light with their dark side forward. A variation of this is seen in the partial lighting

Sound made visual (Welles *Othello*)

of people and things, the constant suggestion that only part of the truth can be seen, only part of the real nature of a person noticed.[57]

Olivier consistently associates Ophelia with light. And as with lighting, colors can clarify conflicts (Capulets against Montagues, English versus French), signal shifts in tone (the draining of color from Zeffirelli's *Romeo and Juliet*), establish an overall atmosphere, or create associations.

Composition is a complex tool in film since it also involves creative use of *montage*, the juxtaposition of image with image. If *within* a shot Polanski may contrast the external beauty of Lady Macbeth, her red hair blowing against an intense blue sky, with her voice-over prayer for cruelty enough to kill Duncan, if Kozintsev may set Lear's royal commands ("Know that we . . .") against a shot of Lear playing with the fool by the fire, if Zeffirelli in *Taming of the Shrew* may place the wedding guests in the top half of the frame and dogs gnawing hungrily on bones in the bottom half, *between* shots the possibilities are infinite. Those who find the written word more expressive and subtle than the visual image might consider the number of meaningful contrasts possible between two shots—contrasts of one color with another, stability with instability, a large pattern with a small detail, one rhythm with another, obscurity with clarity, light with dark, stasis with movement, and a hundred other such juxtapositions. Much of the explosiveness of Shakespeare's verse, Peter Brook has pointed out, results from montage. Words and images constitute many messages, "often crowding, jostling, overlapping one another. The intelligence, the feelings, the memory are all stirred. . . ." Using "free verse on the open stage enabled him to cut the inessential detail and the irrelevant realistic action: in their place he could cram sounds and ideas, thoughts and images which make each instant a stunning mobile."[58]

Entrances in Shakespeare often duplicate shock cuts: "Enter Lear, with Cordelia in his arms"; (upon Duncan's expression of amazement at his complete trust of Cawdor) "Enter Macbeth." No wonder then that filmmakers use montage extensively. The filmmaker may seek a comic effect, as when in *As You Like It* Paul Czinner dissolves from the ludicrous, mustachioed, melodramatic villain, Oliver, to the wiggling posterior of a swan; or he may underscore the unity of a mood, as when Welles, in *Chimes at Midnight*, dissolves from rebels hanging motionless from gibbets to the solitary, sick king, and from sleepless Henry, hemmed in by huge stone columns and peering out through barred windows, to his melancholy son Hal before a stagnant, glassy pond. He may establish a parallel, as when Welles, in *Othello*, dissolves from jealous Bianca, clutching the handkerchief, to Desdemona, worried about its loss; or he may reveal unspoken thoughts, as when in Schaefer's version Macbeth registers the prophetic nature of his act as he hands the scepter and crown to Banquo, who in turn hands them to a young boy.

Often scenes are punctuated by associative pairs of shots. Schaefer dissolves in successive shots from Macbeth's brutal kiss of Lady Macbeth to the murderers waiting for Banquo (one of them whittling a stick), linking sex and violence; from dead Banquo's bloody face to the roast pig brought in to the banquet being held in his honor; from Ross's whispers about armies on the way from England (cause) to Lady Macbeth staring out the window at the dawn and Macbeth guzzling wine (effect); from Macbeth resolving to execute each violent thought to the aftermath of such thoughts; and from the burning Scottish village strewn with bodies to England with its sunlight and green trees. But often, in much more subtle ways, such associations and comments are made within scenes as well.

From the days of so-called silent films, music has been used to under-

The inner made outer: the anguish of Henry IV (Welles *Chimes at Midnight*)

Dissolve: Sleepless Henry IV to melancholy Prince Hal (Welles *Chimes at Midnight*)

31

score or counterpoint with the tempo and rhythms of physical motion. It has been used to clarify dramatic conflicts, create moods, give a sense of period, provide unity, bridge transitions, punctuate bits of business, and heighten meaning and effect in scores of less easily verbalized ways. Shakespeare himself often used music brilliantly in his plays—Iago's drinking song and Desdemona's willow song, Titania's lullaby, the gravedigger's song—and the filmmaker may simply follow the playwright's directions. Shakespeare has provided another kind of musical accompaniment in his plays however, the music of the words, which has not always received kind treatment in films. Subtle verbal harmonies are often obliterated by the heavy syrup of cliche movie music. Similarly, it sometimes seems that the director is striving with full orchestra to provide the emotional power which his actors cannot. Castellani's *Romeo and Juliet* and Yutkevitch's *Othello* serve quite well to illustrate both faults. They help us understand Brook's decision to strip *King Lear* of musical hyperbole, and help us appreciate critical pronouncements that "additional music has more frequently proved a hindrance than a help in conveying the dramatic poetry."[59]

Nevertheless, William Walton's music for *Henry V* is very successful in underscoring the film's great variety of visual styles. Nino Rota's boisterous "Where is the life that late I led?" captures Petruchio's character and the dramatic moment perfectly. And Miklos Rosza's careful development of separate themes for each major character contributes much to Mankiewicz's *Julius Caesar*. There is no hindrance in the obscene rasping pipes which accompany the play within the play done in *commedia* style in Richardson's *Hamlet*, the festive ceremonial music by Walton which dies off in Olivier's *Hamlet* when the observers realize the duel is in earnest, and the ironic religious music of Olivier's *Richard III*. Even more powerfully ironic are the angelic chorus which is juxtaposed with the shrieks of wounded horses, clashes of iron, and cries of pain in the battle scene of *Chimes at Midnight*, the sour bagpipe music signalling the presence of the witches in Polanski's *Macbeth*, and the haunting chants of the chorus and forest spirit in *Throne of Blood*. And in at least two instances this side of opera and ballet—Reinhardt and Dieterle's *Dream* with Mendelssohn's music, and Kozintsev's *Hamlet* with Shostakovich's score—films heavily saturated with music succeed in part because of it.

Finally, to round out our survey of nonverbal expressive means in realizing Shakespeare on film, let us consider an element used less creatively than almost any other—nonmusical sounds. It has been said that they "have almost no place in the presentation of Shakespeare."[60] Yet Shakespeare's own company used many acoustical "props"—owls, clocks, cannon, tolling bells, battle sounds, crowing cocks, thunder, and so on.[61] Many of the most memorable moments in Shakespeare films are inextricably bound up with such sounds: the crackling of the flames as Lady MacDuff stares in wordless horror at her slaughtered children in Polanski's *Macbeth*, the hollow thud of the gravedigger's hammer as he nails on the lid of Ophelia's coffin in Kozintsev's *Hamlet*, the slam of the massive door which seals in Othello and Desdemona in Welles's film. Welles is often acclaimed for his acoustic artistry because sound in his films is often highly subjective: the dripping noises in the cave in *Macbeth* which suddenly accelerate madly, the soft, slow, irregular ringing of the alarm bell which greets Macbeth's call to arms (Seyton's body is swaying from the bell rope). His *Othello* includes the fine aural collage of celestial chorus, thunder, pounding waves, mandolins, wind, a clanking alarm bell, shouts, barking dogs, and notes from a harpsichord which serve as a transition from Venice to Cyprus, and the blend of laughing soldiers and whores and the cries of gulls as Othello wakes from his fit and stares up at the ramparts.

The sheer power of discreetly heightened "natural" sounds often creates meaning as well. There is a grim rightness in sensual Gertrude's horrible, panting death in Richardson's *Hamlet*. The battle which we hear but never see under the fog at the beginning of Polanski's *Macbeth* suggests a brutality and ferocity that literal images seldom achieve. Sounds in Castellani's *Romeo and Juliet* often articulate tomblike spaces eloquently, such as the echoing clank as Romeo smashes a huge iron candlestick on the cathedral altar, or the grinding sound of the tomb lid as Romeo pries it off, suggesting the weight of the forces working to separate the lovers. The birds shriek with laughter as the lovers make fools of themselves in Hall's *Dream*. Whether expressionist, as in the rush of water at the moment of Roderigo's death in Welles's *Othello*, or realist, as in the crunching sound of a knife piercing bone as Macbeth kills Duncan in Polanski's film, nonmusical sounds are often important interpretative tools.

To speak with precision and understanding about style in Shakespeare films, we must go far beyond categories which divide films according to their relative distance from the language of poetry and the theatre or which measure in some simpleminded way the relative distance of the film from the original play. We must gauge the truth of the actors' performances and the power of the director's aural and visual images, which often must be thought of as free translations, cinematic equivalents, or re-creations rather than attempts at transparent presentations of Shakespeare's poetic and theatrical images. We should always seek the *why* of filmic techniques, ask how they are integrated into overall patterns which constitute a significant style appropriate both to the spirit of Shakespeare's work and to the collaborative artist's vision. (Clearly the same cinematic style could never suit both *As You Like It* and *Hamlet*.) Shunning pedantic fervor, we should ask how the restructuring from play to film constitutes an interpretative act—inquire in such a manner that we learn about both play and film. (Is it true that all good films stress physical action and plays stress emotional and reflective reaction? Is it more effective on film to show the killing of Duncan, or to leave it to our horrible imaginings?) Style describes many things—acting style, the personal themes and techniques recurring in a particular filmmaker, the genre and period of the play, the proportion and relation of verbal to visual meaning, and much more.

In its largest sense, however, style deals with the integration of all expressive effects. Peter Brook praised Kozintsev's *Hamlet* precisely because his "structure is inseparable from his meaning." The film is "a search for over-all meaning as opposed to the many and varied, sometimes dazzling, attempts to capture on the screen the actor-manager's view of the play as imagery, theatricality, passion, color, effects."[62] A unified style need not imply simplistic narrative clarity, reductive concepts, or a single level of dramatic illusion. The strength and truth of the play within the play in Richardson's *Hamlet*—a parodic event in which Claudius becomes a red-nosed clown, Elsinore a flimsey cardboard castle, the cuckolding of King Hamlet a game of sexual leapfrog between the Queen of Hearts and her two royal studs, and the murder as a festive dance around the Maypole turned grotesque as the King is strangled in the brightly colored streamers and the self-crowned murderer leaps into the Queen's arms—its strength and truth is its duplicating in terms of visual style the insane discord in

Hamlet's mind. Stylistic truth and unity come from the overall vision of the actors and the film artist. Said Orson Welles,

> With me the visual is a solution to what the poetical and musical form dictates. I don't begin with the visual and then try to find a poetry or music and try to stick it into the picture. The picture has to follow it. And again, people tend to think that my first pre-occupation is with the simple plastic effects of the cinema. But to me they all come out of an interior rhythm, which is like the shape of music or the shape of poetry. I don't go around like a collector picking up beautiful images and pasting them together. . . . I be-lieve in the film as a poetic medium . . . poetry should make your hair stand up on your skin, should suggest things, evoke more than you see. The danger in the cinema is that you see everything, because it's a camera. So what you have to do is to manage to evoke, to incant, to raise up things which are not really there.[63]

# Max Reinhardt and William Dieterle's

# *A Midsummer Night's Dream*

*A* MIDSUMMER NIGHT'S DREAM IS SHAKESPEARE'S REVERIE ON
the interpenetrating themes of moon, madness, metamorphosis, acting,
enchantment, imagination, love, dream, and death.[1] Like a dream, the
comedy is both lucid and mysterious. Move close, and the *Dream*
"hath no bottom." It becomes a dazzling overlay of intricate patterns
of character, theme, language, and action. Step back, however, and
the discord becomes musical, the overall pattern—a blend of the
pastoral movement from civilization to the forest and back again, and
the movement of dream-vision poems from waking to sleeping to
waking—becomes clear. The wood near Athens is as much an experience as an actual place ("wood" in Elizabethan English meant mad),
at once lyrical and grotesque, liberating and frightening, benevolent
and vengeful. This magical Dionysian world, "a vision of a state outside time and society and morality; the world presented as an ecstatic
state of liberty where no action has irreversible consequences and all is
mere play,"[2] became in Shakespeare's analogical mind a distorting-
mirror image of Theseus's Apollonian world, as the audience is invited
to "look not with the eyes, but with the mind."

The *Dream* is a preposterous mixture of traditions and styles, incorporating Theseus and Hippolyta from classical legend, young lovers
who seem to have walked out of an Elizabethan anthology of love
poetry, Stratford workmen, and fairies from English folklore, all in-
habiting a world with a distinctly Ovidian flavor. The language ranges
from stately blank verse to earthy prose, from Petrarchan conceits and

Puck's spritely rhymed verse to the ludicrous bombast of "Pyramus and Thisby." The action ranges from the sublime to the ridiculous. If we accept Roger Moore's definition of Baroque as "a splendid pomp and monumentality resulting from yoking together many varied kinds of experiences, often wildly disparate, into a single unity,"[3] we can perhaps understand why the *Dream* has so often been produced as a vast balletic-operatic extravaganza with huge casts, elaborate scenery, and lavish costumes. The scale may seem wrong, but the style is correct and the impulse toward idyllic vision Shakespearean.

The first and most glorious of these was Purcell's *Fairy Queen* (1692), in which Shakespeare's rustics and fairies are joined in the second act by "Fairy-Spirits, Night, Mistery, Secresie, Sleep, and the Attendants, Singers, and Dancers," in the fourth by "Spring, Summer, Autumn, Winter, and their Attendants. Phoebus: A Dance of the Four Seasons," and in the fifth by "Juno, Chinese Men and Women. A Chorus of Chineses. A Dance of 6 Monkeys. An Entry of a Chinese Man and Woman. A Grand Dance of 24 Chineses." In addition, the production was graced with splendid decor.

> The Scene changes to a great Wood: a long row of large Trees on each side: a River in the middle: Two rows of lesser Trees of a different kind just on the side of the River, which meet in the middle, and make so many Arches: Two great Dragons make a Bridge over the River; their Bodies form two Arches, through which two Swans are seen in the River at a great distance. . . . While a Symphony's Playing, the two Swans come Swimming in through the Arches to the bank of the River, as if they would Land; there turn themselves into Fairies, and Dance; at the same time the Bridge vanishes, and the Trees that were Arch'd, raise themselves unright.[4]

A production at Covent Garden in 1816 concluded with

> A Grand Pageant, Commemorative of the Triumphs of Theseus, Over the Cretans—the Thebans—the Centaurs—the Minotaur, Ariadne in the Labyrinth—the Mysterious Peplum, or Veil of Minerva—the Ship Argo—and the Golden Fleece,[5]

causing William Hazlitt to resolve that "poetry and the stage do not agree together."[6] Charles Kean's biographer, Cole, recalled in Kean's 1856 production of the *Dream*

> the noiseless footsteps of the "shadow dance" on the moonlit greensward, with the undulating reflections . . . : the wood peopled with

37

its innumerable fairy legions . . . the melodious music composed by Mendelssohn . . . the perpetual change of scene and incident; the shifting diorama; the golden beams of the rising sun glittering on the leaves; the gradual dispersion of the mist discovering the fairy guardians, light and brilliant as gossamer, grouped around the unconscious sleeping mortals; the dazzling magnificence of the palace of Theseus. . . .[7]

Herbert Beerbohm Tree's production in 1900, with its live rabbits scampering among real trees, elicited similar lyricism:

[The forest] with a carpet of thyme and wild-flowers, brakes and thickets full of blossom, and a background seen through the tall trees, of the pearly dawn or the deep hues of the night sky. . . . The mind recalling it seems to dwell upon some actual beauty of nature, instead of a painted arrangement of canvas and pasteboard . . . a splendid Duke's palace, which, as soon as the mortals have retired, is filled with the fairy throng. There they dance, and, as they wind in and out, gradually the pillared hall glows with mysterious light, every pillar a shaft of fire, with little points of light starting out here and there at the touch of Oberon's wand. Then the fairies are dismissed. . . . They troop off, and slowly the hall darkens again. The glow dies away, the stage is swallowed up in gloom, the lights in the house are suddenly turned up, and the play is over. It is as if the audience were rudely awakened from a pleasing vision.[8]

The Reinhardt-Dieterle *Midsummer Night's Dream,* with its magical disappearances, fairies suspended by wires, *Chinoiserie,* and elaborate sets, its music by Mendelssohn, emphasis upon dance, and attempt to create in its viewers a sense of wonder and awe, is a summing up of this stage tradition. Max Reinhardt sought, like many actor-managers before him, to create a dream of beauty and delight:

In Shakespeare's lovely fantasy, I have always seen, above all, a cheering, hopeful reminder that since Life itself is a dream, we can escape it through our dreams within a dream. When stark reality weighs too heavily upon us, an all-wise Providence provides deliverance. Every one has a secret corner into which he can retire and find refuge in Fancy. "A Midsummer Night's Dream" is an invitation to escape reality, a plea for the glorious release to be found in sheer fantasy.[9]

The film imitates the play's astounding amalgamation of disparate elements. The shimmering production numbers choreographed by

Bronislava Nijinska and Nini Theilade bear more than a little resemblance to the Busby Berkeley creations for Warner Brothers' 1930s
musicals. The design of the forest blends Arthur Rackham's illustrations
for the play with Teutonic, Grimm's fairy-tale fantasy. Acting style
varies from the sighing, fist-to-forehead silent-movie grieving of Verree
Teasdale as Hippolyta, to awesome amateurishness in matinee idol and
crooner Dick Powell as Lysander, to Olivia deHavilland's spunky
American college girl Hermia, to Ian Hunter's Standard British
Shakespearean Thesus. Against heavy doses of stock farce by the
Warner Brothers stable of comedians, Mickey Rooney's mischievous
American street-kid Puck, and Victor Jory's fierce tough-guy Oberon,
is set an ethereally beautiful, shimmering blonde Titania by Anita
Louise (she does not act, but dances, poses, and sings), and Jimmy
Cagney as Bottom, blending innocent weaver, Chicago hood, and Ugly
Duckling.

Theseus and Hippolyta in Athens

Reinhardt's spectacle begins in Athens. Port and palace are huge
and filled with crowds and activity. The garish tableaux are brilliantly
lit, emphasizing hard, shiny surfaces—shields, breast plates, helmets,
satin, jewels, sequins. The frame is flooded with laces, brocades, pat-

terned hangings, tassled canopies, swirling pillars, and curving steps. Windblown plumes, hair, flames, and banners catch the eye, and our ears are filled with fanfares, a hymn in praise of Theseus, and orchestral marches. Everything in Athens bespeaks luxury, civilization, and sophistication. The notes of disharmony sounded pose no real threat in the overall atmosphere of triumph and celebration. One senses that in this atmosphere of romantic comedy, melancholy, serpentine Hippolyta will not hold out long against genial, generous Theseus, and that harsh Egeus will not have his way. Theseus does not take him seriously, and even in the opening scene the jealous, angry father cannot keep Hermia and Lysander apart. The more literal notes of disharmony during the singing of a pious hymn to Theseus reflect the rustics' good-natured exuberance as they bellow "Trumpets and fifes!" and lovers with the healthy instincts of kids being naughty in church.

Bottom and Company in Quince's workshop

Quince's carpenter shop provides a brief respite between the splendors of Theseus's court and Oberon's gothic forest. It is small, dark, lit by a candle which etches the outline of tools on the walls. The textures are simple and rough—wood, coarse cloth, leather—the faces richly comic, and the characters identified with earthy details, such as

Flute's nibbling on sunflower seeds, Snug's scratching his head, Quince's peering over his tiny spectacles, and Bottom's nervous, violent gestures and ranting as he provides his own sound effects by whistling and rattling a thunder sheet and out-roars Snug. Here King Quince holds court at a workbench and his major problem is a set of giggling actors who either fit none of the parts or want to play all of them.

Reinhardt and Dieterle's ethereal forest, with shimmering white balletic fairies racing through the trees and up moonbeams to the delicate strains of Mendelssohn's music, carries on the spectacular stage tradition. Deer, owls, frogs, birds, and a unicorn inhabit a world of intensely back-lit ferns and rushes, lush grass and pools, flowers, and huge oaks. Shakespeare's lush imagery and lyricism have been stripped from the text (where, given these actors, they would only have been an embarrassment) and embodied in chords of birch trees, cascading musical streams, and swirling fog and fairies shot in soft focus through gauzes or through smeared sparkling sheets of glass. It is a film of carefully choreographed movement, where the swirl of Titania's fairies around a tree matches the swirl of Puck as he spirals upward on a branch to fetch the "love-in-idleness," where the flow of Titania's white veil is echoed in the billowing black cape of Oberon. So fluid are the lines and shapes of the film that some critics suggest it is much more a film of Mendelssohn's music than of Shakespeare's play. "The total graphic feeling is like a flow of bright palace crescendos, dusky forest cadenzas, pizzicato glimpses of glistening dew drops, and largo passages of mysterious and lovely moonlit creatures—the whole thoroughly and ornately orchestrated for the eye."[10]

This is a remarkable interpretative film, for not only does it incorporate the tradition of idyllic and spectacular productions, it is also a precursor of the "darker Dream" which has fascinated modern critics and directors.[11] Alongside the innocent playfulness, genial humor, and cotton-candy fantasy in Shakespeare's dream play are numerous undercurrents which are unfestive, grotesque, erotic. This was sensed by early illustrators, William Blake and Henry Fuseli,[12] but among critics it was G. Wilson Knight who in 1932 observed that in the *Dream* "the night is a-glimmer with moon and star, yet it is dark and fearsome; there are gentle birds and gruesome beasts. There is a gnomish, fearsome, *Macbeth*-like quality about the atmosphere just touching nightmare."[13] Contrary to the dominant comic movement are moments of murderous hatred, jealousy, threatened rape, sexual humiliation. Sadistic

Oberon, "King of Shadows," has a Satanic air about him (Titania is another name for Proserpina), and chaos-loving Puck seems very much at home with dawn-fearing "damned spirits" wandering from their wormy beds. Even if things finally come out well in this dream, Lysander and "Pyramus and Thisby" remind us that oppression, war, sickness, and death lay siege to lovers in the real world. Confusions and metamorphoses are funny, but there is something frightening about them as well. If the world of the play is benign and beautiful, it is also one in which the seasons alter, causing diseases, floods, rotting crops, and dead cattle. Spiders, beetles, worms, ounces, cats, wolves, owls, bears, lions, and boars must be warned away from the sleeping Fairy Queen. In the epilogue Puck urges us to dismiss the play as a fanciful dream. But who trusts Puck?

Harley Granville-Barker toyed with golden oriental fairies and a certain strangeness in the forest scenes on the stage in 1914-15. But this 1935 collaboration between directors of very different sensibilities was the first production on stage or screen to give anything near full weight to the play's darker elements.

> The overall tone of the film is dark in the Dieterle style. The saturnine figure of Victor Jory's Oberon, a sinister presence in many scenes, is typical, more so when he is "disguised" as a tree, little more than a gnarled shape from which his face peers enigmatically. Undoubtedly Dieterle is also responsible for the effective use made of the complex forest sets; the gloomy wood which he achieves provides the best possible background for the shimmering Anita Louise and such spectacles of special effects as the fairies' weaving a web of sleep over their Queen.[14]

This mixture of light and dark puzzled more than a few critics. Otis Ferguson put his finger on obvious structural weaknesses in the film, but he was perhaps too quick to dismiss some parts as "so many independent sideshows on a midway."[15] More recently, commentators have objected that

> the director interpolates other non-dramatic but intriguing goings-on, some of which are really disturbing. For instance, the grotesquely disguised midgets who play for fairy concerts (and "speak" in incoherent grunts) are ugly and unwholesome rather than charming. Reinhardt's Oberon (played by Victor Jory) is a solemn, humorless, rather threatening figure, a gloomy bogeyman commanding armies

of batmen out of a Dracula movie. Is the audience supposed to feel happy when the reunion of Oberon and Titania is celebrated by having his batmen capture her glittering follies-girl attendants?[16]

Wilson Knight, on the other hand, remarked in 1936, "I was impressed by the way the producer brought out, *what is in the poetry*, the nightmarish fearsomeness of the wood and its wild beasts. This was interpretative work with authority in incident and imagery, whereas the average stage-production leaves you with the impression of blue-bells and tinsel. I liked Oberon on his black horse. . . ."[17] A newspaper reviewer noted that "the sensitive lenses have caught the nightmarish spirit of the drama,"[18] and John Russell Taylor found that the "fairy sequences . . . distil precisely the slightly cruel, slightly sinister poetry that Shakespeare achieved in words. . . ."[19]

Much of the energy of the film is generated by this clash of the Reinhardt style and the Dieterle style, of ornate escapist fantasy and dark vision. Against the sticky sentimentality of the little Indian boy lost and abandoned and the "true love" between Hermia and Lysander are set the troll who spits water in the boy's face and Puck who gleefully terrorizes all the mortals in the forest and mocks their sufferings (while riding on weeping Helena's skirts, he wipes his nose on them). Against angelic Titania gathering flowers, singing, weeping with the moon for "some enforced chastity," is set fierce, jealous Oberon with his black stallion and virile, bat-winged train. Against Bottom's idyllic reign as King of Fairies is set his terror when Puck makes him aware of his transformation.

The central panel of this dramatic triptych—Titania embracing an ass—is both hilarious and grotesque. With Puckish humor, the directors composed the image as a parodic "Mother and Child," and punctuated her soprano lullaby "Sleep On" with little contented hee-haws from Bottom. (There *is* something holy about the marriage of Bottom and Titania, something as important to the overall design as the marriage of Reason and Imagination in Theseus and Hippolyta.) Despite some glimmerings of sensuality in Olivia deHavilland's Hermia, there is nothing particularly erotic about the lovers, Oberon, Bottom, or Titania. Instead, the eroticism of the play has been transferred to still another couple who dance an allegorical conflict between Moonlight and Night to Mendelssohn's "Nocturne." As the original souvenir booklet describes the ballet, it

43

tells the story of the creatures of the wood who are happy only in the moonlight and wage war against the approach of darkness. The lovers are asleep in the wood when Puck appears, heralding the departure of the moonlight. Across the meadows comes the chariot of Oberon, and close to him are countless elves, fairies and night creatures.

Suddenly, there appears a startling, iridescent creature. She dances wildly, finally taking refuge beside Titania. Then Darkness itself, an awesome creature, emerges from the wood and woos the dancer. She tries to flee, but he throws his veil over her, and she is forced to succumb. The fearsome being lifts her high and she is swallowed up in the blackness of night.

In what Pauline Kael called "an exquisite and magical moment on film,"[20] Oberon descends in a glittering chariot trailing hundreds of feet of billowing black cloth. Expressionist images of his slaves flow past the camera in close-up: ecstatic sleeping women, bald men ("exiles from light") with melancholy faces, swirling goblin-musicians playing and dancing behind gauze. The whole scene serves as an epiphany of idyll and nightmare as the shadow of Oberon and his train passes over the faces of the sleeping lovers.

When Titania, Bottom, and the lovers awaken, fantasy and nightmare dissolve in hilarity as Quince, Bottom, and company perform the tragi-comedy of "Pyramus and Thisby" in Theseus's ornate great hall. Like Shakespeare's other plays within plays, this one is a complex event. It is a glance at the strengths and fragilities of his own art. It is an inadvertently comic variation on the theme of parents against lovers sounded at the beginning of the play. And it is a test of the temper of this renewed society in Athens—its humanity, its flexibility, its imagination.

From Shakespeare's time to the present, "Pyramus and Thisby" has generated more ingenious comic stage business than any other scene in English drama. (Improvisation began with the performances of Shakespeare's own company in which Thisby lost her sword at the critical moment and was forced to commit suicide by stabbing herself with the scabbard.[21]) Unlike the actors in Peter Hall's more recent film, who play sincere, earnest amateurs, the rustics here are unabashed comedians using traditional gags—incessant giggling, rampant forgetfulness, double takes, the deadpan—to milk as many laughs as possible. But still the humor of the hilariously inadequate tragedy comes through.

Titania and Bottom in the forest: Madonna and Child

The erotic conquest of Moonlight by Night

Wall, with a brick and bucket of mortar and wearing a painted cloth, is so nervous he forgets his own name. Bottom's helmet flies off when he tosses his head back to bellow his opening line, and he spits on his hands before his moments of passion like a good workman about to undertake a heavy lift. Looking more than a little ridiculous in what looks like a ballerina skirt over his armor, he shatters both dramatic and social decorum by striding across the room and up the steps to the throne to explain ever so patiently to Theseus that "deceiving me" is Thisby's cue. Moon, tottering precariously on a chair, suffers the humiliating realization that his lines are utterly superflous, and is unlucky enough to have his valiant little dog engage Lion in combat.

Pyramus and Thisby

Most preposterous, however, is Joe E. Brown as Thisby, sporting a huge fake flower (she is "de-flowered"), a Goldilocks wig, and a judiciously padded dress. He tries and fails to remember to smile glamorously, to hold his hands in a dainty posture, and to speak in falsetto. He trips over words ("as Shaproc . . . as Proshoc . . . as Sha . . . as I to you") and, being nothing if not consistent, trips over his petticoat too. Like Pyramus, Thisby pulls Wall's "chink" to her mouth as if being interviewed on a radio show, and "she" is more than a little embarrassed at having to hide hands which are hardly "pale as milk."

The climax of the buffoonery is Thisby's death. At the crucial moment she cannot find her weapon. "*Come* trusty sword," she wails. Out of desperation she knocks on Pyramus's armor and borrows his weapon, but suddenly finds herself with *two* swords as Quince comes to her rescue. What to do? With impeccable logic she sharpens one on the other as if to carve a turkey, then politely returns Pyramus's sword (he repeats his death tremors once again). At the moment of truth, she giggles as the icy blade slides down her bodice, pokes herself gingerly in the breast, and executes a bone-crushing dive onto the unfortunate hero.

Sensitive modern directors have often found disharmony between the courtiers' response to the rustics' play and our response. There is a certain narrowness and lack of generosity in the flat jokes and satirical jibes of the snobbish, condescending onstage audience whom the amateur players strive so mightily to entertain. Shakespeare seems deliberately to cut across the festivity and good humor—perhaps to suggest to us what kind of audience we should not be. Perhaps it was to reveal that Athens did not benefit from its encounter with the wood as much as it might have, that the return to civilization and harmony is made at the cost of much of the freedom and wonder of the world of Oberon.

Reinhardt and Dieterle underscore this disharmony with a stunning *coup de théâtre*. After the play, when the rustics go backstage to prepare for their burgomask dance, the smiling courtiers sneak away. Mendelssohn's triumphant music sounds, the camera holds on the dancers' feet, and they storm forward in a jubilant, clumsy chorus line. Suddenly the frame freezes and the festive music stops. Cut to the empty hall. Cut to the shocked reactions of the rustics who are mocked by background music. Cut to the aristocrats who, having neither thanked nor rewarded the players, go up the grand stairs to bed. Long before John Hancock's widely acclaimed black comedy version of the *Dream* in 1966–67, in which the rustics were herded away by faceless armed guards, un-Shakespearean sentimentality was stripped away. And in much the same way, the usual lyricism and harmony of idyllic interpretations are undermined. True, the magic returns as Oberon and Titania glide in among the pillars and fill the palace with the fluid movement, glitter, and music of the forest. But mischievous Puck has the last word. He terminates the decorous procession which Athens prescribes as the appropriate prelude to consummating the marriages by blowing out all the lights. Then, from the door of Theseus's and Hippolyta's bedchamber he speaks his ambiguous epilogue. What, one wonders, does Puck, who delights in chaos and tormenting mortals, intend behind those massive doors?

The central conflict of this film is couched in the opposition of black and white—male/female, Night/Moonlight, jealous hatred/love, evil/innocence. There is another visual theme in the work, however, which makes it even more Ovidian and Platonic than the play—the theme which can be summed up in the associative chain: reflection–echo–mime–shadow. In this film of a play so full of structural parallels, pairs, and mirror scenes, the glistening floors of Theseus's palace reflect the figures who walk and act upon them. In the forest, Bottom becomes Narcissus, first falling out of and then into love with his own image in the water. In the forest, moments of great humor for us and great terror for the mortals results from Puck's parodic talents. His answers to their cries—"Lysander!" "Oh dear heart speak!" "puppet!" "maypole!" —are raucous, distorted echoes which give the forest a nightmarish solipsistic feel. When Puck leads the duellists astray in the fog, we sometimes see *two* Pucks. When he becomes fire, he splits in two, forcing Flute to jump into a pool.

To act a part is to be a reflection, a double, and the link between echoes and theatre is established in the rehearsal scene. Quince, the interpreter of the playwright's interpretation of reality, has his stage directions and gestures mistaken for lines and gestures in "Pyramus and Thisby." Flute repeats everything back to him, including his anger at being misunderstood. Miming may be ineffective for the Indian boy who tries to fly like Titania's fairies, but Puck's imitative magic is potent. He transforms Bottom into an ass by miming its features. He puts the lovers to sleep by mirroring their every word and gesture. (One of the many visual gags has the imitation ass scare the rustics' real one away.) All of this repetition and counterpoint is, of course, reinforced by Mendelssohn's music in which themes and styles associated with the different parts of the plot—horns for Theseus, passionate strings for Helena, light strings for the fairies, heavy, raucous tunes for the rustics—are subtly varied and blended in a harmonious whole.

This echoing and mirroring is also used to embody the organic unity of the *Dream* in which there are many mysterious links between the real, dream, and play worlds. Philostrate, the stuffy, formal manager of mirth in Athens, parallels the shrieking satyr-joker of the forest, Puck. The snakes adorning Hippolyta's dresses and the undulating pillars of Theseus's palace reappear in Hermia's erotic nightmare in which she grasps the pearl necklace around her neck and dreams a serpent ate her heart away. The huge statues of lions in the palace are echoed in Lion of "Pyramus and Thisby" who symbolically deflowers the heroine by staining her mantle with blood. Theseus's chariot and white chargers are repeated in the rustics' ass-cart and Oberon's magnificent chariot of Night, and his scores of little oriental attendants at the end recall the Indian boy in the forest. Pronounced shadows recur in workshop, forest, and court. The spiralling of the fairies around the trees in the forest recalls the pillars of Athens and foreshadows the twining of ribbons around the Maypole at the festivities before Theseus and Hippolyta's wedding, just as the anthropomorphic willows of the forest serve as counterpoints to the humans decked out as Moon, Wall, and Lion in the play within the play. The hysterical laughter of Bottom and the lovers recurs in Hugh Herbert's Snout. Titania, with her smile, graceful movements, soprano voice, and gently tilted head, represents that vision of feminine loveliness which Quince was trying to create with the none-too-malleable material of Joe E. Brown. These and many more details are not mere decoration, but interesting explorations of the merging of inner and outer worlds in Shakespeare's play.

If one comes to the Reinhardt-Dieterle *Dream* expecting a faithful and literal presentation of the play, it is impossible not to make harsh judgments. Let the outraged British director Sidney Carroll bare the film's shortcomings from this point of view for all time:

> The most tolerant view I can take of this Reinhardt-in-Hollywood affair is that it is a splendiferous cinematic German-American version of "The Babes in the Woods". . . . A little Indian boy is . . . the central figure of a grand kidnapping adventure, and the pivot of the story. The boy is pursued by the demon king (Oberon) on horseback, protected by the fairy queen (Titania), and is eventually replaced in her affections by an American gunman called Bottom.
>
> Bottom at the head of a gang let loose from the Palladium Crazy Week goes off into the woods with a real donkey and cart, is watched by a Tom Sawyer Puck, while in the backwoods Colum-

bine Theilade disports with a troupe of smoke-screen dancers. The true local color is secured by a quartette of American college co-ed lovers. A masked jazz band of gnomes relieves Mendelssohn's music with a clamour of noise reminiscent of the menagerie of the modern danceroom. No expense has been spared with either costumes or scenery completely to eliminate Shakespeare from the picture.

Mr. Carroll summed up the work as "this frightful nightmare of crudity and childishness, this restless phantasmagoria of mingled Teutonic and Transatlantic buffoonery," a film with "little or no regard for Shakespearean poetry," with only actor (Ian Hunter as Theseus) who has "the slightest idea of proper Shakespearean diction and bearing."[22]

To other critics, the film's obvious flaws are offset by some sparkling virtues. The work is a bold effort to interpret and translate Shakespeare in cinematic terms and puts to shame the faded, rather dull efforts which came between it and Olivier's exuberant *Henry V*. Particularly in the performances of Puck, the rustics, Hermia, and Helena, it was a blow in the ongoing battle to free actors from the staid, elocutionary style and to replace it with acting less polished, perhaps, but livelier, more energetic, closer to modern experience. Finally, despite its excesses (what baroque work does not have them?), the directors skillfully integrated the traditional view of the play as idyllic fantasy with the darker, post-Freudian *Dream*, and in doing so made an important contribution to the interpretation of Shakespeare in performance.

# Peter Hall's *A Midsummer Night's Dream*

IN REINHARDT AND DIETERLE'S *DREAM,* ATHENS IS AS MUCH OF a fantasy as the forest. The overall movement is from one dream world to another. In Hall's film with the Royal Shakespeare Company, the pastoral pattern is more definitely invoked. We move from the daylight, rational, civilized world of Theseus to the cluttered, naturalistic rustics' shed, to the dark, wet greenery of the forest, and after sundry confusions and outbursts of irrationality we withdraw once more to the protection and order of Athens. Unlike the earlier film, this one retains Shakespeare's sense of conflict within the seasons. Said the director,

> The *Dream* is quite clearly a play about an English summer in which the seasons have gone wrong. It is winter when it should be summer; everywhere is wet and muddy. This is described by Titania in a central speech. This is why I shot so much of the film in the rain, during a bad-weather period lasting about six weeks. Titania's speech explaining this has often been cut in the past, yet it is the essence of the situation. The King and Queen of the Fairies, embodying animal nature, are quarrelling, and their quarrels have upset the balance of nature. This is what the play is all about. It is not a pretty balletic affair, but erotic, physical, down to earth. All this, but with great charm and humor as well.[1]

Stylistically, the film mirrors this pattern. The director first roots us in "normal" realistic settings and film conventions, then pulls the rug out from under us, imposing upon us the same disorientation and release that the lovers experience in the wood. After journeying cinematically from the sterility and monotony of the court, through transitional jump cuts with the lovers and Dutch Realist tableaux with the workmen, to an anarchy of visual and verbal styles in the forest, the conflicts between film styles are resolved. In the end, Hall, like the characters in the play, makes a concord of discord.

The opening of a Shakespeare film gives the filmmaker a certain freedom from the demands of the narrative, an opportunity not only to create atmosphere and set tone, but to establish motifs which will be used throughout the film. It is the director's overture. Hall's *Dream* begins not with Theseus's conciliatory words to Hippolyta but with a succession of images and sounds under the credits. Under the title of the play is an image of symmetry and harmony. Three large trees and a country house in the distance are reflected in a large pond. Bottom (the pun is inevitable) mirrors top, illusion mirrors reality, much as the forest mirrors Athens, "Pyramus and Thisby" mirrors the lovers' plight, and Shakespeare's comedy mirrors our own lives and dreams. Under the names of the actors who play the rustics is a bridge, appropriate enough since they serve as a transition between court and forest. Then follows a series of images which prefigure Titania's long speech about "an English summer in which the seasons have gone wrong."[2] We glimpse the dislocations of space and time we will experience later in the forest—images of various places whose spatial relations are not clear and of one season dissolving into another in sequences violating nature's cycle: a rain-dimpled pond, brilliant green sunlit grass, rocks covered with snow and ice, white clouds and blue sky, autumn leaves floating in the pond. Against the hope expressed in all the greenery is set the ominous rumble of thunder, dark clouds, and a shadowy gravestone covered with moss. Hall invokes both major elements of comedy—the celebration of the renewing cycle of the seasons, which includes marriage and procreation, and its necessary complement, death. In the sounds accompanying this collage of images is posited Shakespeare's sense of the underlying harmony in man and nature: Theseus's distant hunting horns gently blend with the sounds of thunder, falling rain, and the cries of birds.

From the disharmonies of nature we shift to what at first seems to be harmony in society. A man adorned with symbols of authority (a chain and a staff) strides purposefully along a path lined with evenly spaced servants standing at attention. The carefully trimmed grass, neat paths, and parallel rows of trees which continue beyond the horizon foster, like the grounds of Versailles, a feeling of mastery over nature. Like the solid neoclassical English house which stands for "Athens" in a play with only a thin veneer of classicism on it, these formal grounds suggest man has succeeded in imposing order, stability, and logic on the fluid, luxuriant growth of nature (which has its own very different kind of order). But appearances are deceiving. The mastery is only an illusion of mastery. As this figure moves into the courtyard and stands at the center of his artificial universe, we suddenly cut to Theseus and Hippolyta. We have been beholding not the Duke, but his prissy, snobbish Master of the Revels, Philostrate.

Our first impression of Theseus as he woos willing Hippolyta is of a man of reason and restraint, impressive in his own way but lacking flair, a bank president perhaps, or a judge. A sudden cut to a close-up of Egeus's unpleasant, angry face, as he incongruously wishes Theseus happiness and then demands his daughter's death for disobedience, jolts us but not the Duke. As Theseus deals with the conflict, we notice that his Georgian palace mirrors his personality. While the outside of the building is solid and well-proportioned, the inside is bland and unimaginative. Its inhibited barrenness is light years away from the crowds, music, and splendor of the court in the 1935 film. In this most functional of monuments, there are no strong contrasts of light and shadow, no unexplored corners, no mysteries. The walls and curtains, drained of color, hover unpleasantly between green and grey. The regular patterns formed by bannisters, vertical folds in the curtains, pillars, and symmetrically placed royal chairs bespeak rigidity and correspond to Theseus's strict reading of the law in upholding the power of Egeus over Hermia (despite the hints of wry humor around the edges of his speeches). The camera angles down at the courtiers, placing them against the black and white grid on the floor, measuring them by and trapping them in marble patterns, intimating that citizens of Athens, like chess pieces, move from square to square according to a prescribed manner even in serious conflicts. The editing and cinematography are chaste and ordinary, save for the telephoto lens which reduces motion, renders the images two-dimensional, and makes the characters visually as flat as the emotions they express.

Inside Athens the illusion of power over nature is maintained. Behind Theseus's head we see, doubly framed by a decorative border, a tapestry depicting people amidst greenery. Leafy patterns are em-

The courtiers in Athens

broidered on the collars of the male courtiers. Everywhere nature is tamed, made decorative. The costumes of the court are dull, unflattering, arranged in a spectrum from Hippolyta's black, to Egeus's dark grey, to Theseus's moderate shade, to the light grey-greens of the suitors, to the still lighter grey of Hermia. The captive Amazon's suggestive black leather dress, thigh-length boots, and serpentine arm bracelet (a borrowing from Reinhardt) are deceptive, for in fact Hippolyta is domestic and dull, the director having obliterated all trace of her conflict with Theseus. It is a bland opening scene, unrelieved by Lysander's wit or Egeus's comic rant (here not comic at all, but the ranting of a nasty, middle-aged lawyer, angry at a broken contract, jealous of the youths).

When Hermia and Lysander are left alone, we see that it is not merely dukes and fathers that stand between them, but the sterility, stasis, silences, and greyness of Athens itself. Placed at opposite edges of the screen, the lovers are separated by large, heavily shadowed chairs of state. When they move together to embrace, the blank wall behind them forms a neutral background for Lysander's lyrical lament (the first beautiful thing in Athens), "the course of true love never did run smooth," but it is also an emblem of the oppressive blandness they must

flee. Even when we are most drawn to the lovers, however, harsh lighting, cruel close-ups, and unflattering angles heighten the blemishes and
lines in their faces—faces not chosen for their stereotypical beauty.
Even in adolescent lovers, there is something ugly about man in such
a setting, a fact which neither the temperate tones of Theseus nor the
impassioned lyricism of Lysander can disguise. In the court of Athens,
man is without spontaneity, joy, grace, physical beauty.

As Lysander and Hermia make plans to flee Athens, Hall introduces
themes and techniques which serve as transitions to the fluid, cinematically free forest scenes. Momentum, regular rhythm, and continuity
are provided by the text while jump cuts disrupt our sense of realistic
space.[3] A tension is established between what sounds like a conventional, clearly articulated stage performance and visuals which whisk
the star-crossed lovers from the grey interior to a flat boat on a pond
bordered with greenery to a spacious lawn where they tell melancholy
Helena of their flight. (As they lie on the lawn, there is a suggestion
that the lovers' flight will not be altogether successful: the path we saw
Philostrate walk upon earlier passes behind, visually *through*, their
heads intimating that whatever their intentions they will take "Athens"
with them.)

The plot propels the lovers further and further from Theseus's court.
Helena's soliloquy, unified in imagery, rhythm, and tone, is matched
with radically dislocated shots and fragments of spatially unrelated
motions as she moves from Athenian death (a chapel with gravestones)
to a phallic monument (the more erotic death of the forest) to the
emblematic bridge. Deliberately jerky hand-held shots reflect her state
of mind and drive us further from the transparent photographic style
of the court. Her direct address of the camera breaks down the fourth-
wall convention observed earlier, anticipating similar soliloquies by
Oberon, Titania, Puck, Bottom, and Hermia in the forest, and her
speech ends on a note of surprise. The sound of a bird taking flight
makes her turn suddenly and the lens throws her out of focus. But
contrary to film convention, the off-screen glance and rack-focus lead
not to a shot of the bird, but to moon-faced, bespectacled Quince, play
in hand, preparing to cast the parts for "Pyramus and Thisby."

Quince's workshop provides a further break from the court. Low-
key lighting (lending a touch of the mysteriousness of the forest),
extreme contrasts, and varied textures are, much to our relief, pleasing
to look at. Everything is concrete and alive in contrast to the abstract,

Bottom and Company

antiseptic, aristocratic world of Theseus. The blocking is appropriately stagelike as they cast their tragedy, Quince's players facing forward and bunching together in tableaux. Yet the scene does not seem static because of the conflicts, noise, range of verbal styles, and a set of richly comic faces unparalleled in Shakespeare films. On their lunch hour, the workers display an energy and an ease unknown in the rarified heights of their "betters." They sprawl, scratch themselves, munch onions and huge sandwiches. Around them chickens cluck and flies buzz. A dead rabbit, victim of a tragic end not yet made immortal by the pen of Quince, hangs from a beam in the background. The dominant color is a deep earthy brown. Tools etch interesting shadows on the wall. Homespun prose and ludicrous bombast are spoken with great verve and intensity, and the workers roar, coo, and laugh with infectious zest. Here, as in the court, the conflict is over authority, and Hall has rightly perceived and underscored the parallel. But the diplomacy of Quince (a comic self-portrait by Shakespeare the playwright-director) far outstrips that of Theseus as Quince persuades his prima donna Bottom that it would be improper for him to imitate protean Puck and play all the parts.

When we enter the forest in Hall's film, we leave behind the naturalistic world of Athens and enter the world of dreams. From the beginnings of cinema, theorists have noted the similarities between dreaming and watching a flow of images on the screen. Freed of narrowing demands for realism, the fluid imagery of film is especially well-suited to the task of capturing the forest of the *Dream* as a landscape of the mind. Shakespeare creates through poetry and theatre imagery a bewildering wonderland of warped time, space, and scale, a place in which characters' identities split and merge. The wood is filled with clashes of realism and artifice, mixtures of self-conscious lyricism and linguistic ornament. Shakespeare's plot is filled with hilarious and grotesque juxtapositions, paradoxes and surprises, endlessly layered events linked together in a mysterious grand design.

Reinhardt and Dieterle created this moon-drenched world of the imagination with the fluid, stylized movements of ballet, the marches, delicate melodies, and buffoonery of Mendelssohn's incidental music, glitter and gauzes which obscure vision, and intense back-lighting which gives Puck and the forest a surreal look. But in Hall's view, *A Midsummer Night's Dream* "is not a pretty, balletic affair, but erotic, physical, down to earth. All this, but with great charm and humor as well...."[4] His seminude, ambivalent vegetation spirits inhabit a glistening green world of tangled branches, vast areas of deep shadow, and sudden appearances and disappearances (Puck vanishes with a "swish" as if sucked up by some huge vacuum cleaner). Shots in the wood blend elements of reality with blatantly antirealistic techniques. Spotlights, shaped by star filters, shine directly into the camera, creating tension between visual attraction (the lights) and dramatic interest (characters). Their glare often invades the integrity of the human images, making them seem unreal. Editing is often disjunctive and rapid—when Oberon and Titania first meet, segments of their movement toward each other overlap, and in one series of nineteen shots each image lasts for between 1/6 and 5/6 of a second. Motion in the forest is often altered or speeded up, and at the end, when harmony is restored, Oberon and Titania seem to drift disembodied through the air in slow motion as they come together again and again to the delicate sound of a celeste.

The performers' articulate, beautifully paced readings and relatively subdued acting disguise the radical unreality of the forest. For example, there is very little consistency about whether it is night or day. Time seems as fluid and free as the fairies' movements. Backgrounds shift wildly and without warning as the spirits move with the speed of a thought from backdrops of pure white or pure black to tangled dark branches, leaves, pink flowers, or the reflection of the moon in the water broken up into dancing circles and stars by a telephoto lens. The fracturing of naturalistic surfaces in a medium which some theorists limit to the "objective rendering of reality" is enhanced by continual changes in composition, unexplained alterations of light, and Hall's blithe disregard for color matching. The forest is a collage of a thousand shades of green, and with each shot faces change color.

Puck and Oberon

Little attention is given to consistency. Oberon's horns (Oberon as Satan? Oberon as cuckold? Oberon as satyr?) change from scene to scene, as do the muddy patches on the lovers' faces and clothing. Groupings and compositions also lend to the surreal air. Puck's feet enter the frame in close-up with their toes wagging frantically. Subsequently, his legs seem like huge tree trunks while Oberon, who usually towers over Robin Goodfellow, looks up at him from the ground where he is buried up to his chest. When Oberon awakens his queen, he does something rarely done in film—he enters from the top of the frame. And in the same shot, Bottom's reclining body becomes an horizon, the "landscape" of the shot. Usually film directors arrange a consistency in screen placement, as when in Burge and Dexter's *Othello* Iago inhabits the left part of the screen and Othello the right. This is done when Puck and the fairy first appear, Puck being to the right and the fairy to the left, but just before Oberon and Titania enter, the pattern is reversed. From then on in the forest scenes there is little consistency in screen position. Anyone is likely to appear anywhere in the frame. Even the sounds of the forest are unreal—jungle birds inhabit a wood near Athens, and voices and sounds are abnormally heightened, rendered in such a clean selective way that no sense of acoustic space harmonizing with the visuals is given at all.

Hall's magic, like Shakespeare's, has a purpose. The assaults on our viewing habits and the violations of conventions serve as an analogue for what happens to those other dreamers, the lovers, Bottom, and Titania. Athens is dull and confining. Those who flee, rebel against male authority, or take an heroic identity upon themselves through the mysteries of tragedy find exhilarating freedom and visions of wonder. But they also find a frightening world of reflections, disorientation, and flux. For dreamers and audience in this film, the patterns of logic and identity which we use to make sense of things break down. Assumptions which ordinarily give meaning to a chaos of thoughts, feelings, and sensations become useless or disintegrate and we are left alone like Alice in Wonderland or the looking-glass world. In being true to the dream experience, Hall has gone some distance toward what Peter Brook and others have called for—a style which liberates Shakespeare's multilayered, fluid, imagistic verse from slow, literal, naturalistic film textures and images. But unlike the one director who has gone beyond Hall in achieving this freedom, Orson Welles, Hall has left the text virtually intact.[5] Furthermore, not only do avant-garde techniques complement the verse, as in cuts which are located consistently at the end of verse lines or in caesuras.[6] They embody meaning, as when color fades of red, blue, and orange underscore the unnaturalness of the alterations in the seasons as Titania describes them.

Like Shakespeare, Hall is interested in the clash of styles. The clumsy, homely, earth-bound rustics, bunched together and facing forward in the forest, are spectacularly unlike the immortals, who are completely at home in the moon-drenched greenery. It is droll to see toothless Starveling, lantern in hand, quake with fear beneath the moon when he is told that he must impersonate Moonshine. Each world comments upon the others. Bottom, who never stops being himself no matter what part he is playing (the mark of a true star), blends Theseus's dignified calm with earscratching requests for hay and dried peas. Titania is erotically freer than the clinging young ladies from Athens, but she is just as silly, and the young men who spout bombastic protestations of love make asses of themselves just like Bottom.

Bottom and Titania

In contrast to the fairies, who move instantaneously through the forest, the lovers slog through streams, become lost in the fog, and crawl on their hand and knees through the tangled undergrowth ("use me as your spaniel," says Helena to Demetrius). The irony of their flight becomes apparent, for they have fled from one prison to another. Cold, wet, hungry, exhausted, and frustrated, they suffer in what they thought was going to be another Garden of Eden. Though Oberon takes pity on them, the forest seems hostile to the lovers and their Athenian trappings. Birds jeer at them when their confusions become greatest. When Hermia is left alone by Lysander, the ominous sounds of the forest become deafening. As faces become smeared with mud, and hair tangled like the branches, their Athenian identities slip off: "am I not Hermia? Are you not Lysander? I am as fair now as I was erewhile" (she is a mess). Apart from Helena, attractively played by

Diana Rigg, particularized by tugging at her pretty dark hair and clinging to sundry trees and men, the lovers seem interchangeable. They are
reduced to a common denominator when their uniforms, starched
shirts, and pretty dresses—symbols of Athenian restraint and decorum
—are torn and soiled.

Sexual drives are closer to the surface in the forest. When Hermia
makes Lysander "lie further off" on their first night together, he simply
leaves her (granted he is "under a spell") for Helena. The friendship of
the two young women descends to bitter jealousy and a most un-
maidenlike Hermia attempts to scratch Helena's eyes out. To be
Athenian in the forest is to be ridiculous. Lysander and Demetrius
attempt to channel their conflict into the civilized form of chivalric
combat, but when they salute each other with their swords, turn, and
march lock-step into the forest to fight to the death, they succeed only
in becoming hopelessly entangled in the shrubbery (a bird shrieks in
derision overhead) and later lost in the fog. Puck manipulates the
mortals like puppets. Only Bottom among the Athenians manages to
adapt to the wonders of the new world, and only he knows what to do
with his dream when he awakes: not explain it, but (like Shakespeare)
transform it into a work of art.

Bottom: "I have had a most rare dream"

The final movement of *A Midsummer Night's Dream* is a return through the workshop to the court, a recovery of sanity for those who have been "wood." Theseus and Hippolyta with their hounds, huntsmen, and daylight invade the forest and dissipate its magic. Awakened by Theseus's horns, the lovers are confused and vulnerable. Like them, we also are jolted by the rush of bellowing hounds at the camera. The young rebels who thought they had escaped Athens have been running in circles. Suddenly they find themselves "onstage," huddled in a tableau under the Duke's oak before a crowd. But Athens has changed. Theseus overcomes Egeus's will and ratifies the arrangement of the lovers which his alter-ego in the forest, Oberon, has with such difficulty arranged. The plot of the lovers' "play," which ends tragically in both *Romeo and Juliet* and its parody, "Pyramus and Thisby," has been altered by Duke and King, and the lovers follow the royal couple to the temple to be married. They do not understand their dreams any more than Bottom does. Like a movie audience, they go off to live their lives knowing that something has been done to them but not knowing exactly what.

Standing in a doorway, looking out past the formal lawn to the forest, Theseus and Hippolyta reaffirm that Athens has changed for the better. As Theseus skeptically equates the minds of the madman, the poet, and the lover, his orderly mind is bodied forth in two chandeliers with lighted candles arranged in hierarchies and resting symmetrically behind him. But as he becomes more involved in imagination, a close-up reveals unexpected ambivalence in his words. His tone shifts to wonder and admiration and the candles behind him are thrown out of focus. Theseus's chandeliers are echoed in Hippolyta's earrings, suggesting that part of her is aligned with his rationalism. But her imagination is symbolized by a brilliant, irregularly burning torch set at an angle behind her head as she argues the antithesis of her husband's view, that the dreams of the lovers grow to "something of great constancy." "Pyramus and Thisby," we note, is illuminated both by the light of the chandeliers and by the open flame of the hearth, suggesting more than one perspective on Quince's tragical comedy.

Shakespeare concludes his comedy of misunderstanding with a tragedy of misunderstanding, a stroke considerably beyond the powers of the Quinces of the world. Athenian decorum, already stretched by the rebellion of the youths and by Hippolyta's influence on Theseus, crumbles. The Duke shocks the snob Philostrate by choosing to hear a workman's play of tragical mirth. The players transform the sterile room of the opening scene. Bottom and company bring with them their low-key lighting, rough-textured fabrics, straw, rich dark browns, delightfully comic faces, and stagey tableaux. The customarily stiff compositions of Athens become unbalanced, and geometrical rigidities of blocking break down.

That Theseus's servants have been invited to watch the play suggests a loosening of class barriers for the sake of communal festivity. Athens' deadening abstractness, which included its commitments to The Law, is shattered by the downright physicalness of the rustics and their properties. So literal are they that, even with Herculean efforts by the audience to quicken their fiction with its imagination, they manage to defeat dramatic illusion altogether. Their naive earnestness, worlds away from the professional clowning of the Reinhardt-Dieterle film, is to no avail as the spirit of Puck seems to dog their every move. One of Wall's bricks shatters in his hand and dust from his leather apron sets the tragic hero coughing. In addition, he suffers excruciating tickles on the hand with which he forms the "chink" as the lovers provoke guffaws among the menservants by announcing that they are "kissing Wall's hole." Mop-headed Thisby's voice repeatedly drops down out of falsetto, Bottom's sword becomes entangled in his belt at the grand moment of his suicide, and Moonshine—poor Moonshine—not only does his part melt away under the heat of the courtier's jibes, but his candle goes out at the crucial moment. This disaster occasions Bottom's greatest victory. He responds with such a thundering set of alliterations ("gracious golden glittering gleams") that he seems to conjure up the light and the audience roars and claps its approval.

Shakespeare designed "Pyramus and Thisby" to be more than a humanizing, decorum-shattering farce, however, and Hall brings this out nicely. Bottom and Quince, the former the only mortal to see the immortals, and the latter a partaker of the mysteries of imaginative creation, are the only players garnished with the bright green leaves of the realm of Oberon and Titania. Their tragical comedy and its miraculous effect on Theseus's whole household have some intimate connection with what happened to the lovers in the forest. Pyramus and Thisby swear by "Helen" and "Limander," and both Demetrius and Theseus refer to the rustics as asses, the latter's remark bringing a puzzled look from Bottom as he lies dead on the floor. As in the Reinhardt and Dieterle film, the play within the play tests the courtiers.

But here they pass with flying colors, and Hall hardly hints at the sourness of the earlier film. Athens has overcome its rigidities and enters into the fun, aided by judicious cuts of several unfunny jokes and snide remarks. Through laughter and the exchange of knowing looks, the young lovers sympathize with the rustics and the lovers they play, and yet also see the ridiculousness of lovers eager to die for love. Since they will be the inheritors of Athens, the regeneration seems genuine. This feeling is reinforced during the burgomask dance, for there is no barrier between the dancers and those who clap to the dance. They are all one.

The regeneration only becomes truly complete, however, when the fairies bring their magic to Athens and bless the marriage beds. By filling Theseus's house with their music, sparkles, fluid movements, nudity, greenery, and sudden appearances and disappearances, they conclude the integration of styles so crucial to the structure of the play, bring full circle the pattern of the dream. Perfect harmony has been achieved on aesthetic and thematic levels. Well, almost perfect harmony, for, true to the play, Hall's Puck invokes dangerous forms of magic and the darker themes of death, disease, and madness articulated in the 1935 film. Puck circles us in the dark (recapitulating the movement from house to forest to house) inviting us with a wry grin to dismiss the play as an idle dream. Suddenly he snaps his fingers and it is morning. Daylight is also an illusion. The sunlit facade of Theseus's house and the sweetly singing birds now seem a trick played on us by a mischievous fairy. This *Dream* by Shakespeare and Hall and Puck stands everything on its head. Do we wake or sleep?

Hall's detachment, his refusal to let his actors emote, his shunning of music to create a festive feeling, and the deliberately dull opening scene alienate many people, especially those who like the Reinhardt-Dieterle extravaganza. The radical cinematography, which, because of the way it is used, makes the film extremely interesting, disturbs people accustomed to more conventional films. This *Dream* is full of playful touches. The encounters of genial eye-rolling, puppetlike Bottom and Judi Dench's beautiful, nude queen of fairies in heat are sublime. Helena's clinging to phallic objects, her comic chases of Demetrius through the forest, and her sucking her thumb as she sleeps by him under the Duke's oak are amusing. One recalls with pleasure Demetrius sitting amazed in the middle of a stream where angry Hermia has pushed him, Puck's pause-filled impatient exit as Oberon keeps thinking of new things for him to do, Puck's putting the ladies to sleep with kisses and covers of hay, Quince's barely perceptible frowns as Bottom crosses him, and Oberon's devilish boy who knocks out skinny, shivering Cobweb left to guard Titania. One of the great double takes on film is registered by onion-munching Snout, who looks back at the script upon seeing Bottom with an ass's head to find the lines in "Pyramus and Thisby" which would explain such a change, and Bottom's operatic gurgling series of deaths as Pyramus and the pummeling he takes from lamenting Thisby consistently bring down the house. Still, this is not a film that *strains* to entertain.

Something of what Hall was after is evident in his discussion of his many close-ups. "I made the *Dream* in close shot not because of lack of money, or because it was likely to be shown on television. I wanted it close shot because this seems to me the only way to scrutinize cooly the marked ambiguity of the text, and the cinema can do this better than the theatre."[7] Sometimes, as in Theseus's speech on imagination, or Oberon's "I know a bank where the wild thyme blows" where the shift in tone is punctuated by a tight close-up, this worked fairly well. But often it puzzles audiences by short-circuiting the connection between the actor's face and his/her lines. Film audiences read close-ups as invitations to think about the psychology of the characters; they respond well to judiciously used close-ups in a work like *Hamlet*. But in a play where the real interest lies in the overall pattern and not in the characters, perhaps close-ups are less appropriate. Despite these flaws, rarely has Shakespeare's verse been spoken so well on film, few directors have experimented so boldly with cinematic style and Shakespearean meaning, and few actors have surpassed Paul Rogers as Bottom. It would be a pity to allow a film made for the small screen, but much more colorful and alive on the large screen, be used up by one television performance.[8]

# 4

# Franco Zeffirelli's *Taming of the Shrew*

LIKE THE *DREAM, THE TAMING OF THE SHREW* HAS MORE
than one layer of reality. The main story of the marrying of Baptista's
daughters is framed by another story—the duping of Christopher Sly—
which distances the main tale, shares themes with it, and casts a certain
ambivalence over it. Also like the *Dream, Shrew* is part romance, focus-
ing upon love and based upon the stock New Comedy situation: the
old block the coupling of the young, the blocks are removed, marriages
are celebrated, and harmony is restored. In other respects, however,
*Shrew* differs from the later comedies. It has fewer characters of complexity and warmth. It is not as genteel and aristocratic in tone—less
lyrical and fantastic, less witty, less philosophical, less sentimental about
love. The deluding of the drunken tinker by aristocratic pranksters into
thinking he is a lord awakened from a bad dream is less genial than
Bottom's dream. There is something cruel about it, and though the
ending has either been omitted by Shakespeare or is lost, we sense that
Sly must inevitably be disillusioned.

This comedy is not set in some never-never land—Illyria, Arden,
a wood near Athens—but in Warwick, Padua, and the country near
Verona. It has a tough, bourgeois, urban strain and a note of crass
materialism which counterpoints with, and to some extent undermines,
the romance. Despite his talk of winning his daughters' affections,
Baptista is a merchant driving a hard bargain. He goes along with
Petruchio and the false Lucentio because he thinks they have gold and
social position, not because they have won Bianca's and Kate's love.

Petruchio comes to "wive it *wealthily* in Padua," and though his motives may change during the course of the play, commerce never entirely disappears. Uncharacteristic of romantic comedies, which take us to the threshold of marriage but not—like *Othello* or *Winter's Tale* —inside, the marriage of the hero and heroine comes in the middle of the play and, as in *Merry Wives of Windsor*, their remaining struggles remove some of the idyllic gloss from that institution.

The most realistic element of the play, however—the one that offends modern sensibilities the most—is the taming of Kate. George Bernard Shaw, posing as an irate woman who had just seen the 1888 producing starring Ada Rehan, labelled *Shrew*

> one vile insult to womanhood and manhood from first to last.... Of course, it was not Shakespear. Instead of Shakespear's coarse, thick-skinned money hunter who sets to work to tame his wife exactly as brutal people tame animals or children—that is by breaking their spirit by domineering cruelty—we have Garrick's fop who tries to "shut up" his wife by behaving worse than she.... In spite of [Petruchio's] ... winks and smirks when Katherine is not looking, he cannot make the spectacle of a man cracking a heavy whip at a starving woman other than disgusting and unmanly.[1]

To a feminist, *Shrew* is either a piece of male chauvinist wishful thinking, asserting that woman's will can be broken and in the end both she and the man will be the happier for it, or it is a confirmation that the rebel in comedy—and, by implication, in society—must ultimately toe the mark. Neither of these is very funny (or perhaps we should say both are *painfully* funny).

Kate has been interpreted in many ways. Perhaps she is a real shrew, full of self-hatred, contempt for kindness and love, and uncontrollable rage, who is shouted down by a male shrew, trained by a lion tamer, or subjected to primal scream therapy by "Dr. Petruchio." Perhaps she is a neglected daughter who envies the favorite Bianca and seeks both the love and the figure of authority in a husband that she missed in her father. Perhaps she is not a shrew at all, but merely shrewd, playing the same game Bianca plays but angling in a different way and for a better prize. Whichever Katherine predominates, viewed with cold, Monday-morning eye, *Shrew* is not entirely humorous, especially if Kate's final speech is taken at face value.

But *Shrew* contains farce as well as romance and realism. It is a play not for a sober Monday morning but for a drunken Saturday night, a vacation from morality, psychology, and seriousness, in which we can sit back and laugh at a caricature of the battle of the sexes, free of the need to be understanding and fair or even to pass judgment. From this perspective, it is enough that there be plenty of knockabout physical humor, that the struggle be lively and entertaining and the action varied (as in any monster movie). It doesn't really matter who wins (would the play really change if, as in *Merry Wives*, the women tamed the men?), for the enjoyment is in the intrigue, curses, and pratfalls, in seeing con artists conned and the everyday world turned into a madhouse.

Franco Zeffirelli, in his boisterous film of *Shrew*, which pits Richard Burton against Elizabeth Taylor, plays up the romance and sentiment, tones down the realism, and revels in the farce. Petruchio and Kate are in love from the moment they set eyes on each other. Their struggle, really a mutual taming, is "the old game"—they test each other, school each other (the other schoolmasters are fakes). When they come to an agreement, it is much more like real-life marriage than the pallid Lucentio-Bianca soap bubble which is pricked in the end. Crass, drunken, self-serving, and materialistic at the beginning, Petruchio, without being rendered impotent, becomes civilized, witty, and dignified by the end. Twice Kate chooses Petruchio over the collection of fops and old men in Padua: by maintaining silence behind the stained glass window when Petruchio announces their wedding on Sunday, and by following him in the rain when he leaves her at Padua's gates and rides toward his crumbling, moth-eaten mansion.

Petruchio's "taming" of Kate in this film has several dimensions. He is the plebeian, taking down a peg a spoiled, egotistical, well-fed, rich girl, teaching her about humility, patience, and recognizing a will other than her own. He is the bohemian teaching her to disdain wealth and luxury, to avoid the bourgeois obsession with appearances and a confusion of values by subjecting her to wetness, cold, fatigue, hunger, pain, and the ridicule of her inferiors. Petruchio, who tests the silver of Baptista's goblets before broaching the subject of marriage and cries "my twenty thousand crowns!" as Kate jumps out the window to escape him, changes too. Like most good teachers, he learns as he teaches.

> To me she's married, not unto my clothes.
> . . . . . . . . . . . . . . . . . . . . . . . . . . . . . . .
> Well, come my Kate; we will unto your father's

68

Even in these honest mean habiliments.
Our purses shall be proud, our garments poor,
For 'tis the mind that makes the body rich;
And as the sun breaks through the darkest clouds
So honor peereth in the meanest habit.

Petruchio is also a playful actor who, unlike the uncreative maskers and unconscious hypocrites of Padua, enjoys taking on roles, is self-aware, and has a sense of irony.

In the beginning, Kate is encased in the role of "shrew," cast in it by frightened, ineffectual men and crafty (though on the surface, submissive) Bianca and kept in it by her refusal to capitulate. She is trapped in a negative image of everything in Padua that she hates, and in that sense she is an imitation of it. Petruchio, her knight in tarnished armor, opposes the frozen, the negative, the uncreative. As D. A. Traversi said, "Petruchio is in effect revealing the *real* Kate to herself. . . ."[2] In cursing him, fighting him, fleeing him, Kate is infinitely more alive and inventive than in dealing with lesser men. Perhaps she learns humility, but she also learns not to be tied to the literal when she must say it is seven o'clock when it is two, or when she must call the sun the moon. In one of the funniest scenes in the film, Kate learns that her husband's "commands" are an invitation to humorous invention. With delicious, devilish innocence, she greets grey-bearded Vincentio as a budding virgin whose parents are blessed in "her." Greeted with his bewildered look as he peers around the head of his horse, she realizes her "mistake" and delivers a mock apology for having her eyes dazzled "by the . . . sun?" (she looks to Petruchio; he nods yes). By raining blows on his servants (the first time we see Petruchio he chases Grumio around the fire, boots him, and rams him into Hortensio's door), making impossible demands, and causing the faults he scolds (he trips the servant who brings the water), by decimating the fashionable clothes prepared for Kate to wear to Bianca's wedding and placing the blame on the poor craftsmen, Petruchio shows Kate her own image. He forces her to see that she must be more forgiving. "Patience," she says, "I pray you, 'twas a fault unwilling." "I pray you, husband, be not so disquiet. The meat was well if you were so contented."

PETRUCHIO:   First kiss me Kate, and we will.
KATE:   What, in the middle of the street?
PETRUCHIO:   What, art thou ashamed of me?

KATE:     No sir, God forbid, but ashamed to kiss.
PETRUCHIO:   Why then let's home again. Come sirrah, let's away.
KATE:     Nay, I will give thee a kiss. Now pray thee, love, stay.

(In the film, Kate holds her own, for she gives him a most unsatisfying peck on the nose.) What he demands, in place of both conformity and rebellion, is tolerance, strong bonds between people, kindness, forgiveness.

For Zeffirelli, Kate's "submission" at the end is a kind of *rite de passage*, a demonstration that she understands what Petruchio has been trying to teach her. After a taste of domestic warfare with Petruchio, a close look at the meanness and vulgarity of the widow and Bianca, and a glance at the children playing with the dogs before the lavish banquet table, Kate seizes the opportunity of the wager to make a pact with Petruchio. With delightful irony, she, who has terrified men by smashing furniture, bellowing, and raining blows on them, bodily hauls the widow and Bianca before their husbands and describes the *frailty* of women. Using her new-found sense of role playing, she uncovers the real shrews and feeds the males present such an eloquent and unconditional surrender to male domination that they are all taken in. But the speech isn't really to them; it is to Petruchio. Beneath her irony, she enunciates the paradox at the heart of love in all of Shakespeare's romantic comedies: give all and you will get all. Kate's fluid shifts in tone, playful hyperbole, love of doing the unexpected, and obvious awareness of her double audience constitute her farewell to the narrowness and rigidities of Kate the shrew. Her offer of "love, fair looks, and true obedience" to Petruchio's "*honest* will," an important qualification, confirms her new-found humility and expresses gratitude for his freeing her from a sterile role. This time there is no hesitation when he asks for a kiss. And if the audience has missed the point and thinks Kate's spirit broken, to the delight of the crowd in the film while Petruchio triumphs over the losers of the wager, Kate sneaks out of the room and makes him begin the chase anew.

Zeffirelli has little use for the realism in the play. For instance, Shakespeare's refusal to be "poetical" and lyrical in the play has been overruled, for the film is loaded with pleasant but syrupy melodies in the best Hollywood tradition. (This is one of the few Shakespeare films where the audience comes out humming the music.) Broad comic acting emphasizes the typical nature of the characters: stooped, pathetically outclassed Baptista, Hortensio the effeminate fop, the pantaloon Gremio, Lucentio the handsome young suitor, Grumio and Tranio the tricky servants, the pedant laden with books and peering through spectacles, the Puck-like Biondello, who peers like a faun through the greenery while Lucentio and Bianca make love in the garden. Whatever ironic perspective Shakespeare provided by making the main action a crude entertainment for a drunken, deluded tinker trying in vain to get his "wife" into bed is gone, for like many theatrical directors, Zeffirelli has omitted the frame story altogether.

There are touches of vivid realistic detail in the film: the children taunting the "wife-stealer" in the stocks and the "drunkard" in the cage near Padua's city gates, tough-looking men and whores, Gremio's bad breath, Hortensio's getting hairs from his false beard in his mouth, Petruchio's ugly, gap-toothed servants, giant dogs eating meat scraps by the banquet table at Bianca's wedding, the ticks Petruchio picks from his dog and shows to squeamish Hortensio, the filth that covers everything at Petruchio's seedy, gothic house, and the downpour that drenches Petruchio and Kate. But these are used for comic effect, and work to heighten the colorful, rich portrait of renaissance Italy. From the opening moments when Lucentio and Tranio, riding in a gentle summer rain, spy Padua haloed with a rainbow beyond a pastoral vision with shepherds, sheep, and greenery, the film is a beautiful idyll bathed in golden and rose-colored light. The central stylistic device, derived from the language of a play uncharacteristically lacking in verbal ornament, is the epic catalogue, the heaping on of detail. Reading verbal floods in Shakespeare—like Gremio's description of his city and country houses, the verbal portraits of Petruchio's outrageous wedding costume and the desecrated marriage ceremony, Grumio's list of tasks the servants were to have performed, and Petruchio's enumeration of rich garments Kate will wear to Bianca's wedding—Zeffirelli created visual equivalents in shots full of sensuous surfaces, color, and motion. Vicariously we devour fancy dishes and drink fine wine, eat symbolic apples, roll in the grass, lie in huge soft beds, sing bawdy love songs, swing on a trapeze and then drop into a bin of raw wool, splash with choirboys in the fountain outside the church, and ride through the rain.

Apart from sentimental romance, Zeffirelli's major emphasis is upon farce. The film delights in harmless violence and festive destruction. Kate smashes shutters and stained-glass windows, splinters music stands and lutes, rips out the bell rope which Petruchio tugs upon so daintily, and tears loose a railing to hurl at him. Petruchio drunkenly knocks over wine glasses and pulls down curtains at Hortensio's house, smashes through railings and brick walls, and falls through the roof in Baptista's barn. He pummels and spits upon his servants, bisects a hat with a family sword causing the haberdasher to faint, tears dresses, hurls food, overturns the dinner table, and makes a shambles of the wedding bed.

This *Shrew* revels in farce's extravagant expenditures of energy and comically accelerated actions: wooing and winning in half an hour, running down the aisle at the wedding, rushing down a muddy mountain on a donkey, spinning half-plucked chickens on a spit. It delights in absurdly complicated situations, as when an avalanche of babbling suitors and schoolteachers falls upon bewildered Baptista, or distracted Vincentio confronts fraudulent versions of himself and his son. It has farce's shallow characterizations and lack of reflective passages. Above all, its primary structural device, the chase, which is repeated in endless variations, is straight out of the Keystone Cops. Tranio chases Lucentio, the singers chase Bianca, Gremio and Hortensio follow Tranio who follows Lucentio who follows Bianca home, and both Lucentio and Petruchio pursue their servants. In the longest chase of the film, Petruchio pursues Kate until he catches up with her at the altar. But the pattern of pursuit does not stop there. Kate rides after Petruchio and Grumio in the rain, the servants chase the chickens with meat cleavers, and so on to the end of the film where Petruchio's chase of Kate is renewed (this time, we suspect, she will not run too hard).

In filming *Shrew*, Zeffirelli obviously provided a pleasant vehicle for Richard Burton and Elizabeth Taylor. But he also redefined, perhaps even revealed, its central action. For most critics and directors, the essence of the play is the "taming" of Kate, or at least the mutual taming of Kate and Petruchio; and certainly the director's radical compression of the Bianca plot makes them even more prominent. But, important as it is, the "taming" is not the heart of the film. Rather, it is the good-natured but thorough assault of Kate and Petruchio on Padua and Paduan values. Zeffirelli turns loose two rebels against hypocrites, greedy pantaloons, time-servers, blind idealists, tricky maidens, and crafty widows. They declare war on respectability, duty, religion, sighing literary romance, and narrowing materialism.

In a fine discussion of *Shakespeare's Festive Comedy*,[3] C. L. Barber argues that *A Midsummer Night's Dream, The Merchant of Venice, Love's Labour's Lost, As You Like It, Twelfth Night* and *Henry IV*,

Petruchio and Kate: Lord and Lady of Misrule

*Part 1* are rooted in saturnalian festivals and other outbursts of "folly" —May Games, the Lord of Misrule, Morris Dances, Masks, Disguisings —which survived in Elizabethan England from the middle ages. In complaining of the European cousins of these revels in 1445, the Dean of the Faculty of Theology at Paris seems almost to be writing a commentary on Zeffirelli's *Shrew:*

> Who, I ask you, with any Christian feelings, will not condemn when priests and clerks are seen wearing masks and monstrous visages at the hours of Office: dancing in the Choir, dressed as women, panders, or minstrels, singing lewd songs? They eat black-pudding at the horn of the altar next the celebrant, play at dice there, censing with foul smoke from the soles of old shoes, and running and leaping about the whole church in unblushing, shameless iniquity; and then, finally, they are seen driving about the town and its theatres in carts and deplorable carriages to make an infamous spectacle for the laughter of bystanders and participants, with indecent gestures of the body and language most unchaste and scurrilous.[4]

Ultimately, if anthropologists are correct, both these festivals and comedy go back through Rome and Greece to ancient seasonal rites of the death of the old year and birth of the new.[5] "The holiday occasion and the comedy are parallel manifestations of the same pattern of culture, of a way that men can cope with their life."[6] By removing Shakespeare's frame story of Christopher Sly and replacing it with a frame of his own—the saturnalian revels of the students of Padua— Zeffirelli emphasizes that *Shrew* is also a "festive comedy" saturated with the exhilaration of holiday, that Petruchio and Kate are allied with the saturnalian forces which stand the everyday on its head and turn reason inside out. As Zeffirelli sees it, the comedy is not primarily about a taming, but about a release of Dionysian energies. As in Alf Sjoberg's *Miss Julie* and Fellini's *Amarcord*, the opening saturnalian ritual defines what follows.

When the film opens, Lucentio and Tranio arrive in Padua on the first day of the new academic year. It is first celebrated solemnly as they witness a beautiful cathedral service in which a boys' choir sings and a Bishop leads the students in prayer. But suddenly a cannon is fired and pandemonium reigns as Zeffirelli provides us with a marvelous condensation of saturnalian motifs. Death, the archenemy of comedy, is mocked as a decorum-shattering funeral winds its way through the streets. A mitred Bishop wearing a mask of a pig strides with great dignity at the head of the procession of mourners carrying a staff crowned with a grinning skull sporting a rakishly slanted turban. In place of the beautiful choir music, we hear raucous songs and obscene chants. The "corpse" (the Old Year) is a skinny, lecherous old man in a white nightcap and nightgown who will not stay dead and has to be forcibly restrained from attacking women (some of them students in drag) along the way. He is treated most indecorously—pummeled with a broom, shaken, tossed high in the air and caught on his bier. The figurative royalty of the procession are the King and Queen, repre- sented by giant masks, but the real queen—the Madonna—is a giant whore who displays her mammoth breasts and strides brassily down the street on foot-high chopines. Chivalry, embodying the height of medieval civilization and encompassing religion, feudal loyalty, and romance, is reduced to a ludicrous knight on a hobby horse, wielding a padded, three-pronged lance. Nearly everyone in the procession wears a mask, many with animalistic features, symbolizing the casting off of civilized identities for more elemental ones. What seems to be an un- expectedly romantic, gentle song sung by several revellers to Bianca, as a figure in a beaked mask lowers a hook to lift her veil, turns out to be bawdy: ". . . give me leave / To do for thee all that Adam did for Eve / I'll do it well, gentle maid, I'll do it well."

This rowdy procession with its chaos of shouts, songs, and shrieks of laughter, completely disrupts the daily routine in Padua, routs serious- ness and pretensions to dignity, overturns the hierarchies of power, and dissolves boredom and drudgery. It challenges the populace, tests their sexual prowess, creative energy, thirst, appetites, and late-night en- durance. It renews communal feeling by replacing social and economic competition with an orgy of hospitality. Part of the idyll is that modern urban paranoia is banished and creative anarchy reigns, cementing the society together and making life—fraught as it is with failure, sickness, and death—more tolerable.

This new frame was a perceptive stroke, and it is interesting to see how many of its themes carry over into the other parts of both play and film—the theme of masking, for instance, of confused or transformed identities. Everyone in the play wears a mask of some sort: Lucentio and Hortensio the masks of "schoolmasters," Kate is "the shrew," Petruchio "the patient wooer," Tranio is "Lucentio," and Bianca "the meek and dutiful daughter." Vincentio has the dreamlike experience of meeting his own double. The overturning of hierarchies also recurs: daughters and sons rule the fathers, servants become masters. In both the opening procession and the rest of the film the central activity is male pursuit of the female. Kate refers specifically to the Madonna-whore when she shrieks at her father "would you make a whore of me among these mates?" Above all, it becomes clear that in assaulting conventional society, Petruchio and Kate are Lord and Lady of Misrule, two bulls crashing through the Paduan china shop. Their courtship burlesques courtly love. Petruchio, who has absorbed Christopher Sly's coarseness and love for the bottle, is no genteel poetical wooer, and Kate, who hurls stools and kegs at suitors and breaks lutes over their heads, lacks the disposition of a Maiden Fair. Their destruction, like that in the Marx brothers' *Night at the Opera*, is an expression of contempt both for culture and for things (recall Petruchio's schoolings), an assault on the old order. The life of decorative luxury, condensed by Zeffirelli into the wine glasses, rich curtains, stuffed bed, and bath water strewn with rose petals at Hortensio's house, is put in its place by Petruchio's bumblings and smashings, socks with holes, and delicate swishing aside of the rose petals to dampen his fingers so as to daub his eyes and ears.

The wedding of Kate and Petruchio is, like the funeral procession, a travesty and a sacrilege. Petruchio arrives two-and-a-half hours late, drunk, dressed in garish clothes (traditional for the Lord of Misrule) including a huge striped pillow adorned with pheasant feathers, carrying dead game birds, and blowing kisses to ladies in the crowd. Enraged, Kate invites him with a smile, then shoves him down the steps, puts down her veil, and races down the aisle, with Petruchio, the children, and guests scrambling in behind her. And all the while, an

Mock funeral and mock wedding

incongruously beautiful, slow "Gloria" is sounded by organ and chorus in the background, recalling the opening religious ceremony. Once at the altar, Petruchio falls asleep, has a coughing fit, gulps down the holy wine with an oath, shoves the mousy, protesting priest to the floor, fumbles for the ring and laughing stupidly displays it to the crowd. He caps his performance by stopping Kate's mouth with a kiss at the "will" of "*I will not!*" The traditional wedding dinner is deflated in midjollity as Petruchio carries Kate out into the rain and leaves the guests to celebrate without them. It is replaced by the inelegant, parodic repast of half-plucked chickens and pudding poured over someone's hat, served by filthy, leering cutthroats amid the wreckage at Petruchio's house; and even this is delayed by Petruchio's comically prolonged grace and then destroyed as he rages that the meal is not fit for the starving bride. The wedding night becomes a blow on the head with a warming pan, a bed ripped apart, and—for the groom—a night on a hard bench.

Also following Shakespeare's lead, Zeffirelli turns the wooing of Kate into a mock epic, continuing the travesty of chivalric valor in the opening procession. When Petruchio, Hortensio, Gremio, and the rest back away in fear upon hearing Bianca scream, our hero boldly declares:

> Think you a little din can daunt mine ears?
> Have I not in my time heard lions roar?
> Have I not heard the sea, puffed up with winds,
> Rage like an angry boar chafed with sweat?
> Have I not heard great ordnance in the field
> And heaven's artillery thunder in the skies?

> Have I not in a pitched battle heard
> Loud 'larums, neighing steeds, and trumpets' clang?
> And do you tell me of a woman's tongue?

Then a spirited Sousa-like march is played by a totally anachronistic full marching band on the sound track as Petruchio strides down the street, followed by lesser mortals, to ring the bell at Baptista's house. In another display of comic heroism, Petruchio, while casting the commercial values of Padua in the teeth of the guests ("she is my goods, my chattels") "rescues" Kate from the bridal dinner (like Erroll Flynn) to the accompaniment of shouts, thunder, and lightning flashing against Grumio's pathetically short sword (Petruchio has lost his).

In "comedies of the green world," as Northrop Frye calls them, it is usual at the end for "a new society to crystallize around the hero."[7] The Lord and Lady of Misrule do not reject order altogether. They simply seek a period of release from imprisoning things and rigid identities in order to humanize society and make discoveries about themselves. Like the lovers and Dukes who flee to the forest in *A Midsummer Night's Dream* and in *As You Like It,* or Bassanio who voyages to Belmont to hazard for Portia, Petruchio and Kate journey from the city to their decrepit country house, where they are reborn. But once Kate has invaded the male enclave and restored it to order, and the seeds of harmony between herself and Petruchio are sewn, like the other voyagers, they make a return. The concluding banquet celebrates a new harmony between parents and children, the old order and the new.

Still, in the film the reconciliation and transformation at the end are not complete. At the dinner Bianca's mask drops, now that she is a wife, and, as was foreshadowed in her earlier outbursts of temper, she becomes a "shrew." The joke is on the newly married men, for not only have they lost the bet, they have yet to fight the battles that Kate and Petruchio have fought, and, quite frankly, they don't look up to it. As in Shakespeare, the hero and heroine do not remain at the center of the supposedly renewed society but assert their superiority by leaving it. Petruchio is ultimately bored with Padua ("eat and drink, eat and drink") and finds chasing the playful, inviting Kate much more interesting. For once the rebels in a comedy are not absorbed by society, but maintain their independence to the last.

Zeffirelli has not made a perfect film of *The Taming of the Shrew.*

Though the cuts in the Bianca plot, which has not aged well, are justified and well executed, and the new opening is both functional and entertaining, one misses Christopher Sly and the doubleness he lends to the play proper. One could do with less mindless baritone laughter from Richard Burton and more acting, and one would like to see as much care lavished on the lines as on the decor and the farce. Nevertheless, it is a better and more thoughtful film than the surprisingly vitriolic attacks on it by many critics would lead one to believe.[8] Given the broad style of the play, with its obvious humor and shallow characterization, it is unreasonable to demand the same subtlety and sophistication we demand of films of *Hamlet*. And, certainly given the sober temper of our times, there is nothing wrong with Zeffirelli's attempt to revive in Shakespeare's comedy a film version of the Saturnalian Revel.

# Franco Zeffirelli's *Romeo and Juliet*

S HAKESPEARE'S SOURCE FOR THE STORY OF ROMEO AND JULIET
was Arthur Brooke's *The Tragicall Historye of Romeus and Iuliet,
written first in Italian by Bandell, and now in Englishe by Ar. Br.*
(1562). In his "Address to the Reader," Brooke spoke of

> a couple of unfortunate lovers, thralling themselves to unhonest de-
> sire; neglecting the authority and advice of parents and friends;
> conferring their principle counsels with drunken gossips and super-
> stitious friars (the naturally fit instruments of unchastity); attempt-
> ing all adventures or peril for the attaining of their wicked lust;
> using auricular confession, the key of whoredom and treason, for
> the furtherance of their purpose; abusing the honourable name of
> lawful marriage to cloak the shame of stolen contracts; finally by all
> means of unhonest life hasting to most unhappy death.

In the story itself, however, he abandoned his heavy moralizing and
showed great sympathy for both the young lovers and the Friar, and
rather than tying the tragic ending to character and divine justice,
rooted the cause in Fortune.

Certainly Shakespeare trusted the tale and not the teller. One of his
most popular plays, written when he was about thirty and also at work
on *A Midsummer Night's Dream, Romeo and Juliet* is an exuberant
celebration of young love—its excitement, passion, and lyricism. Despite the ominous Prologue, which foretells the sacrifice of the young to
"bury their parents' strife," critics often note that this love story has
many of the characteristics of Shakespeare's romantic comedies: the

79

fool Mercutio, the bawdy, funny Nurse, the stereotypical villain Tybalt, the blocking of the loves of the young by the values and laws of the old, ornamented verse, domestic detail, and even the motif of dreaming. Only with the death of Mercutio does the story become a tragedy of Fate and begin its breathless race toward the tomb.

What Romeo and Juliet lack in depth of character they make up in energy, beautiful innocence, and spontaneity. If the arc of their rise and fall seems unusually intense and brilliant, it is because it is set against a rich, dark background. Love clashes with hate, the ideal with the real. Romeo and Juliet's romance avoids sentimentality because it must pass through the fires of the Nurse's jokes and meandering, trivial, pragmatic mind, Mercutio's bawdy wit, the demands of duty and honor, the ugly rigidities of the old, and the feud, which though bound up with Fate seems to have a life of its own. Shakespeare's pattern seems true because it is never a simple one. If the parents want to live their lives over again through their children, they also have great affection and hope for them. Blended with the impulses of the young toward rebellion are hot tempers and the need to prove their maturity, which keep the feud alive when the old are ready to let it die. Analogous to the literal tragedy that the young and innocent are sometimes cruelly cut off in life is the figurative one that youth, innocence, spontaneity, passion die as we grow older—they are sacrificed to meaningless conflicts, adult responsibilities, and accommodating oneself to a fallen world.

Zeffirelli's *Romeo and Juliet,* based loosely on his energetic stage production for the London Old Vic in 1960, is the most popular and financially successful Shakespeare film yet made. It shares with his *Shrew* rich colors and textures, elegantly reconstructed Renaissance interiors and costumes bathed in idyllic golden light and resembling paintings by the old masters. It is spectacular, extravagant, full of nervous motion, energy, camera movement, rapid cutting. We find the same frenetically active extras and strenuous physicality in the clowning of the Maskers before Capulet's ball and the fights in the square that we find in Petruchio's pursuit of Kate and their destruction of Paduan proprieties. (The saturnalian pattern is at work here too, but the outcome is deadly, not festive.) The director fills his frame with motion, people, and things in an effort to give the film a realistic solidity, fullness, and spontaneity. At times it becomes almost operatic in its excess. As in *Shrew,* there is so much music that one expects the actors suddenly to burst into song. Yet the acting, far from being operatic, is in a fresh, nontheatrical, nonelocutionary style. The director uses a pared down text, often interrupts the flow of the lines with entertaining gestures and sounds, and generally keeps the talk out of the way of the action according to the convention of film realism.

Critics have been harsh with Zeffirelli's rash, reckless style. John Simon complained of what he called "centrifugality."[1] In comparing *Romeo and Juliet* with Kozintsev's *Hamlet*, Ronald Hayman argued that

> wasting visual effects is quite as bad as wasting words, and where Kozintsev is tautly economic, Zeffirelli is loosely lavish. Each visual detail, each movement of the actors and each movement of the camera means something in Kozintsev, whereas Zeffirelli's camera wanders all over Verona, grabbing at anything that catches its eye, and putting in movements (or even dances like the gratuitous Moresca at the Capulet's ball) for the sake of their immediate photogenic appeal.[2]

Though we may question whether a "tautly economic" style would really suit this play, there is truth in Hayman's objections. Zeffirelli's films sometimes veer out of control, lapse into visual cliches, caricatures, and sentimentality, wander between muddled motivations and geography and a tendency to make everything simple and obvious. Still, he is no mere mindless popularizer of Shakespeare. Like *Shrew*, *Romeo and Juliet* is a critically underrated film which has some interesting dimensions. When he has things under control, Zeffirelli's images embody interpretative truths about the play very well.

The panoramic opening shot of *Romeo and Juliet* (a tribute to the opening of Olivier's *Henry V*—he even has Olivier reading the prologue) strikes many as a conventional establishing shot, an attempt to be "scenic." But Zeffirelli is doing here what the critics have not credited him with doing—using imagery in a significant way. To begin with, the shot provides a visual equivalent to the godlike, distant, formal tone and style of the prologue which contrasts so vividly with the passion and violence inside Verona's walls. As the camera pans over deathly still Verona, bathed in early morning light, the city is shrouded in fog. There is a formal rightness in this image, for the white shroud is one of the central motifs of the film. It recurs in Mercutio's white handkerchief, which at various times becomes his apron as he kneels in

81

mock prayer and mimes the priest "dream-ing of an-o-ther ben-i-fice" (a glance at Friar Laurence?), his needle work (not long after, we see Juliet sewing), his contraceptive as he plays the gossip and the bawdy jokester with the Nurse, his deathlike mask ("blah, blah, blah") and washrag in the hot square, and finally his bandage which hides the bloody fatal wound and is rubbed in Tybalt's face by Romeo. The white shroud also appears in the Nurse's veil ("A sail! A sail!"), in the sheets and gauze curtains in Juliet's room, and in the winding sheets in Juliet's funeral and covering the corpses in the Capulet tomb. Opposing the fog-shrouded city of death in the opening shot is the burning circle of the sun. The camera zooms rapidly in on it (an overused device in this film) until it fills the screen with blinding orange light, making of it a symbol of the opposing passions of the play. It represents not only the love of Romeo and Juliet (the sun greets them in bed and shines at their funeral), of Romeo and Mercutio, and of the Nurse and Juliet, but also the general hatred unleashed in the feud—the frustrated rage of Tybalt, Mercutio, Romeo, and Prince Escalus. The symbol captures the underlying unity of emotions which come together dialectically at the end of the play.

Zeffirelli's splashy style is evident in the two big scenes of the film, Capulet's ball and the fatal duels in the square. Each is shamelessly milked for emotion, the dance for the tenderness and lyricism of young love, including the sticky sweet song "What is a Youth?" and the fights for the raw excitement of seeing mockery and tests of skill turn into a fight to the death as well as the shock and pain of seeing Mercutio die while his friends laugh, thinking it is another of his jokes. Each scene is filled with spectacle: the ball with swirling costumes, candles, torches, glasses of wine, heaps of fruit, diffused gold backgrounds, and the comic faces among the guests (including a tall, homely, moon-eyed girl who stares down at Juliet), and the duels with Mercutio's clowning and playing to his audience even in his bravura death, and the vicious, dirty, unromantic fight to the death between Romeo and Tybalt, shot in the midst of the dust with a hand-held camera and punctuated with nervous bursts of cuts, climaxing with Tybalt's running on Romeo's sword (a grim repetition of the accidental stabbing of Mercutio) and his sightless corpse falling on top of Romeo. Yet, in these scenes Zeffirelli does more than just immerse his audience in action and spec-tacle. Each scene presents a complicated pattern of characters, relation-ships, and themes central to Zeffirelli's interpretation of the play.

For Zeffirelli, language is primarily a key to character. He is more interested in "the poetry of human relationships" than in ideas, imagery, and the music of the words,[3] and he is not timid about fleshing out characters roughly sketched by Shakespeare. Lady Capulet, for example, is at the hub of the continuing feud. In her appearances before the ball, we learn that her marriage to the older Capulet is not a happy one. As the camera tastelessly zooms in on her sour face and a violin comically whines on the sound track, it is all too evident that Capulet has learned about girls being marred by early marriage and motherhood from personal experience. Capulet's remark to Paris that Juliet will be his only heir and, later, his joking lament for his lost youth at the ball suggest that he is impotent, that what is left of his marriage is the social arrangement. Lady Capulet, on the other hand, is still young, vain about her looks (we see her primping and being made up), uncomfortable with a nearly grown daughter, in need of the Nurse when she must broach the subject of marriage, in need of Capulet when Juliet is disobedient. At the ball we learn more about the conflict between Lady Capulet and her husband. He is a *nouveau riche*, lacking the polish and refinement of his guests, while she is a daughter of the old aristocracy, embarrassed by her *gauche*, gregarious spouse, positively withering in her irony as she reprimands Capulet and Tybalt for quarrelling at the ball (with a hostess's smile: "*well said* my hearts!").

In a sense, the Capulet marriage is a recapitulation of the larger conflict between the Capulets and the Montagues, who, Zeffirelli said, "are a noble, military family who have gone to seed. They are in decline. They produce only students—Romeo learns verses and Benvolio carries books. The Capulets are a rich merchant family, full of social climbers, men of wealth as well as men of action."[4] Louis Gianetti notes that the bright colors worn by middle-aged, clean-shaven Capulet contrast with the dark robes of grey-bearded Montague.[5] Lady Capulet's refusal to help Juliet is thus more clearly motivated in the film. She is anxious to shore up the respectability of her family with an alliance with Paris; she is uneasy in the role of mother and annoyed that Juliet's stubbornness has subjected her to Capulet's anger. Underneath, too, one guesses that she welcomes the opportunity to subject Juliet (obviously Capulet's favorite) to the unhappiness she herself suffers by marrying her to a man she does not love. Lady Capulet is further implicated in the feud in that her refuge from her husband is handsome, virile, young Tybalt, her dancing partner at the ball, the "young princox" who submits to her when he will not to his uncle. The intensity of her grief when, with her hair down, she cries to Prince Escalus for justice (revenge) reflects the loss of much more than a favorite nephew.[6] This frustrating relationship also clarifies the keenness of Tybalt's anger, his anxiousness to prove his manhood, to uphold family honor, and to prevent Juliet from "consorting" with Romeo.

In the duels, Zeffirelli is once again interested in "the poetry of human relationships." There is deep friendship, even love, between Romeo and Mercutio. Mercutio's mercurial showmanship seems aimed at Romeo, and his anger, when Romeo is off sighing for love or making a milksop of himself before Tybalt, is tinged with jealousy. How could a friend abandon male comradery for "a smock?" These feelings, along with the oppressive heat, general boredom, and shallowness of Benvolio, make Mercutio push Tybalt too far and set the wheels of Fate in motion. The combatants are natural opposites. Tybalt fights with strength and skill, Mercutio with resiliency, wit, and a talent for doing the unexpected. Tybalt frightens and threatens his victim (he puts a sword to Mercutio's throat and lets him sweat, cuts off a lock of his hair), While Mercutio ridicules his (by bandying words while baptizing himself in the fountain, whistling nonchalantly when cornered, doing pratfalls and running in mock fear, arming Tybalt with a pitchfork, and forcing him to retreat by sharpening one sword on the other before his face). This ingrained antipathy between Mercutio and Tybalt—Tybalt's need to humiliate an opponent, Mercutio's need to flirt with danger (very near a death wish)—and Romeo's guilt, first at abandoning Mercutio and then at causing his death, come together to accelerate the tragic movement begun at the ball.

Zeffirelli's *Romeo and Juliet* does not have particularly distinguished readings of the verse, being in this respect at the opposite end of the spectrum from the articulate readings of Olivier's films or Peter Hall's *A Midsummer Night's Dream*. This was in part lack of skill and in part artistic choice. "What matters is modernity of feeling rhythm, modernity inside. The verse must always have an intimate rhythm, the rhythm of reality. It must never become music."[7] The ball and the fight heighten the contrast in the film between the young who *do* and the old who *talk*. "What Zeffirelli suggests is that the means of communication between the young, or those who understand the young, is not essentially words, as it is for the older generation, but gesture and action."[8] Romeo and Juliet fall in love at the ball through looking and touching more than through words. Tybalt need only look at Juliet to know what has happened. In the duel, and earlier when he sports a death mask, raves in an empty square, and lifts up the Nurse's skirts, it is what Mercutio does as much as what he says that makes him so bawdy, irreverent, erratically alive. Like the lovers, the young bloods of the square "speak" with their bodies and their "weapons." The young distrust the rhetoric of the old: Juliet asks "what's in a name?" Mercutio responds to Benvolio's echoing of parental cautions with "blah, blah, blah," and Romeo is so impatient with Friar Laurence's tired saws while awaiting Juliet that he fills in the next word each time the holy man pauses. The impotent old, on the other hand, talk and talk, give worldly advice like the Nurse, send tardy letters and lend spiritual guidance like the Friar, or lecture and threaten like Capulet and the Prince. They seem overly deliberate, unspontaneous, slow compared with the young. That is why they are unable to help or even to understand.

Zeffirelli not only used the ball and the duel scenes to entertain, to further characterization, and to contrast young and old, he also displays something of Shakespeare's analogic habit of mind by underscoring the parallels between rituals of love and hate. Both scenes are ironic. Capulet intends the dance to provide a respite from the feud, to be a gesture of peace, a ritual of harmony in which his enemies are welcomed as his friends. Instead, it pours fuel on the glowing coals. Like Benvolio, Romeo tries to keep the peace in the fight scene, but he only manages to make "worm's meat" of Mercutio and Tybalt and get himself banished from Verona and his new wife. The good intentions of old and young go for naught. Hence, the ball and the fights are thematically linked by the motif of the circle,[9] which was first introduced in the opening shot of the sun, and is echoed later on the church floor at the marriage of Romeo and Juliet. The dance is choreographed as a symbolic feud, beginning with two separate circles of dancers and shifting to two concentric circles moving in opposite directions. In an analogue of the overall movement of the play, after the dance the crowd merges into one static circle as a singer of a melancholy song of love and death performs. The "dances" of the duellists also take place in a circle formed by spectators. Following Shakespeare, Zeffirelli shows that love and hate, and the rituals Verona has generated around these passions— the dance and the duel—are intimately related. In *Shrew* Zeffirelli found a play which celebrates the liberating and creative aspects of love. In

*Romeo and Juliet* he found a play which focuses on *eros*, the destructive aspect of love (between Capulet and Lady Capulet, Romeo and Juliet, Romeo and Mercutio, the Nurse and Juliet, Lady Capulet and Tybalt, Friar Laurence and Romeo).

In many ways, this film is a "youth movie" of the 1960s which glorifies the young and caricatures the old, a Renaissance *Graduate*. While Romeo acquires a stubble of a beard and defies the stars, and Juliet learns that she must stand alone when her parents and the Nurse abandon her, we have little sense that they grow up. They are Adam and Eve in the Edenic greenery of Capulet's garden and never lose the golden aura of innocence which insulates them from reality. Romeo's way of opposing the feud is to wander the streets alone sniffing flowers and sighing with melancholy, avoiding his parents and friends, playing at love. Through cuts in the text, Romeo is not forced to take advantage of the ugly, dehumanizing poverty of the apothecary, nor is he guilty of a second murder, that of Paris.

Juliet begins the film as a laughing girl running playfully through the house, becomes a credible teenager in love at the ball and in the balcony scene, and at least starts to mature when, abandoned by her parents, she turns to the Nurse for comfort and finds none. Shakespeare expresses the moment verbally:

> Ancient damnation! O most wicked fiend!
> Is it more sin to wish me thus forsworn,
> Or to dispraise my lord with that same tongue
> Which she hath praised him with above compare
> So many thousand times? Go, counselor!
> Thou and my bosom henceforth shall be twain.

Zeffirelli says it with fewer words. Sadly advising Juliet to forget Romeo and marry Paris, forcing herself to praise the County, the Nurse makes up the bed in which Romeo and Juliet hours before consummated their marriage. To her a little straightening of the sheets can make everything as it was before. Juliet's response is simply "go!". The Nurse reaches out to touch and reassure her, but Juliet backs away. The Nurse goes to the door, looks back for the conciliatory look she had always found before, and, finding none, backs out of the room, crushed, bowing as she closes the door like one of the common servants. This, however, is the extent of Juliet's growth.

Finally, there is no real sense of maturity or eroticism in their love. As Pauline Kael wickedly remarked, theirs is a "toy marriage."[10] It is damaging that Mercutio seems to feel and know more than Romeo and Juliet. He dies in irony and anger. They sob uncontrollably at losing each other. The limitations and the virtues of Zeffirelli's portrayal of Verona's youth are summed up in John Russell Brown's description of the original stage production.

> All the youth of Verona were at ease. Running and sauntering, they were immediately recognizable as unaffected teenagers; they ate apples and threw them, splashed each other with water, mocked, laughed, shouted; they became serious, sulked, were puzzled; they misunderstood confidently and expressed emotion freely. . . . [Zeffirelli] gave prominence to a sense of wonder, gentleness, strong affection, clear emotion and, sometimes, fine sentiment, as well as to high spirits and casual behavior.[11]

In comparison to the young, Brown noted, the old lacked conviction, and this carries over to the film. Their grief is not particularly moving. They often seem two-dimensional (in the zoom-in on Lady Capulet's face or Friar Laurence's leering at Juliet through his test tubes). The Prince has his moments of ferocity when breaking up the opening brawl on his magnificent, nervous horse with the sun burning behind him, and again at the conclusion. And the Nurse, a delightful mock nun who is eager to find in Juliet the daughter she lost, steals wine at the ball, refuses and then takes Romeo's money, rages at Mercutio, is human throughout—right to the moment when she stares stunned at the bodies of the two lovers at the end. But in general the older characters are less convincing, seem hastily sketched in, and this causes an imbalance. What keeps the film from being totally one-sided is the fatal, self-destructive urge in these youths. They are reckless, bored, cynical —children of the feud, just as a generation of Americans were children of Vietnam. They are *implicated* in keeping the feud going. It provides them an outlet for feelings of jealousy, insecurity, and rage not merely at the old and everything they are responsible for but at mortality in all its forms. Even Romeo is not always glamorized, turning into a bloodthirsty animal as he goes after Tybalt. In this sense, Zeffirelli does preserve Shakespeare's balance between old and young.

In shaping the text for the film, Zeffirelli and his fellow scriptwriters accelerated the already rapid sequence of events, reduced speeches to stress the inarticulateness of the young, and stripped away much of the self-conscious verbal artifice which clashes with realistic surfaces and colloquial readings. For example, Escalus's ornamented image is cut:

> What, ho! You men, you beasts,
> That quench the fire of your pernicious rage
> With purple fountains issuing from your veins!

Extended conceits are removed, such as Lady Capulet's urging Juliet to "read o'er the volume of young Paris' face" (the figure is elaborated in "beauty's pen," "margent of his eyes," "unbound lover," "gold clasps," and "golden story"). The film avoids the formal idiom of Juliet's grieving over the death of Tybalt or of the Capulets' mourning over the supposed death of Juliet. In the play Romeo uses oxymoron to embody the fundamental paradox of love and hate:

> Why then, O brawling love, O loving hate,
> O anything of nothing first create!
> O heavy lightness, serious vanity,
> Misshapen chaos of well-seeming forms,
> Feather of lead, bright smoke, cold fire, sick health,
> Still-waking sleep, that is not what it is!
> This love feel I, that feel no love in this.

Zeffirelli uses *visual* contrasts, shows the maimed survivors of the brawl and their mourning kin as they interrupt flower-sniffing Romeo's talk with Benvolio (Romeo throws the flower on the stones, walks away in disgust). Some of Zeffirelli's cuts (especially those in the cumbersome final scene) are usual on the stage and rescue what is in some ways an immature play from its own excesses. Some are compensated for by adequate gestures and visual imagery, such as the fierce, proud look on Tybalt's face as he turns to see Juliet sighing over Romeo at the ball, replacing "I will withdraw; but this intrusion shall / Now seeming sweet, convert to bitt'rest gall." Some substitutions are less successful, as when a dull shot of Italian countryside replaces,

> The grey-eyed morn smiles on the frowning night,
> Check'ring the eastern clouds with streaks of light;
> And flecked darkness like a drunkard reels
> From forth day's path and Titan's burning wheels.

In keeping with the anti-intellectual tone of his films, Zeffirelli makes a philosophically thin play even thinner by cutting the Friar's thoughts that "The earth that's nature's mother is her tomb. / What is her bury-ing ground, that is her womb," and his wonder at a world where the vilest things do good and virtue can become vice. Also, occasionally cuts result in missed dramatic opportunities. For a director who under-scores the structural and thematic relations between the Capulet's ball and the duels, as well as between the balcony scene and the deaths of the lovers, for example, it was a remarkable oversight to omit Shake-speare's striking transition from the Capulet's festive wedding prepara-tions to mourning and funeral preparations when Juliet is found dead.

Many have complained that Zeffirelli's ornate brand of realism is in-appropriate to tragedy. Certainly one would not like to see *King Lear* in this style. Yet in view of the strong elements of romantic comedy in the first half of *Romeo and Juliet*, the bright colors, constant move-ment, and rich detail seem true to the original. And often Zeffirelli foreshadows the darker, bleaker moments to come by cutting across this festive style: when Mercutio is bellowing in the empty square bathed in eerie blue light, when Juliet pauses in the shadows of Capulet's courtyard, and when Romeo is pursued along a dark, tunnellike street. The dust and stone of the hot town square contrasts with the warm, colorful interiors, and the imprisoning walls and mazelike streets sym-bolizing centuries of tradition and a social system hardened against change underscore the central theme of this and Castellani's film— "youth against a hostile society."[12]

Most important, the style of the film changes radically after the death of Mercutio; it is drained of its busy look and festive colors. Juliet's room dominated by whites, the somber tones of Friar Laurence's cell, the dark of Capulet's house, the subdued funeral for Juliet, Romeo's shadowy house in exile, the Capulet's tomb, and the desolate wind-blown square filled with mourners in black—all these serve to erase the festivity and effectively embody Shakespeare's shift in tone. And Zeffi-relli not only shows his protagonists imprisoned in colorlessness and stone, he shows them imprisoned in a pattern of events. Visually, he emphasizes the symmetry of the escalating conflicts from the opening brawl to the deaths of Mercutio and Tybalt to the deaths of Romeo and Juliet. Three times the Montagues and Capulets come before the Prince, and three times he chastizes them, but only the last time, when the cost has been great enough, do the families see that they are destroying themselves by allowing the feud to continue. The love which blos-somed in a garden withers in a tomb. The shrouded city becomes a tomb. As in *Throne of Blood*, the artistic patterning which provides the work with coherence and meaning becomes an embodiment of Fate which enmeshes the principal characters.

Some films of Shakespeare's tragedies end with a close-up of the face of the hero (Richardson's *Hamlet*, Brook's *King Lear*, Mankiewicz's *Julius Caesar*), placing emphasis upon the individual fall. Some conclude with a movement outward or upward, the society being involved in a final ritual (Welles's *Othello*, Olivier's *Hamlet*, Kozintsev's *Hamlet*). Some are circular (Kurosawa's *Throne of Blood*, Welles's *Macbeth*, Polanski's *Macbeth*), stressing the continuing power of the pattern. Zeffirelli's conclusion is a blend of the latter two. In the end the rituals of love and death merge. The bells which continually remind us of passing time, and celebrate the wedding, now become funeral bells. The Montagues and the Capulets, who streamed twice before into the square in parallel linear movements, now form a single procession as they bear Romeo and Juliet to be buried in their wedding garments. All the people we care about are dead, and with them have gone spontaneity, energy, and innocence. The silence in the sunlit square is broken only by the tolling bell, muffled footsteps on the stones, and the whistling wind. Compositions are rigidly symmetrical as the families gather on the steps of the church. The chaos of the brawls has been replaced by order, but it is a dead order. The camera picks out somber faces (especially the Nurse's), which reflect guilt, recognition, a sense of loss. Then emphasis shifts to the Prince and the Shakespearean theme of "responsibility learnt in adversity."[13] In the sole outburst of passion, the Prince's formal pronouncement, "all are punished," becomes a howl of rage and pain, "All are punished!"

As the two families file through the cathedral door toward the camera and the credits pass over the screen, there are gestures of consolement and reconciliation. The feud is over. But when they have all filed past, and the credits are through, the camera holds on the castellated wall towering over Verona's empty square, echoing the second shot of the film and providing a final symbol of division, war, imprisonment, continuity with the past. If *this* conflict has ended, conflict itself has not.

Zeffirelli's *Romeo and Juliet* is in most ways superior to the films by Cukor (1936) and Castellani (1954). It has energy, humor, and life where the others do not. No one would be tempted to say of it, as George Bernard Shaw said of Forbes-Robertson's production in 1895, that "the duel scene has none of the murderous excitement which is the whole dramatic point of it."[14] It avoids the static, ornate prettiness of the studio sets of the 1936 film, yet despite some excesses, never becomes a distractingly beautiful travelogue of Renaissance Italy the way the 1954 film often does. Leonard Whiting and Olivia Hussey are credible and likeable lovers as Leslie Howard and Norma Shearer or Laurence Harvey and Susan Shentall are not.

However, one may like the film for all its action, emotional power, and sense of theme and structure and still be aware that this *Romeo and Juliet*, transforming tragedy into a story of sentiment and pathos, is a less mature work than Shakespeare's. It is not merely that the hero and heroine do not ripen in understanding. It is that their deaths are conceived too simply. The sorrow, the sense of loss, the sexual overtones of "death" are present at the end, but the insight and defiant anger are missing. Neither Romeo nor Juliet senses the larger pattern. They never see what a corrupt and flawed world it is that they are leaving, never give any indication that they know how they contributed to their own downfall, and never understand that love of such intensity not only cannot last but is self-destructive. Sorrow at losing each other is not coming to terms with life or death. The clear-sighted calm and sense of inevitability with which Shakespeare's tragic hero and heroine greet their end have disappeared.

# 6

## Joseph Mankiewicz's *Julius Caesar*

*J*ULIUS *CAESAR* IS SHAKESPEARE'S MOST CLASSICAL PLAY. THIS gives it a certain grandeur and strength. But it lacks the variety in language and dramatic situation which characterizes his other major works. Despite tentative gestures toward humor, *Julius Caesar* "lacks much of the lower register."[1] The serious actions are never seen from a comic point of view, and without the usual Shakespearean elements of romance and fantasy the play strikes many as his least imaginative effort. The play's chief activity is men arguing, orating, manipulating each other with words: the tribunes harangue the people, Antony and the people urge the crown on Caesar, Cassius ensnares Brutus, Portia persuades Brutus to reveal the plot to her after he has argued with the conspirators about the way to conduct an assassination. We see Calpurnia and Decius Brutus sway Caesar, Antony talk the rebels into letting him live, and Brutus reason the crowd into accepting Caesar's murder. Antony incites the people to riot, and Cassius and Brutus quarrel over money and tactics. As in courtroom drama, the suspense lies in who will make the most persuasive case, the interest in how people will respond to pressure.

Structurally, *Julius Caesar* is as lucid and straightforward as a work of Roman architecture, falling neatly into two parts: "the conspirators' action and Antony's counter-action"[2]—the first climaxed by the murder of Caesar and by Antony's stirring words, and the second by the death of Brutus followed by Antony's eulogy. The narrative moves with clean logic from cause to effect and is built upon numerous pairs of contrasting events: Caesar's impressive entrance and limping exit; the storm and the battle; Portia's pleading and Calpurnia's pleading; the murder of Caesar and the murder of Cinna; the quarrels which pit Antony against Octavius and Cassius against Brutus; Brutus's shaking the conspirators' hands to prove his sincerity, Antony's to dupe them; Cassius's suicide and Brutus's suicide. Mankiewicz underscores these parallelisms, large and small, so that, like the play, his film is an impressive march of events with a certain regularity and ponderousness to it.

Language in *Julius Caesar* reflects its narrowness of tone and dramatic situation. It is symbolically right that the only poet in the play, Cinna, is slain, for here there is no playfulness, no beauty or lyricism, no dense structure of poetic images. The power generated by the words is a cumulative power, as the devices of formal rhetoric provide regular channels for the passion. There is something distant and impersonal about the idiom. Characters habitually refer to themselves in the third person, and we find little individualization of characters through imagery or other stylistic devices. Though there are colloquial bursts like Casca's description of Caesar's "foolery," though Shakespeare contrasts Brutus's logic and Antony's theatrical appeal to the emotions, overall the work has a uniformity foreign to the other plays. Even in domestic and private scenes, characters *orate*—the fluid, subjective, meditative style in the soliloquies of *Hamlet* or *Macbeth* gives way to half-public discourse. This unity of form and language can generate great power, but it also entails risks, for as the viewers of many high school productions have found, the play teeters on the edge of boredom and ridiculousness. As John Gielgud wickedly commented, "there is always the danger of the effect of a lot of gentlemen sitting on marble benches in a Turkish bath."[3]

This simplicity of surfaces is deceptive, however, for *Julius Caesar* is a difficult play. The work does resemble Shakespeare's other stories about "the killing of the king," so that it is tempting, despite the prejudices of "democratic" modern audiences, to view it as a conservative, cautionary tale.

The Elizabethan age believed in the personal ruler as a terrestrial analogue of deity and, as reference to the assassination of Caesar in other Shakespeare plays emphasizes, that particular murder was the classic example of outrage, the greatest secular crime in history.[4]

From this point of view, Caesar is seen as a Roman Henry V, a legendary hero and ideal governor who, though he had physical infirmities like other mortals, with his strong, just rule and conquests brought order and prosperity to Rome. The play tells how rash, envious Cassius and other malcontents persuade honorable Brutus (misguided idealist? self-deceiving abstractionist?) to join with them to kill a great man. It tells of the chaos which results and is quelled only when justice (revenge?) is performed and strong leadership is restored—tragically, a leadership which contains within it the seeds of more civil war. It is, in short, another Shakespearean tale of the Fall in which the sacred harmony and order of the feudal system is shattered and modern power politics is born.

At the opposite extreme, one may view the central theme as "Liberty versus Tyranny."[5] As in Orson Welles's anti-Fascist New York production in 1937, performed in modern dress without scenery, it is the story of a heroic attempt to save the Roman Republic from absolutism; but the attempt tragically fails because of the people's desire for a dictator, Brutus's utopian high-mindedness, Cassius's love for and inability to overrule Brutus, and Antony's cunning. Brutus becomes the central character, a martyr for liberty, the classic liberal intellectual allied with men whose motives are less pure than his own, lacking the ruthlessness of his enemies and unable to persuade the people that they must not create—and he does not want to become—another Caesar. Caesar becomes the vain tyrant who confuses his will with Rome's, and Antony his pupil who, after avenging the death of his friend, slips easily into the role of ruler. Rome, in short, is and remains a fallen world, peopled by heroic but flawed men.

Because both views are persuasive but incomplete, many subscribe to a third: that the play is a grim, realistic portrait of a *coup d'etat* in an unheroic world where motives are mixed and certainty is non-existent. Perhaps Shakespeare felt compassion for people dragged down by human weakness, for a civilization debased and ultimately destroyed by some vast, inexorable power hostile to greatness in men or nations. Often one senses real pathos as men in the face of annihilating forces cling to each other, pit love against those forces (Portia and Brutus, Cassius and Brutus, Caesar and Brutus, Antony and Caesar), and exhibit true nobility as they confront their fates. On the other hand, perhaps with that frightening detachment and dark laughter one senses behind plays like *Troilus and Cressida*, Shakespeare the ironist looks down godlike, amused by man's vanity, his fickleness and pettiness, his penchant for destruction and self-deception. Whatever Shakespeare's attitude, *Julius Caesar*, from this point of view, is to be valued because, unlike *Richard III* or *Henry V*, it is an unbiased portrait of an assassination and its aftermath, replete with interventions of chance, errors of judgment, complex motives, and paradoxical situations—a portrait which will remain true as long as there are leaders feared or hated enough to make it worth trying to kill them.

Shakespeare is in his histories equally distant from the typical Elizabethan moralistic-deterministic interpretation of history (the working out of God's plan, the Tudor Myth) and the economic determinism of modern Marxist history. As in his tragedies, events issue from character. History is viewed as a clash of great personalities in whom are embedded contrasting ethical and social values. One of the most praiseworthy aspects of Mankiewicz's film is its refusal to sentimentalize, popularize, or oversimplify. Mankiewicz and his producer John Houseman had the sense and courage to forego both the expected DeMille epic and Wellesian modernizing and to place the emphasis on the characters, reaffirming that "Shakespeare's *Julius Caesar* remains, basically, a tragedy of direct, personal strife. Its scenes call for intensity rather than for grandeur."[6] Not only are the four major characters skillfully cast and directed, they are carefully balanced to preserve the ambivalence which is the life of the drama. It may be accurate, in speaking of Mankiewicz's handling of the "clash and conflict of political ideas and personalities," to say

the futile effort of Brutus, for the noblest of principles, and Cassius, for the most practical of reasons, to stem the tide of caesarism, is made tragically clear. The people in the play want and need a dictator, whether it be the deaf, epileptic, superstitious, and arrogant Caesar, or the demagogue Antony, who can callously "cut off some charge in legacies" after using Caesar's will itself to turn the mob to his own purposes.[7]

But it is also necessary to underscore the weaknesses, self-delusions, and egotism of the men opposing Caesar and Antony.

From the opening quotation from Plutarch in Mankiewicz's film, it is apparent that we will not see a worshipful portrait of Caesar:

Upon Caesar's return to Rome, after defeating Pompey in the civil war, his countrymen chose him a fourth time consul and then dictator for life. . . . Thus he became odious to moderate men through the extravagance of the titles and powers that were heaped upon him.

Producer John Houseman spoke of their effort to evoke modern history.

> While never deliberately exploiting the historic parallels, there are certain emotional patterns arising from political events of the immediate past that we were prepared to evoke. . . . Hitler at Nurenberg and Compiegne, and later in the Berlin rubble; Mussolini on his balcony with that same docile mob massed below which later watched him hanging by his feet, dead. These sights are as much a part of our contemporary consciousness—in the *black and white* of news-reel and TV screens—as, to Elizabethan audiences, were the personal and political conflicts and tragedies of Essex, Bacon, Leicester and the Cecils.[8]

Roger Manvell noted echoes of Nazi Germany in the film's Caesar and Rome: the mass rallies and public spectacle, the stiff-armed salutes, the political police, and proliferating images of the leader.[9] Our faith in Caesar's popular support is undermined as the people slink away in shame when scolded by the tribunes for cheering the conqueror of their former idol Pompey, and later swing to Antony's side not so much out of love for Caesar's memory as out of greed and love of an emotional, highly theatrical show (Caesar's body and his will are the chief props).

Despite his imposing size, Louis Calhern portrays Caesar's weaknesses more than his strengths. That fear, vulnerability, and softness at the core which Calhern brought to the part of the lawyer Emerich in *Asphalt Jungle* is skillfully used by Mankiewicz as a contrast to his massive power. Caesar's public might is emphasized by Miklos Rosza's recurring Caesar theme, the emblem of the eagle, the many images of Caesar—his fountain statue in the middle of the square, decorated with flowers and later seen in the storm, the huge statues which decorate Caesar's porch or dwarf Cassius and Brutus in a gallery as they speak of overthrowing him. But Mankiewicz also stressed Caesar's personal weaknesses—his deafness in one ear, his epilepsy, his inability to hide his fear of Cassius. He stressed Caesar's crassness in making a public matter of Calpurnia's barrenness, his near-drowning, his being shaken by a fever and whimpering like a girl. This Caesar is a weak man who drives himself with a steel will, unyielding, whether it is about giving a reason for not appearing to the Senate or about the repealing of a banishment. For such a man, to bend is to break. In a play full of waverers, this may seem admirable, but it also makes Caesar appear mindlessly rigid, prey to clever men like Decius Brutus who win him over by appealing to his pride and ambition and by assuring him that he is immune to flattery.

Caesar is an egotist, but his personal loyalties are strong. He takes a fatherly tone toward Antony, greets the conspirators warmly when they come to fetch him to the Senate house and invites them in for a bowl of wine (suggesting a Last Supper). His love for Brutus is total, and the moment when he stares in disbelief and sorrow as his friend stabs him, and then resignedly accepts death, is the most moving in the film—much more so than the deaths of Cassius and Brutus at the end. Caesar's character is filled with contradictions. How can one reconcile Caesar's shrewd analysis of Cassius's character with his ignorance of who his enemies are? He denies the crown three times, but is this a show like that put on by Richard III for the people of London, or is it a man mastering his inclinations toward absolutism? Is Caesar's generosity and love of the people real, or does it live only in the rhetoric of Antony? The doubleness of the man is captured when, as he announces to Calpurnia that he will go to the Senate house, he stands beside a larger-than-life statue of himself. The private man and the public image stand side by side inviting comparison.

James Mason's Brutus is an accurate portrait of a man who means well, has integrity, inspires loyalty in everyone, and loves both Caesar and Rome, yet he betrays and murders his friend and plunges Rome into civil war. Apart from Caesar, Brutus is the only character who thinks beyond the pragmatics of the present to the larger pattern, but Mason stresses the slow, almost mechanical way he thinks, moves, and speaks. His general statements about the corrupting nature of absolute power, about justice, and about the uselessness of external gestures like oaths seem true enough. Yet such abstractions have little to do with the blend of ungovernable forces, contradictory personalities, and mixtures of high principles and vested interests which constitute politics in the real world. (An irony in the play not preserved in the film: the rebels are defeated because Brutus's initially victorious troops fall to spoil rather than go to the aid of Cassius.) Hence Brutus seems terribly naive, an idealistic, unspoiled Adam in a fallen world. He prides himself on his ability to think things through dispassionately (twice we see

97

him with a book—in his first scene with Cassius and in the ghost scene),
yet neither he nor the other conspirators anticipate what will happen
once Caesar is dead. Brutus can plan a sacrifice with equanimity, but
he shrinks in horror at the actual butchery, at the scarlet hands with
which he must gesture to the crowd. He can scold Cassius for raising
money by vile means, and in the next breath rage at him for not providing money to pay his legions. He is an idealist, yet a bumbling
tactician who lets Antony live and speak over Caesar's body, who gives
up the advantage of the mountains to do battle on the plain head to
head, Brutus fashion. Above all, he is an intellectual totalitarian, this
rebel against tyranny, an unyielding defender of absolutes even with
those wiser and more experienced than he.

When we see inside Brutus, though, we get a very different picture,
one of wavering and indecision. Visually, Mankiewicz stresses Brutus's
desire to retreat from action to contemplation by having him back
away when pressed by Cassius, Portia, and wounded Caesar in turn.
From the first, Cassius and others know more about Brutus than does
Brutus himself. As described in the script,

> The Soothsayer blunders toward the tunnel. He is stopped by a
> guard. Then he fumbles for the stairs. Brutus takes his arm to guide
> him. The Soothsayer feels of Brutus' toga, of his face and hair. He
> pulls away abruptly. He leaves the stadium.

Up to the moment of his suicide, we realize in retrospect, he is never
really sure what he should have done: "Caesar, now be still; / I killed
not thee with half so good a will." Unending indecision is his tragedy.
The definitive image of Brutus is when, alone in his symbolic ruined
garden littered with shattered urns, Brutus is "with himself at war,"
when the ugly tangle of branches casting shadows on the wall serves as
an objective correlative of his confusion, his inner "phantasma or hideous dream" as he marries self-persuasion with self-deception.

John Gielgud's portrait of Cassius is narrow but intense. Sensing
more in the part, Eric Bentley objected to a Cassius "reduced to the
vulgar abstraction of personal jealousy."[10] But within its limited scope
—and not all critics would agree that Shakespeare provided material
for more—it is a good performance. Cassius's massive inferiority complex and his anger at others' fear and envy of Caesar are powerfully
realized. This scowling Cassius is cool and shrewd when not pressed,

but he lacks self-control, bursting into a personal and irrelevant attack on Caesar's physical weaknesses when he had intended to reason Brutus into rebellion, rashly threatening suicide when it appears Popilius will disclose the plot, raging against Brutus before their troops the night before battle. He is crafty, able to manipulate Brutus and organize the conspiracy, and has courage as he braves the storm or mocks frightened Casca. He sees through Antony's mask, and compared to Brutus is the better strategist. But he is no leader of men, and he has a fatal weakness for Brutus—love not only for the man but also for his stoic calm, considered resolution, idealism, and firmness of purpose.

To the extent that we view Caesar as a dangerous, pompous, power-hungry tyrant, we share Cassius's intense disgust at the spectacle of Rome bowing before him. And unlike Brutus, Cassius knows himself. His desperation seems born of an inner knowledge that, should Caesar become absolute ruler, he will succumb out of fear like the rest. His cynicism and fatalism are rooted in a clear understanding of a Rome entirely at odds with Brutus's abstractions and ideals. Seeing the end, Cassius even enjoys the irony that he will die on his birthday. Next to Brutus's cold reserve, rash, envious Cassius is the more sympathetic man. If we may seize on a physical detail as a symbolic summing up of a character, we note that Cassius is nearsighted. "His eyes are narrow, and blink a little—a manifestation which gives added pathos, at the moment before his death, to the words "My sight was ever thick.' "11

Our attitudes toward Antony change radically as the film progresses. Until Caesar's death he is a minor character: athlete, reputed reveller, follower of Caesar who assures him that Cassius is not dangerous. Then suddenly, in the space of three scenes, he becomes the central figure. In the first scene, he walks a thin line between unbelievable rejection of Caesar and a blunt expression of loyalty which would force the conspirators to kill him. The tears and request to speak over the body seem real. When alone, however, Brando's animal ferocity is unleashed, and Antony attracts us to him as he sets out to revenge the death of his friend. In his speech to the people, we are still with him as he slowly lets his rage against the murderers surface and turns the crowd against them. Contrasting the film with Welles's prewar, anti-Fascist production, Houseman said in retrospect, "the casting of Marlon Brando as Antony completely reversed the structure of the play. Now it was

Marc Antony they were rooting for and the twelve hundred cheering bit players and extras massed on M.G.M.'s Stage 25 were merely reflecting the empathy of future audiences."[12]

But this formulation is too simple, for accompanying our admiration for Antony's cunning, boldness, and loyalty to Caesar, is a growing uneasiness as we see a man exploiting his own emotions and the mob for political ends. By the end of his funeral harangue, this uneasiness turns to active dislike. He *calculates* his displays of "sincere" feeling, uses the body of his friend for a theatrical prop. Originally Mankiewicz intended to retain Antony's final line. The script reads: "His sweaty, tense expression relaxes into a grim smile. 'Now let it work. Mischief, thou art afoot. Take thou what course thou wilt.'" But in the shooting, the line became superfluous, for Brando's sardonic smile says it all. Antony is indifferent to the chaos and destruction he turns loose; like the conspirators, we have been taken in. In the next scene the real Antony surfaces again and we back away in revulsion, for what the conspirators feared in Caesar has been realized in Antony. After casually condemning his sister's son and turning Octavius against Lepidus, Antony is left alone. He strolls over to the balcony of Caesar's apartment, looks out over Rome and stretches himself as though to embrace the whole empire. Then he stares reflectively at the statue of Caesar, turns it toward him, and smiles at the ironic result of the assassination. Picking up the list of political enemies to be executed, he ambles to Caesar's eagle-crested chair and sits as music crescendos in the background. Caesar is dead. Long live Caesar.

In battle Antony engages in no foolhardy heroics. He sits above, smiling, and stage-manages as his troops decimate Cassius below. In the final scene, there is a recollection of the old Antony as, in contrast to distant Octavius, he walks to the side of dead Brutus and speaks his final warm tribute. This final act qualifies but does not erase Antony's brutality and link with Caesarism. The strength of Brando's performance lies in his blend of sympathetic directness and dangerous ferocity. The definitive image of Antony occurs in his prolonged entrance to join the conspirators by the body of Caesar. As he moves along a corridor lined with pillars, light and shadow are alternately thrown across his face, embodying the problem faced by conspirators and audience alike: Who and what is Antony?

Comments on the visual style of Mankiewicz's *Julius Caesar* range from praise for its "satisfying unity of style," its appropriate "austerity," and its "dynamic inner force and . . . absence of externals,"[13] to dismay at its "tastelessness," "blandness," and "staginess."[14] If we are seriously concerned with a cinematic style that suits the action, themes, characters, and language of the play, then we must grant that Mankiewicz and Houseman made many of the right choices—the black and white of documentaries (contrasted to the garish color of Burge's 1969 version) despite the antidocumentary studio feel, a cool restrained look tending toward abstraction and deliberately ugly to prevent identification with the characters and their world. The greyness and lack of contrast of the film, added to the lack of depth caused by flat lighting,[15] give it the appearance of a frieze, and its starkness and ambivalence are heightened by the absence of reaction shots and point-of-view shots. The characters, filmed from eye-level mostly in medium and long shot, have a statuesque feel. A technical advisor recalled, "I remember Mr. Mankiewicz remarking once that in directing the big speeches he had kept in mind the conventional motions and style of classical oratory."[16] Mankiewicz's shots are often rigidly frontal and composed in geometrical patterns—circles, triangles, and squares. In general, however, individual shots call little attention to themselves. In classical Hollywood style, the force and movement are linear as the action is propelled forward and emphasis placed on the actors and their lines.

From the accounts of those involved, one might expect considerable emphasis upon physical detail and setting in Mankiewicz's *Julius Caesar*. P. M. Pasinetti wrote of the way in which "object and properties help characterize backgrounds and people," of how much research went into giving the work both accuracy and "the feeling of a city alive and functioning," with graffiti on the walls, litter in the streets, and construction under way—a claustrophobic Rome, without the spacious sterility of the public monuments in Washington, D.C.[17] John Gielgud, recalling a set "with real sheep, pigeons, dogs, goats and dirty water running in the gutter," felt that "Herbert Tree's ghost must have breathed approval."[18] He remarked that "the elaborate scenic backgrounds, the milling crowds, filling the screen at one moment or receding at will to a respectful distance, allow the characters to fill the foreground, dominating Rome and its unruly citizens with ease." He spoke of Mankiewicz's skill in "devising close-ups, and also in many details illustrating key moments in film terms—(the blind Soothsayer with his staff of jingling bells, rising slowly from the steps where he sits half hidden by the crowd—Casca's sweating forehead as he moves

through the crowd of conspirators to strike the first blow at Caesar)—
and, above all, in the striking contrasts of close-ups, distances, and
angles."[19]

The film is by no means devoid of significant detail. One recalls a
tree split by lightning and still smoking, the shadows and disarray of
Brutus's garden, the bells on the Soothsayer's stick. There are intimations, as well, of the central poetic images of blood, tempest, fire, and
animals in this play so barren of imagery. And as Robert Hapgood
points out, the director has carefully developed the motif of rise and
fall:

> Shakespeare himself provides literal counterparts to the metaphorical
> ups and downs of power in Rome, as when Caesar's former under-
> lings stand over his fallen body. But Mankiewicz makes these still
> more graphic by setting almost all of his picture either on steep
> steps or on a mountain. One instance among many is when Cassius
> suits the action to word at "we have the falling sickness," descending
> the stairs from above Brutus and Casca to below them. The sense
> of rise and fall extends to many aspects of the production. Caesar's
> body is not raised at the end of Antony's oration (as it is in Shake-
> speare), yet the effect of Caesar's rise is achieved by the elevation
> of Marlon Brando's voice at the last syllable of "ruffle up your
> spirits" and on all of "when comes such another." The most success-
> ful effect is the downward camera-angle when Cassius beneath a
> towering statue of Caesar speaks of him as a colossus and of himself
> as an underling. At that moment I see Cassius as he sees himself.[20]

The pattern is even used in the music when, in the scene of Brutus's
death, the Caesar theme grows louder and eventually drowns out the
Brutus theme. Caesar's fountain statue in the square evokes Calpurnia's
dream of Caesar's image, "which, like a fountain with an hundred
spouts, did run pure blood," and often statues visually contrast with
characters. The night storm scene in the square, echoing the dark, rain-
slicked streets and menacing shadows of *film noir*, establishes a sinister
atmosphere and evokes Hollywood gangster films, children of *Julius
Caesar* and *Little Caesar* which also portray with irony and ambivalence
power struggles, violence, killings, and tainted revengers.[21]

In general, however, places and things count for little in this film.
One should contrast it with the Wellesian imagery in the student film
of *Julius Caesar* by David Bradley (1950)—its low-angle shot of the

dark silhouettes of Caesar's train and the bent figure of the reaperlike Soothsayer moving in opposite directions, its faces emphasized by raking light and black backgrounds, its poetic images of its storm and dream sequences. Vivid and apt images like the skull-like lamp on the table as the triumvirate determines which enemies are to die, and the wasteland setting of sand and grotesque stumps which contrast with the impressive man-made order of Rome, confirm one's feeling that in Mankiewicz's film the action is not powerfully *seen*. There are memorable dramatic moments, but no memorable images. In seeking restraint and a distancing effect, Mankiewicz often succeeded only in making scenes bland and visually dull.

When this happens in film, sometimes the script is at fault; but in this case the script was an imaginative one, full of atmosphere and significant detail. The problem lay rather in the design, lighting, and framing of the images. For instance, the contrast between civilized Rome and the wasteland into which Brutus and Cassius are driven is present in Mankiewicz's script, but it is hardly noticeable in the final work. Pasinetti suggested a ritual of sacrifice before the battle,[22] and Mankiewicz, perhaps intending to echo Brutus's "sacrifice" of Caesar, described "Some sheep, herded by religious men. Camera follows them to THE RELIGIOUS AREA. Here preparations are being made for a sacrificial killing." But in the film as Cassius and Brutus throw incense on the fire, the camera brushes past so quickly that there is little chance for us to register the significance of what is going on. In the script, Mankiewicz carefully describes the acts of the mob: looting, beatings, men smashing wooden tubs, scaffolding, booths, and stands, and heaping them around Caesar's body, citizens rushing in with lighted torches, smoke drifting up past Antony. In addition, he asserts the grim presence of the Soothsayer: "Camera remains upon the Soothsayer. Illuminated by the light of Caesar's pyre, his sightless eyes are focussed vacantly before him." But in the film, all this is unemphatic background for Antony's turn and smile, just as the fine shot of Caesar's pyre burning at night is mere background for the titles and music which bridge the lapsed time between the riot and the day before the battle.

Given the sketchy rendering of this thematically and dramatically important violence, the senseless mob murder of Cinna the Poet becomes all the more important. In the script it is worked out in detail, including Antony's indifference as a "strong curtain." At its climax,

Cinna trapped in the center of the Forum. Crowds rushing on him from both directions, he scrambles up the steps of the capitol toward camera, screaming "Cinna the poet! I am Cinna the poet!"

The crowd is after him. Cinna trips and falls. He is caught by the heels, and dragged by the heels screaming, down into the center of the Forum. From above and about camera, more citizens rush down into the Forum.

Cinna's body is blotted from view by the mob as it smothers him within it. . . .

Past Antony—as Cinna's high scream is lost in the roar of the mob. They disperse as quickly as they gathered. Cinna's body sprawls almost alone on the floor of the Forum. . . .

Close—Antony. He stands overlooking the Forum. His look is an impassive one.

But though the scene was shot,[23] it was eventually cut in its entirety. The parallel with the murder of Caesar was thrown out along with a chance to alleviate the oppressively static nature of the film, probably because the scene does not directly further the plot.

Mankiewicz's script is by no means always superior to the finished film. Few will lament the loss of an opening scene in which a toddling little girl decks Caesar's image with flowers and is watched simultaneously by her proud parents and by scowling Flavius and Marullus. Often something of the intended effect is preserved. This is true, for example, with the symbolic prop of Lucius's harp, first seen when the innocent boy falls asleep while dutifully playing for Brutus. The moment in the film in which Octavius's soliders find the mangled harp on the battlefield is a strong one. The soldiers bring it to him. He looks at it in bewilderment, throws it down, and then rides on, allowing us to register the temper of Rome's new rulers, to realize that something important has been destroyed along with Brutus. But imagine the following if it were filmed by Bergman, Welles, or Kozintsev:

Throughout the scene, there is the silence of bloody defeat. Some moans from the wounded; occasionally a cry or two, as they are dispatched by Octavius' men.

A Close Shot of the musical instrument which has been so closely identified with Lucius. It lies smashed on the battlefield. One of Octavius' officers stoops into the shot, picks up the instrument. He crosses the battlefield, carrying it to Octavius. The angle widens as he crosses: the battlefield is disclosed.

The distinctive implement of war, which has been identified with

Brutus, lies overturned and smashed. Octavius' men are busy with looting, and with salvaging weapons. Occasionally, in the b.g., the moonlight picks up the flash of a sword as the wounded are dispatched.

Octavius, remote as always, stands to one side, accompanied by some generals, surveying his triumph. The officer hands Lucius' smashed instrument to him. Octavius looks it over curiously, then shrugs and tosses it aside.

Mankiewicz's dramatic point comes through, but the brutality and the eerie wasteland effect do not.

So it goes with smaller details. The ominousness, the visual jolt of the soldiers in black who arrest Flavius and Marullus is lost. A piece of Egyptian sculpture meant to evoke the Roman Empire and perhaps Cleopatra hardly registers at all in the overplayed "dramatic" moment heightened by a musical crescendo as Calpurnia shuts the doors on stubborn Caesar and the conspirators. The "distinctive implement of war" associated with Brutus has been pruned away from a battle which unfortunately resembles a stock Indian ambush, and the suicides of Cassius and Brutus, against a setting sun in the high country with jagged trees and boulders, read better than they look. The problem was not in translating from play to film, but from script to film.[24] Still, if we find Mankiewicz's film visually disappointing—a kind of mirror opposite of Welles's early efforts where sheer graphic power overwhelms the acting—it is only because few Shakespeare films can match it for its integrity in dealing with the original, its narrative drive, and its fine characterizations.

# Orson Welles's

## *Chimes at Midnight (Falstaff)*

SHAKESPEARE'S SOURCE FOR THE *HENRY IV* PLAYS WAS EN-
glish history as filtered through Holinshed's *Chronicles*. There the
material was shaped into a blend of moral and political exemplum and
biblical parable. Holinshed tells of the troubled reign of Henry Boling-
broke after he usurped the crown from Richard II, of a life of constant
rebellions, suspicion, fear of assassination, guilt, and sickness, all interpreted as God's punishment for the unlawful seizure. He also tells
of the reconciliation of Henry with his Prodigal Son, Hal, who sheds
his lawless companions, fights bravely, and becomes a legitimate successor who rules well and wins glory in France, only to die tragically
two years after his marriage to Katherine of France. Shakespeare retained enough of the moral and political instruction in Holinshed to
encourage many critics to view the plays as essentially a presentation
and amplification of the tale of personal and national penance and
reform. But in the playwright's hands it also became a marvelous and
varied entertainment, a powerful drama of conflicts between fathers
and sons, and a profound exploration of the impact of the Renaissance
on Elizabethan England—all of which serve, with the personal conflicts, to raise the plays to mythical status.

Shakespeare, it bears repeating, lived in a period of transition from
the Middle Ages to the Renaissance. He looked back on the feudal
system, with its sense of divine order in the universe and purpose in
history, its land-based economy and static social order, institutions, and
hierarchies, its widely though not universally accepted values and

body of knowledge expressed in Latin. But he also seemed to intuit the decay of that order and the shattering impact of protestantism, empiricism, capitalism, nationalism, and the explorations of the New World which gave birth to the modern world. As an artist writing for an increasingly secular, urban audience, for a kind of theatre and company unknown to London before the 1590s, and in a language just beginning to rival Latin in subtlety and range, Shakespeare was a product of the new. His mind is an epitome of the dynamic, questioning age which produced Montaigne, Cervantes, Bacon, Galileo, and Machiavelli. At the same time, Shakespeare had strong allegiances to the old. He was a child of Stratford as well as of London who saw that change was not always for the better, that things were being destroyed which were precious and irreplaceable, and that the new forces which were being unleashed might bring the time, as Albany says in *Lear*, when "humanity must perforce prey upon itself, like monsters of the deep."

This double perspective permeates Shakespeare's *Henry IV* plays. Falstaff, the landless knight, and Hotspur, who rides and does battle even in his sleep, may represent the decline of chivalry, but the freedom, good humor, and affection of the fat sovereign of the tavern, and the playfulness, innocent trust, idealism, and biting wit of Hotspur make them the most appealing characters. Set against them are strikingly familiar students of Machiavelli, the humorless, brutal, heartless users of men: Worcester, Northumberland, Henry IV, Prince John, and eventually Hal. In Falstaff's unmasking of "grinning honor" and the naiveté of Hotspur, Shakespeare exposed fatal flaws in the feudal system. In the betrayals of friendship and kinship, the boundless opportunism and unprincipled manipulations of the New Man—made comic in Richard III but horrible in Iago, Edmund, and Lear's cannibalistic daughters—he gave us a prophetic vision of the bloody repressions and revolutions, assassinations, world wars, genocide, and pitiless exploitation between nations which constitute modern history.

With passionate ambivalence, he shows us in the tetralogy from *Richard II* to *Henry V* war as a reflection of national pride, as a proving ground for men, and as a glorious adventure. But he also shows us Falstaff milking money from draft dodgers and gathering the sick and poor for cannon fodder. He shows us the cynicism of the common soldier, war as mutual butchery, war as a ploy for suppressing rebellion. By revealing different aspects of the action and by moving characters

King Henry IV at court

King Falstaff in the tavern

from one situation to another, Shakespeare forces us constantly to change perspective, to shift our sympathies, to reassess cumulative meanings. The ultimate realist, he traps us in a maze of emotions, ideas, and motivations—pride, fear, ignorance, ambition, love, duty, pragmatism, idealism, imagination—which bears little resemblance to the simple moral framework of Holinshed.

The *Henry IV* plays have several overlapping themes and patterns. There is conflict between the generations, young virile Hal and Hotspur against sick, past-ridden, crafty, impotent, guilty old men—a conflict parodied by Falstaff as he descends on the travellers in the Gadshill robbery crying "they hate us youth." Each of the fathers has a characteristic way of trying to control Hal. In Welles's film, Henry IV "stands well in the background, gaining his majesty from high walls around him. Motionless, he lets the freezing rigidity of the setting work on Hal until it breaks him down. Falstaff in the inn, on the contrary, is constantly moving, shouting, cajoling, approaching Hal."[1] There is the equally universal conflict of holiday versus everyday, the individual's need for joy, fluidity, and release against society's need for order, duty, and constraint, the need for power and immortality against the limitations placed on man by nature. In the clash of Falstaff and his world with Henry and his world, we see a man "out of all compass" in body and spirit, night reveler, punster, protean role-player, court jester, rebel against all limits, an embodiment of the comic spirit, take on everything in life that demands that we take it seriously. Incorporating these themes is the pattern of death and rebirth. Henry IV, having killed Richard the King, suffers and dies (like Oedipus) to rid his kingdom of a plague, and is replaced by the son he feared might kill him. Falstaff too is a sacrificial figure—heaped with the sins of both the community and the wayward Prince and banished like the human and animal victims described in Frazer's *Golden Bough*. Spring replaces Winter and the curses of disease and sterility are removed.

In adapting the *Henry IV* plays, Welles confessed that he lost much of their humor and entertainment value.

Falstaff is a man defending a force—the old England—which is going down. What is difficult about Falstaff, I believe, is that he is the greatest conception of a good man, the most completely good man, in all drama. His faults are so small and he makes tremendous jokes out of little faults. But his goodness is like bread, like wine. . . . And that was why I lost the comedy. The more I played it, the more I felt that I was playing Shakespeare's good, pure man. . . . You discover in making the film that the death of the King, and the death of Hotspur, which is the death of chivalry, and Falstaff's poverty and Falstaff's illness run all through the play. Comedy can't really dominate a film made to tell this story, which is all in dark colours.[2]

Though he has focussed on the triangle of Hal, Henry IV, and Falstaff by paring away scenes which do not involve them and by reshaping scenes and language, Welles has still managed to render powerfully the personal, political, and mythical dimensions of the original plays. More important, in spite of obvious sympathy for Falstaff, Welles has succeeded as few interpreter-adaptors have in preserving Shakespeare's double perspective, the tensions, contrasts, and discontinuities which give the drama life.

The interesting thing about this story is that the old King is a murderer, an usurper, and yet he represents the legitimate idea. So

Hal is the creation of a legitimate Prince who must betray the good man in order to become a hero, a famous English hero. The terrible price of power which the Prince has to pay. In the first part of the play, the Hotspur subplot keeps the business of the triangle between the King, his son and Falstaff (who is a sort of foster father) from dominating. But in my film, which is made to tell, essentially, the story of that triangle, there are bound to be values which can't exist as it is played in the original. It's really quite a different drama.[3]

Different, and yet not so different. One must speak with Daniel Seltzer of a "*reimaging* of the text," a "dramatization of the play's *sub*text, . . . that line of intention, of motivation, that might exist beneath the actual words of a script."[4]

From the beautiful long shots of Falstaff and Shallow walking through a dead winter landscape and the close-ups of their reminiscing by the fire to the final scene when Falstaff's coffin is wheeled out of the innyard, Welles's tragedy, suffused with nostalgia and a sense of loss, refutes the commonplace that everything that happens in film is in the present tense. As in *The Magnificient Ambersons*, we find "action embedded in reflection,"[5] saturated in pastness.

The film was not intended as a lament for Falstaff, but for the death of Merrie England. Merrie England is a conception, a myth, which has been very real to the English-speaking world, and is to some extent expressed in other countries of the Medieval epoch: the age of chivalry, of simplicity, of Maytime and all that. . . . Almost all serious stories in the world are stories of a failure with a death in it. . . . But there is more lost paradise in them than defeat. To me that's the central theme in Western culture: the lost paradise.[6]

While Zeffirelli gives us a heightened, colorful, spontaneous past, Welles's distant sounds punctuated with silence, subdued lighting (he had hoped to give the whole film the texture of an old engraving, but the lab was unable to do it),[7] and spare interiors and landscapes show the fifteenth century filtered through memory and imagination. That is why this "Fall" seems so irrevocable, and the bursts of wit, playfulness, and good fellowship seem superficially ineffective. They are not so much dramatizations as evocations, remembrances of things past.

Not that *Chimes* is devoid of humor. Who could forget Falstaff in his tentlike monk's robe being chased through a forest of skinny trees at Gadshill, or his ignominious fall to the ground from the winch before a horse could be guided beneath him before the battle? Who could forget his lumbering strides first one way and then the other to avoid charge and countercharge: "this knight in rusting armor, this belligerent armadillo, waves the troops on to idiot battle, then steps prudently aside."[8] There are funny shots of Falstaff dwarfing the young page who follows him everywhere, wearing a pan on his head with a Kris Kringle twinkle in his eye, peeking out of a trapdoor like Satan out of Hell on the Elizabethan stage, emitting vapor from his helmet as he lies "dead" after the battle. And the comedy is not limited to fat Jack. Silence, who bears a striking resemblance to a prominant former public official, with a pig in his lap and endless stuttering, is a perfect complement to Shallow, lean of aspect and full of squeaky inane speeches. There are rich comic contrasts as well in the scenes with Hotspur and his wife—between Hotspur raging in his tiny bath-tub and the huge suits of armor which surround him, between blasts from heroic trumpets on the battlements and Hotspur dropping his bathtowel and engaging in love play with his beautiful Catherine. Yet the film is a disappointment to audiences seeking in it the broad hilarity of Zeffirelli's *Shrew.*

Beyond the reasons already suggested for the film's somber tone—Welles's sympathy for Falstaff and everything he stands for, and the muted pastness of the film—we might consider others. The first is that Welles is not a great comic actor or director. He cuts or races past good comic moments and then tries to milk laughs from unfunny sit-uations—Sir John in the john, Doll throwing plates at Pistol as he sticks his head through a hole in the wall like the target at a carnival. One feels Welles straining to be funny or trying to patch together things shot months apart, with painful results. His marvelous sense of timing in static scenes of lyricism or somberness, or in frenetic, frag-mented action scenes, fails him in moments of comedy in ways that quick cuts or fluid camera movements cannot disguise.

Second, *Chimes* is the most *personal* of Shakespeare films. Reputed to be a great conversationalist, wit, entertainer and charmer of women, Welles remarked: "the more I studied the part, the less funny he seemed to be."[9] Perhaps he saw too much of himself in Falstaff. To a man who directed and starred in a masterpiece and has since staggered through three decades of underfinanced, hurried, flawed films, scores of bit parts, narrations, and interviews which debased his talent, dozens of projects which died for want of persistence and financing, the story of a fat, aging jester exiled from his audience and no longer able to triumph over impossible obstacles with wit and torrential imagination might well seem tragic. In dramatizing the simultaneous betrayal and self-destruction of Falstaff, one can see Welles exploring a career of squandered talent and of rejection by an industry which, as Pauline Kael said, labels any serious artist "trouble-maker," "a difficult person," "self-destructive," "a man who makes problems for himself,"[10] just as the court saw in Falstaff a misleader of youth, a feeder of riots, and a vulture of the royal coffers.

Finally, one senses that while Welles the actor idealized Falstaff, Welles the director was more true to Shakespeare's double perspective. Though he suppresses Falstaff's most despicable act[11]—stabbing Hotspur in what the text euphemistically refers to as his "thigh"—and surrounds him with admiring if not very admirable worshippers and an aura of Father Christmas, some of his other traits are far from amusing. His obvious intention to use Hal once he is King, his crassness toward Doll, his cynical drafting of the poor, and his greed all serve to qualify our admiration. Furthermore, even at the very end Hal is not unlikeable. He has real affection for Sir John as well as for his father, and he is well aware of how his "friends" are trying to use him. Hal knows he must be his own man and not be absorbed by one of his "fathers," and he knows the cost of being King. In a sense, it is his tragedy too.

Seen one way, *Chimes at Midnight* has a two-part structure, the two halves being divided by the battle at Shrewsbury. Before the battle, life for Hal is an idyll of jests, robberies where the money is given back, impromptu plays, late-night revels, and sporting with girls among tuns of wine. Rash young Hotspur, ranting against the King at court or against a cowardly rebel in a bathtub, is attractive because of his energy and spontaneity, and Falstaff is likeable because of his affection for Hal, his wit, and his love of play. As the battle approaches, however, the seamier sides of Falstaff, Hotspur, and Hal come out. Falstaff, driven from his festive inn, becomes ugly as he victimizes the poor and leaves Doll to the unwanted embraces of Mistress Quickly's customers. Hotspur is both gullible—easily taken in by his crafty uncle Worcester—and suicidal, as he eagerly seeks battle despite the odds. Hal becomes increasingly aligned with his cunning, imperious father. After the battle, England becomes a land of sterility, disease, and death —Hotspur is dead, Falstaff's staff has fallen and like the King he is dying, diseased Doll is ironically pregnant, weary, melancholy Hal and bitter, cynical Poins sit by a still pond. By the end, Falstaff and the King are dead, Falstaff's seedy followers are imprisoned, and charming, Dickensian Shallow has become a greedy scavenger who wants his thousand pounds. Hal has risen to his duty and become Henry V, meeting the national need for order, health, and a direction, but at a cost. As king he must betray his friends, join a hypocritical moralistic revulsion against humor, freedom, and improvisation, and, glorious adventure or not, follow Henry IV's advice to "busy giddy minds with foreign wars."

Seen another way, *Chimes* follows the familiar Shakespearean pattern of juxtaposing parallel actions—three up to the battle and two after it —which mirror and comment upon one another. In *Chimes*, as in the plays, the scenes with Falstaff's followers and the rebels carry the least dramatic weight. Despite certain parallels—Hotspur's hasty dressing for battle and Falstaff's being "armed" in a monk's robe by Hal for the robbery, for example, or Hotspur's bravado and Pistol's— the central thematic contrast is between tavern and court. In terms of visual style, the tavern stresses horizontals and diagonals, fluid camera movement, and alternations between cold emptiness and Brueghel-like feasts and dances. The court stresses verticals, static shots, and alternations between the agonies of the isolated King and carefully ordered ceremonial processions.

Yet there is a certain unity between them as well—both seem hostile to human trust and companionship, like the wintery exteriors and bleak battlefield. The robbery at Gadshill in holy robes is a parody of the battle at Shrewsbury in chivalric armor. In each enterprise thieves cannot be true to one another, and in each Falstaff proves that the better part of valor is discretion. The improvised play at the tavern, where first Falstaff and then Hal play the part of Henry IV, comments on the masking at court where the King feigns strength and the Percies loyalty until Henry forces them into rebellion by denying ransom to Richard's true heir, Mortimer. King Falstaff, ruling from his tavern chair, parodies King Henry in his high throne. Henry's precious crown becomes a dented cooking pot, and the political and military support the Percies provided Henry against Richard II becomes Hal and Poins's comic lifting of gigantic Falstaff onto his throne where, as at the real court, rays of divine light play down upon his godlike majesty. Both King-fathers die false deaths and are "reborn"—Falstaff on the battlefield and Henry in bed by the crown—and each time Hal is there to reveal his feelings. As their masks dissolve, each old man asks for music. Beneath Falstaff's jollity we see sadness and fears of dying and being forgotten. Beneath Henry's cold, hard exterior we see a suffering, guilty man envious of his subjects and hated, he suspects, by his son. Both contrast markedly with contented, nostalgic Shallow, whose real past has been obliterated, transformed into the antics of a mythical "mad Shallow of Clement's Inn." After the battle, over the body of Hotspur, the two kings meet, but it is a silent standoff and Hal refuses to commit himself to either. When Hal and Falstaff meet again, Hal has become a new man (his rebirth is real, not a sham like Falstaff's or Hotspur's) and the results are fatal to the fat knight. Out of a brutal dialectic of court and tavern, the world of Henry V is born.

Seen still another way, *Chimes* is a series of scenes acting one argument: a farewell. Welles noted that Hal's leave-taking from Falstaff "is performed about four times during the movie, foreshadowed four times."[12] Accompanying Hal's partings from Falstaff at the tavern, on the battlefield, and again at the tavern before the final one at court, are many other painful separations: the Percies' forced leave-taking from the King, Hotspur's parting from his wife, the soldiers leaving the village to go off to war, Falstaff's departure from Shallow in the rain, Hotspur's farewell to his men before battle. We witness Hal's farewell to Hotspur, sick Henry's riding off from his son after the battle, Falstaff's leaving weeping Doll at the tavern gate, Hal's two partings from his father, Falstaff's exit from court after being rejected, and his final exit in a coffin at the end. Partings of course occur in any narrative. What makes them so important here is the dramatic emphasis they receive. Welles portrays people alienated, people driven apart by death and the forces of history, people betraying each other.

*Chimes* is intermittently a great film, yet as Pauline Kael said of its chances with the masses, "there ain't no way."[13] Stylistically, the film is very different from the splashy baroque of *Macbeth* and *Othello*. In the 1950s one could not imagine his saying: "what I am trying to discover now in films is not technical surprises or shocks, but a more complete unity of forms, of shapes. The true form, the interior, the musical form of a picture. I believe that you should be able to enjoy a picture with your eyes closed."[14] One reviewer commented, "part of the letdown one feels on first seeing his *Chimes at Midnight* is that it seems so unastonishing: a film of great sobriety, some bleakness, only intermittent visual flair, a film which seems to turn its back on brilliance."[15]

*Chimes* has occasional examples of the earlier Wellesian rhetoric: epic, low-angle shots of the rebels, Falstaff, and the King; a shot in which the camera sweeps down as Worcester returns to the rebel camp, obscuring him with hundreds of spears; rows of knights on proud chargers with their lances bristling against the sky and archers in orchestrated patterns which echo Olivier's *Henry V*. Also recognizably Wellesian are the brutal poetry of the battle, the camera moving down through the rafters in the Brueghelesque inn, and the extreme high-angle shot of Hal helping his dying father to the throne. There are even motifs deliberately carried over from Welles's *Macbeth* (the gallows with hanging traitors, the castle high on the rocks, the briarlike bar in the window) and *Othello* (sunlit flowing banners, forests of spears, Eisensteinian close-ups of blaring trumpets), suggesting, as Charles Higham has noted,[16] that the three films constitute a trilogy of Autumn, Summer, and Winter. But the most striking quality of this film is its simplicity. Hal's symbolic gesture of throwing autumn leaves on Falstaff before the robbery, or the witty direct translation of a verbal image to a visual one as Doll climbs over recumbant Falstaff making him indeed a "huge hill of flesh"[17]—these stand out because there are so few overtly conceptual effects in the work.

*Chimes* is also a difficult film because of its oblique casting and unsettling characterizations. Jeanne Moreau's sour, drunken, crazy Doll, Tony Beckley's Poins as cynical friend and lover of Hal who is so bitter at their parting, Margaret Rutherford's meek, gentle Mistress Quickly, Michael Aldridge's caricature of a caricature of Pistol, and Norman Rodway's barely likeable Hotspur—all have unpleasant, puzzling aspects which jar with the lucid performances of the three principal roles, Keith Baxter's Hal, John Gielgud's Henry IV, and Welles's Falstaff. The most important reason for the film's inaccessibility, however, is its incredible unevenness. Between scenes of true genius—the battle of Shrewsbury, the rejection of Falstaff, the scenes with Falstaff and Shallow, Henry's two death scenes, and the conclusion—are sketchy, rushed-through and patched-together scenes that bewilder and bore. But these things are obvious to anyone who views the film. The critical problem is to see past them in order to do justice to the film's excellences.

Welles's battle scene invites comparison with the battle on the ice in *Alexander Nevsky* and the battle of Agincourt in *Henry V*. For Peter Bogdanovich, Welles's battle is

> infinitely more realistic than the one in Olivier's *Henry V*, but it is also superior in other ways—as film it is more complex, works on many more levels, is even, in an agonizing way, more beautiful because of a vividly conveyed sense of grief. Olivier's sequence has in its pageantry some of the charm of an ancient tapestry, but Welles's is comparable to the war paintings of Goya.[18]

Lasting about ten minutes from the lowering of the knights onto their horses to Hotspur's death, and consisting of just under three hundred shots, Welles's battle is a grim, violent realization of feudal warfare. Never pretty, it has the terrible lyricism and beauty of the rugby matches of Lindsay Anderson's *This Sporting Life*.

> We shot with a big crane very low to the ground, moving as fast as it could be moved against the action. What I was planning to do— and did—was to intercut the shots in which the action was contrary, so that every cut seemed to be a blow, a counterblow, a blow received, a blow returned.[19]

In this conflict, beginning with chivalric splendor and ending with death throes in the mud, it is not merely the sight of men silhouetted against the sky skewered with lances, slashed with swords, pierced with arrows, and beaten mercilessly that is affecting. It is also the *sounds*—the shouts of jubilation, the clash of steel on steel, the swish of arrows, the dull thud of a club crushing a skull, the shrieks and groans of the wounded, and the whinnying horses brought down with arrows. Set against this grotesque dance of butchery is, first, the rotund, armored figure of Falstaff as he nimbly flees from tree to bush and provides respite from the violence, and second, an angelic chorus which sounds above the cacophony of the fighting and provides an ironic commentary on it. What ultimately deflates Hotspur's illusions of glory in war, demonstrates the destructiveness of the rivalry between the nobles, and casts a melancholy pall over the land is not Falstaff's speeches against "honor," or the failure of his plea for good fellowship in sack. It is this brutal slaughter in which everyone is implicated. Against the Battle of Shrewsbury, the crimes of the fat knight look small indeed.

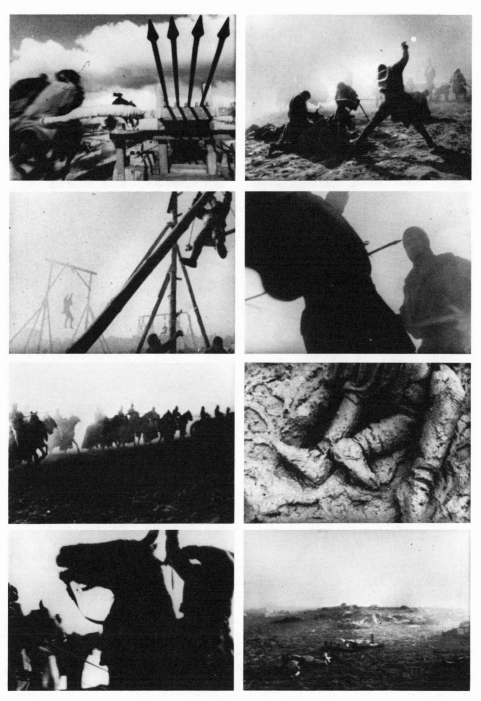

The Battle of Shrewsbury

The rejection of Falstaff

The climax of the film is the inevitable confrontation between Henry V and Falstaff. Welles builds toward the moment by creating momentum behind the King's coronation procession as he rides and then walks in state through his subjects. Then Falstaff breaks through the orderly ranks of soldiers and subjects, halts the procession and music, eliciting cries of shock as he calls out to his "sweet boy." He shatters public ritual and demands a show of personal loyalty. But Hal has become Henry V, holiday turned to everyday. With his back still toward Falstaff, the King cuts him down with two lines: "I know thee not, old man. Fall to thy prayers." Impressively imaged from a low angle against rows of spears and banners and the high vaults of the cathedral, Henry rejects the past as a dream from which he has awakened, bids Falstaff think on death, cuts off the white-haired jester's laugh with a declaration that he is a new man, and brings him to his knees with a decree of banishment.

This much has been public proof that he has reformed. Then Henry's voice changes in tone. His feeling for the man he is destroying surfaces as he promises Falstaff money to keep him from evil. Finally, it seems, Falstaff is cornered and the triumph will be Hal's, but it is not so. Shifting from the high-angle shots of bewildered, hurt Falstaff to a low angle which restores to him his kingly stature, we see the jester smile for the last time—in recognition of the grim humor that this is the way it must be, that Hal must play the comedy in earnest, betray both Falstaff and himself in order to follow his father's path. Henry studies the understanding smile and, unable to bear it, turns to go off into legendary history. A long silence, and then to muffled drums and a low sustained musical note we hear the clatter of armor and weapons as the procession moves wordlessly on, leaving Falstaff to be hounded by pitiless Shallow, who demands his thousand pounds. Falstaff exits alone, dwarfed by vast walls and arches, watched by the young page who has witnessed his story from the first.

Welles's big scenes are usually great ones, but the excellence of *Chimes* also lies in fine subdued moments. "Welles' films *are* showy, but this is only one side of them. The other, quieter side gives a far better clue to what his films are all about."[20] Foremost among these are the nostalgic scenes with Falstaff, Shallow, and Silence. Before the King's death, Falstaff sits drinking and staring into the fire, caught between stuttering Silence, who is comically and pathetically unable to spit out a whole sentence, and frail ancient Shallow, who babbles endlessly about the myth of his madcap youth (a glance at madcap Hal?), who repeats himself like the refrain in a ballad, and asks after people who have been dead twenty years. Shallow

> senses the passing of time only by the changes in the price of live-stock. This is the way of human existence: "To be or not to be" interests some; other only care how much bulls bring now at Stamford fair.... Shallow is not only an insignificant man, he is the Great Insignificance. This figure embodies all the inanity of the existence of a man who lacks the gifts of thought, desire, action, pleasure, and pain.[21]

Welles's selections from the Shallow scenes capture their essence with unerring instinct.

SHALLOW. Ha, cousin Silence, that thou had seen that that this knight and I have seen. Ah, Sir John, said I well?
FALSTAFF. We have heard the chimes at midnight master Robert Shallow.
SHALLOW. (laughs) That we have, that we have, that we have. In faith Sir John we have. Jesu, Jesu the mad days that I have seen. And to think how many of my old acquaintances are dead!

SILENCE. We shall all f-f-f-f-f
SHALLOW. 'Tis certain, 'tis certain. Death, as the Psalmist said, is certain to all. All shall die. (long silence) How a good yoke of bullocks at Stamford fair?
SILENCE. A good yoke of b-b-b-b-b
SHALLOW. Death is certain. And is old Double of your town living yet?
SILENCE. D-d-d-d-d
SHALLOW. Dead? Jesu. 'A drew a good bow, and dead.

This note is sounded once more. After his father dies, Hal lifts the crown and announces in ringing tones, "Now call we our high parliament!" With nice irony, Welles cuts to Shallow and Silence drunkenly singing and dancing in a vast empty barn. Again the blend of humor and pathos, the sodden silences, the sense of freedom (what would Henry IV not have given for such a night?), the iteration of the theme of death. Now, however, Silence's tongue is mercifully liberated by wine: "We shall be merry now. Now comes in the sweet of the night." And Falstaff sits on the far side of the huge room, dwarfed by a network of huge beams over his head—emblematic, perhaps, of the political forces which have caught up Hal and will soon crush the fat knight. These moments of stasis and melancholy reflection, as much as the dramatic conflicts, lie at the heart of *Chimes*.

In two other muted scenes, we see Henry Bolingbroke—who in *Richard II* as a brash young man of action looked on unfeelingly as the King discovered his own mortality, found the crown a hollow cipher, and melted in tears—remove his mask of state and reveal the raw wounds beneath. Sick, sleepless, and alone, he looks out a castle window with the shadow of a bar across his face, musing at "how many thousand of my poorest subjects are at this hour asleep." Gentle strains of cello, harp, and oboe sound in the background. The King's isolation is emphasized by long shots which imprison him with massive pillars, and the poetry of suffering sounds—"Then happy low lie down! Uneasy lies the head that wears a crown." It is as beautiful, moving, and restrained a moment as in any Shakespeare film.

After spending his strength in hunting Hal and the crown, the cold, austere figure with death-mask face (he is to Hal what the ghost is to Hamlet), distant from his people, slippery with his allies, speaks to his son. Gregorian chant echoing in the background, he reveals his agonizing guilt at having usurped Richard II's crown and plunged his country into civil war, his pain in seeing that his whole life has been a play acting the argument of his rebellion against Richard, and his fears of the men who helped him do it and of a son whose rejection threatens to make it all meaningless. In the end, however, remorse gives way to cunning as he urges Hal to "busy giddy minds with foreign wars." As Hal turns to face his new subjects, one shot shows him distant as his father always was, undefined in the smoke and sunlight. Another shot shows the dead father behind the son—not only can Hal not escape duty and the past, he has in a sense been inhabited by the spirit of his father.

The sad, still ending of *Chimes* is set up by ugly scenes of ongoing life—smug lords gloating over the King's "fair proceeding" (Nym comments sadly "the king is a good king, but it must be as it may"); Henry announcing to cheering subjects that he will make war on France and ordering Falstaff released from prison (musing that it was "excess of wine that set him on"). Indifferent Poins, munching an apple denoting the "end of innocence,"[22] walks past Falstaff's empty tavern throne and goes out into the innyard where his followers lament Falstaff—"the king has killed his heart." After Mistress Quickly's threnody about Falstaff in Arthur's bosom, the men slowly push Falstaff's huge coffin out of the tavern gates, recalling his taste for women and his joke about the flea on Bardolph's nose being a soul burning in Hell. The fortress looms in the distance and, as in the opening shots, is juxtaposed with the tavern. While the coffin is wheeled out, the camera booms up out of the innyard to take the larger view of history, contrasting with the personal view of Falstaff's grieving friends. With grim irony, an impersonal narrator (the voice is Ralph Richardson's) pronounces Holinshed's ringing enthusiastic judgment, and the sight of Falstaff's solitary funeral is juxtaposed with fine words about a prince who "put on the shape of a new man," of his "prudence," "policy," and "honor," of a man who "left no friendship unrewarded." A deeply flawed good man has died betrayed, and humor, holiday, personal loyalty, innocence, charity, and youth died with him. Under the credits we watch a film loop of rows of soldiers and subjects at Henry V's coronation, and hear endlessly repeated muffled drums as though the world is locked in a deadening cycle. There *are* great scenes in *Chimes at Midnight*, and the film will be remembered for them. As with Falstaff, next to such virtues, its flaws seem slight.

# Laurence Olivier's *Henry V*

*HENRY V* IS A CLASSIC AMONG SHAKESPEARE FILMS, THE FIRST to be both an artistic and a popular success. It is a unique blend of realism and artifice, a bold departure from the singleness of style of earlier Shakespeare films. Made in a difficult period in England's fight for survival against Germany, it is brimming over with high spirits, bustling with activity, and full of shifts in mood, fluid motion, and changes in color and texture.

What Shakespeare wrote in *Henry V*, and what the film has splendidly caught in its own fashion, is a fanfare; a flourish; a salute to
high adventure; a kind of golden and perennially youthful exalta-
tion of man's grim work.... The opening and closing scenes are
represented as taking place during the first performance of the
piece at the old Globe Theatre, and are played deliberately broad
for comedy. Speech, gestures, and make-up are formally exaggerated;
players and audience mingle in a kind of stylized puppet play....
With the gathering of the English fleet at Southampton, however,
the film breaks loose.... From that moment onwards, the picture
is a beauty. It moves with a flowing line, a rhythmic pattern of mass
and color, that has only been equalled on the screen in the best of
the Disney fantasies. One rich composition after another fills the
eye; the light airy tracery of the French court scenes; the blazing
canvas of the battlefield; the deep, whispering quiet of a darkened
camp waiting for morning; bold, massed groups, single heroic figures; a quaint formal flower garden for a fairy-tale princess, a rearing
and curvetting of caparisoned chargers for a couple of Kings at
war.[1]

Olivier was perfectly suited to Henry as he conceived him—a bold adventurer with something of the likeable madcap about him—and the minor parts are graced with a masterful touch of caricature. This *Henry V* is a blend of history and storybook romance, a tribute both to the glories of the English Elizabethan and Medieval past and to Englishmen in 1944. Stylistically, the film is a miracle of lucidity, order, and harmony. As an interpretation of the play, it is notable rather for its clear, broad outlines and strokes of bravado than for subtlety or complexity of theme or character.

The central conflict is still between the English and the French, but it is defined somewhat differently in the film than in the play. Our impression of the English is bound up with Olivier's robust recreation of the Globe with its dynamic actors and vigorous audience. It is a bristling, lively place, democratic in the sense that commoners, gentlemen, and nobles watch the same play—a quality which carries over into Henry's fellowship with his soldiers in France. The audience, far from the passive, respectful, and often bored audiences of modern theatre, is quick to mock the blunders of the actors, to cheer Falstaff's name and chief comedian, Pistol, to guffaw at bawdy jokes, and to applaud madly at Henry's stirring response to the Dauphin's tennis balls. Henry, of course, attracts the most attention, and his eloquence, self-confidence, and blend of humor and earnestness merge two English heroic identities—Henry, the conqueror of France, and Shakespeare's star tragedian Richard Burbage, conqueror of Elizabethan audiences. But there are others who characterize the English as well: Exeter, dressed in deep reddish brown tastefully ornamented with gold, who boldly brings Henry's demand for the crown to the pastel French court; old-fashioned, hot-headed, loyal Fluellen, who, with Gower and Jamy, sets off the comic cowards; and cynical Michael Williams, who displays another valuable English trait—the Falstaffian instinct for self-preservation. The sadness of Falstaff's followers at his death and the brooding of the soldiers on the night before the battle give the English depth, while the French show no feelings save pride and fear until the final scene. At the opening, though Olivier does what he can to slur over the fact, England is the aggressor, but in France that role soon gives way to the more admirable one of the hard-working underdog—the closely knit group of plain-speaking, honest, loyal, pious men who get the job done.

France, in contrast, is viewed as a decadent, overcivilized country, peopled with beautiful women and shallow, vain men. Our first glimpse of the French court (we were "behind the scenes" in England in a different sense) reveals the addle-brained king seated sans crown on the floor, a sleeping soldier leaning against the empty throne, and bored, idle nobles occupying themselves with games, studying paintings, or looking out the window. The room is full of decorative swirls, gilt, and pretty things—the product of jaded tastes and oversophisticated, effeminate sensibilities. The ludicrously small gates of Harfleur are so flimsy that they seem in danger of being blown down by the English trumpets. Save for the battle, there is very little movement in the French sequences.

> His main method is to keep the scene relatively static so that the actors always seem to belong to the pictorial composition. Camera movement is negligible and characters tend to move from one formal pictorial arrangement into another. The result is closer to a succession of separate, beautiful composed pictures than a single coherent dramatic scene.[2]

The French are snobbish aristocrats, constantly waited upon, isolated from their soldiers, busy drinking wine, eating luscious banquets, and playing games. Even war, until Henry teaches them otherwise, is to them a playful pageant. Apart from the brave, cynical Constable and bold Montjoy (Henry has to have *some* worthy opponents), France is filled with men so silly and weak that they create "unnatural" inversions: the Herald is nobler than the king and braver than the blustering braggart Dauphin, and the women are so much more decisive than the men that they look to the English for sons of mettle. The French are, in short, deluded fools living in a fairy-tale world.

In shaping the script, which contains about half the lines of the play,[3] Olivier and his aides Alan Dent and Dallas Bower not only shortened the original, but made interpretative omissions designed to heighten the polarity of the English and the French. According to Olivier, "the difficulty in Henry's character is in its complete straightforwardness."[4] This is especially true in the film because many of the contradictions in Shakespeare's portrait have been eliminated and its less favorable traits softened. Shakespeare opened his play with a striking contrast between a flowery, stirring epic chorus which portrays Henry as Mars, and a deflating scene in which two politic churchmen resolve to urge the king to make war on France and to provide him with money so that he will not stay home and seize church monies and lands. Olivier, in contrast, after swooping down into the Globe and having the chorus deliver the prologue, provides us with a stage farce of misplaced scrolls and crooked mitres, the churchmen becoming straight man and clown. The emphasis shifts from Shakespeare's mixture of self-interest, deception, pride, and longing for adventure which leads to war (including, if one is familiar with *Henry IV, Part 2*, a plan to "busy giddy minds with foreign wars"), to a good-natured, gutsy acceptance of a personal challenge from the Dauphin.

Similarly, the director has cut Henry's cunning entrapment of Cambridge, Scroop, and Grey, his sentencing them to death for collaborating with the French, as well as smaller details like the vivid image the king uses when speaking to the French ambassador:

> We are no tyrant, but a Christian King,
> Unto whose grace our passion is as subject
> As is our wretches fett'red in our prisons.

He omits also Henry's threats to King Charles that "hungry war" will open its "vasty jaws" and leave widows, orphans, and maidens weeping, and his vicious threats before the gates of Harfleur, laced with images of defiled daughters, "naked infants spitted on pikes," and the heads of silver-haired men smashed against walls. Olivier removes Henry's cool agreement that Bardolph be hanged for stealing a crucifix, his worries before battle about inheriting the guilt of his father, who usurped the crown from Richard II, and his tactical decision in battle to have his soldiers cut his prisoners' throats. Gone too are Henry's joke on Michael Williams, his indelicate reference to Katherine as a good "soldier-breeder," and the chorus's deflating reminder at the end that Henry V died soon after his triumph, that the golden age was followed by the troubled times of Henry VI, "whose state so many had the managing / That they lost France and made his England bleed." Accompanying this tidied up image of the king is a softened view of Falstaff's followers in the subplot. There is a world of difference between Pistol's line in the original, "Falstaff he is dead, and we must earn therefore," and the line in the film, "Falstaff he is dead, and we must yearn therefore" (a reading from the Third Folio). At the end of a sad leave-taking, Pistol in the film no longer spells out his real reason for going to war—"Let us to France, like horse-leeches, my boys, / To suck, to suck, the very blood to suck!"—and we are spared the boy's disgusted list of Pistol's base exploits.

In the midst of a war, the pressures on Olivier must have been very great to make an entertaining nationalist film uncomplicated by Shakespearean irony. Certainly the patriotism is there to complement the escapist fantasy, the hymn to Britain's past glories, and the "twentieth-century conception of a sixteenth-century conception of a historical fifteenth-century king."[5] He does not use strict allegory with one-to-one correspondences, but what Raymond Durgnat calls "sliding symbolism."

> We can find an analogy in *Henry V*, where the English are the English but Agincourt is D-Day, where the French are the Germans, until Henry courts Katherine, whereupon the French are probably the French. Such "contradictions" are typical, also, of Freudian dreamwork, where symbolism is dominated less by the "objective" correlative of each mental entity than by polarities in an emotional situation.[6]

For example, it is our emotional reaction to the killing of the boys in the English camp that suggests the Nazi slaughter of the Jews rather than its place in an intellectual pattern.

Nevertheless, it is to Olivier's credit that in spite of these pressures he retained a few of the complicating elements of the play and made something more than a brilliant showpiece of propaganda. The most important of these is the interpolated death scene of Falstaff. It is possible to follow the reasoning of Harry Geduld that

> Olivier's addition of the death scene can be justified first as an unequivocal reminder that Henry has renounced his former waywardness, and secondly as an indication that corruption in the attractive guise of frivolous irresponsibility has been exorcised from the kingdom. The English have serious affairs to settle, and Falstaff's rascality is a distraction that must be removed before the campaign begins.[7]

But we then must share this critic's puzzlement over George Robey's performance as Falstaff, which gives "little more than the impression of a horror-stricken, hollow-eyed old man being cruelly spurned in his hour of greatest need." Perhaps the scene, with its low-key lighting and somber passacaglia suggesting fate or death,[8] should be taken as a reminder of the darker side of Henry's character, of the *cost* of king-ship. Remember that the cheers at the mention of Falstaff's name in the Globe are still ringing in our ears. Certainly anyone familiar with the ambivalent treatment of Falstaff in the *Henry IV* plays should have no difficulty in seeing this stroke as Olivier's qualifying of other idealiz-ing parts of the film. (To this end, he even suppresses the humor and bawdy in Mistress Quickly's "dizzying blend of comedy and noble piteousness"[9] as she describes his death.)

Furthermore, if Falstaff is dead in this film, Falstaffism is not. His talent for parody survives in Pistol, whose speech is filled with bom-bastic epithets stolen from old plays. His knowledge that discretion is the better part of valor lives on as Pistol cries "On! On! On! On to the breach, on to the breach," as he looks for a place to hide (a fine contrast to and mockery of Henry's "once more into the breach"). Pistol also shares the rotund knight's knack for getting into comic situations which lay bare serious actions elsewhere in the play. After the confrontation between Fluellen and Pistol, it is difficult to avoid noticing that Henry is risking the lives of his men to make France eat a leek. Falstaff's way of smelling out the lies hiding behind official abstractions, of riddling soph-istries with holes, reappears in the scene before the battle where they force Henry to face things he would rather not face: an innocent boy wonders who will account for all the dead and wounded, a cynic is sure the king will be ransomed when they are all dead, and a blindly obedient subject, oblivious to both self-interest and morality, will follow the king anywhere and do anything for him. Finally, the spirit of Falstaff hovers over Henry as the former pupil muses on the empti-ness of "ceremony" in a speech reminiscent of Falstaff's skeptical catechism on "grinning honor" in *Henry IV, Part 1.*

Even in an antiheroic, antimilitaristic, post-Vietnam era, Olivier's film arouses enthusiasm with its glorious battle sequence. But it is not entirely accurate to label it "just a decorative pageant."[10] Agincourt may begin as a splendid show, but the tone shifts with the slaughter of the boys in the English camp. The splendid charge descends to a grim, unheroic standoff of hundreds of soldiers mired in the mud, and over a shot of the corpses of young men in the foreground and masterless horses racing over the ironically green, body-strewn battlefield in the background, a Te Deum is heard. These somber moments, in concert with the emblematic shots illustrating the ruin brought to France by war described by Burgundy near the end, have nothing approaching the gruesome power of the battle scene or the scenes with melancholy, dying old men in *Chimes at Midnight*. But they make themselves felt nevertheless, and a series of unfestive minor themes and moments in the film reinforce them. For instance, Olivier leaves the conflicts between Nym and Pistol and between the King and the cynical soldier unresolved. He retains the grotesque link between Mistress Quickly's feeling the parts of Falstaff's corpse, Princess Katherine's lesson in English names for parts of the body which is riddled with off-color jokes, and the young soldier's worries about "all those legs and arms and heads, chopped off in a battle." And he did not omit, as he could easily have done, the half-touching moment when Pistol, thoroughly exposed, beaten, and humiliated by Fluellen, tells us that his Nell has died of the malady of France and he must turn bawd and thief. It is true that "*Henry V* is, ultimately, a movie about the strengths of discipline, determination, leadership and union in a common cause, and the hollowness of arrogance, ostentation and indecision."[11] But the film is about other things too.

The idealization of Henry results as much from Olivier's performance as from his shaping of the text. He is a splendid, likeable, handsome young prince from a fairy tale. Olivier begins as Burbage the Globe actor, clearing his throat and setting a smile before making a grand entrance to win over the audience with thundering words and big gestures. (As in the recent television production of *Long Day's Journey Into Night*, in which Olivier plays an aging actor who loves Shakespeare, a certain resonance results from his status as the Burbage of his age.) Olivier gets away with the transition from Burbage to Henry because Shakespeare—observer of Elizabeth and Essex, author of so many plays in which the kingdom is a stage and kings players—wrote into the part the theatricality of renaissance princes. In the play, this showmanship may have undertones of fakery and "seeming." In the film, it is a delight because Henry is healthily aware of his outrageous panache and is not secretly manipulative like Shakespeare's less likeable politicians. Even his restraint is ostentatious as he smiles and leans casually on the arm of his throne before rising and shaking the rafters with his reply to the Dauphin's challenge.

Henry shows ease and a superior sense of timing when he nonchalantly tosses his crown onto the back of his throne, when at Southhampton he grasps the royal seal in midspeech, flourishes it to make a point, stamps it on the waiting hot wax, and sweeps on to supervise the loading of the ships, or when at the end of his St. Crispin's Day speech he leaps from a wagon onto his horse. In battle he is a fine horseman who can pluck a sword from the ground while riding full tilt, a resourceful fighter who, when disarmed by the Grand Marshal, unhorses him with a blow of his armored fist. He can be forgiving, as when he releases the unnamed man who slandered him, yet he drives a hard bargain with the defeated French. He is generous, sensing in Montjoy a kindred spirit and rewarding him liberally, frank when he reveals his army's weariness to the enemy, and of course splendidly eloquent—when he urges his men "once more into the breach," the camera slowly pulls back and up, freeing Olivier to cut loose and showing how he is welding his men into a unit.

Though Olivier's Henry is not a portrait of much depth, he does convey the king's discovery of his growing verbal and political power.

> His blood-raising reply to the French Herald's ultimatum is not just that; it is a frank, bright exploitation of the moment for English ears, amusedly and desperately honored as such, in a still gallant and friendly way, by both Herald and King. His Crispin's Day oration is not just a brilliant bugle-blat; it is the calculated yet self-exceeding improvisation, at once self-enjoying and selfless, of a young and sleepless leader, rising to a situation wholly dangerous and glamorous, and wholly new to him. Only one of the many beauties of the speech as he gives it is the way in which the King seems now to exploit his sincerity, now to be possessed by it, riding like an unexpectedly mounting wave the astounding size of his sudden proud awareness of the country morning, of his moment in history, of his responsibility and competence, of being full-bloodedly alive, and of being about to die.[12]

Even Henry's horse seems to share his excitement, shaking its head vigorously when the Herald offers ransom before the battle.

Olivier shows also the maturing of the man and the leader in the long night before battle. When he faces doubt, mortality, the loneliness and responsibility which weigh on all Shakespeare's kings, he becomes more human, less of a plastic icon of the Ideal King. James Agee noted

> the difference in tone between Olivier's almost schoolboyish "God-a-mercy" and his "Good old Knight," not long afterward, measuring the King's growth in the time between with lovely strength, spaciousness, and cleanness. . . . It fully establishes the King's coming-of-age by raising honorable, brave, loyal, and dull old age (in Sir Thomas

Erpingham) in the King's love and esteem to the level of any love he had ever felt for Falstaff.[13]

In this scene, at least, he is a man of contemplation as well as action. After winning against the odds on the battlefield, he enters the lists once again, but this time there is no risk—Katherine cannot, and does not want to, refuse him, and they both know it. Nevertheless, he plays the wooing game, to give her pleasure and to prove himself once more a man for all seasons, addressing her with a mixture of roughness and delicacy, of royal bearing and unrepentent naughtiness. He decimates both the French language (*"donc vostre est France et vous estes mienne"*) and the courtly love tradition ("clap hands and there's a bargain"), and is utterly charming in winning the princess. As far as *this* film is concerned, they live happily ever after.

Olivier's *Henry V* merits praise for many things, not the least of them being the clarity and energy with which the verse is spoken unashamedly as verse, but without the dull incantation that plagues many English productions. As a film, however, its most original and interesting aspect is its structure with which both visual style and music are in complete harmony. The work begins as a documentary recreation of a performance by Shakespeare's company at the Globe on May 1, 1600. "We are not in the play, we are in an historical film about the Elizabethan theater, that is to say, we are present at a film of a kind that is widely accepted and to which we are quite used."[14] While the camera gives us occasional glimpses backstage, the overall feel of the cinematography is theatrical, and this is reinforced by the broad acting styles, placards announcing changes in setting, and spontaneous interactions between actors and audience.

When we shift to Southampton, we move from theatrical artifice embedded in Elizabethan realism to a scene as it might have been staged on the illusionist nineteenth-century stage with realistic properties, a large crowd of extras, three-dimensional ships (the mast in the shape of a huge cross emphasizing the religious cast of the scene), and an obviously painted canvas backdrop portraying the town, countryside, and the sea. At the Boar's Head, the style is somewhere between illusionist theatre and the "realism" of studio sets of the 1940s. The dynamic camera work introduced as the camera pulls back and up from Henry to the ship's crow's nest continues as it sweeps slowly up to and through the window of the room where Falstaff lies dying. Olivier adds other explicitly filmic devices too, such as the lyrical dissolves to Mistress Quickly when she drifts slowly into the frame toward Falstaff, and to the dark exterior of the tavern as his mournful followers come out. The French court scene is acted out as a tableau with distorted scale and perspective and composed panels reminiscent of medieval manuscript illuminations.[15]

In the centerpiece of the film, the battle, the director climaxes his movement toward film realism by using location settings, hundreds of extras, and violent motion covering a great deal of space. But at the same time he holds that realism in check by shifting from a theatrical style to Eisensteinian montage as he juxtaposes the rush of charging French horses with the harsh diagonals of English pikes and arrows, involving close-ups with long shots which provide a detached overview. After Agincourt, the pattern reverses, and we pass through a lovely painterly winter tableau and the delicate tracery of the French court to arrive once again at the Globe, Walton's music shrinking from full orchestra and medieval styles to Elizabethan theatre music once again.[16]

Olivier, in short, has made *Henry V* a play within a play—a Shakespearean enough device—by enclosing it in a frame. And, as in Shakespeare, the pattern of the whole is echoed in the form of its parts. The jewel of a garden scene set in the make-believe French palace in which Katherine looks down to the palace gate as knights ride out, enters the garden with her attendant, makes a circular tour of it while taking her English lesson, and then leaves, pausing once more to look down as the knights return, mirrors perfectly the overall pattern of the film: a movement outward followed by a return. The quasi-allegorical nature of the film is reflected in the emblematic scene in which an Englishman, an Irishman, a Welshman, and a Scotsman—each wearing an appropriate emblem—resolve to fight for Henry despite their differences. Different parts of the action are tied together by recurring symbols and echoes. The Constable's black armor decorated with gold suns, seen first standing empty in the French tent before the battle where it symbolizes the empty vaunting French, is last seen when it is worn by that professional coward and scavenger of the battlefield, Pistol, when he is forced to eat the leek. Reminders of the Globe frame saturate the central parts of the film: the Globe flag and trumpeter are echoed on the battlefield, the arch over the inner stage is duplicated by the arch into which a banquet is crushed at the French court, Henry encircled by his men on a wagon resembles Burbage surrounded by spectators at

The Battle of Agincourt

the theatre, and Henry "directs" the spectacle at Agincourt, as Geduld notes, "conducts" it with his "sword-baton" like the choir master above the stage.[17]

This framing of the action was a cunning stroke in a number of ways. It allowed Olivier to heighten the virtues of film poetry and film realism by exposing and transcending the limitations of the theatre—though, as Agee complained, the image of the Globe is in ways a false and condescending one.[18] It permitted him to gloss over an opening scene which is out of harmony with his view of Henry, and to take advantage of the natural pattern of an audience's emotional and imaginative involvement so that the humor and romance occur in theatrical scenes and the serious action occurs in realistic ones. The frame afforded Olivier scope for originality and an opportunity to expand on the implications of the name of the Globe—that it opens out and reflects the real world. It permitted him to preserve a structure which contrasts the individual death of Falstaff (while thinking on God) with the mass slaughter of soldiers (whose leader in a dark night of the soul also puts his cause into the hands of Heaven), which juxtaposes the strength of King Henry with the weakness of King Charles (in the film, a blend of Richard II, Merlin, and court fool), and which pits English values against French values. Most important, it permitted him to "play" with style in a Shakespearean way, to shift and blend styles scene by scene, matching Shakespeare's metadrama with metacinema. The marriage of Henry and Katherine on a thematic level is a perfect match of "male" aggressiveness and courage with "female" beauty, delicacy, and refinement. It resolves the dramatic conflict by bringing harmony and by promising, like the marriages at the end of so many of Shakespeare's comedies, renewal. But the wedding also represents a marriage of styles—theatrical and illusionist, film realist and painterly—in the film as a whole. As Bazin said, "there is more cinema, and great cinema at that, in *Henry V* alone than in 90% of original scripts."[19]

*Henry V* is a much richer play when seen as the last part of a tetralogy including *Richard II* and *Henry IV, Parts 1 and 2*, and Olivier's film therefore makes an interesting contrast with Welles's *Chimes at Midnight*. In *Chimes* we witness the decline and death of Merrie England. *Henry V* is a vivid re-creation of it: "the film isn't about the historical Henry V, or even about Shakespeare's idea of Henry V. It's about *The Demi-Paradise*, Britain as happy home of poet and warrior alike."[20] Against the somber story of the self-destruction

Snowy stylized Agincourt, the Royal
marriage, and a return to Elizabethan
London

and betrayal of Falstaff and the ironic triumph of the New Men,
starring an aging director and ending in an asymmetrical image of
death, is set an exuberant blend of heroic epic and romantic comedy
starring a youthful director and ending in symmetry, order, and
harmony. While Welles's film takes itself very seriously, Olivier's rich
confection is playful both in its performances and in its techniques.
Against the darkness, the bleak wintery landscapes, the vast cold interiors, the coarse textures, and the pervading sense of pastness in
Welles's underfinanced black and white film we find brilliant, lucid
images, decorative compositions, a variety of seasons including a festive
winter patterned after the February illustration for the Limbourg
brothers' *Tres Riches Heures du Duc de Berry,* and heightened costumes and movement in Olivier's well-financed Technicolor work
which sports the saturated colors of a Hollywood musical.

Welles uses oblique casting, restrained naturalistic acting, and
difficult, complex characterizations. Olivier uses broad, simple characterizations. *Chimes* uses a single level of illusion and is an uncompromis-
ingly personal film which alienates popular audiences. *Henry V,* on the

other hand, shifts easily from one level to another and was conceived from the first as a popular film intended to unite a country and express a national spirit. In the later film, despite occasional moments of humor, war, death, and betrayal kill off the comedic elements of the original. In the earlier film, from the backstage scenes showing boy-actresses using oranges for breasts and the actor of Ely being as silly offstage as he is on, to Nym's cuckolding Pistol and then declaring "I cannot kiss, that's the humour of it," and Pistol's brandishing his truncated sword, to Fluellen's bellowing for Gower to be quiet on the eve of the battle, to the French Constable's pouring acid comments on the bright hollow words of the Dauphin, to Henry's mocking his own awful French, comedy predominates. In these films we see reflected Shakespeare's shifts in tone and technique from the *Henry IV* plays, where laughter gives way to death, disease, Machiavellian politics, and Hal's carefully orchestrated reformation and betrayal of his saturnalian friend, to *Henry V*, which on its surface, at any rate, is a jubilant patriotic hymn. But we also see two different cinematic sensibilities at work for fundamentally different artistic purposes.

# Laurence Olivier's *Richard III*

SHAKESPEARE'S *RICHARD III* IS A GARGOYLE ON THE GREAT cathedral of English history. It is not really a history play, even though it uses real names and events and describes the climax to the violence and chaos which followed the short-lived glories of Henry V. Rather, as Olivier says in his preface to the film, it is the dramatization of a a legend—a legend concocted by Tudor historians writing to glorify and confirm the legitimacy of Queen Elizabeth's ancestor, Henry VII (Richmond). The original title labels the play a tragedy. If it is, it is a medieval tragedy of the kind found in a work Shakespeare knew well, *The Mirror for Magistrates*, "wherein may be seen by example of other, with how grievous plagues vices are punished and how frail and unstable worldly prosperity is found, even of those, whom Fortune seemeth most highly to favour."[1] In telling the stories of, among others, Henry VI, Clarence, Hastings, Buckingham, and Jane Shore, this poetic work shows the high brought low, murderers haunted by the ghosts of their victims, and wrongdoers crushed in the gears of the great metaphysical machine, Divine Justice.

Two things, however, make Shakespeare's medieval tragedy different from the others. First, its charming, Machiavellian, grotesque, Faustian hero Richard—a wit, a self-conscious actor of great skill, a renaissance wolf among medieval sheep. Second, its medieval tragic structure is fleshed out with a unique blend of Senecan gothicism, melodrama, farce, and irony. It is gothic because Richard the Macabre takes such *delight* in killing his enemies, because the women in the play are attracted to his diabolism and deformities (playing Beauty to his Beast), and because the characters are haunted by premonitions and ghosts. It is Senecan melodrama because it is full of exaggerated actions, sensational scenes, wooden rhetoric, flat characters, and simple moral polarities (or inversions of same). It is farce because Richard has so *many* victims and we are so detached from the violence that it becomes funny. It is ironic not simply because the victims are ignorant of their impending doom, but because the "normal" world by which Richard is measured and condemned is rotten to the core—riddled with guilt, cowardice, sickness, and indecision, a dying world, in fact, which the villain-hero pulls down with him leaving to the "outsider" Richmond the task of restoring health and harmony.

As an interpreter of Shakespeare, Olivier has never shown much interest in the social and political dimensions of the plays. Film is not for him a tool for analytical thought, for exploring the interactions of men and historical forces. He has chosen to film plays in which these elements are not central. In the comic image of exasperated Canterbury becoming lost in a heap of scrolls and Ely throwing them up in the air in disgust, Olivier has provided in *Henry V* an emblem of what in his view Shakespeare has done with the complicated, intractable material of English history—namely, thrown it away and created fiction and myth. In *Henry V* links with earlier plays were minimized. In *Hamlet* he discarded Fortinbras and the larger action and focussed on Hamlet's personal struggle. Even in Burge's *Othello* his intensely psychological portrait made it primarily a tragedy of character. In a penetrating essay, however, Constance Brown has argued that in *Richard III* Olivier retained the socio-political dimension and gave us a "portrait of tyranny." By opening the film with the abstract image of the crown, "symbol of divinely sanctioned authority," and introducing into the text the coronation of Edward VI from *Henry VI, Part 3,* the director focusses his work on the "parabolic curve from legitimate king to tyrant to legitimate king."[2] She even asserts that Olivier intends the audience to see a connection between Richard and Hitler, as Caesar and Hitler were linked in Mankiewicz's *Julius Caesar.*

There is no question that the theme of the crown is important to the film. The theme of the fall and rise of the state is even underscored in good Elizabethan fashion by the changes in the seasons. The story begins with the "glorious summer of this son of York," moves through the deadly, sterile, yet perversely decorative winter of Richard's discontent, and ends on the parched plains of Bosworth Field, where Richmond's triumph heralds the coming of spring. Nevertheless, Olivier's real emphasis lies elsewhere. In cutting down and clarifying what Olivier once referred to as "an absolute delta of plot and pre-supposed foreknowledge of events" up to the arrival of the Princes,[3] and in removing Margaret and her curses, he has shifted the emphasis away from history and the working out of Divine Justice. As Alice Griffin remarked,

> in insisting on clarity for the benefit of the millions who will see the film, Sir Laurence unfortunately has sacrificed the larger signifi-cance of the work. He cuts out the character of the virago Queen Margaret, who runs like a thread through Shakespeare's text, re-minding Richard, his fellow sinners, and the audience, that retribu-tion will come. And in so doing, Olivier narrows his scope from the execution of divine justice on doers of evil to a chronicle of Richard and his pawns, and his theme from the falls of princes to the punish-ment of one man. But within this smaller framework the film is a *tour de force*, in one opinion the best of the Olivier films to date and the best of motion picture Shakespeare.[4]

One need only contrast Olivier's *Richard III* with the political drama of Mankiewicz's *Julius Caesar* or the intense social consciousness of Kozintsev's *King Lear* to see that his theatrical talents and antirealist sensibility led him to make a very different kind of work.

Shakespeare, we have noted in discussing *Chimes at Midnight*, was an artist caught between the medieval and modern worlds. One sees this conflict everywhere in his plays—between the loyal servant Adam in *As You Like It* or Kent in *King Lear* and the Oswalds and Osrics of the world, between the idealism of Othello and the pragmatism of Iago, between poetic, myth-believing Richard II and terse, blunt Boling-broke, between aristocrats playing love games and tolerant of fools and drunks, and middle-class, status-seeking, puritanical Malvolio in *Twelfth Night*. In *Richard III* Shakespeare depicts another aspect of the decline of the medieval world and rise of the modern. It is a play of hollow ceremonies, ineffectual rituals which fail because the ideals and beliefs on which they were based are dying.

> The Renaissance . . . was a moment when educated men were modi-fying a ceremonial conception of human life to create a historical conception. . . . Shakespeare's plays are full of pageantry and of action patterned in a ritualistic way. But the pageants are regularly

interrupted; the rituals are abortive or perverted; or if they succeed, they succeed against odds or in an unexpected fashion. The people in the plays try to organize their lives by pageant and ritual, but the plays are dramatic precisely because the effort fails. This failure drama presents as history and personality; in the largest perspective, as destiny.[5]

If Olivier has made an historical film, it is in the sense that, out of respect both for Shakespeare's thematic interest in ritual and for his sure instinct for theatrically explosive scenes, Olivier showed how rituals, faced with Richardism, can no longer make the world cohere and have meaning.

The film opens with the coronation of Edward IV, which is decorative and impressive in its own way. Yet we hardly pay any attention to it. What is really arresting is Richard, ominously dressed all in black, prophetically crowning himself in the foreground and obliterating the image of the "real" coronation in the background. We are taken not with the distant rhetoric of Edward but with the angular profiles and sly looks of Richard and Buckingham, and in particular Richard's unblinking gaze straight into the camera. The pomp and circumstance, festive music, and carefully orchestrated symmetrical movements as the procession moves from one room to the other are made silly by the coy glances of a sensuous and beautiful woman (Jane Shore, the King's mistress) who, despite the presence of the Queen, makes eye contact with Edward and physically cuts a diagonal across the official flow as she passes through his followers.

Later, a funeral procession, in which pale, lovely Anne and an orderly line of chanting monks follow a coffin, is interrupted by Richard, who draws his sword, barks a command to set down the corpse, disarms a soldier who tries to resist, and scatters the monks. He then proceeds to woo the shocked, grieving widow over the body of her husband (in Shakespeare it was her father-in-law) whom he has murdered. Soon after (for Olivier has broken one scene into two, perhaps for the sake of credibility), Richard completes his conquest in a kind of perverse Annunciation. He jars her out of her angelic, frescolike posture of prayer, forces her away from her husband's tomb and up against a pillar, and, in his own erotic ritual, gives her his sword, rips open his doublet, and, seizing on her inability to kill, embraces and kisses her passionately. This ritual ends with a "wedding" delicately suggested in the film by Richard's grotesque shadow falling on Anne's white dress as she waits in terror and anticipation by her bed, her face obscured in the shadows. Delicate, but clear enough in meaning.

Still other rituals are undermined by Richard. Christ-like Clarence, superbly played by John Gielgud, prays for peace and forgiveness as he is shaken by a terrible dream of drowning and by pangs of guilt. But he little suspects that the god who watches over him is quite other than the one in heaven—we see, as he cannot, the shadow of his twisted brother (who with nice irony, *does* send him to a death by drowning) on the window of his cell door. Later, Edward's ceremony of peace-making among the nobles is shattered by Richard's casual announcement that the King's order to execute Clarence has been carried out. Edward, who had hoped to end generations of rancor with a few words and gestures in order to die at peace with himself, staggers around the room trying to shift the blame on others and dies a horrible death, haunted by guilt and the knowledge that the bloody conflicts will go on. Even the mourning of the King is parodic. Hastings and Jane Shore, after their hands meet as they piously fold Edward's hands on his chest, frame the image of the King and weeping Queen and look deep into each other's eyes as they anticipate their sexual union. The picture of Richard and Buckingham, speaking in low tones, hands carefully folded, standing solemnly at the foot of the bed gazing upon the dearly departed, *looks* reverent enough. But what are they discussing? How to take custody of the Princes and get rid of the Queen's allies.

The crowning blow to medieval ritual is Richard's coronation. He even turns the planning of it (though at this point the rite is still ostensibly for the Prince) into a murderous practical joke. Richard theatrically traps Hastings, who sits confidently at the head of the table, painted angels on the wall hovering protectively over him. By crying treason and baring his withered arm, Richard condemns Hastings for hesitating to accuse Jane Shore of witchcraft. The other prelude to Richard's coronation is the marvelous mummery put on for the Lord Mayor and the citizens of London. Holy, otherworldly Richard, flanked by chanting monks, reluctantly agrees to accept the crown only after the repeated and earnest entreaties of his fellow thespians, Buckingham and Catesby. The coronation itself is a burlesque. The cry "may the King live forever" sticks in Stanley's throat. Richard drags his faint Queen unceremoniously to the foot of the raised throne, orders all to stand apart (setting the ordered ranks of his followers in complete disarray), slowly ascends in his grotesque manner, and sits holding the emblems of royal power, stunned, staring into space, hypnotized by the prospect of limitless dominion. From this moment on, everything he does is a nightmarish parody of the Elizabethan ideal of the Christian-Humanist King.

All other rituals having failed, the action shifts from a man-made to a natural setting and England resorts to a more primitive rite, the boar hunt. This sole authentic ritual in the film is strikingly foreshadowed as Richard is encircled in his dark, empty throne room by torch-bearing messengers bringing word of new attacks. Then it is viciously carried out on the battlefield. In Shakespeare, Richmond kills Richard in single combat: "Enter Richard and Richmond, they fight, Richard is slaine." In Olivier's film, the killing is a communal one. Far from the neat, orderly rites of Christianity, the soldiers brutally tear at Richard like mad dogs, skewer him on their spears, purging his evil from themselves and their country. In killing him, they reach back to the ancient pattern of the killing of an old, sterile king linked with the dying year, as well as to the scapegoat pattern in which the sins of the community are heaped on a sacrificial figure, the figure is destroyed, and a new king is crowned.[6]

Apart from the patterns of ritual, the heart of Olivier's *Richard III* is Richard Crook-back—twisted Lord of Misrule, feudal Al Capone, sinister self-aware parodist monster.

> Sir Laurence, incarnating that evil genius, the treacherous, witty, spleenful and ever-unrepentent villain, plays Richard in a spirit verging on the Victorian melodramatic. He savours his wickedness with relish, sharing, in close-up, his cynical and mirthful contempt for his victims. Gleefully, he takes perverted joy in the world's dislike of him, revels in his plots, glories in his hellish ministry. Rage he knows, and despair, but never gloom or self-pity.[7]

Some object to the shallowness of Olivier's portrait. Those who view Shakespeare's *Richard III* as a serious, bloody, morbid play urge upon us a portrait of more psychological realism. To them a thoroughly evil man

> becomes interesting only when evilness is given a shadow, a cleavage, a psychological background. . . . Richard's intellectual insight should be contrasted with the manic complex of the cripple, his very crippleness ought to contrast with a sexual attraction of highly unique quality. But Olivier depicts Richard just as unequivocally as

he depicted Henry—he replaces uprightness with a completely self-integrated wickedness. The clarity and consistency of Henry, which contributed so essentially to the charm of the film, makes Richard into an uninteresting figure. In Olivier's splendid and fascinating acting, Richard is manic, but not demonic.[8]

Yet, Richard III is not Macbeth. It was only in 1595 with *Richard II* that Shakespeare really began to explore the inner lives of characters. Earlier, under the influence of Seneca and Marlowe, he made his central characters interesting in more external ways. In the case of Richard III, he portrayed not a psychological and metaphysical mystery like Iago, or a case study for the sociologist and psychoanalyst like Edmund the Bastard, so much as a full-blown stage-villain, a blend of the traditional comic devil of earlier English drama and the bogeyman who haunted the nightmares of Elizabethan Englishmen asleep over wine and a copy of Gentillet's *Contre-Machiavel*. We are not really frightened by Olivier's entertaining Richard, who is a handsome devil. If we have sympathy for him, it is not of a sentimental variety. Rather, it is a sympathy of the imagination for a man more cunning than his adversaries, a brilliant wit and poseur, a Dionysian reveller who bursts the moral confines of society and dips his hands in blood. Richard's cynicism and self-awareness are so complete that they annihilate the pathos of his situation.

Like Shakespeare, Olivier nods toward the "human" Richard. He hints at the deep-seated feelings of neglect since childhood, the envy of the pretty, well-formed Princes, the masochist's need for punishment, the insatiable lust for power which drives him to destruction. Olivier shows that, like most practical jokers, Richard has no sense of humor when the joke is on him, least of all, as young Richard of York learns, when it comes to the cosmic joke of his humped back, short leg, and deformed hand. Olivier lends several authentic touches to Richard's hatred of romance, music, dancing, fertility, and harmony which places Richard among Shakespeare's other unfestive outsiders—Malvolio, Shylock, and Iago.

In Olivier and Shakespeare, however, the real emphasis is upon Richard the virtuoso role-player, who rivals protean Falstaff in his appeal to audiences. Much of our pleasure is in watching Olivier the consummate actor play Richard the consummate actor, shifting easily from "concerned brother," to "repentent murderer" and "flattering wooer," to "plain honest man overflowing with righteous indignation," to "friendly peacemaker" and "dutiful son," to "jolly playful uncle," to "pious unworldly man" until he becomes king and need pretend no longer. Richard as parodist is pure delight. Quite against the demands of his part when "the people" beg him to become king, he riffles through the Bible as though it were a picture magazine, revealing the shallowness of all the characters' commitments to Christian values. If poets "descant" (create variations) on their beloved's beauty, he will descant on his own deformity. And, just as Olivier constantly threatens to overflow the part he plays with such relish, Richard flirts with giving himself away by telling Edward, for example, that "by G his issue disinherited should be" or sadly noting after Clarence's death that "some tardy cripple bore the countermand." Olivier is more a splendid entertainer than psychologist or realist, but rarely has so external a performance fit the work so well.

Physically, Olivier's Richard is very striking—long sharp nose, piercing eyes, jet black hair with spears of it cutting into his brow, a gloved claw of a hand. He is good-looking, having a Byronic attractiveness, limp and all, and is extremely mobile compared to the static characters around him both at court and in battle. His list to one side often makes him the most pronounced diagonal in the frame; the camera shows him askew in a world in which he does not belong, and this feeling is confirmed by his habit of staring into and confiding with the camera.

Ronald Berman remarked after a screening of *Richard III* on Public Television that Richard is the only character in the play who *thinks* very much. At times he seems to be thinking about his double performance (one for the other characters, one for us). He not only shatters the moral and social conventions of society, but right from his brilliant opening soliloquy,[9] breaks out of the fourth-wall convention of realistic film, placing himself both inside the fictive world and outside it. Olivier also stresses Richard's power by having him look down on his victims from heights when they are unaware of his presence, and the camera consistently takes his point of view. His entrances are always calculated and spectacular, and his costumes either boldly declare his evil nature (Satanic blood red or funereal black) or parody "high fashion" by juxtaposing it with his own deformity. Richard's comic hubris is irresistible. Each gesture has flair, as when, after his opening soliloquy about the crown, he jauntily tosses his cap over his shoulder

and says "Tut! Were it further off I'd pluck it down." He is delightfully improvisatory, light-hearted, casual, as Ms. Brown notes.[10] He
very nearly gives the murderers Clarence's *reprieve* rather than the
death warrant. So much a virtuoso is he that at times one feels he is
hardly bothering to deceive his victims at all, choosing rather to terror-
ize them, to hypnotize them as a snake does a rabbit.

In the film Richard's opponents are weak and stupid, but they do not
seem evil as they do in Shakespeare.

Richard is an arch-villain operating against a group of victims who are
at worst gullible, and at best innocent, bewildered sheep who suddenly
discover a fox in the fold. But Shakespeare's original, thanks largely
to the offices of Margaret, leaves no doubt that Richard is simply a
smarter villain amongst a pack who morally and ethically are no
better than he.[11]

They do not succumb to the fox because of past sins and guilt, but, as
in Ben Jonson's *Volpone*, because of their greed, vanity, lust, fear,
ambition, innocence, and superstition. Olivier's gallery of two-dimensional gulls is one of the great delights of *Richard III*. The pale, nervous
Queen weeps, wrings her handkerchief, and takes comfort from professional optimists. The fat Lord Mayor of London smiles his idiotic
smile and tries to sound wise by parroting the Cardinal about Hastings
("I never looked for better once he fell in with Mistress Shore").
Skittish, carrot-topped Dorset strides about trying to look noble in a
ridiculous thimble of a hat.

If the lesser characters have any depth, it is forced on them by Richard, for, dramatically speaking, he is the Prime Mover. Buckingham
and smirking Catesby positively glow when in his service—being evil
moons to his evil sun. When faced with death, Richard's victims have
moments of contrition and insight which *almost* arouse sympathy. Anne
must face the grossness of her giving in to fear and desire and perhaps
glimpses the intimate relation of love and hate. Hastings learns the
folly of complacency and foresees the sufferings of England. Stanley
sees that blind obedience or compromise will not work and that he
must support Richmond even at the risk of a son. And Buckingham
learns that what he read in Richard as shrewd pragmatism was in fact
compulsive madness and that he is doomed for the very reason he
should have been rewarded.

The audience too is forced by Richard to undergo an awakening.

Having had our feelings and moral sense anesthetized early on and having enjoyed vicariously Richard's clever treachery and sadistic delight in destruction, once he is crowned we look forward to his destruction, for he is no longer entertaining. Now Richard, pressured by his enemies and hounded by the ghosts of his victims, experiences the terrors of the victim, and we await the satisfaction and dark humor of the hunter hunted, the trickster tricked. Richard's last, grand gesture is therefore directed as much against us as against his enemies. Wounded and encircled like Claudius in Olivier's *Hamlet*, shaken by orgasmic death throes while embracing his sword, he defiantly holds it up toward the skies in his deformed hand before dying.

Stylistically, Olivier's elegant, decorative *Richard III* resembles his *Henry V*. We find in it the same tableau effects, emblems, and fairy-tale neatness (it must be the *cleanest* movie ever made—everything is freshly painted and even the sheets in Clarence's cell are spotless white and carefully pressed). We find the same vivid colors and rich dark costumes which make the chief characters stand out against stylized, pastel settings. The "mood" scenes of Clarence in the Tower and Richard in his tent with their dark browns and somber music resemble the death of Falstaff and the contemplative night scenes before the battle of Agincourt. Edward's court is not terribly different from Charles VI's. Though the level of illusion is much more uniform in the later film, within each shot one finds a unique blend of realism, theatricalism, and painterliness, even in the battle scenes. Still, in *Richard III* this style is put to different use. Its festive carnival air, akin to musicals like *Meet Me In St. Louis*, becomes grotesque when Richard is turned loose in it. The artificial set emphasizes the unnaturalness of Richard's actions, and the bright, highly saturated colors contribute to the hysteria generated by Richard's sudden, deadly moves against friends and enemies.

The critic who noted a similarity between Olivier's Henry and his Richard was correct.[12] Richard's youthful energy and spirit of high adventure as he tears through opponents like paper dolls make it seem that some wicked witch has cast a spell on the fairy-tale Prince and transformed him into a troll. Richard's wooing of Anne resembles a twisted version of Henry's wooing of Katherine. But the effect of Olivier's performance, like the effect of Walton's festive music, changes drastically because of the ironic context. All Richard's courage and talents are turned to destruction of a corrupt world. Walton's fanfares and flourishes, so impressive in Henry's world, here mask pitiful weakness and evil. The religious chant, used so effectively after the battle of Agincourt, here is sung by two wrinkled little monks who stare wide-eyed and helpless at Richard. Throughout, the religious music serves as an incongruous backdrop for treachery, treason, and murder. The ceremonies of Henry's world are dead—they are still decorative and colorful, but the corpse has indelicately begun to stink.

Visual imagery in *Richard III*, as in Olivier's other films, is simple but effective, especially when the director shows flashes of Richard's ironic wit. He shows delicious humor, for instance, in the scene where the little Prince, dressed in red, sits on an empty throne in the distance playing at being King while in the foreground Richard and Buckingham, framed like two benefactors at the sides of a religious tryptich, conspire to kill him. As spritely Richard goes along a gallery to woo Anne, Olivier arranges it so that a series of winged dragonlike gargoyles comes into view, and helpless painted angels, recall, look on as Richard ensnares Hastings. Olivier also orchestrates humorous dissolves, from the blood running down the axe blade at Hastings's execution to the dripping rag used by a maid to clean some steps, from a bell set wildly spinning by Richard as he slides down the rope to many bells ringing in honor of his coronation, from the blend of blood and wine which flows from the Tower down into the Thames after the murder of Clarence to Mistress Shore placing the King's silver wine pitcher back in its little holy niche. Olivier has a cultivated sense of sardonic detail. Before Buckingham goes out to dupe the Lord Mayor and citizens, he wolfs down an executive's lunch (wine, bread and butter, scallops) with great relish. At the dramatic moment when Richard relents outside and calls the supplicants back to tell them he will accept the crown, we notice that two blinkered horses stand conspicuously in the foreground.

There are also effective serious themes and motifs in the film— Richard's shadow, for instance.

After the initial scene with Anne, in the abbey, Richard declares: "Clarence beware! Thou keepest me from the light. But I will plan a pitchy day for thee." As he speaks, the camera wanders away from him to his shadow stretched over the stone steps of the abbey. He starts to move down the steps as he speaks, and the shadow occupies more and more of the screen until, on his last words, it swallows up the screen completely—just as Richard's tyranny will swallow up England; just as every tyrant swallows up the country he rules.[13]

As the film develops, Richard's Jungian shadow passes over everything and everyone. Even his accomplices are associated with it: Buckingham's shadow merges with Richard's after they decide, by Edward's body, to capture the Princes, and the shadow of the murderers falls upon the crucifix in Clarence's cell as they enter to kill him. The crown, another important image, has already been touched upon. When interest flags, however—and this happens often enough in its two and three-quarter hour length to be troublesome—it is not for lack of serious themes. It is because Olivier's sense of irony and witty invention fails him.

To those who view the play as a serious horror story, perhaps Roman Polanski would have been a more suitable director. To those who view *Richard III* as a history play in the same sense Shakespeare's other history plays are, nothing less than a full text will do. To those who demand from every film everything film is capable of doing, its technique is frustratingly simple, for outside of some thematic and illustrative flourishes there is rarely a complex relation between language, composition, acting, and sound. The clever composite set, which compresses time and space and the emphasis upon the actors' broad gestures —Richard struggling toward the throne through an imaginary wood or Anne spitting in his face—is sure to displease those who wish directors to obliterate all traces of Shakespeare's theatrical background. Still, if the essence of the play is the diabolic comedian Richard and his shattering of the medieval world order, then Olivier has captured this essence. And if we look carefully at Shakespeare's style in *Richard III*—its relatively external, broad characterizations, wooden rhetoric, and elementary structures—then Olivier's lucid, elemental style suits the play quite well. His *Richard III* properly remains one of the most admired and popular of Shakespeare films.

# Defining *Macbeth*:

# Schaefer, Welles, and Kurosawa

$M$ACBETH is the shortest of Shakespeare's tragedies and the simplest in its statement: *Thou shalt not kill.* In the words of Coleridge, it contains "no reasonings of equivocal morality, . . . no sophistry of self-delusion." With eyes wide open to the hideousness of his offense, a brave, imaginative, and morally sensitive man commits a stealthy murder for gain. . . . The retribution is as appalling as the crime—his soul's slow death in self-horror, degradation, loneliness, and despair, then his bloody extermination.

Alfred Harbage[1]

THE LACK of any sense of the hero's moral relationship to society —intensified by the play's supernatural aspects and by the hallucinatory, almost solipsistic nature of Macbeth's ambition, which is too compulsive to admit of rational calculation—turns the drama farther inward than in any Welles film until *The Immortal Story*. We are in a theatre of the subconscious.

Joseph McBride[2]

FOR KUROSAWA the pattern of repetition is destructive and it is this pattern which his free heroes attempt to destroy. . . . The hero . . . tries to realize himself. His fault—not ambition or pride, as such—

is his failure to realize himself completely. . . . It is perhaps because he is here exclusively concerned with limitation, negation, death, that Kurosawa—for the first time—created a formal film. . . . It is a finished film with no loose ends. The characters have no future. Cause and effect is the only law. Freedom does not exist.

Donald Richie[3]

Each interpretation of *MACBETH* strikes a new balance among Macbeth, society, and Fate, as it acts through the Weird Sisters and Lady Macbeth. Each film constitutes an exploration of the misty borderlands between tragedy and melodrama. *Macbeth* is a splendid piece of theatrical entertainment, full of fine images, gothic thrills, and splendid speeches. But for our culture it is also the classic incarnation of the historical fact of the unleashing of the Renaissance Spirit— secular, individualistic, self-conscious, capitalistic, amoral, questing— upon the traditional Christian moral and social order. It is, in addition, an incarnation of one of man's oldest rituals—the cleansing of the kingdom and restoration of order by the hunting down and killing of a scapegoat-King associated with autumn and sterility, bloody Dionysian revels, and evil. Any director will, consciously or unconsciously, shape the rise and fall (or is it a fall and rise?) of the criminal-hero, give it a tone and a context, and if not resolve its paradoxes at least define their terms. But as with all of Shakespeare's mature works, no single set of perceptions and formulations can encompass everything that is there. In their films of *Macbeth*, George Schaefer, Orson Welles, and Akira Kurosawa have each made a different kind of work and embodied a different understanding of the meaning of the play; yet all three incorporate important dimensions of the original.

George Schaefer's film, starring Maurice Evans and Judith Anderson, presents the play in its most familiar aspect, as the story of a crime against the moral, social, and natural orders, followed inevitably by a prolonged and terrible punishment—a cautionary tale against murder and "the danger of ambition."[4] The force of the story resides first of all in the unnaturalness of the deed—the killing of a sleeping, white-haired old man who is a kinsman, guest, good and generous king, godlike father figure. It lies too in its choking atmosphere of blood,

149

darkness, and fear. When the valiant killer brings the butchery of the battlefield home and preys on the weak, fear forces Banquo into silence, MacDuff to flee, leaving his family unprotected, and corrupt, ambitious lords to stay and serve the bloody tyrant. The long scene in which Malcolm tests MacDuff by chronicling his own moral degeneration shows the degree to which the suspicion engendered by Macbeth has spread like an infection. Nature becomes chaos, shaken by tempests. Owls become clamorous and horses turn cannibals. Macbeth and Lady Macbeth become microcosms of the Hell they have made of Scotland as they are plagued by sleeplessness, hallucinations, paranoia, guilt, self-hatred, despair, insanity.

The heart of Schaefer's film is its contrast of the moral disease of the Macbeths with a healthy, regenerative nature. It opens with panoramas of the spacious, scenic highlands on which the rebels against Duncan are defeated. After that battle, leafy trees, water, and intense blue skies decorate the arrival of Duncan to Macbeth's castle, just as they serve as a backdrop for his funeral procession through the open countryside. Bright green leaves decorate the outside of Macbeth's stone castle as he resolves to kill Banquo, foreshadowing the sunshine kingdom of England where the forces of good gather, the open fields where cheering allies cut down green pines to bear against the stone walls of Dunsinane and (in contrast to the helpless physician) bring health to the kingdom and make Macbeth's castle once again a "pleasant seat." In like manner, the feast with shared food, music, dancing, and good fellowship around the fire reaffirms and celebrates the bonds which are broken by the Macbeths, bonds which are only renewed when men band together to destroy the evil king and queen.

The difficulty with Schaefer's work is not in its conception, which is true to important parts of the play, but in its execution. The decorativeness, the prettiness of the film—its landscapes and costumes heightened by crude Technicolor, night scenes lit with garish, operatic reds, blues, and golds, and images characterized by excessive clarity and solidity (the film was made for television)—is fatal to the play's murky atmosphere of evil. The work as a whole is characterized by a "directness that rather precludes subtlety of perspective and nuance," a style "appropriate, perhaps, for Racine and Corneille, but not suitable for Shakespeare's more open form."[5] The performances, unfortunately, are as mundane as the images. Evans's Macbeth, "a greeting-card king, rosy-cheeked, lustrous hair, red and blue plaids over his dressy armor,"[6] and Anderson's Lady Macbeth achieve some measure of pathos as they suffer, but "good taste" in the form of censored violence, tempered eroticism, and pedestrian cinematography rob their parts of both terror and grandeur. There is so little of the heightened, passionate intensity, so little of the "haunted ferocity"[7] of Shakespeare's characters that Macbeth's literal fall from great height at the end seems preposterous hyperbole.

While Schaefer's film depicts a world shaken by a murderous fever and restored to health and order, Welles's film shows a world permeated from the beginning with evil. Christian values, symbolized by the Celtic cross, constitute a fragile, man-made order which is helpless before the natural forces of chaos embodied in gnarled trees, swirling fog, and the witches. Macbeth does not violate nature in this phantasmagoria, he is a child of it—molded of clay in the hideous birth which opens the film. Welles's imagination is so fully engaged by the evil atmosphere and characters, and the "good" characters are so weakly conceived and acted, that a reversal of values takes place—"fair is foul, foul is fair." Duncan, Malcolm, the "Holy Father" (Welles's creation), and Lady MacDuff seem pathetically weak, huddle together in fear, show no positive qualities. They exist merely as a negation of evil. MacDuff becomes admirable only in confronting and killing Macbeth, and Banquo is a slippery, calculating, passive version of Macbeth, sharing his ambition but lacking his will to act. Though weakened by inadequate performances by Welles and Jeanette Nolan, Macbeth and Lady Macbeth show more courage and energy, are more fully alive, than the other characters. Their unrelenting journey to the end of night and their terrible suffering make them more human than the cardboard figures which surround them.

This is an "expressionist" *Macbeth*,[8] a "violently sketched charcoal drawing of a great play."[9] The hero and heroine seem drugged or asleep and shaken with horrible nightmares. In place of natural growing things are blasted trees etched against a bleak cyclorama. The sterility of the Macbeths is generalized as MacDuff's children are murdered. Their sick eroticism blended with violence (Lady Macbeth sensuously stroking the fur of an animal skin, or embracing Macbeth as the axe falls on Cawdor's head) underscores the Freudian undertones of dripping caverns which give birth to monstrous acts. Visually, the film is filled with distortions—vast foreground figures dwarfing those in the background, axe-blades and hands spread across the screen, shadows on rough walls or passing ominously over human figures. As in Brook's *King Lear*, the atmosphere is of unrelieved primitiveness. Windows and rooms are crudely hewn out of rock, and the wet rough walls capture the savagery of Macbeth's time and his debased nature in a way that the decorative Bosch-like paintings on the walls of Macbeth's armory in Schaefer's film could never do. Welles places concrete details in the film not to ground it in reality but to serve (as in dreams) as emblems: grisly traitors' heads on tilted crosses against a blank grey sky, candles lit in an ineffective ritual intended to protect man from Satan, the shining carcass of the roast pig with its grinning face at the banquet, a sword passing before the blank eyes of the voodoo doll as Macbeth hallucinates a dagger.

What seems important to Welles is not the moral and social dimension of Macbeth's acts—indeed, the political motivations for Macbeth's acts hardly exist—but the subjective experience of pushing deeper into the heart of darkness. Congruent with the psychodramatic aspect of the medieval morality plays which influenced Shakespeare, and true to the Elizabethan pattern of microcosm and macrocosm (though lacking its moral and social grounding), the world of the play becomes an externalization of Macbeth's drunken, fear-crazed mind. The innerness of the *Macbeth* world so apparent in the play and so conspicuously absent from Schaefer's film accounts for the increasing unreality of a film "emptied of any precise historical reference."[10] Landscapes shift from cliffs to blank spaces to Stonehenge-like rock formations. Our vision becomes distorted like Macbeth's when he stares at his haggard face and ludicrous out-sized crown in the twisted surface of a polished shield, or sees guests and Banquo's ghost alternately appear and disappear. The murderers who hover in gnarled trees and descend like vultures on their prey are more like Macbeth's vision of the killing than the event itself. As in Kafka, space is radically compressed and journeying seems an act of the mind—with a few steps Macbeth traverses the distance from his aspiring castle atop a mountain to the hill where the witches reside. Intense close-ups and voice-over soliloquies isolate Macbeth in his own Hell. There is an increasing sense of vertigo and warped perspective as overhead shots show Lady Macbeth falling to her death on the rocks below and Macbeth casting a huge shadow over a Rorschach-test floor. Discontinuities of vision, which climax in the cut to the clay idol as Macbeth is beheaded, are matched by discontinuities in behavior. Lady Macbeth passionately kisses Macbeth in the sleepwalking scene, then screams and retreats from him in horror. If the Macbeths are heroic, it is because they test the outer limits of solitude and human suffering, journey beyond good and evil.

In the end, the moral and social order, strengthened it seems by the struggle, closes, temporarily healed of its disease. The troops roar approval as MacDuff tosses the tyrant's head down to them, and they raise their torches and crosses to the sky hailing Malcolm king. But in Welles's version two truths are told at the conclusion (something which became clearer in the final version of the film). The first is spoken by MacDuff: "the time is free." But on the heath the witches with their forked staffs watch, waiting before the castle, which now seems a huge deformed crown surrounded with mist. Cut to rolling fog, evoking the despair in the face of chaos in Macbeth's "tomorrow, and tomorrow, and tomorrow" speech, and the outlines of the witches are superimposed over the fog as one of them ominously intones the second truth: "peace, the charm's wound up." True not to the letter of Shakespeare's conclusion but to the spirit of his play and the lesson of history, there will be another Macbeth, another assassination and closing of the circle, another mythical quest, confrontation, and acceptance.

Akira Kurosawa's Japanese *Macbeth, Throne of Blood* (more accurately *The Castle of the Spider's Web*), has been called "the finest of Shakespeare movies" by Grigori Kozintsev, a "masterpiece" by Peter Brook.[11] It is a highly formal work with images of great force and beauty, a blending of the Japanese equivalent of the western—the medieval Samurai film—with the conventions of Japanese painting and the Noh drama.[12] Stylistically, the film "realizes an admirable synthesis of an aesthetic of brutality, of movement, of exacerbation of the senses and an aesthetic of nobility, slowness and meditation." It "plays marvelously on the antagonism between realism and symbolism."[13] Kurosawa has stripped the poetry from the lines and infused it in the movements of characters and camera, contrasting settings and costumes, and beautifully composed images.

If Schaefer renders *Macbeth* as Christian parable told from the point of view of society, and Welles as individual nightmare, Kurosawa renders it as a tragedy of Fate, a grim tale in which malevolent powers fill a man with illusions and then destroy him. *Throne of Blood* echoes with the Forest Spirit's dark laughter, resembling a child's amoral delight as it watches a fly struggle in a web. Kurosawa is not ignorant

Cutting for contrast: Washizu/Macbeth and the Forest Spirit

of moralistic tragedy. In fact, *Throne of Blood* contains an added play within the play, sung and danced by an old actor at the banquet, which begins: "all of you wicked, listen while I tell of a man vain, guileful, vile, who though ambitious, insolent, could not escape his punishment."[14] But as the director shows, such works of art have no effect upon those driven by fear and ambition to violate the bonds of kinship and duty (Washizu simply halts the performance and calls for more wine). In *Throne of Blood*, the tragedy is that man is caught between two orders: the moral order, which he has invented but which he is unable to hold himself to, and the impersonal natural order, which refuses to be contained by the terms good and evil—in fact, resists all attempts to define or make it meaningful. The Forest Spirit dares man to take his fate in his own hands, then frustrates his longings for immortality, ensnares him in labyrinths inside and outside himself, and drives him to destroy himself (the rebel traitor committed suicide, Washizu is killed by his own troops). Man belongs wholly neither to the castle nor to the forest. He wishes to be Job or Satan, but can realize the perfections of neither. He is doomed to make futile journeys between them until the fog descends.

Kurosawa underscores the irony of the story first of all by framing it—a device used for very different effect in Zeffirelli's *Taming of the Shrew*. After the titles, superimposed over a still of the tangled forest, we see distant mountains in a dense fog and the ruins of the once invincible fortress. The camera slowly pans down the slope of a mountain to a grave marker, and as its inscription is revealed, a somber god-like chorus chants:

Behold, within this place now desolate stood once a mighty fortress,
lived a proud warrior murdered by ambition, his spirit walking still.
Vain pride, then as now, will lead ambition to the kill.

The fog slowly clears revealing the fortress intact, and the story of Washizu is acted out. Washizu strives and is destroyed and the fog returns. The castle is obscured and once again the chorus sings of the fortress and the proud warrior, adding, "still his spirit walks, his fame is known for what once was, so now is still true. Murderous ambition will pursue beyond the grave to give its due." Far from suggesting a nostalgic journey into the past (compare *Chimes at Midnight*), this somber frame with its images of desolation increases our sense of entrapment and the futility of Washizu's struggles, for it was all settled long ago. The mighty fortress has been levelled. Both good and evil are dead and their world has been swept away. "Still his spirit walks." Perhaps this suggests that Washizu will spend eternity fighting in Naraku (the Buddhist Hell).[15] But it also suggests that Washizu lives on in other men, that unlike the good whose names are forgotten, the crimes of Washizu grant him an immortality recorded by the grave marker and perpetuated in its artistic equivalent, Kurosawa's film. All traces of the restoration of health and harmony and an ongoing social order stressed at the end of Schaefer's film have been obliterated. "Washizu is destroyed not by his judges but by his peers who suffer from the same malady. Order is not established because it springs from men who are themselves without order."[16]

Donald Richie has noted that the extreme formality of this framing device carries over into other parts of the film. Washizu is trapped in a vast pattern which he but dimly perceives. The larger actions of the film are symmetrically arranged. Washizu follows in the footsteps of Lord Kuniharu who preceded him, and the Lords who preceded Kuniharu, so that one feels a ritual effect when waves of messengers bring news of rebellion against the Forest Castle. The slow procession of Lord Kuniharu to Washizu's castle (which Washizu senses is a ruse) mirrors the suspenseful approach to the Forest Castle by Washizu with the body of Kuniharu (another ruse). Three times Washizu visits the forest—in the opening when he and Miki first encounter the spirit and become lost, in the middle when pursuing Noriyasu and Kunimaru (Malcolm), and toward the end when alone he seeks assurance from the equivocal spirit that he will not be defeated. Then, with crushing irony, the forest visits him and he is destroyed.

Like Shakespeare, Kurosawa renders insanity visually as endless repetition. Shattered by guilt and the grimly just stillbirth of her child, Asaji (Lady Macbeth) is locked in an endless ritual of washing her hands. This action echoes the endless winding of thread from one spool to another by the forest spirit (an analogue of the Greek Fate Clotho's spinning the thread of life, and of Kurosawa's act of creation—film too winds from spool to spool, and the director, like the spirit, has god-like power and detachment). Asaji moves from one form of death—an impassive exterior and actions governed by a steel will—to another. As in Shakespeare, foreshadowings are fulfilled with mathematical precision. The cry of the raven when Washizu's servants stare in horror at the blood-stained walls of the room where a traitor committed

A mighty fortress and a parodic hut of sticks

A labyrinthine forest versus cool, geometrical interiors

suicide, repeated when Asaji persuades Washizu to kill his Lord, fore-shadows the swarm of birds which rushes the fortress as Kunimaru's men cut down the trees. Asaji predicts that Washizu will be killed by the arrows of his own troops. The ominous rack of arrows in the forbidden room, prominent in the shots of Washizu immediately before and after the murder, foreshadows Washizu's spectacular death by arrows (which blend the feathers of the birds with the wood of the forest). And the prolonged struggle of the messenger mortally wounded by Washizu not only looks ahead to Washizu's final ferocious struggle to survive, but echoes the nightmarish appearance of Miki's (Banquo's) ghost—"The time has been / That, when the brains were out, the man would die."

The central polarity in *Throne of Blood* is between the forest and the fortress. The forest is full of deceptive appearances and paradoxes: both "foul" and "fair" as it rains and shines, it shifts as in a dream from tangled vines to clearings, to misty images of Golgotha. In self-defense against the labyrinth, man builds fortresses which give the illusion of safety and power. "Behind the flimsy walls man makes to seal himself off from an amoral nature, there is a lucid, quiet geometry that is assaulted throughout the film and, in the end, shattered."[17] Ironically, the fortress is never conquered from without—it doesn't need to be. Washizu opens the gates with the body of Lord Kuniharu, and Miki's troops have only begun their assault when their enemy is killed by his own men, just as Asaji is destroyed from within by her own child. Part of the Spirit's laughter is at man's reliance on spears, arrows, armor, horses, and castles. It *parodies* these things by taking the shape of a helpless old woman seated in a mockery fortress of sticks. As in *Richard III*, man attempts to use ceremony to impose meaning, define boundaries, impose control (the banquet, Asaji's precise planning and movements). But the attempt fails. "Like Shakespeare, . . . Kurosawa uses the interplay between ceremony and irrational spontaneity as a dramatic metaphor for Macbeth's conflict between duty and ambition."[18]

In such a divided world, man can be heroic only in a very limited sense. War leads not to safety but to more war. The defense afforded by the labyrinth proves an illusion as Noriyasu triumphs over it by ordering his troops to ignore the paths and ride straight through. But for Washizu, such rigidity leads to disaster. "The right-angle or perpendicular becomes a graphic symbol for conflict and rigidity of attitude that leads blindly to disaster."[19] Stoic Asaji with her frozen mask and deliberate movements tries to imitate the geometry of the fortress, but inevitably she is overtaken by the labyrinth within. All of the characters are filmed with icy detachment, almost exclusively in medium and long shot (in contrast to Welles and Polanski). The characters' costumes, movements, and postures make them resemble insects (Asaji a praying mantis, Washizu and the other armored soldiers bugs with wings). Macbeth in Shakespeare is a man of imagination, sensitivity, nobility, and eloquence. Violent, visceral, external Washizu is a trapped animal fighting for its life. He and the other characters "speak only when they can't communicate any other way, and then in language that is terse, unadorned, brutally functional."[20]

In the beginning of *Throne of Blood*, the Spirit gives Washizu and Miki a glimpse into the abyss. They are told that in the face of a vast emptiness, loyalty and rebellion are equally absurd.

Men are vain and death is long
And pride dies first within the grave
For hair and nails are growing still
When face and fame are gone.
Nothing in this world will save
Or measure up man's actions here,
Nor in the next, for there is none:
This life must end in fear.
Only evil may maintain
An after life those who will
Who love this world, who have no son
To whom ambition calls.
Even so this false fame falls.
Death will reign; man dies in vain.

There is nothing benign or harmonious about this natural order. One can obey the demands of honor and kinship; or one can obey nature, as the banners on the backs of Washizu and Miki indicate—the scorpion preys, fights, is devoured by the female, and the rabbit multiplies, then becomes prey. Either way nature triumphs in the end, reducing individuals into heaps of bones and obliterating the mightiest of fortresses with an endless succession of "tomorrows."

The Scorpion (Washizu/Macbeth) and the Rabbit (Miki/Banquo)

A moral tale of disease and healing, a hideous nightmare of crime and retribution, an ironic tragedy of fate: *Macbeth* is all of these and more (one would like to be able to write of the heroic, Satanic grandeur of Olivier's Macbeth, which was not filmed because he could not raise the money in the 1950s). If the film versions of *Macbeth*—including Polanski's recent effort—have not been blessed with performances in the title role of the power of Scofield's Lear, Olivier's Othello, or Smoktunovsky's Hamlet, they have provided us with interesting perspectives on one of Shakespeare's greatest plays.

# II

# Roman Polanski's *Macbeth*

ROMAN POLANSKI HAS MADE SO BRUTAL AND BLOODY A *MAC-beth* that it is difficult to respond to on an aesthetic level at all, much less think about its relation to Shakespeare's play. In the tradition of the "Theatre of Cruelty," the film assaults us with bleak landscapes, grotesqueness, and disgusting carnage. It is so "contemporary" a work (that other Pole, Jan Kott, is in the background), with its cynicism, political assassinations, warfare, reign of terror, and reverberations of the Manson murders, that it goes to the opposite extreme from all those "respectful" stage performances of the play featuring blustering readings of famous speeches by middle-aged actors. But we must keep the violence in perspective. If we look beyond the initial publicity about nudity, Kenneth Tynan, and Playboy productions, beyond what at first seems to be a blend of exploitive sensationalism and superficial naturalism, we can see that Polanski has made quite a good film, thoughtful in its interpretation-translation of the play, filled with significant imagery, subtle connections, and imaginative creations.

The opening shots of Polanski's *Macbeth* are among the best of any Shakespeare film.[1] Striking in themselves, they work well to establish the atmosphere of the play, and articulate motifs and techniques which radiate throughout the work. The opening shot, a lurid pink orange sunrise which changes through time-lapse photography to the flat light of day, establishes a half-lit world of dawns (it is dawn as MacDuff and Lennox come to wake Duncan, at the coronation of Macbeth, and as Malcolm and his troops move behind the trees toward Dunsinane) and dusks (Duncan's arrival at Macbeth's castle, Banquo's death). It establishes an aesthetic pattern of the beautiful juxtaposed with the ugly and enunciates an overall movement from Macbeth's bloody reign to at least a temporary peace. This land we survey is "equivocal" (appropriate in a play of equivocation), a tidal flat alternately dry and inundated by the sea in an endless cycle of change. The empty, sterile beach anticipates a number of such spaces in the film—the desolate ruins inhabited by the Weird Sisters, Duncan's darkened courtyard where Macbeth watches Cawdor's body sway in the wind, the vast plain surrounding Macbeth's castle (which is, like Macbeth, strong but vulnerable in its isolated height).[2] The camera often lingers on these spaces—the courtyard inside, which empties as Macbeth looks down on people rushing to escape the sudden downpour, the still dark castle before the murder ("Now o'er the one half-world / Nature seems dead . . . "), the empty corridor as Duncan's sons flee in fear, and the deserted castle in which Macbeth is finally hunted down (designed by Wilfrid Shingleton to convey "a feeling of emptiness"[3]).

The witches' crooked stick piercing the frame establishes a pattern of penetration or rape by hands and swords[4] (Duncan's sword drawn to remove the chain of office from Cawdor's neck, the bloody grooms' daggers, Young Siward's drawing on Macbeth), and the stick itself is linked with the forked sticks and crosses outside the witches' ruins (recall Welles's *Macbeth*), the trident-shaped beams at Inverness, trees of Birnam Wood hacked down by the murderers and Malcolm's troops, the log Macbeth places on the dying fire before hearing of Lady Macbeth's death, and the logs and the staff figuring in MacDuff's fight with Macbeth. The witches themselves are "fair" and "foul," two of them old crones and one a young girl, possibly pretty under her rags and stringy hair.[5]

The circle inscribed in the sand recurs in the crown which falls from Duncan's head and which in the end is given to Malcolm, the iron collar around Cawdor's neck, and the coronation where Macbeth is raised on a circular shield, the Thanes and stones serving as the jewels in a huge crown. It recurs in the bucket and basins in which the Macbeths wash their hands, the witches' cauldron, Macbeth's matching goblets which underscore the parallel of the two "banquets" he attends, and the ring to which the baited bear is chained. The crying gull (foreshadowing the women's screams which later fill the air) hovering above the witches is linked to a whole zoo of birds and

The opening scene

animals, many of them present in Shakespeare's verse. Polanski has set his medieval Scots among cackling geese, squawking chickens, crowing roosters, squealing pigs, barking, howling, whining dogs, neighing horses, shrieking owls, croaking ravens, and of course the growling caged bear and the hunting hawks perched ominously behind Banquo as Macbeth asks him where he will ride (they also appear later perched on the arm of Banquo's ghost and in MacDuff's castle). The noose buried by the witches evokes the brutal hanging of the surviving rebel soldiers (do Macbeth and Banquo look on impassively, or do they ride away because they have had enough?), the hanging of Cawdor, and the hook on the rope that swings ominously over the well after the murder of Duncan, perhaps suggesting a connection between Macbeth and that archetypal figure T. S. Eliot called "the hanging man" in "The Wasteland."

In a film of killings, ringing metal on metal, and apparitions of silver weapons in the air or sticking in blood-red royal hangings, the emblematic value of the dagger needs no explication. The severed hand is the first of a seemingly endless line of horrors in "Golgotha triumphant":[6] soldiers hung or killed with spiked iron balls, Duncan's bloody captain, Cawdor's suicidal leap, the nightmarishly prolonged stabbing of Duncan. Audiences are jolted by the minced bodies of the grooms, Banquo axed in the spine, the murderers pushed into a flooded dungeon, the apparition of a bloody child being removed from the womb, the butchering of MacDuff's children, Seyton shot between the eyes with a crossbow, soldiers slashed in the eyes, axed in the guts, and stuck in the throat by bold Macbeth, and, capping off a work "supped full of horrors," Macbeth skewered on a sword (he smiles with relief) and beheaded. But the hand, being a piece of a man, also underscores the witches' love of destruction, discord, fragmentation. They live in a ruins, brew potions with pieces of animals, and show visions with heaps of armor, teasingly incomplete predictions, and discontinuous planes of reality (mirrors within mirrors). The pouring of baboon's blood on the buried icons is mirrored by Lady Macbeth's pouring the drug in the grooms' wine, Macbeth's ritualistic pouring of the wine for the murderers, and the sacrilegious link of blood and wine.

Vaguely orgasmic grunts and squeals as the witches carry out their grisly ceremony suggest the perverted sexuality between Macbeth and Lady Macbeth which permeates the film, the eroticism not only of her breathless invitation to murder while lying on a bed and at the bear baiting where she is hypnotized (attraction and repulsion) by the bloody spectacle, but of Macbeth's repeated plunging of the knife into Duncan on that same bed, and the rapes and murders at MacDuff's castle. As the witches move off, two in one direction and one in another, they infect the air, disappear into a fog (it reappears at the end when Malcolm's troops approach Macbeth's castle) which, when it clears, shows the aftermath of the battle we have heard all too vividly but only seen with our inner eye. The grating, squealing wheel on the witches' cart as they hobble off blends with cries of a gull and the squeak of a violin to form a grotesque chorus, much as the slow, sour bagpipe music, played as Duncan approaches Macbeth's castle and each time we see the outline of the witches' ruins, contrasts with the harmony and spritely tempo of the dance music and Fleance's song at the feast for Duncan. Like many of the "naturalistic" sounds of the film—the dripping of the water as Lady Macbeth waits tensely while Macbeth kills the King, her quiet ringing of the alarm bell (soon after, it is rung loudly), the grating sound of a sword being sharpened on a grindstone and the whishing sound of arrows as Ross tells MacDuff of the murders—these have important emotional overtones.

As the witches exit, their shapes are dimly reflected in the wet sand, and when they disappear into the fog, they vanish suddenly like apparitions. Polanski's *Macbeth* is filled with reflections and hallucinatory visions: Macbeth's vision of the dagger, his image reflected in a puddle which he obliterates with a bucket of bloody water, the dream in which Fleance and Banquo come to kill him with an arrow. Recall too the ghost in the banquet scene, the elaborate series of reflections and mirrors in the second witches' scene, Lady Macbeth's horrible imaginings at night and seeing drops of blood on her hands in the day. The witches' exit is slow, giving us time to contemplate. Polanski often punctuates important dramatic moments and encourages audience participation by holding shots longer than we expect. Duncan's fateful ride toward Inverness is painfully prolonged as Lady Macbeth watches from the ramparts and the sky becomes darker and darker (toward the end the fleeing thanes follow a similar winding path as they abandon Macbeth). The director provides sustained shots of Banquo staring at Macbeth (the man who offered "honor" the night before) as he learns of Duncan's murder, a coronation scene in which the symmetry of concentric circles, the beauty of the sunrise and white robes, and impressive ritual contrast with the hatred and ambition behind the masks, and Lady Macbeth's contorted body lying in the courtyard.

Polanski has not made a film composed totally of gothic horrors. There are scenes of normal life—a happy wife greeting her husband home from the wars, people sweeping a room, Lady Macbeth strewing flowers on the King's bed, musicians in red liveries filing through the courtyard where servants catch pigs and chickens for the royal banquet, the hostess dancing with her guest. We see proud Banquo mouthing the words as his son Fleance sings to the King and anxiously looking for signs of approval, children playing blindman's buff, a man brushing a horse's tail, a mother giving her son a bath and feigning anger (but really being pleased) at his saucy wit. But these scenes of normality do not offset the brutality. They only intensify it. The welter of everyday details and ongoing normal life heighten the unnaturalness and sterility of the Macbeths. Even normal motion is disturbed. "It is the stability of the social life evoked in these scenes that the Macbeths seem to violate, and the use of speeded up film in Duncan's murder indicates how far their crime signifies a disruption of the natural rhythm of life."[7]

There is precious little humor in Polanski's *Macbeth*, and most of that is saturated with irony. While it is funny to see the Porter urinate against the wall while MacDuff and Lennox cool their heels outside the gate, we know they will never wake Duncan with their knocking. As in Shakespeare, the Porter's joke that wine is "an equivocator with lechery"—"it makes him stand to" (he raises his huge gate key) "and not stand to" (he lowers it)—is too directly related to the themes of equivocation and the impotence and sterility of the Macbeths to be merely funny. It is but one of the film's many "double" speeches, including Duncan's remarks about making Macbeth "full of growing," Macbeth's ironically true "Had I but died an hour before this chance, I had lived a blessed time," Ross's effusive parting from Lady MacDuff and his assurances to MacDuff that his family was "well" and "at peace." The laughter in this film is cynical or manic laughter. The witches howl mockingly at Macbeth when one of their number cries "by the itching of my thumbs, something *wicked* this way comes." Malcolm and Donalbain giggle hysterically in Macbeth's vision. Henchmen laugh at rape and murder in MacDuff's castle and chuckle at Macbeth's accusations against Duncan's sons and his Hell's Angels antics of bravado. When the humor is the filmmaker's rather than the characters', it is all the more ironic. Fleance's song to the King, who sits next to Macbeth as he contemplates murder, is entitled "your eyen two will slay me suddenly."[8] The game of blindman's buff in which a servant lunges after MacDuff's children introduces the scene in which soldiers pursue and butcher them. Seyton's ringing the alarm bell is as futile as when it was rung after the murder of Duncan: his call to arms becomes a signal to kill him, loot the castle, and flee.

The play that for George Schaefer became a moral, political, and theological lesson, for Welles a nightmare, and for Akira Kurosawa a tale of irony becomes for Polanski a naturalistic portrait of meaningless violence acted out in a wasteland. The film projects a much darker view of human nature than does the play. Shakespeare does not disguise the fact that Banquo is stirred by the same thoughts that stir Macbeth, so it is no surprise that Polanski follows suit. But in Shakespeare the traitor Cawdor "confessed his treasons, implored your Highness' pardon and set forth a deep repentence." In Polanski, Cawdor is a thug whose sardonic farewell, "long live the King," before jumping off the ramparts with a chain around his neck, indeed strikes wonder in Duncan and his sons, but not because of a change of heart. They are disturbed because, like Macbeth at the end, the rebel is bold and unrepentant in his death. He shows a courage which is lacking in both Duncan, who does not fight but merely receives reports about the wars, and his two sons, who flee from Macbeth's castle rather than risk death to become rulers. The long scene in which Malcolm tests the loyalty of MacDuff by confessing himself treacherous, greedy, and lustful has been cut, and with it went his declaration that the "taints and blames" he laid to himself are strangers to his nature. Malcolm, in fact, is a very unsympathetic character. At the crucial moment when Macbeth tells Lady Macbeth they will "proceed no further in this business" and walks away leaving her weeping in shame and indignation, it is Malcolm's smug vaunting of his power that persuades Macbeth to kill Duncan: the newly proclaimed Prince of Cumberland forces Macbeth to fill his goblet with wine like a common steward, adding with heavy irony, "Hail, *Thane of Cawdor*."

Underscoring Polanski's critical treatment of the Scots nobles—a treatment perhaps closer to Shakespeare's source, Holinshed, in which Duncan's "feeble and slothful administration" of the laws and "too much of clemencie," his killing his predecessor, and his violation of the laws of succession by naming his son Prince of Cumberland qualify our condemnation of Macbeth[9]—is his portrait of Ross, who becomes an important character in the film. It is Ross who at the beginning brings Cawdor to Duncan lashed to the rails behind his horse, who conveys the chain of office to Macbeth when he is made Cawdor, and who kneels to help him onto his horse. He is among those who shout "Hail, Prince of Cumberland!" at the feast for Duncan and later stare at Macbeth suspiciously when he announces that he killed the grooms. In contrast to MacDuff, who does not attend the coronation of Macbeth, Ross is one of the inner circle of thanes who lift the new King on the shield, crying "Hail Macbeth! King of Scotland" (Banquo remains mute). Ross is the play's mysterious third murderer (he is unsuccessful in killing Fleance only because Banquo shoots his horse out from under him) who leads his accomplices to a dungeon where they are disposed of—he pushes the second to his death with the man's own crutch.

It is Ross who invites Macbeth to the table where Banquo's ghost waits in the banquet scene, who sets up the slaughter at MacDuff's castle while assuring Lady MacDuff with equivocal truisms ("things at the worst will cease, or else climb upward to what they were before") and holding MacDuff's son ("my pretty cousin, a blessing on you"). When he is passed over for advancement and Macbeth rewards the flattering weakling Seyton with the chain of office (a direct parallel to Macbeth's earlier situation), Ross flees to join Malcolm. With an earnest look, the man who arranged the rape and murder of MacDuff's family breaks the news to him. In the end, not only is Ross not caught and punished, he becomes part of the new order. It is he who takes the crown from Macbeth's severed head, wipes off the blood, cries "Hail Malcolm, King of Scotland," and presents it to him. There is no true cleansing. The crown and the men who wear and serve it are tainted.

Shakespeare's tragedy ends with Malcolm naming his thanes Earls, calling home exiles to end the isolation of kingship, dealing with the men who served Macbeth, and doing "what needful else that call upon us, by the grace of Grace . . . in measure, time, and place." MacDuff cries meaningfully "the time is free!" The time is not free at the end of Polanski's melodrama, for there will be no end to the chain of ambitious killings, repression, and fear. In the concluding scene a rider approaches the ruins of the witches and the sour bagpipes sound again. It is Donalbain, Malcolm's younger brother, whose limp links him with the young murderer and whose looks were as dark as Macbeth's when Duncan named Malcolm successor. He takes shelter from the rain under the ruins as Macbeth and Banquo did. Hearing the witches' chanting, he goes to investigate. The film's final image is a sustained long shot of the ruin in the rain with the horse outside awaiting its master. On the sound track is a sound loop—a series of guitar notes and drum beats repeat under the credits. There is no reassertion of normal rhythms and domestic detail. As in *Chimes at Midnight*, history seems stuck like a needle on a scratched record.

In addition to its political cynicism, Polanski's *Macbeth* is notable for its emphasis on the theme of fathers and sons. The Macbeths are opposed by Duncan and his sons Malcolm and Donalbain, Banquo and his son Fleance, MacDuff and his children, Old Siward and Young Siward. The director even elaborates the theme, making the murderers father and son (Macbeth nods in turn to the older and the younger man as he speaks of "*you* and *yours*"). The acts of Macbeth and Lady

Macbeth grow out of their sterility (in this version Lady Macbeth has not given suck). Having no investment in the future, they allow their ambition to flower. Their sexuality becomes twisted. She "conceives" a murder and pants in the courtyard while above blood-splattered Macbeth's vicious thrusts into Duncan bring it into being. She becomes strangely excited at the bear-baiting. In his futile but heroic struggle to control the future, Macbeth attempts to impose his own sterility on the world. He kills the sons of MacDuff and Siward, and very nearly Fleance as well. By warring on domesticity and creating around him a "society" of male cutthroats, he is taking revenge on the natural order, making his own apocalypse, causing the world to die with him. In this sense Polanski has put his finger on one of the reasons why *Macbeth* fascinates us so much. It is an extreme assertion of the individualism at the root of western social and economic systems which makes us unable to accept death.

Polanski's symbolism is less obtrusive and schematic, less influenced by Eisensteinian rhetoric than that of Welles and Kozintsev. Meaning seeps through and around naturalistic sounds, actions, objects. The grating sound of a sword being sharpened on a grindstone assaults our ears as Ross tells MacDuff his family has been slaughtered. Open gates and doors recur and express a feeling of vulnerability and disturbance: the door of Duncan's room left open by the fleeing sons, the creaking door of the witches' ruin when Macbeth awakes from his visions, the gates of MacDuff's and Macbeth's castles which are treacherously left open so that the invaders meet no resistance. Twice Macbeth drops a goblet—one of wine at the banquet intended to cement the bonds between men, the other of the disgusting brew at the witches' "banquet," which is an inversion of the first. The camera ruminates on Macbeth's determined, wordless lacing of his boots as Banquo warns that the spirits of darkness often win us by telling truths—in his act lies his answer. It pauses often on the steps Macbeth and Lady Macbeth repeatedly ascend until at the end the pattern is reversed—she lies dead in the courtyard and his head and trunk tumble down. There is more than a suggestion of "bloody instructions, which, being taught, return to plague th' inventor" when the fire, which fills the screen after the carnage at MacDuff's castle, does so once again as a ball of fire is catapulted into Macbeth's castle. We sense it too when Duncan's crown, which falls from his head as he gasps out his life, is seen in the grisly shot of Macbeth's severed head.

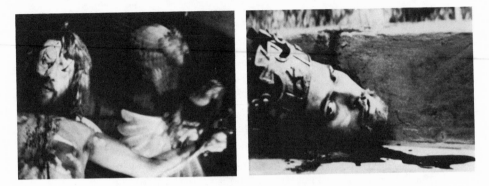

Grotesque surrealism and realistic gore

Like other filmmakers, Polanski, to penetrate surfaces, strives to make the inner outer. When Macbeth is on the brink of deciding not to kill Duncan, we read the tension not on his face but in the intercut close-ups of the sword dance of the grooms where naked feet pass rapidly between the blades of razor-sharp swords resembling the imaginary dagger he sees soon after. Apart from Macbeth's visions, the supernatural is absorbed in and hinted at through the natural. At the banquet, as Macbeth sits "rapt" beside his jovial royal guest thinking on the retribution which follows murder, a sudden gust of wind blows a window open. The curtains billow out, and the lamp on the table is extinguished, plunging the room into darkness. Immediately Banquo rushes to close the window, a servant races in with a torch to relight the lamp, and normality is restored—an ominous sign for Macbeth.

Realistic surfaces serve as a springboard for hallucinatory moments. "What I like," says Polanski, "is a realistic situation where things don't quite fit in."[10] A good example is the chilling banquet scene. When he is invited to sit, a quick glance tells us that Macbeth is right. The table *is* full. But the director holds the shot and we look more closely. The smiling lords beckoning him to the table are frozen in a tableau. Then one of the guests moves slightly and a pale, accusatory finger slowly creeps around his shoulder as he turns to grin bloodily at his host. The director draws not only upon the overt emblems taken from the play— the imagined dagger, Lady Macbeth's candle, panicked horses, the washing of hands, the baited bear, the crown—but upon carefully chosen details: Macbeth and Banquo watching refugees slog down a muddy road, capes dragging in the mud, the bloated, glistening nude bodies of the witches and the frail sleek frame of Lady Macbeth, children poking at the caged bear with sticks, creaking wheels, miserable rainy days, rumpled Macbeth waking in a tent and scratching himself as he walks out into the cold morning air. Macbeth's is a world without the beauty, unity, and harmony often imposed upon works of art by artists playing God—it is a wasteland drained of meaning, peopled by animals struggling for survival.

Like Zeffirelli, Polanski and his literary advisor, Kenneth Tynan, pared down Shakespeare's poetry and compressed the text to suit a realistic emphasis. Often poetic images have been removed: in the opening scene, for example, the bloodied captain's images of two spent swimmers, the sun dissipating a storm, overcharged cannon, the biblical reference to "Golgotha," and Ross's striking image "the Norweyan banners flout the sky and fan our people cold." Several word paintings have been omitted, such as Banquo's description of the "temple-haunting martelet" which lives in Macbeth's castle, and Ross's portrait of Scotland where shrieks fill the air, people are accustomed to funeral bells, and men die before the flowers in their caps wilt. And, as in several other filmed tragedies, soliloquies are rendered voice-over, so that there is a great disparity between the characters' prosaic, shallow, and deceptive public utterances and their rich, imagistic inner thoughts and feelings. Macbeth, in particular, is monstrously out of tune with his world. "His acts are very primitive but his thoughts are very sophisticated."[11]

Casting young, non-Shakespearean actors, Jon Finch and Francesca Annis, as Macbeth and Lady Macbeth was one of Polanski's most controversial directorial decisions. "It's much better to have them played young. There's some sex between them which I want to be understood," he said. "It's much more sympathetic. Lady Macbeth usually nags and nags." Tynan remarked that from the point of view of realism "it makes nonsense to have Macbeth and Lady Macbeth performed by 60-year-olds and menopausals. It's too late for them to be ambitious."[12] The director concurred: "Warriors didn't live to be old men."[13] Though some of the play's autumnal flavor is lost, Normand Berlin is correct—there is a thematic as well as a dramatic rightness about this decision, for a couple beautiful and sympathetic in looks but ugly beneath suits a play in which "fair is foul," in which the central theme is "confusion of values, life as ambiguity, puzzlement, equivocation."[14]

But if the two actors suit the naturalistic surfaces and major theme of the film, there is still something wanting in their performances, for they never really engage us in their suffering. Shallowness, like boredom, is dangerous on the screen. One risks reactions like Pauline Kael's: "The murder of Duncan does not change Macbeth or awaken anything in him."[15] Finch gives a remarkable performance of the *externals* of the character: the handsome warrior come home, the frightened man preoccupied with murder, the haggard, weary, death-wishing killer, the tough guy playing the wit among his henchmen. But the inner conflict is lost. Partly because his hallucinatory visions are so fully realized, we focus on them and not on the man who perceives them. We sense no moral awakening.

> Macbeth at the beginning of the film is just as morose and irascible as he is in the middle, at the time of Banquo's murder; if he hesitates to kill Duncan, it seems to be not for any "milk of human kindness" in him but merely for pragmatic reasons: fear of being found out, a physical repugnance to cold-blood killing, and a psychological aversion to the breach of hospitality. He betrays no sense that the act is any different from killing in battle.[16]

Shakespeare's balance of sympathy and condemnation is absent in the end. Michael Mullin correctly labels Macbeth's fight with unsympathetic, ineptly played MacDuff a "public spectacle." "We adopt the view of history, in which the common good of society outweighs the tragic strife of the individual."[17] And even then, we are not allowed to enjoy the smug "view of history" very long, for the remarkable silent, fast motion, point of view shots of jeering soldiers as Macbeth's head is rushed toward the ramparts give us an ugly picture of ourselves as onlookers ("fair is foul").

Perhaps because there was less weight placed on her, Francesca Annis fares somewhat better as Lady Macbeth. She is a beautiful woman streaked with darkness, impatient, bored with domestic routine while Macbeth is out taking the risks and winning the honor. Her intense ambition is matched with a shallowness which allows her to believe "a little water clears us of this deed" even when her own trembling voice denies it. The garish shots of Lady Macbeth high on the ramparts, against a blue sky with her reddish orange hair flowing in the wind, watching as Duncan and his train approach, heighten the opposition of fair and foul. Her means of persuasion are not the nagging and lecturing of Judith Anderson's queen, but whimpering, tears of shame and disappointment, slashing insults to his manhood. She is good at deception as a child is good at pretending, able to smile, to dance with Duncan, to drug the wine, and to ring the bell. The sight of bloody Duncan completely unhinges her, however, and she faints when she sees the dismembered grooms. She appears to regain her balance until the banquet scene, the turbulance underneath showing only in her strained smile and her attraction-repulsion at the bear-baiting (the camera shows her reaction, not the baiting itself). Then a stunned look, numbness, and weariness set in. Lady Macbeth is sexually rejected by Macbeth, who is busy planning the next murder. Left alone, she shrieks when wakened, and starts at hallucinations of blood on her hands. In the sleepwalking scene, she is nude (her young body contrasting with the wrinkled, misshapen witches) and terribly vulnerable.

Probably Lady Macbeth's best scene is one added by Polanski: hysterical, shuddering, staring in disbelief, she relives the fatal decisive moment by slowly reading over Macbeth's letter announcing Duncan's arrival. This scene, her compulsive rubbing of her hands, and other repetitions of gesture and word suggest, as in *Throne of Blood*, that the Macbeths are locked in an eternal hellish cycle. They kill to be free, to have absolute power, but the deeper they get, the more they lose control over events and themselves. Horrible visions make the bloody past an eternal present. Time has stopped, clotted like blood. There is no safety, no sleep until death.

In the end, Lady Macbeth's suicide is not shown (remember the spectacular leap in Welles's film), only her contorted, bleeding body on the stone courtyard. In contrast to her women who weep, Macbeth hardly seems to react at all. He walks down the stairs thinking "tomorrow, and tomorrow, and tomorrow," stares down at her, measures the distance she fell with a glance, and walks away. Lady Macbeth is not even buried. A blanket is thrown over her, the looters leaving the castle ignore her, and when MacDuff finds the corpse, he registers nothing but heightened desire to find and kill Macbeth.

In *Macbeth*, Polanski challenges the customary definition of pornographic violence: "if you don't show violence the way it is, I think that's immoral and harmful. If you don't upset people, then that's obscenity."[18] Seldom has war been less appealing than in the violent battle we hear and imagine under graphic opening credits, followed by the brutal dispatching of the wounded on the beach. Seldom has a murder by a character whose plans and point of view we share been less of a romantic adventure. The violence is not the central focus of the film any more than it is the central focus of Shakespeare's play. "I'm not preoccupied with the macabre—I'm rather more interested in the behavior of people under stress, when they are no longer in comfortable, everyday situations where they can afford to respect the conventional rules and morals of society."[19] If there is a morality underlying this film, it is neither a theologically based condemnation of murder (this is a Godless world), nor a pragmatic rejection of slaughter as an ineffective means of gaining and holding power. Rather it is an instinctive feeling of disgust and horror at seeing the human body dismembered, pierced, and contorted, a feeling of desolation and emptiness at the spectacle of a man demeaned by ambition until his life becomes "a tale told by an idiot." It is just criticism that the film is more melodrama than tragedy, true that the acting is sometimes weak (Macbeth's soliloquies, MacDuff, the sleepwalking scene) and the director's fertile imagination sometimes flags (all of the scenes with Malcolm's armies). But overall, Polanski has made a strong film with memorable imagery and truth both to Shakespeare's vision and to his own.

# 12

# Orson Welles's *Othello*

Welles's *OTHELLO* IS ONE OF THE FEW SHAKESPEARE FILMS in which the images on the screen generate enough beauty, variety, and graphic power to stand comparison with Shakespeare's poetic images. His visual images compensate for the inevitable loss of complexity and dramatic voltage accompanying heavy alterations in the text. Full of flamboyant cinematography, composed and edited in a "bravura style,"[1] this *Othello* transcends categories, blends antithetical film styles—the deep focus "realistic" style hailed by Bazin and the expressionist montage associated with Eisenstein. If the film destroys the narrative continuity of the play, so much so that voice-over narration must be provided in the beginning, it succeeds in creating an eloquent subjective portrait of Othello's heroic world in disintegration. Plagued with garbled and poorly synchronized sound, the work is filled with haunting music and marvellous aural collages. What the film lacks in acting—that is, subtle characterization and emotional range—it makes up in rich, thematically significant compositions. In short, Welles's *Othello* is an authentic flawed masterpiece.

John Dexter conceived the play in more realistic terms in the 1966 film where it is a story with racial and political overtones. At the core of the Olivier film is a searing, shocking spectacle of a man eaten up with jealousy, consumed with a desire for revenge, a man going mad and reverting to savagery. Welles depicts an epic world in collapse (compare *The Magnificient Ambersons*), a world which is a metaphor not just for Othello's mind but for an heroic, premodern age. For him,

*Othello* is myth. It portrays another lost Eden, another fall from in-nocence in which the serpent fractures unity, harmony, love, and beauty and destroys man with terrible knowledge. When Iago succeeds in undermining Othello's faith in Desdemona, we witness the birth of the monstrous, nightmarish world of Kafka's *The Trial*, or of Conrad's *Heart of Darkness* (two other literary classics which attracted Welles's attention). Othello is engaged in a quest. "The labyrinth is the most favorable location for the search. I do not know why, but my films are all for the most part a physical search."[2]

The visual style of Welles's *Othello* mirrors the marriage at the center of the play—not the idyllic marriage of Othello and Desdemona, but the perverse marriage of Othello and Iago.[3] Part of its cinematic language is born of Othello's romantic, histrionic character. The breath-less exposition and epic imagery derive from his own narrative style.

> Wherein I spoke of most disastrous chances,
> Of moving accidents by flood and field;
> Of hairbreadth scapes i' the imminent deadly breach;
> Of being taken by the insolent foe
> And sold to slavery; of my redemption thence
> And portance in my travels' history!
> Wherein of anters vast and deserts idle,
> Rough quarries, rocks and hills whose heads touch heaven,
> It was my hint to speak.

The film, like its hero, uses hyperbole and personification.

> Heaven stops the nose of it, and the moon winks;
> The bawdy wind, that kisses all it meets,
> Is hushed within the hollow mines of earth
> And will not hear it.

Othello's nature is embodied in Welles's low angles, vast spaces, monu-mental buildings, crowds of soldiers, and processions of mourners. "Gusts of jealousy are paralleled by billowing cloaks, veering birds, and flapping sails."[4] The tracery of Venetian architecture, the brute fortress with its networks of arches, the very sky, sea, and rocks express Othello's downfall. "*Othello* unfolds, then, in the open sky, but not in nature. These walls, these vaults and corridors echo, reflect and multiply, like so many mirrors, the eloquence of the tragedy."[5] Unlike many directors, Welles recognized that

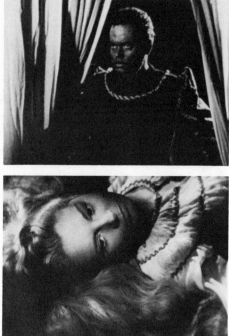

The Othello style

These are people who have more life in them than any human being ever had. But you can't simply dress up and *be* them, you have to make a world for them. . . . In *Henry V*, for example, you see people riding out of the castle, and suddenly they are on a golf course somewhere charging each other. You can't escape it, they have entered another world. . . . What I am trying to do is to see the outside, real world through the same eyes as the inside, fabricated one. To create a kind of unity.[6]

If the film's grandeur, hyperbole, and simplicity are the Moor's, its dizzying perspectives and camera movements, tortured compositions, grotesque shadows, and insane distortions are Iago's, for he is the agent of chaos. In Shakespeare's verbal terms, Iago's masterpiece is to reduce the Othello music to bursts of confused logic, shattered syntax, obsessive repetitions, and unconscious puns:

Lie with her? lie on her?—We say lie on her when they belie her. —Lie with her: Zounds, that's fulsome.—Handkerchief—confessions—handkerchief!

"Since *Othello* is very specifically a drama of concealed perspectives and quickly changing attitudes, Welles's camera imitates this manner.

The Iago style

The treacherous slight-of-hand manipulation of individuals, through which Iago destroys Cassio's career, becomes the motif of the shooting as that action builds."[7] The paranoia Iago generates and the violence he unleashes are expressed in staccato rhythms and sudden movements through shadowy labyrinths. Iago isolates his victim, plays on his weaknesses, fills his mind with troubled images, deceptive surfaces, and contradictions until he loses all sense of orientation and continuity. His satanic artistry, in other words, is not unlike Welles's.

The director stresses the conflicts of the Iago style and the Othello style from the beginning. After a disorienting opening shot in which the camera booms up and then down again on Othello's lifeless face surrounded by darkness, in which the corpse suddenly begins to move away on a bier, there is a jarring shift in scale and composition as we see the horizon filled with processions of mourning monks bearing the caskets of Othello and Desdemona. Then against the even, slow, horizontal movements left to right of the funeral trains are set the spasmodic jerks right to left as Iago is led past in chains and the vertical movement as he is suspended in an iron cage from a huge tower. A solemn mourning chorus and massive low chords from an amplified harpsichord contrast with the shouts of a mob hungry for revenge. A swaying point-of-view shot through the bars (which form a cross echoing crosses in the procession) as Iago peers down from his cage is the first of many shots creating a sense of vertigo, a feeling of tottering instability which climaxes in Othello's epileptic seizure where a huge upside-down wall twists in the frame, in the murder of Roderigo in a Turkish bath, and in Othello's dizzying final fall with Desdemona on their bed.

Shots of great beauty reflect Othello's commitments to Desdemona and the "plumed troops": the shot of the fluidly gliding gondola, the joyous silhouette of his ship with billowing sails against the fortress at Cyprus, and Othello's spiralling ascent (to triumphantly rising chorus and trumpets) to greet Desdemona against a sky filled with white clouds and wind-blown banners. When Othello and Desdemona consummate their marriage the scene begins with a splendid panoramic view of St. Mark's Square in the evening, shot past mechanical figures striking a huge bell in the foreground. In each case, however, the beautiful or the lyrical is shadowed by impending doom. The slow, horizontal motion of the gondola recalls the inexorable movement of the funeral processions. Othello's climb to Desdemona on the heights echoes the earlier descent of Brabantio's spiral staircase by torch-bearing householders as a harpsichord races down a scale—a "symbol of the spiralling rush down to doom."[8] In the love scene, framed by Iago's ominous "I am not what I am" and the fierce storm at Cyprus, the beauty of Desdemona in soft light with her hair spread out on the pillow is offset by Othello's shadow on the curtain, which appears again when he enters to kill her, and by the grill-work motif behind them, which echoes shots of Iago's cage throughout.

Welles, following Shakespeare, uses setting to express theme as well as character. The geography is symbolic geography. In Venice, Iago's attempts to sow discord and inflate conflicts are frustrated. He is but a shadow on the canal, a whisper echoing in the cathedral—a threat, a possibility. The civilized order which holds Iago in check is symbolized by the rich, harmonious architecture, sculptures of heroic man, placid canals, and the elaborate symmetrical altar at which Othello and Desdemona are married. Visually, people are dwarfed by an old and massive order which, if it cannot eliminate human conflict and suffering, can prevent gross injustice and provide a framework for happiness. Within this civilized order Othello is completely in command of him-

Venice versus Cyprus

self, moves and speaks to his own rhythms. In contrast to earlier rapid cuts, his account of the "witchcraft" he used to woo and win Desdemona is rendered in lengthy takes of his handsome profile. Here, and again in his love scene with Desdemona, an otherwise nervous film comes to rest.

In Cyprus, at the frontier of the civilized world, the restraints of Venice are lifted. Art, luxury, and institutions, so evident in the galleries, rooms, and squares of the canalled city, are absent. Armaments and the fortress represent a cruder, and in the end hopelessly inadequate, way of dealing with the "Turk" in man. Group leadership by white-haired civilians is replaced by the individual generalship of Othello. His subjects are not the rich merchants of Venice, but whores, soldiers, and impoverished Cypriots. Glassy canals are replaced by vicious seas which pound at the battlements. And the longer we are in Cyprus, the more the involuted Iago style triumphs over the lyric, heroic Othello style. We move inside the labyrinthine bowels of the fortress, into vaulted halls, long staircases, sewers where the deceptively placid water mirrors endless arches, and the Turkish bath where the sweat and steam lead to a crescendo of rushing water at Roderigo's death. Here Venetian Christianity is overpowered by paganism.

In Cyprus, Christian images appear but are put to perverse use. Iago kneels before a Madonna and Child, but it is to vow to aid Othello in his revenge. Othello's killing of Desdemona is a dark ritual recalling the wedding in Venice, but here he puts out the candles at the altar, the organ music is discordant, and the vows concern murder. Sounds in Cyprus—shouts, the wind, echoing footsteps, slamming doors—become surreally loud. Shapes on the screen are less and less easily

The disorientation of a tilted frame

recognizable: compositions are tense, full of diagonals, and faces are obscured, crossed with shadows or bars, harshly side-lit, or set askew in the frame. Often we see not human figures but their shadows, which distort as the figures move. Twisting corridors entomb Othello and Desdemona, who struggle to escape, while Iago is at home in them. As Peter Cowie suggests, "the bubbling, seething baths are a brilliant reminder of the 'cistern for foul toads to knot and gender in' that Shakespeare speaks of through Othello's mouth."[9]

Characters are often separated by great distances, vertical and horizontal, as when Iago looks down at cashiered Cassio or when Othello watches Desdemona and Emelia from the battlements. Yet accompanying this feeling of alienating distance is an increasing feeling of confinement. Ceilings bear down, walls become overpowering, the world seems to close in. The frame is sometimes masked by walls, pillars, stairs, and windows so that the one constant in film, the rectangular shape of the screen, is changed, bodies and faces being compressed into small, oddly shaped spaces. The exhilaration, the sense of freedom and infinite possibility experienced on the battlements now seem an illusion. The reality, revealed by the inspired prophet Iago, is a tortured, solitary eerily lit face surrounded by darkness.

The bed and the handkerchief are the two central symbolic properties in theatrical productions of *Othello,* and Welles uses them as recurring images in the film. He juxtaposes the marriage bed in Venice, emblem of the union of Othello and Desdemona, first against Brabantio's bed, with a headboard shaped like the galleries of Venice, and then against the grotesquely shadowed bed of suspicion and death in Cyprus. The handkerchief with "magic in the web," symbol of the lovers' mutual commitment and Desdemona's honor, is stepped upon by Othello as he rushes from her side. We see it both on Cassio's bed and in Bianca's hands, and finally it is used by Othello (or is it the wedding sheets?) when carrying out his terrible brand of justice upon her. (In either case, the Moor makes of a symbol of love a hideous death mask.)

But Welles's significant imagery is by no means limited to theatrical properties. Often he reaches for the resonant, multilevelled quality of Shakespeare's dramatic poetry. In some cases, he has sought visual equivalents for poetic images, as in the recurring opposition of dark and light. From the torches lit by Brabantio's hopeful followers to Othello's sustained speech before the Duke in which he moves from light to shadow to light as he speaks, from the flashes of lightning in the

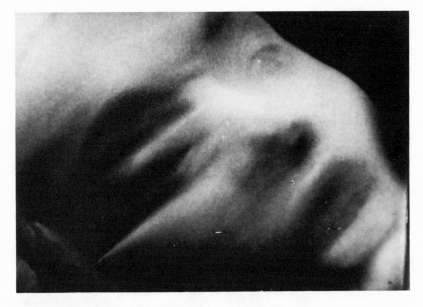

Desdemona's death

Cyprus night to Desdemona's white handkerchief and dress, from the emblem of the sun on Othello's black cloak to the lighted window in the huge fortress tower and the repeated extinguishing of lights toward the conclusion, the conflict and interpenetration of these opposites are stressed.

In Shakespeare, Iago's favorite images are the net, the snare, the web, making him fisherman, hunter, spider. "With as little web as this will I ensnare as great a fly as Cassio." "Will you, I pray, demand that demi-devil why he hath ensnared my soul and body?" says the Moor. Welles holds this image before our eyes, plays variations on it. We see it in a grate through which Desdemona passes to escape her father, in the net which holds her hair in Cyprus, in ships' rigging, in a rack of spears (the tips of which visually penetrate Desdemona as she walks toward disturbed Othello), and in the windows and doors of Othello's bedchamber. Welles repeatedly foreshadows the irony that Iago will be caught in his own mesh: hovering over him and escaping his notice is the iron cage where later the sun will scorch him and the gulls peck away his flesh.

Through cinematic imagery Welles also anticipates Othello's line in Act 5: "Here is my journey's end, here is my butt and very seamark of my utmost sail." Following Othello's farewell to "the plumed troop, and the big wars," a dark ship drifts toward the walls of the fortress and its sail slowly comes down. The director also stresses the animalistic mentality into which Iago leads his victims: Iago takes Cassio and Roderigo past braying asses, treats Roderigo like the gull's own puppy ("drown cats and blind puppies"), and leads Othello among goats ("exchange me for a goat") and screaming gulls. As in the play, images often underscore parallels—Welles dissolves from jealous Bianca holding the handkerchief to Desdemona worried at its loss. Images frequently reflect mental states, as when Bianca's shadow passes over the portal through which Othello thinks he has heard proof that Desdemona is a whore.

Assuming that the essence of Shakespeare does not reside solely in the poetry, Welles draws many of his images from the characters and dramatic situations. Mirrors which Othello peers into embody Iago's technique of turning his victims in upon themselves, of playing upon their impulses toward doubt or self-destruction by showing them distorted images of reality. Iago's power over other characters is stressed visually as he casts huge shadows, looks down from heights, makes sudden appearances, appears fully dressed and armed while others wear nothing but towels in the Turkish bath, and strips the armor from Othello as he begins to work on his fears and insecurities. Welles's *Othello* is not only impressive in the density of its film imagery. It is impressive in its range of expressive images. The tone may be light, as when Roderigo's dog bites his finger or follows him as he goes to murder Cassio, or it may verge on black humor, as when a little stick of soap resembling a hanging man dangles by Roderigo's head in the bath. Some of the best shots are simple ones: the *Seventh Seal*-like silhouettes of the funeral processions against the horizon, or the slamming shut of the round trapdoor at the top of a huge vault above the dead lovers at the end. Yet some effects are only apparently simple, as in the centerpiece of the film—a travelling shot of nearly one and a half minutes' duration of Othello and Iago walking together, stride for stride, along the ramparts of the fortress, Iago questioning, pausing, refusing to reveal his suspicions, questioning again. It is a good shot because the acting is good, and the seeming endlessness of their motion suits the dramatic moment. It is a great shot because of its overlaying of several aural and visual rhythms, each in conflict with the others, which builds a growing sense of unease in the viewer: the regular beat of the boots on the stone and the accompanying movement of their bodies, the rhythm of the waves beating against the shore, the uneven bursts of speech and silence, the irregular appearances of cannon in the notches in the wall, the regular patches of sunlight thrown on the walkers' feet, and the pattern of the irregularly spaced rocks in the sea beyond the ramparts.

As in Fellini, there are images in Welles's films which are eloquent in a mystical way, which have a suggestive vagueness to them akin to Shakespeare's best poetic images. One cannot account simply for the rightness of the moment when the soldiers of Cyprus stare up at Desdemona in silence, when mechanical figures strike the bells of St. Mark's, or when a grotesque chandelier masks Iago's figure as he walks past. Often it is not single shots which work in this way, but combinations of shots. Shot 1: an extreme long shot from almost directly overhead of tiny Desdemona walking between two dark pillars onto a vast piazza with a hypnotic mosaic pattern (scales? shells? tears?). Dissolve to shot 2: the camera rushes up to Othello with a loud roar on the sound track. He moves under an arch, followed by the camera, and a vaguely monstrous shadow falls over his profile. Cut to shot 3: Iago's shadow appears upside down at the top of the frame and lengthens on the glistening cobblestones as he approaches Othello to urge him to kill Desdemona. In these shots the major triad of the film is stated with clarity and force, yet with such complexity of movement and contrast in composition that rational explication is impossible.

Welles also generates electricity in shots portraying the death of Roderigo, a forerunner of the shower murder in *Psycho*. He shows it to us not as a continuous action but as a montage of fragments: Iago's sword flashing in the steam, Cassio falling and grasping his slashed leg, Roderigo's face distorted with fear as he futilely tries to pull open the locked and barred door, his pitiful helpless look up through the floorboards at Iago, the insanely accelerating sound of the mandolins as sadistic Iago looks down at his trapped victim, the spinning shot of the underside of the floor with Iago's sword slashing through it, the unexpected rush of water which blanks out the frame, and thudding low chords from a harpsichord as we stare at the huge tower with the light in the bedchamber window and the cage hanging outside.

In a film with such strong and expressive visuals and sounds, it seems almost unfair to demand more. But in Shakespeare films we *do* demand more, particularly good acting. While the performances in *Othello* are never obtrusively bad, as they often are in Welles's *Macbeth*, still they lack force and variety. Not only are the roles underplayed, they are seldom detailed and personal, lacking the subtextual dimension. In an effort to avoid theatrical excesses, Welles reined in his players too much, so that, as in Eisenstein's films, the actors are most eloquent when used as compositional elements. What subjectivity they possess is derived from their environment or from point-of-view shots. Faces are not emphasized in the film and are seldom expressive when they are. Memorable moments occur not on the lines (in the case of the minor characters, what lines are left them), but between the lines. Brabantio, for instance, is best when, having lost his daughter and been humiliated before his peers, he moves toward the door, pitifully looks back, and then exits in solitude while the others, embarrassed by or ignorant of his pain, busy themselves with state affairs. Bianca is most effective when leaning drunkenly on Cassio's shoulder during the sodden silences which follow the festivities, when fiddling with Cassio's ear while wearing his helmet, or when bustling along the beach to confront him with the handkerchief. Bitter, cynical, middle-aged Emelia is a good foil for Desdemona as she scratches her chin with her thumb and throatily chuckles that women have appetites too, even though her shrill, ludicrous death scene detracts from the film. Flabby-faced Roderigo is good when Welles parallels him with his curly-haired little white dog, or shows him cutting a ridiculous figure in a turban and ragged towel in the steam bath where he has been scratching hearts with "D" in them on the wall. But he is best, perhaps because of the preceding humor, when, terror-stricken, he is cornered and murdered by Iago.

Suzanne Cloutier's Desdemona is a fairy princess, rescued from a wicked father's tower by an adventurous Moorish prince. She wears strings of pearls spiralling down her blonde braids in Venice, and is indeed like a pearl ("like the base Indian, threw a pearl away . . ."). Her wide-eyed innocence and softly lit, angelic beauty, her playfulness when first urging Othello to forgive Cassio, and her stunned incomprehension at Othello's anger and accusations make Desdemona seem out of place among the soldiers and whores of Cyprus. She is a saint, an emblem of love and devotion. Except for feigning sleep and panic just before being strangled, she shows little evidence of humanity, of inner life (Welles has robbed her of important introspective moments by cutting the willow song). Paradoxically, her simplicity and goodness

Othello and Desdemona in darkness

become a horror to Othello and drive him mad. Her opaque whiteness serves to heighten the ugly labyrinths Iago has revealed in him. Ultimately Othello kills her not out of a sense of justice but out of a blend of twisted desire (he kisses her as he strangles her) and hatred for her inhuman perfection. As Parker Tyler put it, "psychologically Othello is very modern because . . . he *desires* to believe in Desdemona's infidelity because he *also desires* to 'kill the thing he loves.' "[10]

Michael MacLiammoir plays a flat, businesslike Iago, a relentless bureaucrat, clinical and disinterested to the point of boredom, a skilled mechanic playing on fear, lust, jealousy, sickness, drunkenness, pride, credulity, and other human weaknesses. Welles instructed his actor to excise all the playfulness, the flirting with giving himself away, the self-consciousness and ironic wit of a man who takes delight in his own demonic powers.

No single trace of the Mephisophelean Iago is to be used: no conscious villainy; a common man, clever as a wagonload of monkies, his thought never on the present moment but always on the move after the move after the next: a business man dealing in destruction with neatness, method, and a proper pleasure in his work: the honest Iago's reputation is accepted because it has become almost the truth.

"And out of her own goodness make the net that shall enmesh them all": to be spoken simply, happily, logically.

Any tendency to passion, even the expression of the onlooker's delight in the spectacle of disaster, makes for open villainy and must be crushed. He must say to Roderigo in discussing the disposal of Cassio, "Why, by making him incapable of his place. . . ." Roderigo looks bland, and Iago continues with a pleasant smile as though explaining to a child why it should brush its teeth, "knocking out his brains."[11]

Except for the killing of Roderigo, more important in the film than in the play,[12] the savagery is drained from the character. His look at the beginning as he peers from the cage at the destruction he has brought about is wide-eyed and blank, Iago's characteristic gestures are small ones: tugging at his dark stringy hair, glancing down to avoid revealing his cynicism, poking at Roderigo with a stick. The disease is hidden and surfaces only in his looks of disgust at Emelia which reveal "the underlying sickness of mind, the immemorial hatred of life, the secret isolation of impotence under the soldier's muscles, the flabby solitude gnawing at the groin, the eye's untiring calculation."[13] From his first words, "I hate the Moor," spoken in a context which stresses sacrilege and impotent envy (the organ plays and the priest recites the marriage ceremony for Othello and Desdemona while Roderigo and Iago, a parodic couple, look on),[14] Welles stresses Iago's humanity. Unlike Shakespeare's character, he is never larger than life. He never threatens to step out of the fiction (his soliloquies have been cut) but remains on the same plane of reality as the others. Said Welles, "I have taken from him the diabolic quality and made him more human."[15] But given the emphasis of the film, this does not seem a good choice. In an interpretation stressing the Fall, Iago's *mythical* quality, the enormity not just of his acts but of his way of thinking and being, is important. Yet here evil follows the definition of the medieval theologians—it has no form or positive qualities of its own, but is merely a negation of good.

MacLiammoir's underplayed, human Iago throws more than usual emphasis upon Othello. But Welles's performance is also damaged by its subdued quality. To put it cruelly, "he never acts, he is photographed."[16] To put it sympathetically, the character has been expressed not through acting in the theatrical sense of the word, but through casting, costume, sound, movement, and setting. "Welles was not attempting to particularize the Shakespearean role in all its nuances; he was trying to generalize it for purposes of film."[17] Unlike Olivier, Welles avoids the big gestures and makes sparing use of his magnificent deep voice. Scenes of bravado are cut or played down. Othello does not face the "bright swords" of Brabantio and his followers, but warns, from high in a balcony, that the "dew will rust them." It is Othello's officers who break up the fight involving drunken Cassio; he appears at the top of a staircase and pronounces judgment from an Olympian height. Welles speaks in muted tones, and holds himself to a narrow emotional range. Othello's power is expressed rather by elongated low-angle silhouettes of his figure against the sky, by harshly side-lit medium shots of his face set against architectural forms. His passion takes the form of sudden movements among grates and pillars, slamming of gates and doors, unexpected appearances of his shadow. We read feeling in swirls of marble or gargoyles beside his head. The subterranean world of Cyprus becomes a metaphor for what Iago uncovers in the Moor—the whole frame "acts" as he is trapped inside himself.

Othello is the only character for whom sound is consistently subjective. The sound of the curtain rings, for example, as he flings the curtains open to look on his shadowed marriage bed is positively shattering. Cassio's laughter becomes surreally loud as Othello hears it echo through the opening in the wall and blend with the screams of gulls and an ingeniously added sound of a softly trilling flute. When Othello regains consciousness on the rocky shore and watches a gull fly toward the inverted fortress wall, the flute sounds again and the bird's cries blend with the laughter of soldiers and whores above (to him, so many Cassios and Desdemonas). The roaring ocean as his passions rise and sudden bursts of music and the echoing alarm bell also help give the film a nightmarish, subjective feel. Even the *quality* of the sound is designed to heighten the effect of the visual style. Noel Burch has pointed out how the jarring juxtapositions of intimate sound "presence" in close-ups and distant, echoing sound in long shots complement an editing style which deliberately omits transitions from actors in stasis to actors in motion, and vice versa.[18]

Welles plays Othello as a truly noble man, great even in defeat—a conception worlds away from F. R. Leavis's deflating "modern" view. Though Welles's usual effect is of stoically contained passion, he has moments of great pathos, when, for instance, imagining his "fountain" Desdemona as a cistern for foul toads, he runs his hand slowly down her body with a look of profound sorrow. Othello's flaw is his greatness. He is "the only character capable of action in a world of impotent observers."[19] But the man of action is trapped in a labyrinth, doomed to destroy goodness inside and outside himself, to realize his guilt, and to execute justice on himself. In terms of balance, this is so much Othello's story that Iago does not even appear at the end of the film, the last shots showing the tragic couple on the bed, and the funeral processions against the horizon. Not until the final credits is the dialectic of the Iago and Othello styles reasserted in the tower and the cage, the masts and ships' rigging, and watery reflections of Venetian buildings with the shadows of ships on them.

It has often been said that Welles's most notable achievement as a filmmaker is "his attempt to invest each shot with an impact and surprise which are greater than any relationship the shot bears to the dramatic content of the film."[20] The many people who dislike Welles's *Othello* do so for this very reason. One reviewer complains that Welles destroyed the tale in order to concentrate on "half a hundred cinematic tricks,"[21] another that Welles "apparently has no sense of narrative, that is, of the procession of incidents, but only an interest in the incidents themselves—no, not even that, but only an interest in separate moments within the incidents, and this just for the opportunity they offer for arbitrary effects, visual and auditory."[22] John Fuegi finds that, "despite the brilliance of Welles's visual and aural imagination, the films fail, because of his willingness to take off after any brilliant effect. . . . Welles simply neglects to ally formal discipline with his immense cinematic intelligence."[23] Joseph McBride calls *Othello* "floridly expressionistic"[24] and Roger Manvell finds that "the large number of strikingly lit architectural shots coming in quick succession on the screen makes the film restless, and to this extent more difficult to enter into. Satiety sets in: so much photographic beauty becomes a drug."[25] On the other hand, those who value this infrequently seen work find that "each fresh viewing of the film strengthens one's opinion that Welles *does* display a remarkable respect for Shakespeare's text, while simultaneously adapting it for cinematic purposes."[26] Increasingly I find myself in agreement with Charles Higham: "despite all the vagaries of shooting, Welles never made a more coherent and beautiful film; the lucid, dashing, vibrant style has seldom been so perfectly wedded to its subject."[27]

# 13

# Stuart Burge and John Dexter's *Othello*

$T$HE WELLES AND BURGE-DEXTER VERSIONS OF *OTHELLO*
illuminate each other in interesting ways, for they are widely different
in style and treatment. Though the 1951 version was shot largely on
location in Morocco and Italy, and the 1965 version—a relatively
straightforward record of a stage production—as shot in a British
studio where the theatrical setting was re-created, it is Welles's work
which seems highly artificed and Burge's the more realistic. By manipulating sound, light, space, form, and motion, and by severely reducing
and rearranging the text, Welles created a mannerist montage of
broken continuities, wrenched perspectives, clashing images, and surreal
sound. As with Van Gogh, the artist's passionate presence is always
felt. In contrast, Dexter cut only about six hundred lines from Shakespeare's more than thirty-two hundred.[1] Burge's three Panavision
cameras coolly, at times almost transparently, bear witness to words
and events which are theatrically flavored, but preserve the human
detail and continuity of ordinary experience. In one work the meaning
and emotional power lie in the *way* the action is seen; in the other in
*what* is seen.

This reversal of traditional definitions of realism in films is comple-
mented by radically different interpretations of the play. Welles's
emphasis is upon the abstract, mythic qualities of a story of violated
trust (apparent in Desdemona, real in Iago and Othello), of a lost
paradise. His images are poetic renderings of Othello's feelings in
terms of shadows, silhouettes, and shimmering water, labyrinths,

towers, and fluttering banners. Dexter's path to the universal is a very different one. "Olivier plays not a tragedy of broken trust, but a tragedy of jealousy. Wild, elemental jealousy!"[2] We watch a noble, self-possessed warrior driven mad by Desdemona's imagined erotic encounters, a magnificent, muscled bull goaded and whipped by jealous Iago, destroyed as much by savage, dark forces within him as by Iago and the strumpet Fortune.

Like Olivier in *Hamlet*, Welles strips *Othello* of its links with the real world. It is "pure" classical tragedy in the distant world of legends and dreams. Dexter, on the other hand, roots the tragedy in a real social and political context, even though literally its world is only sketched in in a sparse theatrical style. Brabantio's fear and loathing at the thought of his lovely white daughter "making the beast with two backs" with the Moor stresses the contemporary *Othello* for modern audiences. While Welles's Othello is everyman, Olivier's is a *black* everyman.

> Persons hypersensitive to racial prejudice could make the charge that this eye-rolling, pink-lipped, tongue-thrusting coal-black Pappy is a demonstration of the most rearguard white man's concept of the "primitive" negro. Persons who like their Shakespeare "poetic" and uncontaminated by any contact with sordid reality could well be appalled by the prosaic rendering of the Moor as a cheeky nigger who has sauntered in from Westbourne Park Road. Such persons would have an element of rightness on their side. Their wrongness would consist of not recognising unbounded magnificence when they see it.[3]

Finlay's Iago is no inexplicable, abstract embodiment of evil, nor is he a symbol for the "Turk" in Othello. This "Iago, bony, crop-haired, staring with the fanatic mule-grin of a Mississippi redneck, was to be goaded by a small white man's sexual jealousy of the black, a jealousy sliding into ambiguous fascination."[4] The ensign's hatred of his general and need to destroy him are a distillation of feelings abroad in Venice. And as in the modern world, racism is intimately bound up with the economics of colonization. Dexter instructed his senators in 1.3 to "chatter among themselves about what really concerns them—namely the effect on their own pockets if the Turks seize a trading center as important as Cyprus: 'Look at the economics of the scene. It's not about religion, it's not about politics, it's about money.' "[5] Othello may be a mercenary who protects and is popular among Cypriots, but nevertheless he is the commander of occupying troops. Bianca is reviled by her people for fraternizing with the enemy: a Cypriot spits in her face as she cavorts with drunken Cassio. Cassio and Montano's fight is dangerous not merely as a breach of military discipline—it touches off a riot which threatens to escalate into full-scale rebellion.

While the generalized acting of Welles's *Othello* makes it lean toward the formalism of *The Cabinet of Dr. Caligari* and *Ivan the Terrible*, the meticulous naturalistic details of the performance in Burge and Dexter's film gives it a realist texture. Often critics categorize and judge film performances solely in terms of volume and scale—if words and gestures are muted and understated, they are "realistic," if loud and hyperbolic (as though people in real life are never so), they are "stagey." But acting style cannot be measured so crudely. There are many degrees and blends between supposed total naturalism and complete stylization. Variables other than volume and scale enter in—verbal and physical rhythm, range, emphasis, tone, structure. If we must stay with the threadbare division between artifice and realism, the flat monotone voices, restrained gestures, impassive masks, and lack of interaction between the characters (exacerbated by discontinuities from shot to shot) lend the acting in Welles's film an artificial feel, while the supple, varied movements, wide-ranging, fluid speeches, pregnant silences, and physical interactions of the characters in Burge's film are much more realistic, despite Olivier's moments of theatrical bravura and the downright un-American articulateness of the actor's readings. Furthermore, those who assume film demands "symptomatic" speech and restrained acting overlook the possibility that, as they are exposed to a wider range of acting styles and become more conscious of the artificiality of *all* performances on the screen, audiences may learn to accept the conventions of stage acting, to enter into the play-film world as they do in theatres, and to respond quite as fully as they do to "behaving." Certainly those with theatre-going experience find Olivier's performance more moving than Welles's.

What graphic style is to Welles's *Othello*, acting style (no less *visual*) is to Burge and Dexter's. In the earlier film, the dialectic between Iago and Othello is expressed in terms of two visual styles, one contorted and imprisoning, the other heroic and liberating, In the later film, it is expressed in terms of the performances of Frank Finlay and Olivier. Iago's gestures are restrained, his costume nondescript, his diction clipped, his speech conversational, staccato, improvisatory. The most intense close-ups are reserved for him, and despite his direct address to the camera-audience, his acting is often close to conventional film acting. Othello, in contrast, is always larger than life, even in his quieter scenes, and in the big scenes Olivier reaches for a grand, breathtaking presence lost to audiences since the nineteenth century. His costumes and gestures are flamboyant, his speeches lyrical and beautifully finished, and despite a West Indian veneer and notes of domestic playfulness and tenderness, the *character's* performance (not merely Olivier's) reeks of the magnificence of the stage. The measure of Iago's inroads on Othello's integrity, faith, and sanity is the degree to which his dry, mundane, "modern" style triumphs over Othello's archaic, grand, heroic one. Iago shrinks the epic figure to human size, changes beautiful fluid gestures to epileptic fits and wild angular thrashing, replaces openness and lyricism in speech with double meanings, gibberish, choking, howls of pain. Othello's recovery in turn is measured in terms of his regaining a humbler, more mature version of his original style. Olivier's triumph is that he liberates film audiences from trivial, demeaning images of man and allows us a glimpse of a splendid, more Shakespearean image of an earlier age.

In a fine study of actors' and critics' interpretations of *Othello*, Marvin Rosenberg suggests that "the actor must not only seek . . . a 'center' for the Moor; he must create an art object in which every gesture, every vocal and facial sign, confirms the wholeness and meaning of the design. This is the only way Othello can be fully known."[6] Burge's film achieves significant style when it shows a great actor creating such a design. By providing a central visual image—a trajectory of words, feelings, and acts from which all the play's major themes radiate—Olivier accomplishes something that the director-ridden art of film seldom permits: an unfettered actor-generated performance.

When we first see Othello, Iago has already roused Roderigo and Brabantio against him. From the beginning we sense tension between calmness and impending violence. The Moor's entrance is without fanfare. He is impressive and knows it, but he never strains to be. Physically, he dwarfs Iago, and his muscular frame shows his age only in a slight paunch and greying hair. His baritone voice makes other voices seem thin and immature. Othello is at ease, happy, quietly humming to himself as he leans casually against a pillar, his sensual nature apparent as he sniffs a red rose. Since the rose evokes Desdemona, whom he has left inside, there is significance in his waving the flower back and forth teasingly under Iago's nose, chuckling knowingly when asked if he is "fast married." The Moor wears a large, ornate gold cross and chain, which dramatically announces an African converted to the religion of his employers. Iago's warning about Brabantio troubles him not at all. Anchored in his royal birth and services to the state, he is secure as successive waves of the Duke's messengers and Brabantio's torch-bearing followers break upon him and recede like waves striking a rocky shore. When he moves, he *chooses* to move, and at his own pace. The contrast of Desdemona's two men is immediately established: Brabantio, the stooped, white-bearded merchant in a dark cloak, barely able to control his rage, pouring out pain, rage, and insults in a quavering voice, and Othello, with white robe and black face and moustache, the cool, deep-voiced foreign warrior, almost ostentatious in his restraint.

When he is on trial before the Duke, Othello's superiority, self-possession, and flair for the dramatic are confirmed. The Venetian Duke, a slight old woman of a man with a high, strained voice and wearing what looks like a nightcap, is a shrewd businessman, perhaps, but he is no warrior, no leader of men. Othello's salutes to him (a slight nod of the head and wave of the hand, a kiss of his ring and graceful tossing of the hem of his robe to his followers) have a touch of mockery to them, just as in his speeches there is "a suggestion of more intelligence below the surface than even the friendly Venetian senators need know about."[7] Brabantio moves between the Duke and Othello, trying to divide them with his accusations, but the Moor counters; moving between the Duke and Brabantio, and hypnotically, eloquently denying his own eloquence, he both recounts and reexperiences his wooing of Desdemona. The asides from his lyricism are not demeaning attempts to ingratiate himself with his hearers. They are joyful recollections of telling her a tall tale about men whose heads grow beneath their shoulders, the delight of *her* "witchcraft" (a blend of forwardness and delicacy), and the wonder of the unspoken feeling that flowed between them. All on stage are rapt. When Desdemona enters and rushes to him it seems as though his words have miraculously conjured her up. For a moment the two are oblivious of everyone else in the room, including Brabantio, who is burning with shame. As they address the gathering, they touch one another with an intimacy that makes talk of war seem out of place. "Even standing together among soldiers or courtiers the sexual promise between them is electric."[8] At

Brabantio's bitter warning "she has deceived her father, and may thee," Othello emits an impatient explosion of breath, takes her hand, vows "my life upon her faith!" and without pause, prophetically commits her into the hands of Iago.

Having weathered storms in Venice and at sea, Othello and Desdemona once reunited in Cyprus are at the pinnacle of their happiness. But such happiness cannot hold. Our point of view at this moment is Iago's—near the camera, he pours poison into our ears as he will later into Othello's. As the lovers are reunited and Cassio the polished courtier greets Desdemona, Iago's gnawing jealousy and slavering voyeurism seep into our response. Like Iago, we sense the irony of Othello's prophetic speech: "If it were now to die, / 'Twere now to be most happy." The joy of the couple spreads to all on stage as Othello announces the Turks are drowned, but Othello senses that the danger is not over, for against a background of drums and shouts, he orders Cassio to see that Cyprus does not "outsport discretion." Robed in white, Othello walks to Desdemona and, while a gentle, melancholy recorder plays, they kiss tenderly and go off to consummate their marriage.

The offstage presence of Othello and Desdemona interacts in an interesting way with the action onstage. Through Iago's leering remarks to lovesick Cassio, the erotic play between the soldiers and their women, and the innate sexual rhythm of revels building to violence, the film underscores Shakespeare's subtextual link between the lovemaking of Othello and Desdemona and the riot. A woman is slashed across the face and screams, and one fight grows to many as the drums accelerate. The alarm bell rings frantically, Montano is wounded, but the climax is cut off as, now in his striped robe and cradling his naked scimitar on his arm, Othello enters. Iago hurls a rioter toward the Moor, and Othello brings him to his knees with one hand, commanding the combatants to hold or die. Shakespeare's text suggests that Othello restrains his anger with difficulty: "My blood begins my safer guides to rule." In the film, these lines are cut and Olivier's Othello is totally in control. The emphasis is less upon his anger than upon his shock and sorrow that Cassio has betrayed him—an emotional note sounded by both Brabantio and Othello in 1.3. At the very moment he dismisses Cassio, sleepy, frightened Desdemona enters. Othello's mental processes are made physical and spatial. Through a theatrical form of montage,

Desdemona is linked with Cassio: Othello's love for her is joined with his betrayed love for Cassio.

Act 3 of *Othello* portrays with perfect psychological truth intense love giving birth to intense hate. Beneath a veneer of self-confidence and civilization in the strongest of men live irrational fear, the need for violence, and an impulse toward self-destruction. Iago plants the seeds of suspicion with one piercing line—"I like not that!"—as he stands midway between Othello and the distant couple, Desdemona and Cassio. (This configuration captures Iago's dramatic function—he constantly mediates between Othello and reality, between us and the action.) From the beginning some frightening ecology of the emotions is at work: Cassio's rise to the lieutenancy generates Iago's envy, Desdemona's love for Othello breeds jealousy in Brabantio, Roderigo, Cassio, and Iago, her honorable love for Cassio and Lodovico gives rise to Othello's insanity. The love between Othello and Desdemona flowers in a world saturated with jealousy, embodied in the yellow cyclorama and the yellow and black striped robe Othello wears.

As Desdemona presses Cassio's suit and reminds Othello that his lieutenant came wooing with him ("took his part"), we sense the first fissures in the foundations of Othello's monumental self-assurance. He softens, can "deny her nothing." But beneath his forced tender laugh, he discovers a weakness in himself not unlike Cassio's weakness for drink; we watch the birth of self-consciousness, a slowly widening gap between what he thinks and what he says. Once Othello is alone, Iago strips him of his defenses—cross, robe, and scimitar, emblems of his Christian values and his office—leaving him in his black tunic unarmed, vulnerable to Iago's assaults. Always the skilled mimic, Iago picks up Othello's note of ill-disguised suspicion. The Moor cannot rest easy until he knows what lies beneath Iago's idle curiosity, and Iago plays him as a skilled angler plays a fish.

Unlike Westerners, who remain isolated from one another, Othello touches people. He "knows" Desdemona physically, and tries to fathom Iago as a suspicious animal might—instinctively, through the senses. He chucks Iago under the chin, places a finger on his forehead and a hand on his chest, puts his arm around his shoulder. But Iago's attack is on a different level, and Othello is helpless against it. He corrodes Othello's faith in Desdemona and himself through abstractions. "Men should be what they seem." "Where's that palace whereinto foul things intrude not?" As Iago describes his own jealous nature, he gives Othello a mold for his chaotic thoughts and feelings. When the time is ripe, he puts Othello at ease with a lecture on "good name," which is an ironic recasting of Cassio's speech on "reputation." They laugh together as comrades. Then, his victim off balance, Iago strikes like a cobra, whining piteously "O, beware, my lord, of jealousy." Shaken Othello, heretofore relatively static, paces, broods as the deep-seated insecurities of a middle-aged man with a young wife, a foreigner among subtle Venetians, a soldier among chamberers, well up. Iago twists Othello's knowledge of Desdemona's passionate nature into suspicion of unnatural appetites. Desdemona enters, and Othello's rage at being robbed of his "good name" gives way to a desperate attempt to forget. He tries to wash away his suspicions by making love to her.

When Othello reenters he is a crazed animal. A giant among men now stoops, staggers about aimlessly, rubbing his hands together (the thought of Cassio has made him impotent), bellowing "false to me, to *me!*" This is one of those scenes that made Kenneth Tynan remark, "watching Olivier, you feel that any moment he may do something utterly unpredictable; something explosive, possibly apocalyptic, anyway unnerving in its emotional nakedness."[9] The wasp stings the bull. Iago taunts, goads, retreats, circles, strikes again—both disgusted and fascinated by a man, so unlike himself, totally without self-control. Othello bellows with pain, strikes contorted angular postures, is split in two as he rages and then weeps for pity, bids farewell to his occupation, and vows revenge. Suddenly he grasps Iago and hurls him to the floor, demands proof his wife is a whore, opens a hidden blade in his bracelet and delicately holds up Iago's chin, leaving his white neck totally exposed. "Strike!" thinks the audience. But Iago escapes with a masterstroke, assuming the tone of a wronged friend, a loyal servant threatened with death for his honesty.

Suddenly the imagery changes. It is no longer a bullfight, but a seduction. Iago adroitly moves behind his victim, plays him, crooning, pouring in his ear visions of sleeping with amorous Cassio, Cassio topping Desdemona, Cassio grossly wiping his beard with the handkerchief. "As [Olivier] grew to a great beast, Finlay shrunk beside him, clinging to his shoulder like an ape, hugging his heels like a jackal."[10] We witness the rape of a man's mind and emotions. Othello, with rolling eyes and gaping mouth, registers each word like a man being tortured. All his basest instincts surface and he is hideously reborn. Iago heats him with righteous anger, obliterates love, reason, and memory, hones him into a tool of revenge. The image is, as Harland Nelson notes, one of spiritual possession, tying together the ambivalent mentions of horns (cuckoldry, the devil) with the panting, frenzied creature raging on the stage.

> Iago kneels with him, holding up Othello's sword as they swear—but point up, so that the sword as cross symbol is turned upside down. This would mean something to Olivier's Othello, just as his tearing the cross from his neck means something a moment earlier. He is superstitious: he clutched his cross to ward off Brabantio's accusation of witchcraft, even in his relatively serene mood before the Senate. Again in this scene he shows superstition, muttering "yet, how nature erring from itself" as Iago's insinuations begin to work. By throwing it away now, and taking his oath before a reversed cross, he is invoking the powers of darkness: and hissing and grimacing later show he thinks they have accepted and now inhabit him, and he acts accordingly.[11]

To audiences accustomed to the often deadening decorum of the classical stage, the intensity and savagery of Othello's jealousy are a jolt. There is nothing noble and refined about a madman screaming "Blood! Blood! Blood!" and choking as his fit comes on. "Tragedy to Olivier is not only an intellectual and emotional experience, but necessarily a physical experience as well—a kind of visceral shock. . . ."[12]

Once again with Desdemona, Othello subdues his huge passion and gestures (flailing arms, running aimlessly as though fleeing a swarm of hornets), but he has lost his self. He has no normality to return to. Unused to dissembling, he finds his every word and gesture embarrassingly clumsy and false. Unable to think of anything else, he takes her hand, but, being warm and moist, it reminds him of her sensuality. Shaken, he resorts to punning and double meaning as he talks of hearts, hands, and heraldry—a form of speech he never used in Venice but it now seems natural to a mind distrusting all surfaces. Unknowingly, Desdemona becomes his torturer: the handkerchief, Cassio, the handkerchief, Cassio. Frightened, she tries to cover her lie by pressing the victory she won earlier, but she also lies badly—her nervousness and guilt rekindle his doubts. Reduced to tears, wailing, praying to his saint, Othello retreats leaving Desdemona confused, ashamed, frightened.

Now Othello is completely in Iago's hands, and Iago takes pleasure in playing his victim, teasing him with visions of Desdemona and Cassio naked in bed. He enjoys the godlike power of the playwright (which Shakespeare surely had in mind) who can take over someone's imagination and fill it with impressions which obliterate reality, who can imprint symbols like the handkerchief so powerfully that they are taken for the things they represent. Iago embraces Othello from behind, makes him beg for more erotic descriptions: "Lie with her, on her," he whispers hypnotically as they sway gently back and forth, "what you will." Burge's camera floats unsteadily back as Othello's shattered syntax and stream-of-consciousness images portray a mind unhinged. Rising on his toes, towering Othello seizes Iago, then releases him and backs away smelling his hands. As Othello becomes more and more disturbed, Iago looks on with disgust. A jarring overhead shot punctuates the climax of the Moor's epileptic fit and Iago dispassionately looks on as Othello falls like a huge oak. The fit is meticulous in its realism— body locked in a twisted, grotesque position, eyes staring, jaw thrust forward. Iago casually strolls to his side, looks down at his handiwork, kneels and places the hilt of a dagger between Othello's teeth—literally preventing him from biting off his tongue, but figuratively fitting him with the pointed tongue of a devil. When Othello comes to, he moans and hisses as the dagger is withdrawn. Iago prods still further, asks if the general has hurt his head. Othello winces at the reference to his cuckoldry. As Othello generalizes about the yoke of cuckoldry borne by all husbands, Iago rubs Othello's back, making him *feel* the yoke physically. When Iago reveals that Cassio was present during Othello's fit, Othello goes berserk, but the mighty warrior has shrunk, for Iago restrains him easily, lifts him as though he were made of straw. The stage image serves as a climax to a series of hints at Iago's homosexual urges—his disgust with Emelia's kisses, his amorous account of sleeping with Cassio, his contempt for men who dote upon and give themselves to women.

When Cassio and Bianca enter, it is Othello's turn to play the voyeur as once again Iago acts as interpreter, mediator between Othello and a couple. Othello's face fills the right of the frame as earlier Iago's did the left. Cassio embraces Bianca, who, like Othello, is jealous because of the handkerchief. But Othello sees not Bianca the whore, but Desdemona the whore.[13] Again Cassio's weakness (before it was drink, now it is his willingness to use Bianca) makes him Iago's pawn. Human nature, deeply flawed in Roderigo, Emelia, Cassio, Desdemona, Brabantio, and Othello, makes good material for Iago's plots. This twisted playwright,

Iago, even has a sense of poetic justice—Othello wants to "chop her into messes" or poison her, but his lieutenant suggests he strangle her in the very bed she defiled. Iago imagines the scene. Othello and Desdemona act it out.

When trumpets announce the arrival of the Venetians, Iago costumes Othello in yellow and black and flicks the foam from his tongue, but as Othello struggles for some natural mode of behavior, every gesture and word is false or double, everything material for his diseased imagination. Standing between Othello in the foreground and Desdemona who greets Lodovico in the background, Iago again plants the idea: "see your *wife* is with him." Enraged, Othello slaps her, calls her devil, orders *her* to duplicate his own wretched performance and feign innocence. Mad with jealousy he plays pimp to his own wife, blantantly offers her to Lodovico, praises her sexual prowess ("she can turn and turn"). For a moment he recovers himself and warmly greets neglected Lodovico, who more than any of the Venetians had supported him and Desdemona. But then with complete disjunction of gesture and tone, he suddenly stoops and hobbles off, wringing the rolled up commission and crying "goats and monkeys!" In his imagination, the whole island is filled with animals lusting after his wife.

Foreshadowing: Othello, Desdemona, Lodovico

When Othello comes to Desdemona, in his mind his bedchamber has become a brothel, Emelia a turnkey for customers, and Desdemona a prize whore. Othello alternately embraces her and hurls her from him, weeps and rages. His love for her is as strong as ever, but now it co-exists with hatred, shattering his unity of being, splitting him in two. In keeping with Shakespeare's tempest imagery, anger, shame, sorrow, love, pity, desire, disgust whip him back and forth like a tree in high winds. Fatally frightened, Desdemona cannot look him in the face. His viciousness and vulgarity terrify her. This is not the romantic story-teller but the killer, the man who has been a slave, fought many battles, and eaten strange flesh to survive. Ugly, bestial, brutal, he treats her worse than Cassio does his whore. When she finally understands what she is accused of, and angrily protests her innocence, he adopts another tone learned from Iago—burning sarcasm. He crosses himself ironically and begs pardon for mistaking her for "that cunning whore of Venice that married with Othello." He summons Emelia, viciously hurls coins at her for his unnatural traffic with Desdemona, and bids her keep their counsel as he leaves.

Othello's murder of Desdemona has always been a shocking spectacle on the stage, whether an impersonal solemn ritual, a brutal attack of a mad animal upon its prey, an act of pity for a fallen creature who must not be permitted to fall lower, or a perverted act of love. Olivier's is a blend of the latter two. Having shut the massive bedroom door with terrible finality, he kisses her tenderly as she sleeps, puts out the light, wakes her and begs her to confess. Then, ignoring her pleas, he par-tially smothers her with a pillow and puts her out of lingering pain (like Welles) by strangling her with a kiss. Under the tutelage of Iago's twisted imagination, Othello perverts the sexual act, creates death on his marriage bed. Yet, unlike the murderous assaults in the dark upon Cassio and Roderigo, there is a terrible beauty to the scene: the murder is done with "dignity and tenderness."[14] In a film intermittently plagued with stale vision,[15] awkwardly angled and framed shots, and ill-timed cuts, this beauty liberates the final scenes, allows the symbolic truth to radiate outward. Figuratively, we all are prey to irrational fear and jealousy, we lose faith, succumb to Iago, kill what we love. This scene suggests that to be mythic and universal, a story need not be abstract.

The charges most frequently brought against Burge and Dexter's *Othello* are (1) that it demeans the play and its hero by adopting F. R.

Leavis's "modernist" view of Othello, and (2) that next to Welles's film the work is without style, virtually non-art. In analyzing Othello's character, Leavis wrote deflatingly of his "obtuse and brutal egotism," his "ferocious stupidity," his "habit of self-approving, self-dramatization," the shallowness of his love for Desdemona, and the lack of "tragic discovery" in the end where all is self-idealization and pride.[16] In molding a context for Othello, John Dexter told his cast, "Othello is a pompous, word-spinning, arrogant black general" (significantly, he added "at any rate that's how you ought to see him"),[17] and Olivier spoke of Othello as "only a goodish fellow who had merely fixed the earmark of nobility on himself," as a man "absolutely in love with himself" who "thinks he is impervious to pride, or impatience, or ill-temper—to all ordinary passions...."[18]

Obviously Leavis's limited "realistic" view of Othello influenced Dexter's and Olivier's thinking. It is dangerous, however, to use ideas which helped performers crystallize a play in rehearsal to "explain" the finished work. The attitudes of the Venetians are not congruent with those of the audience. The conception of Othello with which Olivier moved himself off the dead center of tradition is comically inadequate as a description of his actual performance (one recalls Helen Hayes's story of how she triumphed in a role by thinking about her cat). Contrary to Leavis's view, in order to engage our sympathies and imaginations a tragic hero must be neither a modest, likeable fellow, nor able to verbalize his tragic recognition (Leavis was a truly *literary* critic). Suffering and knowledge in theatre and film are more often a matter of gesture, facial expression, presence. Unquestionably the film reflects Othello's "pride in his stature, his prowess, his power to captivate attention." But it also shows that he is "not vain, but proud," a man who "lives on a more lofty, more intense, more imaginative plane than ever the men of Florence and Venice could ever hope to do."[19] Robert Hapgood correctly observed that Othello's most admirable qualities are deeply qualified by complacency, sensuality, self-pity, and self-consciousness.

Yet Olivier's Othello produces a much richer spectator experience than does F. R. Leavis' essay.... As I read Leavis I can only feel pitying contempt for Othello's self-deluding folly and revulsion toward his "obtuse and brutal egotism." Olivier's interpretation goes beyond Leavis to make me feel sympathy, even admiration, for this Othello, with all his faults. For I have to admire his courage: the greathearted all-outness of his responses, his utterly vulnerable disregard of his self-protection that lay in restraint. In the same way, for all the excesses of Olivier's own portrayal I cannot help but admire its all-outness.[20]

In fact, it is the tension between Olivier's characteristic magnificence and ability to arouse sympathy and the influence of Leavis that lends the film such a startling blend of reality and grandeur.

Burge's is a film of powerful gestures which are as significant and visually striking as sweeping camera movements or strong compositions: Othello recognizing that no man can control his fate and letting his sword crash to the floor, Othello slowly registering in a sustained shot the enormity of what he has done. Said one reviewer, "I would not have believed an actor could have managed this, to make of his body the epicenter of the play and show the cracks going out, brain and heart and nerve and all."[21] Iago's gesture as he faces armed Othello (he thrusts out his arms making a cross and showing he is unarmed) is suitably ambivalent. Does he welcome punishment? Does he invite the thrust of a lover he has made "his own forever"? Is he mocking Venetian Christianity and the code which says a soldier must not strike a defenseless foe? The sheer *range* of Olivier's performance is unmatched on film. He modulates from the small gesture (trying to reestablish the bond with Desdemona, he reaches out toward her, but draws back his hand in shock at the coldness of her flesh) and tender words (he embraces her corpse and speaks in a small wavering voice of unutterable sorrow) to titanic fury and agony as he creates with his arms cascades of liquid fire pouring over his head and wails with West Indian inflection, "Desdemon's daid! Daid!" Then, in his final moments, all traces of self-consciousness and showmanship are gone.

Olivier in the final scene of Burge's film bears little resemblance to Leavis's braggart soldier. Pride and boastfulness have been scourged from him as he asks Cassio's pardon, and weeps, not out of self-pity, but for Desdemona and everything fine in himself that he has destroyed with her. His plea is not that he be excused but that he be understood. Having made that plea, he angrily executes justice on himself and falls, embracing Desdemona. As the camera slowly pulls away from the bed and the lights darken, one recalls not a satire on a self-deluded savage, but a story with a double perspective. It is at once a tale of the ostentatious, proud, sensuous, self-ignorant barbarian who reverts from Christianity to savagery and destroys himself and Des-

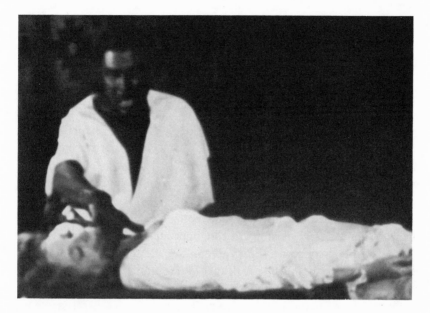

The touch of a corpse: sacrificial whites

demona, and a tale of the Moor of a constant, loving, noble nature, the spirit unfettered in mind and body, corrupted by a civilization which spawned the jealous hypocrite Brabantio, the stupid fop Roderigo, worldly Emelia, Cassio with his weakness for woman and drink, Venetian merchants who hire mercenaries to protect their interests, and envious, malevolent, treacherous Iago.

Complementing this complex Othello is Frank Finlay's complex design for Iago. The character blends modern cynicism with a sneering humor which is sometimes entertaining, sometimes merely sick. His bland surface is broken by perverted lyricism, a need to spread his own disease like a rabid dog, and finally panic and despair as he loses control over people and events. It is a remarkably well-rounded portrait. His hatred has many facets. He hates Othello on pure racist grounds, for his grandeur, for denying him advancement, for rejecting his love, for sheer love of hating. He takes sadistic delight in scheming, skillful deception, exercising power over the beautiful, gifted, and fortunate whom he envies. His desires seem to extend to both Desdemona and Othello. His vast ego is matched by fathomless self-hatred and longing to be punished (hence his constant flirtation with discovery, his greedy overreaching). Above all, he must prove that his Machiavellian, rationalistic view of the world is the correct one, that men and women are vain rutting animals and only cowards and fools believe in honesty and love.

Maggie Smith's Desdemona is neither schoolgirl nor saint, but a mature woman of great beauty, sensuality, and grace, with the courage to abandon her father, home, and friends and go off with her black general to Cyprus. Seldom two-dimensional, she feels for her father's loss and tries to make him understand, yet never wavers in her commitment to Othello. She is affectionate with Lodovico and generous with Cassio, loyal to Othello, full of respect for her husband. But she is also flawed—blind to Othello's faults, afraid, driven into defending the lie that she had not lost the handkerchief, fatally ignorant of jealousy both in her father and in Othello, imprudently insistent for Cassio. Once she is accused, Smith shows glimpses of the tragic perception that life entails suffering and betrayal, that all are implicated, guilty, fallen (she does deceive and betray Brabantio, and in the willow song she inadvertently adds the line "his scorn I approve"). In her last scene, she captures the psychological depth of the part, Desdemona's half-hearted defense and half wish to die (given what has happened, there is no returning to the bliss and glory of their former love), then her last-second anger, panic, and desperate instinctual attempt to live.

Given such performances, Burge could have made a great film. As it is, he only made a good one. Too often the camera is in the wrong place, the editing thoughtless, the lighting and makeup shoddy. The action is seldom powerfully *seen* save in some remarkable moments when one gets a glimpse of a film that would have shattered for all time the widely shared assumption that great theatre can never be great film. Shakespeare's language is effective, however, and in a medium hypnotized by its visual possibilities, that is something to be grateful for. And enough of a strong interpretative vision and some fine performances survive to give us a moving and effective contrast to Welles's baroque vision.

# 14

# Laurence Olivier's *Hamlet*

$M$OST WORKS OF DRAMATIC ART SIMPLIFY HUMAN EXPERI-
ence—select from it, give it an order and a meaning not easily perceived outside of the theatre. *Hamlet* is unusual in that it forces upon
us the uneasiness, bewilderment, and desperation of its hero as he discovers the paradoxes of life.[1] Hamlet is a man divided between a
heroism of action and a heroism of awareness. The first is the province
of Claudius, King Hamlet, Fortinbras, and Laertes, the second the
province of madmen, actors and fools—Ophelia decked in flowers,
the player mourning for Hecuba, Yorick the jester. King Hamlet's
sudden death brings home to Hamlet not only his own mortality but
the crassness of the world which, filled with well-meaning innocents,
time-servers, and preachers of the gospel "best safety lies in fear," goes
obliviously on. Like a prophet, Hamlet is forced by the ghost to see
everything with fresh eyes. Within himself he finds a mass of contradictions and mixed motives which call into question the very con-
cept of "self" and make stoicism and Polonius's advice ("to thine own
self be true") meaningless. Outside himself he finds a world of flux
where "purpose is but the slave to memory," where a loving mother is
also a lascivious whore, and where one has two fathers, one Hyperion,
the other a Satyr—a world best captured in the images of an unweeded
garden, a prison, a sweaty bed for incest, a graveyard. Hamlet wishes
to avoid being a pipe for Fortune or fathers to play upon. He wants to
be a moral agent, to understand why he is performing an act, what it
means, and what its consequences will be. But if in murdering a

murderer you *become* a murderer, if death is a "consummation de-voutly to be wished," if we should use men not "after their own desert" but according to our "own honor and dignity," why kill Claudius? Given self-consciousness, how does one escape theatricality to achieve authenticity as one "acts"?

*Hamlet* is a collage of styles: lyrical, grotesque, grand. It is a play full of grisly humor, oratory, riddles, songs, proverbs, and parodies. And, as its stage history attests, the characters have a shimmering, fluid quality. We find records of Polonius the likeable, well-meaning old man, and Polonius the sly, knowing politician hiding behind a mask; Ophelia a sweet, innocent girl, and Ophelia a spineless betrayer of the Prince; Claudius the hedonistic slime of the earth, and Claudius the capable ruler, sincere lover of Gertrude, and conscience-stricken murderer. Hamlet has appeared as a wigged and plumed thundering hero in performances stressing "robust action rather than the profound thought of the poet";[2] as a pale, melancholy, sensitive youth; as a raging madman; as a sane, courteous Prince of noble bearing; as a thin, bearded cynic who is brutal, snarling, morbid, corrupt, self-hating; as a restless intense intellectual. And each of these captured some truth in the role.

Given the length and complexity of *Hamlet*, it is no surprise that it is seldom performed entire and that actors give us something less than whole characterizations. Even more than most productions, however, Olivier's is a conscious simplification and reduction of the play. Like more recent filmmakers, he has focussed upon those areas of life most congenial to modern playwrights and novelists—the family and the individual psyche. The conflict between Denmark and Norway is thrust to the background, Laertes' rebellion is reduced to a few harsh words spoken in private to Claudius and Gertrude, and Rosencrantz, Guildenstern, the second gravedigger, Fortinbras, and Reynaldo dis-appear altogether. Olivier and his script editor Alan Dent not only pruned away characters and speeches, they rearranged scenes to make *Hamlet* more orderly, less fragmented, more like the movie stories familiar to 1948 audiences. "To be or not to be," for instance, is "ex-plained" by placing it directly after Hamlet's brutal treatment of Ophelia in the "nunnery" scene, not in the more puzzling moment after he has resolved to ensnare Claudius with "The Murder of Gonzago." Following John Dover Wilson's suggestion in his New Cambridge edition, Olivier's Hamlet overhears Polonius's plot to "loose" Ophelia to him, so that Hamlet's divination of the trap is literally explained.

Narrative, theme, and character become simpler as Ophelia's madness, death, and funeral are arranged in an unbroken train, followed by Claudius and Laertes' plotting to poison Hamlet.

What is left after this pruning and shaping is the story of Hamlet's struggles to overcome weakness and to do his duty. This is explicitly stated in Olivier's somber, voice-over recitation at the beginning: it is some "vicious mole of nature," "O'ergrowth of some complexion," or "habit" (that is, intrinsic defect, form of insanity, or scholarly trait of endless deliberation) which brings about a "tragedy of a man who could not make up his mind." Perhaps it seems that, given such extensive cuts, including Hamlet's self-accusations in "Oh what a rogue and peasant slave am I" and "How all occasions do inform against me,"

what actually happens in this film treatment seems to have nothing to do with the "interpretative" declaration with which it begins. Quite the contrary, Hamlet keeps making up his mind with precipitous abandon, and the typically virile playing of Olivier ignores the old romantic conception of the Prince as a kind of overly cerebral young Werther.[3]

But this is not quite accurate. Slow, meditative transitions between scenes and the remaining soliloquies still serve to make the movement toward the climax seem sluggish, and Hamlet, as Olivier plays him, partakes of the sensitive, sighing, romantic young man more than is indicated in such a summation. Olivier's Hamlet is neither all enervation nor all sudden violent action, but a hysteria-ridden blend of both. Mary McCarthy called him "a king of shreds and patches" in a kingdom of "hypocrisy, broken faith, play-acting, imposture."

Sir Laurence Olivier's is the only *Hamlet* which seizes this inconsecutiveness and makes of it an image of suffering, of the failure to feel steadily, to be able to compose a continuous pattern, which is the most harrowing experience of man. Hamlet, a puzzle to himself, is seen by Olivier as a boy, whose immaturity is both his grace and his frailty. This uncertainty as to what is real, the disgust, the impulsiveness, the arbitrary shifts of mood, the recklessness, the high spirits, all incomprehensible in those middle-aged, speechifying Hamlets to whom our stage is habituated, here becomes suddenly irradiated.[4]

Certainly, though, without the opening quotations, which obscure more than they reveal, Olivier's becomes a more complex performance, and the work a more interesting one.

Physical and emotional separation:
Hamlet and Ophelia, Gertrude and Claudius

Roger Furse's *mis-en-scène* for the film liberates the play's language and actions from deadening literalness and reinforces the psychological nature of the drama. The vague Kafkaesque castle, with its large rooms, pillars, corridors, and archways, its misty ramparts and tortuously winding staircases, its bleak stone walls and ominous areas of impenetrable shadow, is as suggestive of the mind's labyrinths as Welles's sweating caves in *Macbeth*. As in Welles's film, the blend of voice-over meditations and large distances between characters helps stress the isolation of the tragic hero. Here the distinct style of the film results from combining this prisonlike setting with a perpetually moving camera, making it a journey. Like Welles's *Othello* and *Throne of Blood*, Olivier's *Hamlet* begins at the end. The camera drifts down from great height toward the castle shrouded with mist to reveal the final tableau of men bearing the body of Hamlet on the top of the high tower. We pause on the ramparts, where, puzzled, frightened, vulnerable, "sick at heart," the men guarding Denmark will confront the unknown. Then we move down the twisting stairs to the paradoxical womblike safety and imprisonment of the castle, past the dark, deserted Great Hall with its huge pillars and long table with two chairs at one end and one at the other, past a larger-than-life portrait of a chivalric figure on horseback (presumably King Hamlet, whose heroic image haunts the court in so many ways—miniature portraits, the ghost, guilty memories, the ghost, his son's face), past the arch associated with Ophelia. The camera finally comes to rest on Gertrude's huge, canopied bed. Dissolve to Claudius drinking wine and the action begins. Throughout the film, this omniscient, heavenly spy journeys along corridors, glides up and down stairs, circles the characters studying them, and in the end retraces its opening journey as it follows the ritual procession for Hamlet—past the graveyard and the firing cannon, the empty chair with a flower on its arm, associated with both Hamlet and Polonius, the altar at which Claudius has prayed, the bed, to the high tower once more.

Though it has clearly influenced Franz Wirth's murky *Hamlet* (1960) and Tony Richardson's recent journey underground where faces take on a hellish red glow,[5] Olivier's choice of an abstract setting and unusual shooting style has let him in for some harsh criticism, not merely from critics of the realist school who detest film artifice of all kinds, but from those who address the proper question: "stylization for what?"

Laurence Olivier tried desperately hard to give *Hamlet* (1948) a worthy visual style, but, as Renoir remarked of its barn-sized sets and deep focus compositions, "you feel dizzy when you look down from a great height? So what? What has that got to do with Shakespeare?" The style *confuses* the issue.[6]

But despite some lapses, Olivier did find a significant style for the play as he viewed it. The heights in the film are not meaningless exercises in vertigo. They are linked to Hamlet's sense of disorientation, to the ghost and to godlike knowledge, and to freedom and aspiration as opposed to the world of compromise, deception, and imprisonment below. The wandering camera not only reinforces Hamlet's disturbed mental state, it links things associatively, as the mind does when moving from thought to thought. Like Hamlet, the camera is on a quest for a meaningful pattern—one which it ultimately finds in the journey at the end of the film.

Just as with amusing literalness some critics complained that Olivier's "geography doesn't make sense" when they tried to "sketch a floor plan of the castle,"[7] many assumed that his modulations into a theatrical look and feel were evidence that he had lost control, that his filmic skills were breaking down and that he was falling back on his experience in the theatre. But the theatricality of the various platforms and "scenes" in this composite set (modelled, like the Elizabethan stage, on man's mind as well as on his universe)[8] was deliberate and serves to underscore Shakespeare's use of the "world as stage" metaphor in the play. Hamlet's problem, like the players', involves the

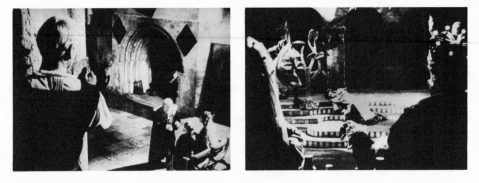

The world as stage

paradoxical relationships between word and act, reality and fiction. The play within the play is but one of the many instances in which, knowingly or unknowingly, characters act out scenes for other characters: the ghostly apparition appears to the men on the ramparts; Hamlet observes the court as a hollow pageant, the courtiers applauding Claudius's performances with gloved hands; Polonius is a spectator to Hamlet's scenes with Ophelia and Gertrude (when he attempts to enter the latter, he is stabbed through the curtain—enter Polonius, dead). And Hamlet and Laertes, like the other courtiers, are caught up in a final deadly play, a ritualized combat which, like the harmless fiction of "The Murder of Gonzago," suddenly takes on grisly reality. Words like "show," "act," "seem," "apparition," "shape," "painting" echo throughout *Hamlet*. While the blatant theatricality of Olivier's *Henry V* and *Richard III* reinforces theme only in certain scenes, here it is bound up with the meaning of the whole.

A moving camera implies a shifting point of view, and *Hamlet* is above all a play of ambivalent and shifting points of view. We become the ghost drifting down into the castle or sweeping behind a pillar in the closet scene. We become Hamlet instructing the players from off-frame or looking with blurred sight at the waves breaking below. We become Ophelia looking down a long corridor at Hamlet or (her dress of madness touchingly resembling a wedding gown) studying her distracted face reflected in a stream. Olivier's play-within-the-play scene is an epiphany affirming that significance shifts with the perceiver; it is a graphic illustration of the subjective nature of reality. As the spectators observe a stylized, mimed murder set to music, the camera slowly travels in a large semicircle behind them, allowing us to see the play from the points of view of Ophelia, the courtiers, Hamlet, Claudius, Gertrude, Polonius, and Horatio. The pantomime becomes in turn a mystery, an exciting fiction, a boring puppet show, an open threat by Hamlet against the king, and a nightmarish revelation of a real murder. The moving camera, taken by many as a gimmick to make a stagey work seem filmic, is a symbol of the impossibility of fixity in a world of flux. The characters have no being, but are constantly in process. Hamlet becomes something quite other than the "glass of fashion and the mold of form." Honor-conscious Laertes becomes the willing tool of a corrupt king. Sweet Ophelia becomes a tousled whore singing bawdy songs. And guilt eats away at the passion of Gertrude and Claudius until, like Lady Macbeth and Macbeth, they are a torment to each other. No single image, verbal formulation, or position of the camera can capture the truth about such persons in process. Says mad Ophelia, "Lord, we know what we are, but know not what we may be."

Many viewers find the most disturbing aspect of Olivier's film neither his reductive stripping away of the social and political dimensions, nor his abstract set and moving camera, but his emphasis upon the Oedipus complex as the "defect" underlying Hamlet's inaction.[9] In Freud's opinion (later elaborated by Ernest Jones),

> Hamlet is able to do anything—except take vengeance on the man who did away with his father and took that father's place with his mother, the man who shows him the repressed wishes of his own childhood realized. Thus the loathing which should drive him on to revenge is replaced in him by self-reproaches, by scruples of conscience, which remind him that he himself is literally no better than the sinner whom he is about to punish.[10]

In public statements, Olivier was somewhat tentative about this view.

> Perhaps he was the first pacifist, perhaps Dr. Jones is sound in his diagnosis of the Oedipus complex, perhaps there is justification in the many other complexes that have been foisted on him—perhaps he just thought too much, that is, if a man can think too much. . . . I prefer to think of him as a nearly great man—damned by lack of resolution, as all but one in a hundred are.[11]

But in the film he reinforces Freud and Jones throughout. Hamlet's self-hatred and guilt are associated with his feeling that his mother's incest has tainted his own flesh. His disgust with sexuality is apparent in the "nunnery" scene with Ophelia in which he labels her "bawd," and he comes near to sadistic assault both with her and with his mother in the "closet" scene. (Shakespeare merely meant by the term "closet" a private room, but since John Gielgud's production in 1936, the bed has become a part of stage tradition.[12]) Olivier's camera lingers often over Gertrude's large, suggestively shaped bed. Hamlet's impotence is indicated by symbolic castration as he drops his dagger into the sea in the "To be or not to be" soliloquy, his inability to strike home with his sword until the end, and his simultaneous fear of and longing for death, "a consummation devoutly to be wished." From the beginning, when Claudius must break up a passionate kiss between mother and son ("Gertrude! Come away!"), Hamlet's scenes with the Queen in her low-cut gowns are virtually love scenes. A setting dominated by archways, corridors, phallic pillars, cannon, and towers echoes the theme further so that the film becomes in a sense an Oedipal cinepoem.

The Freud-Jones interpretation does not narrow Hamlet's character as much as some have argued. Olivier's portrait shows us much more than Hamlet "the ineffective dreamer, the hysteric, the oversensitive scholar."[13] Mary McCarthy's phrase the "king of shreds and patches" holds. We also see his warm feelings for Horatio, his good humor with the players and gravedigger, his tenderness for Ophelia and Gertrude. We see his skill in acting (which permits Olivier/Hamlet, in a nice touch of metacinema, to school the players), his athleticism, playfulness, biting satiric wit, commanding voice, and bursts of energy. Olivier was well aware that his acting gifts were more suited to Henry V or Richard III—in fact, he tried for a time to find another actor for the role of Hamlet. But if it is not his greatest performance, there is no serious imbalance in it. The problem generated by the Oedipal emphasis lies rather in the imbalance between Hamlet and his world—an imbalance heightened by Olivier's pruning away of the play's larger context. In the play, we have noted, Hamlet is a hero of perception. As with *Richard III*, the very fact that Hamlet *thinks* sets him apart from the other characters. Where they draw back—from imagining the progress of a king through the guts of a beggar or the dust of Alexander stopping a hole in a beer barrel, from seeing clearly the guilt, vanity, and self-deceptions that make ordinary life at once despicable and possible, saying with Horatio " 'twere to consider too curiously, to consider so"—Hamlet pushes ahead relentlessly.

In the film, however, the emphasis is almost entirely upon the flaws and weaknesses of Hamlet. His story arouses sorrow and pity, but he is distinctly unheroic, in Olivier's words, "a nearly great man—damned by lack of resolution." The contradictions seem ingrained not so much in the world as in the imaginings of a diseased, unschooled mind. His suffering seems not tragic but pathological. John Ashworth could not argue away Hamlet's delay, but he was right to raise the issue of the essential conservatism of the psychoanalyst's view of Hamlet, according to which Hamlet is sick and needs to be *cured* of his questioning. His rebellion against the prostitutions of Claudius's court is a symptom of his abnormality, not a revelation of its corruption and an aspect of his greatness. Unfortunately, such a view is not unlike that of Claudius and other characters in the play: Hamlet's rebellion against mortality, compromise, the way of the world, and mindless action is labelled immaturity, impossible idealism, madness, and cowardice. Had Olivier provided a much stronger and more sympathetic portrait of Claudius, and used a fuller text, his film might well have stood the play on its head, rooting Denmark's sickness in Hamlet, making him, in G. Wilson Knight's phrase, an "Embassy of Death."[14]

Because of this imbalance between Hamlet and his world, the conclusion of Olivier's film is much less complex than that of the play or of Kozintsev's film, where an equilibrium is maintained. In Olivier's film, Hamlet broods, thrashes about, plays dangerous games, waits like a coiled spring. Then, finally, he overcomes his weakness and acts: he humiliates the skilled swordsman Laertes, commands the doors to be shut upon learning of treachery, climbs to a ramp above, and sails down like an avenging angel to plunge his sword into Claudius—again and again. (Olivier saved the leap for the last day of shooting and executed it himself, knocking Claudius's stand-in unconscious and breaking two of the man's teeth.)[15] Dying, Hamlet occupies for a brief time his rightful place on the throne of Denmark as his subjects bow before him; then, "the rest is silence." After this saintlike death, a ritual procession takes him heavenward and grants him both mythical status and redemption. Gertrude, too, is redeemed, for she *knowingly* drinks the poisoned wine, both punishing herself and making a sacrifice to help her son. With peace between Laertes and Hamlet, and with Horatio the Stoic left to rule Denmark, Olivier's *Hamlet* concludes with a crescendo of regeneration. Shakespeare's sense of waste and ambivalent blend of triumph and defeat give way to an unequivocal sense of fulfillment.

The imagery of Olivier's film, like its conception of Hamlet's world,

A castle of inner experience

is relatively unsophisticated. Montage between shots is hardly used,[16] save for a few blatant examples such as the dissolve from Gertrude's bed to Claudius swilling wine. Rather, meaning is generated *within* shots: the head of Hamlet's shadow falls upon Yorick's skull (fore-shadowing death, and linking him with the role of fool), the ghost seems to rise out of Hamlet's head as it reveals the murder, Claudius and Gertrude slowly ascend stairs to separate rooms while reading Hamlet's letters, signalling his success in parting them. Occasionally properties link characters—the wine cup of Laertes as he gives advice to Ophelia, associating him with Claudius, and the Player Queen's blonde wig revealing the link in Hamlet's mind between Gertrude and Ophelia—and changes of costume are used to some effect. But on the whole, *Hamlet* is a very spare film. There are occasional powerful images—the jagged outline of the steps cutting into Hamlet's figure as he ascends to his mother's room; Hamlet's torch filling the screen at the climax of the play scene when Claudius cries "give me light"—but Olivier generally seeks power through the acting (uniformly compe-tent but nowhere brilliant), camera movement, set design, and block-ing rather than in striking compositions. When the director does consciously compose—as in the tableau of theatrical emblems, the dying king encircled by the spears of his own guards, Ophelia in the sunlight with pastoral landscapes glimpsed beyond, or floating down the stream in a Rossetti-like image, the insets of the murder superimposed over the ghost's description, or the fight of the two ships over Hamlet's letter—he is less effective than when the camera floats through the castle, moves around the characters, or captures them in motion. Save for periodic dissolves into Hamlet's face, iterated images of spying and theatre, thrones, the bed, recurring crosses (Hamlet's sword, the grave markers, Hamlet's entrance in the graveyard scene and final leap with arms outstretched), and rounded shapes associated with Gertrude and Ophelia,[17] recurring visual motifs are few.

Though as a visual director Olivier is overfond of tableaux, he often suits physical movements to the rhythms and meanings of the lines in interesting ways. His use of sound, however, is less inventive. Although there are rare moments like the combination of a beating heart and a moan as the ghost appears, he relies primarily upon an orchestral score by William Walton, which has aged less gracefully than the score for *Henry V*. The music bridges scenes, establishes moods, and identifies characters. Quite properly it is seldom realistic, and occasionally, as in the play scene, where the music is an analogue for Claudius's passion (it builds, he fights it down, and finally it erupts), blending suspense music with a repetitive, strangely sinister dance tune,[18] it has real dramatic power. But on the whole the sheer *ordinariness* of the music takes the edge off the performances and the language. There is nothing haunting, grand, or unpredictable about it. Often the hyperbolic clashes of cymbals, the repeated rushes up scales as the camera sweeps up to the ramparts, or the attempts to "point" speeches like "To be or not to be" come perilously close to unintentional humor.

The difficulty in "imaging" *Hamlet* on the screen is that there are two *Hamlets*. Quite apart from the length of the play, the complexity of the hero, and the incredible range of verbal styles, a director must reckon both with the conflicts within Hamlet and with his outer clashes with other characters. Olivier's dreamy, lyrical film, with its misty ramparts, dissolves, and gliding camera, captures the inner *Hamlet* quite well. Kozintsev's epic Russian version, on the other hand, places more emphasis upon the outer *Hamlet*, and while it may lose some of the brooding psychological power of the earlier film, it is truer to the tensions, paradoxes, and rough edges at the heart of the *Hamlet* experience.[19]

# Grigori Kozintsev's *Hamlet*

KOZINTSEV'S *HAMLET* IS INDEBTED TO OLIVIER'S FOR MANY details—the impersonal mask covering the suffering human face of Hamlet's father, the empty chairs and prominent tapestries and staircases, the tableaux of theatrical props associated with the players, and the symbolic crosses (prominent in the graveyard scene, the voice-over soliloquies, and the concluding funeral procession). Yet the Russian film is remarkably different in both style and interpretation. Olivier's Prince is isolated in a timeless, expressionist rendering of his own mind, its corridors, deep shadows, and winding staircases embodying his confusion and emotional turmoil. The action is theatrically generalized, abstract. What glimpses we get of the world outside Elsinore are distant and stylized—it hardly seems to exist. Kozintsev's Prince, in contrast, inhabits a crowded castle which has a history and is the center of a society rooted in nature—sky, stone, plains, and the sea. The castle becomes, in effect, one of the Dramatis Personae.

Olivier surrounds his king with toadying, formally dressed courtiers, but Kozintsev also provides glimpses of the common people who are affected by the murderous struggle within the castle. Peasants turn the gigantic wheel which raises and lowers the portcullis. They gather to listen as Claudius's proclamation is read to them and as the actor recites the Hecuba speech. They walk the road Hamlet walks when he returns after being "set naked" on the shore, are viciously pushed back by soldiers as Ophelia is buried, and at the end look on in silence as Hamlet's body is borne by. Because there is a context for Hamlet's action, Hamlet's problems are social and philosophical as well as psychological. In his production diary, Kozintsev wrote,

> It is impossible to combine human worth with existence in a society based on contempt for man. To reconcile oneself, to swim with the current, is ignominy. It is better "not to be." This tragedy portrays a man who does not find himself between life and death, but between one era and another. . . . The conflict between Renaissance ideals and the reality of the epoch of primary accumulation of capital was evident enough. This is the germ that sickened those who had the misfortune to realize the depth of the rift. . . . The society portrayed in *Hamlet* is frightening neither by its resemblance to the savage existence of beasts of prey nor by the particular cruelty of bloodthirsty fiends, but by its callous emptiness. The noble and the spiritual have vanished from life. It is not bestial crimes that arouse horror; it is normal human relations which have lost their humanity. . . . The screen must convey the enormity of history, and the fate of a man determined to talk with his epoch on equal terms, and not be an extra, with no speaking part, in one of its spectacular crowd scenes.[1]

Olivier used a screen of traditional proportions. Kozintsev used Sovscope, an epic 70mm format, which permitted him to stress vast horizons, crowds, dances, and processions. The wide screen allowed him to modulate between close-ups isolating significant objects, complex medium shots including subtle gradations of emphasis from background and decor, minor motifs, major themes, to central characters and actions,[2] and extreme long shots isolating a figure against great expanses of castle, sky, or rock, or separating characters horizontally. In Olivier's dreamlike film, dissolves frequently link shots; in Kozintsev's a hardness and precision results from the exclusive use of straight cuts. Olivier's imagery is simple and direct: a bed, a tower, Hamlet's face inverted in the screen as he wakes from the nightmare of the ghost. Kozintsev is at once more of a realist and more of a symbolist. His film retains a greater proportion of the play's complexity and mystery, not merely because his images have a Shakespearean realism and grandeur to them, but because the visual texture is denser, the images and connections more consistently meaningful.

Like Welles, Kozintsev is a true poet of the screen. While there are conceptual patterns underlying his films, they are always rendered in terms of the concrete. There are scores of epiphanic moments in his

*Hamlet:* Yorick's rotten cap and bells sitting at a jaunty angle atop his skull while a flute plays a melancholy but spritely tune in the background, Gertrude's black-gloved hand embracing Hamlet while the drawbridge and huge spiked portcullis close him in, the duel which with its exaggerated shadows seems a grotesque dance of death. Sounds, gestures, and images achieve extraordinary power: the ominous little click of the casket aboard ship (echoed later in Ophelia's casket) as Hamlet shuts in the death warrant for Rosencrantz and Guildenstern, Ophelia's attempts to push a suffocating black veil of mourning away from her face and her drifting through the immense rooms of the castle, the lyrical shot of the willow reflected in the water and the slow pan to her body lying still under its surface, the loud hollow sound of the gravedigger's hammer as he nails the lid on her coffin, and the abrupt contrast between the dark, wind-swept courtyard with skittish horses and creaking gate as Hamlet and the watch stalk the ghost and the brilliant lights, busy, rapid movement, shouts and festive music of Claudius's revels inside.

In Kozintsev, things and gestures "speak": the corpselike dress borne out of Gertrude's bedroom as obsequious Polonius creeps in to consult with the king, Hamlet's intense, deliberate demonstration to the actor of how to pour the poison in the sleeping king's ear, Claudius's subsequent miming of that gesture as he rises during "The Murder of Gonzago" and relives the nightmare of his crime, and Ophelia's disjointed, mechanical dance which is echoed in the gestures of the Player Queen. Gestures, indeed, often lead straight to the heart of a character. Gertrude nervously flutters her fan at the play and repeatedly holds her hand to her breast (even after her death) to hide what is there from herself and others. Hamlet recoils from Polonius's blood, wiping it from his hand on the arras, and gags at the sight and smell of Yorick's skull. Claudius, "a satyr, a sensual beast with moist lips and languid protruding eyes" and "a seducer of women and ministers of state . . . [wearing] all those earrings, laces, chains and signet rings,"[3] smiles his hideous public smile even as his beloved Gertrude drinks the poisoned wine—fear of discovery and habit have made him incapable of an authentic public response.

Kozintsev, like Shakespeare, uses change in costume both to reflect changes in character and to embody the themes of "seeming" and (punningly) "habit." Hamlet's shifts from simple black dress, to mad disarray, to a monastic robe, to a leather fencing doublet, mark important stages in his growth. The Gertrude in jewelled finery and feathers, formal hair style and face frozen in a public mask, jars with the sensuous woman of Claudius's bed, the older, troubled, vulnerable woman who paces before the closet scene in a robe with her hair down. Part of the meaning of Hamlet's attraction to the players is revealed in their jester's costume—the jester being the madman-seer, the detached observer of manners and morals, the self-acknowledged fool who shatters conventions and turns words and scales of value inside out, as well as the sacrificial figure upon whom the sins of the community may be heaped. This association is continued in the graveyard scene where Hamlet mourns the death of the Yorick in himself, "foolishly" resolving to take upon him the sacrificial role. From beginning to end the courtiers of Denmark are linked with death—their wrinkled skull-like faces and suits of mourning give the whole film a funereal air, a pervasive sense of loss and decay. Nothing could express more painfully what happens to beauty and innocence in such an atmosphere than the transformations of Opehlia. First she is a mechanical doll, awkwardly imitating her grotesque dancing teacher, then one of Gertrude's cold court beauties, then an emblem of death as she is imprisoned in an iron corset, metal hoops, and a heavy black dress and

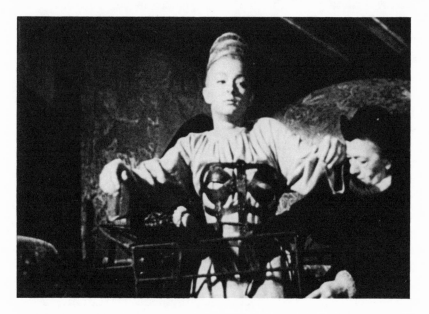

Ophelia caged in iron, surrounded by crones

veil. Finally, she achieves saintlike simplicity and happiness in her mad scenes, and in her death regresses as she lies foetuslike in the still water.

Kozintsev creates not only beautiful and significant isolated images, he creates powerful patterns of images. He invites viewers to register repetitions, associations, and contrasts. Some juxtapositions are elementary ones: a festive satyr-bull with Claudius, a Great Dane with panting, bloodthirsty Laertes, the drum of Claudius's soldier as he reads the proclamation with the player's drum (Claudius is also putting on a play). He links Gertrude's mirror of vanity with Claudius's mirror of conscience, Laertes, demented and single-minded in his quest for revenge, with Ophelia, aimlessly and lyrically mad. Replication of characters confirms their commonness: "the protagonists have their chorus, a kind of echo."[4] There is a whole bevy of cocky, smiling young Osrics, any one of whom might come down the stairs to invite Hamlet in inflated style to accept the deadly invitation to duel. Gertrude's ladies-in-waiting, Fortinbras's soldiers, Claudius's council members all mirror and reveal their "betters," while, in contrast, Hamlet's eccentric dress and movements and disdain for decorum make him unique.

Often, however, the chains of association are more subtle. When Hamlet first hears of the ghost, the camera moves slowly upward revealing more and more of a blazing fire in the fireplace behind him, paralleling his rising passion. Thereafter, dead fireplaces proliferate, stressing Hamlet's inability to stir himself to act in such a world, the dying passion between Gertrude and Claudius, and the cold, dead feeling of the castle. Several times the camera lingers over empty chairs: when Claudius calls upon his "chiefest courtier" and "son" in the first court scene, when Hamlet stares at the chairs of state at the head of the council table, when Polonius's chair is left vacant by his death. Billowing cloth suggests disturbance and is linked with death: we see it in Hamlet's cape as he rides toward the castle and rushes up the stairs, in the curtains and flags of mourning on the castle, in the ghost's flowing cape and the murderer's robe in the play within the play, in the tapestries as Hamlet laughs insanely while dragging Polonius's body away. We see it in the sails of the ship which is to carry Hamlet to death, in Ophelia's mourning veil, and in the tapestries past which Claudius runs bellowing to his death.

The "action" of this *Hamlet* is therefore not solely narrative. As in the original play, there is also action in the images. It is a cinepoem of stone, iron, fire, sea, and earth.

Stone: the walls of Elsinore, the firmly built government prison, on which armorial bearings and sinister bas-reliefs had been carved centuries ago.

Iron: weapons, the inhuman forces of oppression, the ugly steel faces of war.

Fire: anxiety, revolt, movement, the trembling flame of the candles at Claudius's celebrations; raging fiery tongues (Horatio's narrative about the ghostly apparition); the wind-blown lamps on the stage erected for "The Mousetrap."

Sea: waves, crashing against the bastions, ceaseless movement, the change of the tides, the boiling of chaos, and again the silent, endless surface of glass.

Earth: the world beyond Elsinore, amid stones—a bit of field tilled by a ploughman, the sand pouring out of Yorick's skull, and the handful of dust in the palm of the wanderer-heir to the throne of Denmark.[5]

The iron which cages Ophelia is linked with the armor of Claudius's guards, Laertes and Fortinbras and their followers, and Hamlet's father. Iron is brutal, dehumanizing. As with Shakespeare, images come alive in more than one context. The calm reflecting surfaces of the moat and the placid stream in which Ophelia drowns link them with literal and figurative mirrors in the film. But, being water, they also contrast with the sea in its various moods: breaking on the shore in slow motion suggesting the agony of Hamlet's seemingly endless encounter with the ghost, violently pounding on the rocks and then mutely waiting as Hamlet meditates on suicide, placidly lying under the sky as the ghost disappears into the troubled sky whispering "Adieu! Adieu," serving as a background for the play within a play, or racing toward shore as Hamlet sits imprisoned aboard ship.

The director's symbolist vision is in keeping with Hamlet's mode of thought, for more than any of the other characters he perceives life's meanings in terms of *things:* an unweeded garden, a prison, carrion, a recorder, a nutshell, a mildewed ear. Hamlet's gestures serve to make hidden truth apparent, figurative truth literal: he tweaks spies by the nose or tugs on their ears, carries a blazing torch into the chamber of benighted councillors, sets a candle before Gertrude to open her

Hamlet thrusts light into Claudius's Council

eyes, and contemptuously thrusts goblets of wine at the "sponges" Rosencrantz and Guildenstern who soak up the king's favor.

Though this is an intellectual film, containing Shakespeare's most intellectual character, occasionally Kozintsev cuts across these associative patterns with random naturalistic detail. As Hamlet sits on a wagon listening to the Hecuba speech and accusing himself ("O what a rogue and peasant slave am I") beside a tableau of theatrical props (clown, mask, and drum), to his left by a door in the castle chickens scratch for bugs, a man leads a horse past, a woman goes by, followed by two children and a dog. During the play within the play, a rowboat slowly makes its way across the bay behind. As in Brueghel's painting "Icarus," celebrated in Auden's poem, in which the ship and the plowman ignore his tragic fall into the sea, there is a world beyond Hamlet's tragic action which is oblivious to it. The contrast between the vitally significant and the empty clutter serves, furthermore, to heighten our sense of impending doom. "The sense of approaching catastrophe is not only seen in the darkness of the clouds moving over the land, but is perceptible in the accumulation of life's numberless trivia, rendering that life senseless and draining it of spiritual meaning."[6] Hamlet confronts not only incest and murder, but a whole social order drowning in irrelevancies. It is a world summed up by the sublime moments when Hamlet stoops, to the endless consternation of his guards, to remove a stone from his shoe before going to answer for the killing of Polonius, and when the crass, jovial, oblivious gravedigger (another "father" speaking to Hamlet from the grave) eats and drinks even as he is waist-deep in Ophelia's grave. "In Denmark, they are used to everything."[7]

Olivier composes images which make statements. Kozintsev composes images which embody conflicts. He sets Ophelia's lovely face against the ugly powdered masks of the old crones who attend her. There is heavy irony in the seemingly peaceful sleep of Hamlet and the beauty of the dawn following the ghost's revelations, for Hamlet is doomed. While grieved, shocked Laertes cries out "Do you see this O God?" upon seeing Ophelia mad, to the right in the frame is an armored head which fixes him in its expressionless stare. At times the conflict is one of motion. The busy, trivial actions and chatter of the out-of-focus courtiers are set against the slow, meditative walk of Hamlet during his first soliloquy. Fortinbras's army, courageously marching off to fight for a patch of ground not worth farming, is shown moving in two directions at the same time, suggesting perhaps the equivocal value of the enterprise.

Associational cut: Laertes mad to Ophelia mad

The entire opening of the film, in fact, is composed of images of conflict central to the play. Order and fixity versus change, Hamlet's grief and remembrance versus Gertrude's vanity and overhasty marriage—these are captured in sounds, symbols, and motion. Shakespeare opens *Hamlet* with nervous soldiers peering out from the ramparts into the darkness; Kozintsev opens it with a tolling bell (remembrance) and the rhythmic sound of the sea (oblivion). Against a wall of rock we see a brightly burning torch. The rock is immoveable, grey, lifeless—the medium out of which man carves fortresses, crosses, coats of arms, and tombs in an effort to transcend time. Before this ironic background is set the flaming torch, connoting life, passion, rebellion, self-knowledge. It is seemingly in endless motion, yet we know it eventually must consume itself while the rock will remain. The second image is the shadow of the fortress on the sea—an illusion of stasis and solidity superimposed upon endless flux. (Later, Hamlet's shadow against a wall may imply character itself is an illusion.) Through the shadow fortress sweep the waves, connoting ceaseless change, madness, death, forces beyond the control and even the imagination of man. Claudius, like Hamlet, wishes to resist change, to make something that will stand against the ravages of time. His guards, fortifications, council of state, self-portraits, tapestries, ceremonies, and orations are all part of his illusion, shared by the courtiers, that a king can tyrannize time. The Danes fear Hamlet because he represents the threat of cataclysmic change. By the end of the play, the forces of change have swept through the court, leaving Laertes, Polonius, Gertrude, Claudius, Ophelia, and Hamlet dead.

Kozintsev, following Eisenstein, has said "the complex unity of an image is revealed only in the clash of its various features."[8] Elsinore's tapestries and the fortress itself illustrate this complex imagery. By contrasting the dead generations with the living, they help develop the theme of "mortality,"[9] but are by no means limited to this theme. The tapestries furnish warmth and provide cosmetics for the brutal fortress and thus are part of the "seeming" which disgusts Hamlet. They are both a scenic backdrop for and a comment upon the "acts" of the Danish courtiers. Figures in the hangings are artificial, lifeless, distorted, two-dimensional like Claudius's followers. Images of hunting and military conquest, important in the play, are set against flowery backgrounds and arranged in patterns. In these large and numerous tapestries, the individual is overwhelmed by the masses, the larger pattern. Literally and figuratively, they are history, the figures being the shadows of past courtiers, perhaps evoking the heroic, chivalric past of King Hamlet and King Fortinbras, perhaps serving as emblems of the vanity of ambition.

Against artifice, courtly society, and history stands Hamlet, who rebels against lifeless poses and demands that in life as in plays man suit the action to the word, the word to the action. He resists categories and fights heroically against necessity, refusing to be an "instrument" to be played upon by live fathers or dead. Hamlet delays, steps back to contemplate the implications of custom, habit, and duty, becomes the satirist and parodist who thrusts light where it is not wanted, disrupts, provokes, reveals. By becoming aware with Hamlet of the traps awaiting those who would examine the motives and meaning of their actions, by struggling to know, we share his intimations of immortality.

Tapestry figures: Gertrude in public and private

In contrast, Gertrude looks but does not see, like the tapestry figures. The development of her character is made clear by a shot in her bedroom as Hamlet enters—as she stands near the hangings, her dark silhouette makes it seem that she has been cut loose and lifted out of their two-dimensional world. And indeed this is precisely what Hamlet has come to do—to make her self-conscious, to jar her loose and force her into a three-dimensional existence by confronting her simultaneously with the past and the present in the form of the portraits.

Hamlet's victory over the tapestries is short-lived, for they help to destroy him by veiling reality. When Hamlet stabs recklessly through the royal figures on the arras, he is attempting to cut himself loose from time and fate. But as with Macbeth, struggling against fate only enmeshes him further. He kills not Claudius but Ophelia's father, and as Polonius falls, pulling the curtain down with him, the lifeless figures multiply. Behind stand Gertrude's dress forms, mute witnesses to the murder. As Hamlet lugs the guts into the neighboring room, his insane laugh filters through the hangings, which billlow in the wind and take on hideous life. Even Ophelia is linked with the tapestries. Her room is decorated with hangings, and she is often occupied with stitching patterns. In her lyrical madness she seems to escape the restraints and ugliness of the court, but lying dead in the stream she has become once more a solitary, two-dimensional figure.

Stage directors have for centuries followed Hamlet's cue and made Denmark a prison. Kozintsev's massive fortress, drawbridge, portcullis, and moat, the huge staircases, corridors, and walls serve to dwarf people and close them in. "There are doors the better to eavesdrop behind, windows the better to spy from. . . . Every sound gives birth to echoes, repercussions, whispers, rustling."[10] Guards, courtiers, and spies shadow Hamlet. As in Olivier's film, sunshine and growing things cannot penetrate the high walls. Yet, Kozintsev felt that a certain amount of luxury in the castle was also important, for the sickness of Denmark is rather in the expediency, deceits, and hollowness of modern civilization than in the primitive struggles depicted in Welles's *Macbeth* or Brook's *King Lear*. The castle is given a history, showing its evolution from the primitive to the modern. The Medieval style includes the massive fortress, armor, Laertes's family sword, and the stone faces, friezes, and coats of arms. The Renaissance style includes the frescoes, tapestries, maps, books, and sextant. The ugly Modern style is dominated by Claudius's garish trappings—the gilded goblets and lions, smiling statues and portraits.

From the outside the castle is Kafkaesque—seen in fragments only, obscured in the fog, too large and complicated to be taken in all at once (again Olivier's influence is felt). Unable to comprehend the whole, individuals either leave it, as does Laertes, or make over little corners of it in their own image. Polonius has his little throne room in which he can play the petty Claudius (the king's portrait hangs on the wall) and lord it over his servants and children. Pale, blonde Ophelia escapes to her room, fancifully decorated with tapestries depicting flowers, peacocks, and unicorns. Gertrude has in her bedroom her gorgeous dresses and the bed where she can indulge her sensuous nature with Claudius. Hamlet, the student from Wittenberg, has a room which reflects his interests in learning, art, and exploration: books, a sextant, maps, a model ship, a bust resembling Ophelia. Most prominent, however, is a fresco showing Apollo embracing Daphne just as she is metamorphosed into a tree—a reminder of the inconstancy Hamlet finds in Gertrude and Ophelia, and an apt parable of unattainable permanence, beauty, and truth.

In this film the characters are never purely good or evil. They are people with good qualities which have been corrupted by lust, ambition, hate, timidity. Hence they are shown not in stasis but in conflict. When Gertrude vows to be true to Hamlet in the closet scene, the shot casts her strength and loyalty into question—she walks to her bed, leans against the post and stares at it, seems surrounded by the canopy. Even her final gesture as she drinks the poisoned wine despite Claudius's warning is ambivalent. Laertes seems to be all action and firm intent as he seeks revenge for his father's death, but the momentum of his rush through the doors and armed guards is frittered away in a pitiful anticlimax. His paralysis before Claudius is born, not like Hamlet's out of disgust, a keen awareness of the cost to the revenger of revenge, the mixed nature of his own motives, or the problem of the meaning of an act, but out of sheer surprise at the courage and show of innocence of his intended victim. The more he becomes Claudius's figurative loyal son, the more depraved he becomes; the more he strives to recoup his honor, the less he has.

Ophelia in Denmark is a living paradox—supple and young, yet dancing like a puppet to a tune whose rhythm is out of joint, played on a harpsichord with the hesitant irregular pace of the novice. She is innocent and well-meaning, yet easily manipulated by Hamlet and Hamlet's enemies, angelic and girlish in madness, a saint among barbarians, yet paradoxically aged, bawdy, and shrunken as she sings ballads, runs stiffly under the stairs like an old woman recalling games of hide-and-seek, and distributes dead twigs to hatchet-faced soldiers. Claudius is viewed as "a perverted unity of something heavy, coarsely powerful, bullish, and at other moments affectedly refined."[11] His conscience stirred by Hamlet's grotesquely stylized parody of the murder of his brother, he, like Gertrude, is driven toward self-awareness, but his strength damns him utterly and he obliterates the subtly distorted image of his face in a mirror by splashing wine on it. In this film of divided characters, even the ghost has a dual nature: under the impersonal, frightening, godlike iron mask one catches glimpses of the suffering eyes of the betrayed man within.

The most divided character is, of course, Hamlet himself. The director is constantly at pains to show him from a double perspective—the inner and the outer. "The close shot catches the barely perceptible spiritual movement, while the general view shows the movement of historical time."[12] Visually the Prince is portrayed as torn between conflicting passions, values, and ideas. When he appears in Ophelia's bedchamber, he presses her into the bedcurtain and draws her toward him with one hand and shades his eyes with the other as he peers into her eyes as though she were miles away. As he viciously pins her against a railing in the "nunnery" scene, he is at once angry, disgusted by her and attracted to her. Hamlet is both mad and feigning madness. His wildly discontinuous behavior at times seems carefully orchestrated. But his addiction to conflicting rhythms and discordant music as he beats a drum maddeningly against the rhythm of the background music or calls for deafening lunatic flute music to drown out frantic Rosencrantz and Guildenstern, and his demonic laugh as he drags away Polonius's body or lies on the back of one of Claudius's gilded lions as he is hunted for the crime, show that he is being pulled to pieces, drowning in a maelstrom of "show," plotting, guilt, hate, and love.

Hamlet divided

From the moment Horatio tells him of the ghost, Hamlet is in conflict with himself. He wanders into the council chamber, sits at the table, and stares at the two empty chairs of state at the other end. The shot is framed so as to divide his head between opposites—the divine Edenic royal pair he remembers from the past, and the rulers of the corrupt, empty present; amoral, aggressive, "male" action, and moral passive, "female" contemplation; love/hate for his fathers and love/hate for his mother. In the "To be or not to be" soliloquy, Hamlet stands at the dividing point between the hewn stones of the fortress and the natural rocks and the sea. If he returns to the castle, he reaffirms his commitment to life, social action, history, purpose, sanity. If he elects annihilation, he negates civilization, chooses freedom over commitment, personal integrity over duty, madness over Claudius's order and Polonius's sleazy reasonableness. Hamlet chooses, and as he slowly ascends the stairs we notice that they have been worn by centuries of traffic. He has not been the only one to make such a choice. It is, in fact, the essential human choice.

We often see Hamlet on the "shore," on the border between the known and the unknown, what is built or controlled by man and what is not. Like the sentries on the ramparts at the beginning of the play (the scene is omitted in the film), he is on the "windy edge of ordinary time,"[13] perched between life and the grave in the graveyard scene, the play world and the real world as he greets the players from the battlements, between the land and the uncharted seas (recall his navigational instruments) as he contemplates suicide, between the land and the sky as he watches the flight of the seagull symbolizing Ophelia's soul ("what should such fellows as I do crawling between earth and heaven?"). It is from the infinite "out there," which is also the past and Hamlet's "prophetic soul," that the ghost speaks. Like Shakespeare's other tragic heroes, Hamlet is a surrogate figure who tests the limits of human experience, a hero held in awe because he is destroyed while trying to reach out for something more than the Polonius world.

In Olivier's film, the complexity of the central character grows primarily out of his performance. The *context* of that performance, on the other hand, constitutes for many viewers an unfortunate narrowing of that complexity. In Kozintsev's film, the fragmented and conflict-ridden personality grows from within as Smoktunovsky brilliantly shifts from sanity to insanity, introspection to action, hate to love, but it is also captured in scenes in which the perspectives are confused, the concepts paradoxical. In Hamlet's first encounter with the ghost, we expect that it will be Hamlet who will move below in the foreground and the ghost who will be high up and distant, but rather it is Hamlet who appears and disappears against the sky in the high, distant archways, while the glinting armor and flowing cape of the ghost move in slow motion below. Identity in name and blood becomes a visual equation.

The Pirandellian confusions of art and life in *Hamlet* become a visual theme in the film. When Hamlet sits on the players' prop wagon, the initial head-on shot is reversed: art framed by life is turned inside

One stage King and Queen mirrors the other

out and becomes life framed by art. Hamlet shrieks and we cut to the waves pounding on the shore as the pressure on him takes him to the edge of madness. In the play scene, there is not one stage but two, and Hamlet watches them both. Each Player King and Player Queen observes and plays to the other. The most poignant moments in the film come when the characters are unable to see themselves in each other. In the "nunnery" scene, Hamlet and Ophelia look at each other through the bars of a railing (later Gertrude will take Hamlet's place), each seeing the other as a prisoner: he by madness, she by ignorance and the authority and values of Polonius. Both are right, but only because they lack faith in each other. They condemn themselves to be right. Ultimately the most important difference between the 1948 and the 1964 films is one of point of view. Olivier plays Hamlet and sees everything through his eyes and in terms of his personality. Kozintsev directs Hamlet and sees him as part of a larger pattern.

In keeping with the contradictoriness of both Hamlet and the larger pattern, the conclusion of the film blends heroism and irony. For Hamlet and for Denmark it is both a victory and a defeat. Hamlet's fulfilling his father's command, his strapping on the uniform of combat to triumph over Laertes in the King's deadly play and his eventual killing of his murderous uncle to the thunderous ghost theme, is a triumph over despair and inaction. But because the emphasis throughout has been on Hamlet's integrity, his refusal to act mindlessly, the fatal moment when he takes arms against a sea of troubles also represents a narrowing, a reduction in stature, a compromise. Throughout the film one feels that Smoktunovsky's Hamlet is finer than the world he lives in. He is a man whose greatness is much more than the sum of his words and acts, which can never "denote him truly." And this is confirmed in his death. Unlike so many stage and film Hamlets, he does not sit on the throne to become King as he dies; he rejects the office and Elsinore. In keeping with the brilliant earlier scene in which he walks slowly around the room staring in contempt at Claudius's ministers, who are furred pompous toadies, thinking to himself what it is worth to rule such men, wounded Hamlet now leaves, aided by his friend Horatio. He walks outside to die against the rocks overlooking the sea. In this transcendent moment, words, which he has throughout found treacherous, are inadequate. No one speaks from the death of Claudius as he runs howling past billowing tapestries to Hamlet's "the rest is silence." Finally, he is beyond "words, words, words."

The corresponding defeat is that the world has not been transformed by Hamlet's sacrifice. Ironically, Hamlet dies in the posture of the maimed, one-armed cross so prominent in the graveyard scene. Whether this suggests that his attempt to assert Christian values undermined by Claudius has failed, that his sacrifice falls short of Christ's because he has become a murderer, or perhaps that the insights Hamlet has had are the ones that will ultimately destroy Christianity in the modern world, his posture suggests a Fall—a theme sounded earlier in the ghost's description of the murder and in the tapestry behind Ophelia's broken-doll dance. After Hamlet dies, the camera pans to the weathered layers of ancient rock and holds there for a time until we hear the "music" of Fortinbras: the clank of armor and weapons, the rumble of wheels and boots on the stone. The enigmatic enemy from without, the other revenging son, enters and takes over without a blow. Is he a Claudius-like conqueror, or a worldly saviour come to restore health to Denmark? Whatever his arrival portends, it is clear that his triumph is not Hamlet's. Hamlet's knowledge is not tarnsferred to the new king. Fortinbras acts to restore order and to honor the dead hero Hamlet, yet he also negates what Hamlet stood for. In giving

The motif of the maimed cross

him the rites of a soldier, the new king forces Hamlet into an image of Fortinbras, or perhaps of their warlike chivalric fathers. When Hamlet is carried to a "stage" in a long and solemn procession, he becomes a part of the court ceremony, the "show" he had sought to destroy while he was alive. The "seeming" goes on and the world is unredeemed.

In the end, the opening images return—sea and fortress shadow, fire and rock—completing a cyclical motif which includes the huge wheel which raises the drawbridge, and the grim cycle of the clock where Bishop, King, Queen, and Knight are followed in an endless round by the old antic Death. Hamlet's longing for human constancy, which would free man from flux and the whims of time, and Claudius's desire for freedom from conscience and a tyrannical rule over history are frustrated. The conflicts embodied in these poetic images remain. There is no escaping history, no escaping time.[14]

# 16

# *King Lear*: Peter Brook and

# Grigori Kozintsev

A S THE WESTERN WORLD HAS GROWN OLDER, LITERALLY AND figuratively, *King Lear* has replaced *Hamlet* in our esteem as Shakespeare's greatest tragedy. Simone de Beauvoir reminds us in her ferocious assault on our treatment of the aged that *"King Lear* is the only great work, apart from *Oedipus at Colonus,* in which the hero is an old man."[1] Lear and Gloucester represent millions of old people—guilt-ridden parents, dethroned monarchs, powerless, lonely outcasts cursed with clear sight and haunted by memories, suffering failing powers, faced with poverty and imminent death. The story of these two old men is a distillation of the experience of growing old— the desperate need for affection and dignity, the panic and despair, the inevitable feelings of neglect and ingratitude as the world goes on without them. On a more abstract plane, our senescent culture is itself not unlike Shakespeare's aging patriarch, characterized by moral blindness and hardening of the institutional arteries, dangerously armed with a hundred knights. Increasingly, the West, as it loses its hold on underdeveloped countries and its faith in faith and ideologies, and is stung into introspection by grotesque, violent events (senseless wars, manmade famines, terrorism and torture), sees itself in Lear and Gloucester as they journey through darkness and madness, rage against cruel offspring and indifferent skies, and are overwhelmed with a sense of loss. No wonder that sensitive observers, seeing on the horizon food and energy shortages, disasters nuclear or ecological, and the masses seeking security in totalitarian forms of government and indulging in various forms of escapism, discern in Shakespeare's tragedy both "the promised end or image of that horror" and a plea for pity and clear sight.

There are two *King Lear*s. One depicts an irremediable crack in nature, an apocalyptic decline and fall of an archetypal kingdom and its rulers. It is a story of jealousy and lust for power eating away at the bonds of love between parents and children, of blindness and vanity, of men preying on each other "like monsters of the deep." It contains enough physical violence to disturb both the strictures of classical tragedy and the decorum of the modern censor, but like modern works it also assaults audiences with mental cruelty as fierce people humiliate, curse, and mock one another, slash each other with sadistic fervor. As Lear's kingdom is convulsed by evil, man is transformed. When the good are banished or hunted, masters become monstrous mad children, and servants sleazy rodents. Nature, if not an amoral force, seems allied with aggression and brutality. Justice is absent as the play shows Nature shuddering in a nihilist orgasm, evil destroying both itself and the good, leaving behind devastation, emptiness, and men too scarred and stunned to go on living. Lear's pain is generalized, as Christian humanist values—forgiveness, humility, compassion—shatter against his anguished query, "Why should a dog, a horse, a rat have life, / And thou no breath at all?" Civilization is left in ruins. This is Peter Brook's *King Lear*—a bleak existential tale of meaningless violence in a cold, empty universe.

The other *King Lear* is the story of man's journey from unfeeling ignorance to self-knowledge and pity. It is a tale of losing oneself to find oneself, of learning stoic endurance and the nature of reality as the trappings of civilization are stripped away. Despite massive suffering and acts of cruelty, we witness a hopeful progress from crassness, materialism, and willful tyranny ("there was good sport at his making," "nothing will come of nothing," "out of my sight") to fundamental questioning ("who is it that can tell me who I am?" "Is man no more than this?" "Handy dandy, which is the justice and which is the thief?") to ever-deepening understanding ("O I have ta'en too little care of this," "he childed as I fathered," "I stumbled when I saw," "ripeness is all"). If the families of Lear and Gloucester make terrible sacrifices for this knowledge, the man left to rule—Lear's godson and alter ego, Edgar—is no power-hungry tyrant but "a most poor man, made tame to fortune's blows, / Who by the art of known and feeling sorrows, / Am pregnant to good pity," a man who urges at the end what could not be said at the beginning, that we "speak what we feel and not what we ought to say." This is Grigori Kozintsev's *Lear*: a Christian-Marxist story of redemption and social renewal.

Though there is tenderness in Brook's film, and cruelty in Kozintsev's, in overall emphasis these two works taken together constitute a dialectic about Shakespeare's tragedy. Each tells important truths about life and about the play. More clearly than any other pair of Shakespeare films, they suggest that a partial view is not always a false one, that it is impossible to exhaust all of a great script's possibilities in a single performance.

Peter Brook's stark, elliptical *Lear* begins in silence as under the credits the camera pans slowly over the rugged still faces of men dressed in animal skins. No establishing shot tells us where they are; nothing tells us what they are waiting for. (Later we learn that they are Lear's hundred knights.) Inside a dark, crude throne room Lear's court sits in a rigid semicircle before his coffinlike throne. Shakespeare's opening, the superficial chatter between Gloucester and Kent and brief glimpse of Edmund, has been stripped away. The door slams shut with ominous finality, and Lear breaks the oppressive stillness with a single word, which, being isolated is both negation ("no") and command ("know"), encompasses the themes of "nothing" and knowledge.[2] In an emotionless, gravel voice, Paul Scofield's grizzled Lear slowly unfolds his ritual transfer of power to the young. Like Gloucester's hardened view of his bastard son Edmund and Goneril's moribund, childless marriage to Albany, Lear's relations with his daughters are cold, formal. Indeed his whole kingdom seems to have reached dead center. Only cruel physic can awaken and restore it. Cordelia administers the first shock, shattering the symmetry of Lear's ceremony, stinging him into life. Kent and France echo her face to face confrontation with Lear, goad him until he stirs. His long, painful awakening begins as he throws open the door and rushes angrily out into the light. (The movement of the film as a whole is also from darkness to pitiless white light.)

Kozintsev provides a very different context for Lear's rejection of Cordelia. After simple credits, set against a background of coarse cloth to the fool's melancholy music, we see peasants journeying over rocky terrain. A father wheels a sleeping child in a barrow while the mother tends to it—a gentle assertion of an important theme. Ancient carvings on the rocks, together with the harmony of the travellers' shapes with

"Know ..." (Brook)

the boulders against the horizon, suggest the timelessness of the journey. One of the anonymous travellers pauses, raises a curved horn to his lips, and blows a piercing note which echoes in the distance—like *Lear* itself, it is both a call by an artist for us to go on and a gesture of fierce pride signalling man's presence in an inhospitable universe. The groups of travellers become larger until they cover the hillsides like ants. Having gathered, they wait in silence before the massive walls of Lear's castle. Brook's naked confrontations of will are isolated against blank or blurred backgrounds, an empty wasteland. Kozintsev shows us a wasteland peopled, masses of subjects who have suffered from Lear's tyranny, blindness, and neglect, who after his rash, fatal act are ravaged by the civil war and must rebuild when it is over.

Inside, momentum continues to build. Courtiers arrive and gather, not in some vast room of state but in a domestic room with a hearth. Then, for the first time, all movement ceases. The king's entrance is a puzzling anticlimax. Laughter and the jingle of bells from behind the door break the silence. As the childlike waif of a king with a shock of white hair enters, without sword or emblem of office, the fool suggests deception, holds a mask before Lear's eyes. Lear cues a councillor, and as the man reads the proclamation, warms himself by

Lear's daughters (Kozintsev *King Lear*) Rosa Madell Film Library

the fire, plays with the fool, whom he harbors symbolically inside his cloak, and listens with satisfaction. Unlike Scofield's intentional and brutal subjugation of wills, here Lear's love-test seems on the surface an old man's whim, a foolish antic. But hints of gnawing need beneath and the incongruity of his playfulness with Goneril and Regan's desperate fear as they blurt out extravagant praises and rush to kneel and kiss his hands reveal hunger and ruthlessness beneath the childlike mask. It is the beauty and warmth of Cordelia's face—a face as different from her sisters' faces as her light gown is from their dark ones—which exposes the wrongness of what Lear has done. He has turned an intimate family gathering before the hearth into a state occasion for proclamations of loyalty. Like Melville's Billy Budd, Cordelia cannot violate her nature, and without warning the real climax of the scene comes. He curses Cordelia, tears the map giving her portion to her sisters, rages against Kent and France, and to Shostakovich's crescendo of music, scales the battlements. The wizened, childish old man becomes a titan silhouetted high against a clouding sky as he shouts her banishment to the awed peasants below.

In choosing and articulating subsequent scenes, each director pursues the logic of his view of the play, so that by noting major instances of shaping the script, we can see their interpretative visions more clearly. To Brook, for example, Edgar's deception of despairing Gloucester is a pivotal scene which, in accordance with Jan Kott's description, is an absurdist pantomime akin to Beckett's *Acts Without Words* providing a grotesquely comic emblem of Lear's fall.[3] The director duplicates in cinematic terms Shakespeare's blend of blatant stage artifice and imaginative reality. In the play the image of actors on a flat stage has superimposed upon it the dizzying heights conjured up by Edgar's splendid word-painting (Poor Tom-Edgar-Actor is himself a super-imposition). In Brook's film, a long shot shows Edgar and Gloucester struggling along a flat plain. But then, in a series of tight, low-angle close-ups, Edgar and Gloucester seem to climb. The sound of the waves in the distance accords with Edgar's description, and following film convention it makes us imagine an off-screen reality. Set on "the extremest verge," Gloucester bids farewell to Poor Tom, and his final speech of despair is filmed in low-angle close-up—one of the most savagely beautiful shots of a human face ever put on film. As he falls forward, however, Brook jolts us with an illusion-shattering cut to an extreme overhead long shot. From this godlike perspective, we watch a tiny old man take a silent pratfall on a barren stretch of sand. Edgar rushes to his side, and in one of those disjunctions so frequent in the structurally parallel storm scene, the screen is suddenly filled with what seems to be a vortex or a huge inscrutable eye. When the camera zooms back, our disorientation, which parallels Gloucester's, is resolved as we see that it is a knot in a piece of driftwood (a microcosm, not a macrocosm) upon which this piece of human flotsam rests his head. In a kaleidoscopic series of voices, Edgar repeats the act of Cordelia and jars his father back to life. Thus, in emotion, theme, and style, this expressionist, absurd, tumbling off the imagined edge of the world is for Brook an epiphany of the *Lear* experience. In Kozintsev's film, on the other hand, this scene was cut. Gloucester's climactic scene comes later, and depicts his actual death. Seized by a stroke as he staggers with Poor Tom across a parched, cracked plain, he feels Edgar's face before he dies and experiences a terrible moment of revelation: his rash cruelty has been met with compassion, the mad beggar is his son. In keeping with the Russian's view of *King Lear*, absurdist pantomime has been replaced by a scene of pathos and redemption.

Brook warily avoids sentimentality in order to heighten the bleakness of the tale and the power of the scenes between Lear and Cordelia and

Lear and Gloucester. Thus he totally eliminates Edmund's reformation and attempt to save the lives of Lear and Cordelia. Edmund displays not compassion but satanic relish in the grim irony that he should be killed by his brother and that, in the punning sense of "death," he and the two jealous, lustful sisters "marry in an instant." In contrast, Kozintsev follows Shakespeare, suggesting the Christian sense of the underlying goodness in even the worst of men. Edmund is mortally wounded not in the head, the seat of the intellect, but is sliced across the stomach. As he writhes in a fetal position, pitifully trying to hide behind his circular shield, his perception that "the wheel has come full circle" leads to a rebirth which is marked by massive orchestral chords. The more terrible Shakespearean irony is preserved: redemption comes too late. Lear's howls rend the air.

In most great films there is one scene whose beauty and power etches itself on the memory and which in time comes to stand for the whole. In the English film, this scene is Lear's conversation with Gloucester on the beach. The cold ferocity and jagged expressionism of the rest of the film heighten the simplicity, serenity, and almost unbearable pathos as blind subject meets mad king on a barren stretch of sand. Its truth to Shakespeare's blend of the general ("we came crying hither") with the particular (Lear's boots) and its emotional power place the scene near the pinnacle of the artistry of Shakespeare on film. By contrast the Russian's central scene is the capture of Lear and Cordelia, where good triumphs over evil even when about to be destroyed by it,

> goodness encircled by iron, weapons of murder—people gripped by mania for destruction, by hatred. And these same soldiers, having seen these two defenceless people—an old man and a young woman—having heard their voices, fall silent. The prisoners, with bound hands, walk past the ranks of men armed to the teeth, wicked men—like conquerors. This is the beginning of Edmund's defeat.[4]

Edmund's uncomprehending hatred of the beautiful love between father and daughter, which leads him to panic, order them to be executed, and to harangue his men until they cry "Edmund! Edmund!" is in this film the greatest confirmation of the power of this love. Our memory of this luminous moment never fades; it overrides the suffering at the end.

The conclusion of Brook's *King Lear* sums up its absurdist perspec-

Gloucester and Lear on the beach
(Brook)

Contrasting central scenes

The capture of Lear and Cordelia
(Kozintsev) Rosa Madell Film Library

tive perfectly. From the darkness of the opening we have arrived on a gravel beach bathed in brutal white light. As Lear kneels with Cordelia's body, he is surrounded by nothingness. His agonizing slow-motion fall backward—intercut with the remaining characters' determination that Edgar will rule—is a condensed image of the play's action, and when he disappears from the frame, only a blank white screen remains. Both characters and audience have attained sight at a terrible cost, but "sight that once acquired looks only into a void."[5] The feeling at the end is of unrelieved emptiness and hopelessness. The silence seems final. In Kozintsev's view, however, "*King Lear* is not only 'Theatre of Cruelty' but also 'Theatre of Mercy.' "[6] The end is also a beginning. Cordelia will come no more. Lear dies in agony and despair after rediscovering and then losing the treasure of his life. And the cruelty will go on—when the bodies of Lear's family are borne by soldiers in procession, one soldier brutally kicks aside the fool as he sits amidst the rubble playing his melancholy pipe. But signs of renewal are unmistakable. The water associated with Cordelia throughout the film flows through the frame as the camera zooms past the rope in the arch where she was sacrificed. Peasants sift through the charred ruins and prepare to build again. The memory of the beautiful scene between

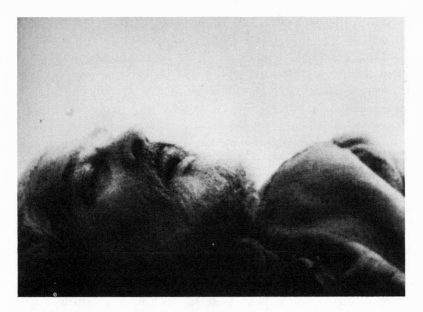

Lear's head falls from the frame (Brook)

Lear and Cordelia remains. Above all there is the final gesture of Lear's godson, Edgar. For the first time in the film, a character breaks the fourth-wall convention. Standing among the smouldering ruins, he stares directly at us, expressing helplessness and sorrow, but also angrily accusing us of not feeling enough, of complicity in blindness and violence, before walking out of the frame to resume his journey. The kingdom has a leader once again, but one, unlike Lear at the beginning, "pregnant with good pity, and made tame to fortune's blows."

Stylistically these two films offer further interesting contrasts. A Hollywood showman's nightmare, Brook's is a raw ascetic *Lear* stripped to "nothing"—a polar opposite of Welles's early, strong compositions, Olivier's painterly tableaux, and Zeffirelli's operatic realism. The film uses Brechtian titles and has the crude surfaces of an early silent film, its dim or washed-out, grainy black and white images almost never being composed for beauty. Close-ups and shallow depth of field give the film a solipsistic feel as brutal faces, often fragmented by the frame, confront one another or stare into the camera. The poetry has been cut to the bone (so anxious was Brook to avoid a dead museum piece that he once considered using a text "translated," as if a foreign classic, by Ted Hughes).[7] Far from traditional theatrical emoting and eloquent singing of the lines, the actors flatten and understate everything, speak in slow, gruff whispers. Their deliveries force each word to strike percussively and then reverberate. Apart from electronic sounds in the storm scene and the fool's discordant songs, the film is devoid of music, its oppressive silences broken only by human voices, the rattle of wooden carriage wheels, whinneying horses, the howling of wind, the crackling of fire. Structurally it is a severely compressed film full of harsh visual and aural transitions. More than one reviewer noted its "disjointed and staccato quality, elliptic camerawork, and violent, mannerist cutting."[8] So much of Shakespeare's exposition is stripped away, so many of the climaxes are sudden violent paroxysms, and so lean is the subplot, that the "naive" spectator may well become lost.

Brook breaks further with popular forms by using Godardian cinematic alienation. This is especially true in the subjective storm scene where almost every realist convention is overturned. It has fractured continuity, violations of screen direction (Lear seems to have a dialogue with himself), and flashing black and white frames. It has distorted images, lightning superimpositions often charged with thematic import (the fool's face upon Lear's, Edgar in close-up upon Edgar in long-shot), and surreal appearances by Lear's daughters. But such alienating techniques are used elsewhere as well, as in the zoom-fades (reminiscent of Welles's *Macbeth*) as Kent disguises himself, the blurred vision in blind Gloucester's scenes, and Lear's hallucinatory visions and dying fall at the end. Flashy and self-conscious in some ways, Brook's *Lear* is in other ways minimalist art, denying itself the bread and butter of many Shakespeare films—decorative spectacle. Though the battle scene in Kozintsev's *Lear* is carefully controlled through point of view, the thematic emphasis upon the suffering masses demands a larger tapestry. But in Brook's character-centered film the battle is not seen but *heard* off-frame as we study out-of-focus images of Gloucester's face. Similarly the duel in the Russian film is a prolonged, exciting contest, while in the English film it is a slow, silent stalking by Edgar of his prey at dawn, circled by soldiers ("the wheel comes full circle"), and a sudden, single blow with an axe.

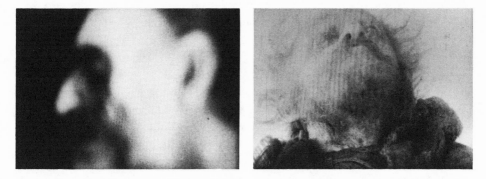

Raw beauty in the shots of blind Gloucester (Brook)

To sum up, Brook's is a cruel *Lear* in two senses of the word. It assaults us with physical cruelty (Kent set in the stocks barefoot in the cold, Edgar placing snow to his chest declaring "Edgar . . . I . . . nothing . . . am," Gloucester's eyes gouged out by casual Cornwall in a butcher-shop atmosphere, Cornwall stabbed and his assailant bludgeoned to death by Regan, Lear and the fool lashed by wind and rain, Oswald speared like a pig, Edmund axed in the head, Goneril and Regan's heads smashed on rocks, Cordelia hung). But it is also cruel in Artaud's intellectual and aesthetic sense, that is, characterized by "rigor, implacable intention and decision, irreversible and absolute determination."[9]

Kozintsev's is a much more romantic film. Scofield's Lear is

> a hard-bitten, despot-king used to ordering people about, getting things done, no nonsense, customarily feeding on flattery and fear. A thorny figure of rigid, cold arrogance, weary, old—but rock-hard, grizzled grey, ramrod straight. . . . This is a hard man to live with: he humiliates his family, makes enemies of his children, wades into folly with a deliberation that must evoke quite a different retribution than that of the titan who stoops to error.[10]

Yuri Jarvet's Lear, equally distant from the archetypal titan embodied in stage tradition by Tomasso Salvini, is a weaker, more pathetic figure whose frailty heightens the incongruity and injustice of the suffering heaped upon him. Though with his knights and fool he comically disrupts Goneril's pretensions to delicate table manners, this Lear is not the ruffian who overturns tables and looses his men to destroy Goneril's dining hall, or blisters his daughters face to face with curses. His violent responses are more inner ones. Though in each film the camera broods over sterile, metaphoric landscapes, Brook's world is the more primitive one, showing life unadorned with art, men huddling in the dark before fires. His vision of Shakespeare's prehistorical Britain sets the fable "so very far in the past that it could be some post-neutron bomb, post-Christian future."[11] Kozintsev's film is timeless in a different sense—a superimposition (as in *Hamlet*) of the Christian middle ages and the predatory renaissance, the furs worn by the characters stressing not only the kinship of men and animals but the pampered isolation of the rich from the poor.

Like the elaborate castle, Shostakovich's orchestral score pushes the film toward Russian romantic epic, giving it a slightly warmer, more lyrical tone. Dramatic climaxes are punctuated by huge orchestral climaxes, transitions are provided by brooding melancholy themes, and the marvellously expressive landscapes are saturated with musical feeling. The music is structurally important, giving the film a denser, more ornate texture. Lear's royal trumpets contrast with the peasant's shrill horn; the death of Cornwall is linked with the death of Edmund. What at first seems the howling of the wind as Lear confronts Goneril and Regan before the storm grows louder is revealed to be a rising and falling six-note melodic phrase (soprano voice?) which recurs and blends with staccato orchestral chords, drum rolls, and sustained piercing string notes to express Lear's rising madness. Above all, Kozintsev's film seems romantic because it builds toward big dramatic moments. In an English stage production which seems to have influenced Kozintsev, the death of Cornwall was a significant climactic moment. A reviewer recorded,

> Mortally wounded, terror and pain in voice and gesture, Cornwall turned to his wife: "Regan, I bleed apace. Give me your arm." Ignoring him, almost disdainfully, she swept past to the downstage exit. He staggered back, groping for support; no one stirred to help him. Open-mouthed, staring eyes, death gripping his heart, he faced the dawning horror of retribution as the jungle law of each for himself caught up on him and he knew himself abandoned even by his wife.[12]

Kozintsev's treatment is even more brutal and animalistic. Regan backs away but stays to watch as Cornwall stares in disbelief, is struck by recognition, and falls. In an elaboration of the theme of the hunt, she goes from room to room searching for Edmund. When she finds him, she savagely rips off his coat and embraces him. Cut to Cornwall's body being laid out on a table. Regan, still excited by her coupling with Edmund, approaches, bends, and passionately kisses the corpse open-mouthed as if to both feed on him and thank him for her freedom.

In the imaging of character and theme by Brook and Kozintsev one can see even more clearly different sensibilities at work. Both artists visualize Shakespeare's animal imagery through costume, by surrounding the characters with animals—dogs, sheep, drowned rats, panicked or dead horses, wild boars—and by underscoring the motif of the hunt as humans are repeatedly pursued like prey. Both bare the force of Shakespeare's pervasive theme of hunger (cries for dinner, craving for love, lust for power)—Brook especially dwelling upon the "tension between imperious surface icily controlled and outraged psychic vulnerability and need driving through it on all sides."[13] In other respects, however, the English film is spare, intensely narrow, and the Russian one varied, full in expression. This is true of tone, for Kozintsev is much closer to Shakespeare in his glimpses of humor—in the fool's antics, in Edmund's mischievous throwing of a stone against the ominously clouded sky, and in the sublime moment when, taking Cordelia's men for enemy forces, surrounded Lear lamely attempts to scale a small boulder crying the hunter's cry, "Sa! Sa!" In Brook, one may connect Lear's disturbed swaying back and forth in tight close-up as he curses Goneril with Goneril's swaying and kneading her leather dress before her suicide, or follow the resonant motif of the broken egg (cracked crown, shattered eyes/globe, sterility) from the fool's punning demonstration of two empty crowns to the eggs smoothed on Gloucester's bleeding sockets, or register the overtones of Lear's gesture of reversing evolution and running back into the sea when pursued by Cordelia's soldiers, and still recognize that the Russian's themes are more numerous and explicit, his metaphoric texture denser.

Few, I think, would contest that Kozintsev's *Lear* lacks the consistently brilliant imagery of *Hamlet*, or that its music is less powerful. Still, one can recall fine and pregnant visual moments: the baroque embodiment of Gloucester's nightmare, as shadows of a barred window (opened by stealthy Edmund?) move obliquely over medieval engravings of Death while wolves howl in the distance; the camera's ironic introduction to Edmund by following Gloucester's ancestral tree upward until it comes to the top where Edgar appears but the bastard does not. As in the earlier film, water and fire form meaningful strains of imagery. In opposition to the water associated with Cordelia, the

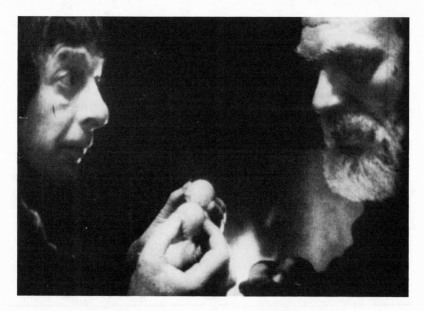

The fool presents Lear with two hollow crowns (Brook)

"envy, hatred, jealousy" behind the war are depicted as a burning flame, seen first in the domestic hearth but soon blazing from the castle walls and in the end destroying the whole kingdom.[14] Man-made emblems of authority are replaced by natural ones as on a hillside—his hair blending with long wind-blown grass—Lear gathers flowers which will serve as his crown. The sight theme, developed by Brook in blurred, fractured images and face-to-face confrontations, is elaborated with great care.

> Throughout the film eyes are prominent, as Kozintsev takes his clue from the punishment of Gloucester, and the verbal ironies of sight and insight that play around that gruesome scene—here represented by a medium shot of the impending spur. The animals throughout the film are all shot for the stolid power of their eyes. As Edmund and Edgar circle in combat, the center of gravity lies in Edgar's eyes, steady and fearless. And there is a crushing irony at the end. Lear and Cordelia are carried off dead, their eyes felicitously closed. Goneril, Regan, and Edmund are carried off with their eyes wide open.[15]

Considering their stage backgrounds, it is not surprising that both directors use theatrical means skillfully in charting human relationships and character—persons detached from one another in the beginning touch each other with tenderness or violence in the end; Lear rigid and upright in the beginning later lies on the ground digging roots or sits on the beach with Gloucester. Both too are masterful in their use of camera movement—Brook in panning slowly over Edgar's shivering naked body ("is man no more than this?") or over drowned rats ("I have ta'en too little care of this"), Kozintsev in sweeping upward movements at emotional peaks or restless tracking shots as characters pursue or are pursued. The Russian, however, more consistently generates meaning between shots through associative montage. This is true within scenes: when Lear asks for his fool and walks out of the frame, for example, the director cuts not to the fool but to disguised Kent, who, like the other good characters, is associated by Shakespeare with "folly." And it is true between scenes: in a single cut—from an extreme long-shot of Lear's train moving right to left, seeming ghostly and unreal in the distance, to a closer, more sharply focussed shot of solitary hunted Edgar moving left to right as he is about to strip himself to rags and join the tattered procession of outcasts—he implies much of the structure of *King Lear* including the parallel/contrast of Lear and his godson Edgar, conflicts of parents and children, the illusions and obliviousness of the rich and the clear sight and sufferings of the poor. Above all, Kozintsev's film makes consistently thematic use of incessant motion. In Brook's film, dead, static scenes are interspersed with Lear's driving movement from his tomblike throne to Goneril's castle, to Regan's castle, to the stormy heath, to the edge of the sea. Kozintsev, however, found *King Lear* "shot through with the rhythms of walking, marching, running. Everything is shaken from its place. Everything is in movement—the wandering beggars, the king's baggage train, the soldiers."[16] Almost every shot both moves and contains motion in this tale of an uprooted and crumbling world. In shaping the text and using the expressive means of theatre and cinema, each director succeeds in conveying not *the* truth but *his* truth about *King Lear*. In each work, the personal involvement of a talented director makes the difference between a dead artifact and a living blend of representation and personal vision.[17]

IN SEVERAL WAYS a comparison of these two recent, complementary interpretations make a fitting conclusion to an exploration of Shakespeare on film. On a purely practical level, they suggest that despite commercial and popular pressures, good film directors and actors will continue to grapple seriously and interestingly with Shakespeare's plays. On an aesthetic plane, they remind us that a good Shakespeare film is a complex blend of filmed performance, critical interpretation, and translation/re-creation in a new medium, requiring the combined resources of literary, theatrical, and cinematic criticism. They remind us that adaptation is a complex form with its own rich assortment of styles and traditions. Paul Scofield's Lear and Irene Worth's Goneril, for example, recall other great performances—Finlay as Iago, Olivier as Henry V, Richard III, and Othello, Mason, Brando, and Gielgud as Brutus, Antony, and Cassius, and Welles as Falstaff. The thoughtful opening scenes by Kozintsev and Brook recall the framing devices of *Henry V* and Zeffirelli's *Taming of the Shrew*. Brook's blend of expressionism and realism draws upon Welles's *Macbeth*, Kurosawa's *Throne of Blood*, and Hall's avant-garde *Midsummer Night's Dream* on the one hand, and evocations of Shakespeare the realist in Polanski's *Macbeth*, Burge's *Othello*, and Zeffirelli's *Romeo and Juliet* on the other. By incorporating elements of Jan Kott's "contemporary" *Lear*, Brook followed the path of Reinhardt and Dieterle, who bared the mixed tones of *A Midsummer Night's Dream*, and Olivier, who underscored the Oedipal roots of Hamlet's delay. The visualization and elaboration of themes (sight and blindness, the hunt) in these two *King Lears*, the often complex relations between word and image, light and dark, stasis and movement, recall the complex textures in works like Welles's *Othello* and Kozintsev's *Hamlet*. In the controlled use of gesture, costume, and setting, the careful shaping of speeches and scenes, and the precise camera movements and composition of images evident in almost every scene in these films we see the artistic core of adapting Shakespeare on film—the quest for significant style.

More remains to be said about Shakespeare on film, but this book is a beginning, not an ending. I choose, therefore, to close with suggestions. It seems that we have had enough defensive propaganda about the differences between literature, theatre, and film. It is time to explore the creative possibilities at their borders and to write criticism which will help us see more and see better. Shakespeareans ought to benefit much more from the fruitful confusion which results from dealing with Shakespeare in performance, and certainly it is time that teachers put films to creative use in the classroom. Artists as diverse as Jean Renoir, Joseph Losey, and Ingemar Bergman and critics such as Sergei Eisenstein and Andre Bazin have done much to break down artificial barriers between theatre and film, and it only remains for students of theatre to realize how much they have to contribute to discussions of literature and film. Film critics should broaden their horizons a bit—reassess the relations of the cinema to other narrative art forms, consider in this director- and actor-centered age the implications of the fact that *all* fiction films are performance-interpretations-adaptations of scripts requiring complex triangulation between film, script, and life. They might consider the ways in which Shakespeare's intricate dramatic structures, rich characterizations, and poetry, often in a figurative sense more "cinematic" than any film, might enrich the cinema. As a group, Shakespeare films are no more permeated with genius than any other "genre" of film. It is time to recognize, however, that many are thoughtful, imaginative works of art, interesting in themselves and as visions of Shakespeare. Should it be so surprising, after all, that the world's greatest poet-dramatist has something to offer an art obsessed with images and dramatic conflict?

# Appendix

# Credits and Outlines of the Major Films

The following are credits and descriptive outlines of all the films discussed in detail in this volume save Schaefer's distinctly minor *Macbeth*. At the head of somewhat arbitrarily divided film "scenes" are the act and scene numbers from the plays from which they were drawn. I have used the revised edition of Shakespeare's *Complete Works* by Alfred Harbage (Baltimore: Penguin, 1969), so that one may see at a glance how the filmmaker has reshaped the play. (See also the detailed lists of cuts in the notes for Hall's *Dream*, Burge and Dexter's *Othello*, and Kozintsev's *Hamlet*.) Credits and outlines of the silent films of Shakespeare are available in Robert Hamilton Ball, *Shakespeare on Silent Film* (New York: Theatre Arts, 1968), and at least partial credits of sound versions in many languages may be found in the following: Max Lippmann, ed., *Shakespeare im Film* (Wiesbaden: Saaten-Verlag, 1964); Roger Manvell, *Shakespeare and the Film* (New York: Praeger, 1971); Charles Eckert, ed., *Focus on Shakespeare Films* (Englewood Cliffs: Prentice Hall, 1972); and Peter Morris, "Shakespeare on Film," *Films in Review* 24 (March 1973), pp. 132-63. Distributors for Shakespeare films may be found in the most recent edition of James L. Limbacher's annual *Feature Films on 8mm and 16mm* (Bowker).

## A Midsummer Night's Dream

United States. Warner Brothers. 1935. Black and white. 35mm.

Directors:  Max Reinhardt, William Dieterle
Script:  Charles Kenyon and Mary McCall, Jr.

Photography:   Hal Mohr, Fred Jackman, Byron Haskin, H. F. Koenekamp
Design:   Anton Grot, Max Ree
Editor:   Ralph Dawson
Music:   Felix Mendelssohn (arranged by Erich Wolfgang Korngold)
Choreography:   Bronislava Nijinska, Nini Theilade
Sound:   Nathan Levinson

THESEUS:   Ian Hunter
HIPPOLYTA:   Verree Teasdale
PHILOSTRATE:   Hobart Cavanaugh
EGEUS:   Grant Mitchell
OBERON:   Victor Jory
TITANIA:   Anita Louise
HERMIA:   Olivia de Havilland
HELENA:   Jean Muir
LYSANDER:   Dick Powell
DEMETRIUS:   Ross Alexander
BOTTOM:   James Cagney

PUCK:   Mickey Rooney
SNOUT:   Hugh Herbert
FLUTE:   Joe E. Brown
STARVELING:   Otis Harlan
SNUG:   Dewey Robinson
QUINCE:   Frank McHugh
NINNY'S TOMB:   Arthur Treacher
MUSTARDSEED:   Billy Barty
FIRST FAIRY:   Nini Thielade
INDIAN BOY:   Kenneth Anger

1. (1.1, 1.2) Watery credits with Mendelssohn's Overture to MND. A poster announces Theseus's victory and coming wedding, offers sixpence a day to players. *The Athenian Harbor*. Fanfares and cheers. Theseus vows to wed defeated defiant Hippolyta. During the hymn "Theseus be Blest" the lovers greet or snub one another, Egeus is alarmed by Hermia's rebelliousness, and the rustics bellow off-key. Theseus and Hippolyta ride off in ornate chariot to Mendelssohn's "Wedding March." Egeus commands Hermia to marry Demetrius. Helena weeps. Quince presents the playscript to his fellows.

2. (1.1) *Theseus's Palace*. Theseus tells somber Hippolyta of his desires. They ascend their thrones and amused Theseus hears Egeus demand death for disobedient Hermia. Lysander and Hermia speak rebelliously. Theseus supports Egeus. Hermia exits weeping and Lysander plans with her to run away to the forest and marry.

3. (1.2) *Quince's Carpenter Shop*. Quince casts his play despite interruptions by giggling Snout, prima donna Bottom, Flute's munching on sunflower seeds, and a roaring contest.

4. (2.1) *Forest*. Establishing shots of trees, animals to Mendelssohn's music. Puck rises and summons his unicorn. Ominous music as fairies emerge from fog. Lighter music as fairies swirl past camera and up moon-

beams. First Fairy and Puck speak of Oberon and Titania's quarrel. Indian Boy follows fairies, frightened by Troll, joins goblin band, rescued, joined by Titania who descends down moonbeam. Threatening Oberon in black demands boy. Titania and her train flee. Oberon sends Puck after "Love-in-Idleness."

5. (2.1, 2.2) *Forest*. Oberon overhears Demetrius reject Helena and vows *he* shall pursue *her* before the night is over. Elsewhere weary Hermia and Lysander lie down to rest. Puck brings the flower to Oberon who says he will go charm Titania's eyes. Oberon sends Puck to charm Demetrius's eyes.

6. (2.2) *Titania's Bower*. Titania gathers flowers with her train. Birds sing and goblins play music as fairies sing her to sleep with Mendelssohn's lullaby. Sinister Oberon charms Titania's eyes.

7. (2.2) *Forest*. Singing Puck rides unicorn. Goblins watch as he mistakenly charms Lysander's eyes. Puck reports to Oberon who realizes the error. A bear flees weeping Helena. Lysander wakes and pursues her with love. Hermia wakes from a nightmare with relief, finds Lysander gone, has her cries mocked by Puck. Puck laughs and mocks as the lovers pursue each other.

8. (3.1) *Forest*. Goblin orchestra plays. Whistling rustics stumble into clearing and rehearse. Bottom exits, is transformed by Puck, and enters. Frightened rustics are pursued by Puck as hound, hog, and fire. Nervous Bottom sings, is hit on the head by a Puck-directed missile, feels his large ears, looks at his reflection in the water, weeps and sadly continues his song. Titania wakes enamoured of Bottom, rejects the Indian Boy, calls her fairies to tend him. A spider spins a wedding veil, sad Titania weeping "some enforced chastity" looks at moon, and a mock wedding takes place to a parody of Mendelssohn's "Wedding March." Oberon picks up the Indian Boy and rides off with him. Titania embraces Bottom and sings him to sleep.

9. (3.2) *Forest*. As Oberon and Puck watch, angry Hermia leaves frustrated Demetrius who promptly sleeps. Oberon charms Demetrius's eyes. Puck fetches Helena who is pursued by Lysander, Demetrius awakes, and two woo one to Puck's delight. Puck summons Hermia. Total confusion and misunderstanding as four lovers babble at once, group and regroup. Hermia pursues Helena, the men march off to duel, and Oberon has Puck blow fog through the wood to prevent harm. Puck leads them astray with ventriloquism, impossible appearances and reappearances. He mimes their struggles and weary collapses, removes the charm from Lysander's eyes.

10. (3.2, 4.1) *Forest*. Seeing Titania embracing the ass, Oberon begins to have pity. Puck warns it "must be done with haste, for night's swift dragons cut the clouds full fast." Oberon's black bat-winged followers swoop over a hill and sweep the moonlight followers of Titania under the billowing

black veil flowing behind Oberon as he descends on his chariot with the Indian Boy. His shadow passes over the dreamers. Goblins dance behind gauze. A muscular black fairy subdues a white one and carries her off into the night. Oberon removes the charm from Titania's eyes, they are reconciled, and they fly off leaving Puck to remove Bottom's ass's head. Bottom wakes, laughs at his dream, is frightened as his laugh becomes a hee-haw. He runs to the stream, is delighted to see his own face once more, dances off singing.

11. (4.1, 5.1) *Court and Forest.* Theseus and Hippolyta journey toward temple in ornate float. The four lovers in the forest awake, laugh hysterically, and join the courtiers where Theseus overbears Egeus's will and vows to marry the couples. Snout rushes off to tell of other marriages. Triumphant chorus as Theseus and Hippolyta ascend throne. Servants bring in platter of food. The rustics enter with their costumes and props. "Invisible" Puck confuses Philostrate so that "Pyramus and Thisby" is chosen by curious Theseus.

12. (5.1) *Court.* Fanfares. Quince delivers the prologue and has to throw lines constantly to giggling Wall as the ludicrous tragedy is played out. Theseus calls for their burgomask, but while the rustics are backstage the courtiers leave, so that the grand dancing entrance halts and the rustics stare at an empty hall. Oberon and Titania glide in and bless the marriages. Fairies sing and dance. As the lovers go to bed, Puck blows out the lights, puckishly delivers epilogue from Theseus's bedroom door.


A MIDSUMMER NIGHT'S DREAM


Great Britain. Royal Shakespeare Company, Alan Clore, Filmways. 1969. Eastman Color. 35mm.

Producer:   Michael Birkett
Director:   Peter Hall
Photography:   Peter Suschitzky
Design:   John Bury, Ann Curtis
Editor:   Jack Harris
Music:   Guy Wolfenden

| | |
|---|---|
| THESEUS:   Derek Godfrey | EGEUS:   Nicholas Selby |
| HIPPOLYTA:   Barbara Jefford | LYSANDER:   David Warner |
| PHILOSTRATE:   Hugh Sullivan | DEMETRIUS:   Michael Jayston |

HELENA: Diana Rigg
HERMIA: Helen Mirren
OBERON: Ian Richardson
TITANIA: Judi Dench
PUCK: Ian Holm
BOTTOM: Paul Rogers

QUINCE: Sebastian Shaw
SNOUT: Bill Travers
FLUTE: John Normington
SNUG: Clive Swift
STARVELING: Donald Eccles

1. Titles over disjointed shots of rain in pond, trees reflected in pond, grass, ice-covered rocks, autumn leaves in pond, country house in distance, figure in authority striding along servant-lined path to stand by Georgian house, all to sounds of French horns, birds, rain.

2. (1.1) *"Athens"/English Country House.* On a balcony, Theseus and Hippolyta anticipate their marriage. They greet Philostrate in courtyard. Inside a stark grey green main hall they hear harsh Egeus demand death or obedience from Hermia. Despite his alarm at Demetrius's wooing of Helena, Theseus overrules rebellious Hermia and Lysander, exits with others leaving them to lament the crosses lovers have to bear. In a boat on the pond Hermia and Lysander plan to flee to the forest and be married. They join Helena on the grass and tell her of their plan. By various buildings, bushes, a stone memorial and a bridge Helena reveals her plan to tell Demetrius of the lovers' escape and to follow in hopes of winning him.

3. (1.2) *A Shed near "Athens."* In a messy lean-to with deep shadows and clucking chickens, Quince casts "Pyramus and Thisby" and tames his prima donna Bottom while he and his fellow workers are on their lunch hour.

4. (2.1) *A Forest, Night.* Owl hoots against green-tinted sky. A girl fairy scatters glitter in starry black sky, splashes water in half-buried green Puck's face, hears him recount his exploits. Quick overlapping shots and screeches as Oberon, Titania, and their equally nude trains rush toward confrontation over the Indian Boy. Slow color-fades (red, purple, orange) and wildly shifting backgrounds punctuate their quarrel. With the moonbeams dancing in water behind, Oberon sends Puck for the flower. Oberon watches Helena chase scornful Demetrius, vows *he* shall pursue *her* with love. When Puck appears with the Love-in-Idleness, Oberon says he will charm Titania's eyes and sends Puck to charm Demetrius's.

5. (2.2) *Titania's Bower, Night.* Fairy children playfully keep Titania awake with their lullaby, then sing her to sleep. Oberon and his train arrive. One knocks out the sentinel with a huge club; Oberon charms Titania's eyes.

6. (2.2) *The Forest, Night*. Lost and weary, Lysander and Hermia decide to sleep. He lies by her, but she modestly insists that they sleep apart. Mistaking him for Demetrius, Puck charms his eyes. In pursuing Demetrius, Helena stumbles across Lysander, who awakes passionately in love with her and chases her. Hermia has a nightmare and wakes to find herself alone. Incongruous jungle noises.

7. (3.1) *A Forest Clearing near Titania's Bower, Night*. Quince and company huddle with their lanterns, clear up production problems of the killing, lion, and wall. Starveling looks up in fear when told he must impersonate Moon. They rehearse. Bottom exits followed by Puck, then reenters with ass's head, frightening off the others—even Tom Snout, who gives up munching on his onion to look in the script for a stage direction with an ass in it. Puck pursues them. Bottom sings, waking Titania who is in heat. She cuts off his attempts at escape, embraces him, calls her fairies to serve him, leads him to her bower and entwines herself about him.

8. (3.2) *The Forest*. Enter Puck's feet with toes flapping. Oberon, up to the chest in the ground, hears with delight that Titania loves an ass. Enter Hermia pursued by Demetrius. She asks for Lysander, angrily pushes Demetrius into a stream. He gives up, sleeps. Oberon angrily sends the bungler Puck to fetch Helena, charms Demetrius's eyes. Puck appears, followed by Helena and pursuing Lysander. Demetrius wakes and both men woo Helena. Enter Hermia whom Helena thinks is in on the "jest." The confused, mud-splattered lovers shout, plead, accuse, threaten. Vixen Hermia pursues her former friend Helena up a tree. The men draw, turn, and march off to duel over Helena, only to become hopelessly entangled in the bushes. Puck mischievously laughs. Oberon has him blow fog through the forest to keep the duellists apart. As each distraught lover comes to the Duke's Oak, Puck puts him to sleep and tosses hay on him. "Jack shall have Jill / Naught shall go ill..."

9. (4.1) *Titania's Bower*. Titania fondles Bottom's ass's ears. Fairies scratch his hairy head, leave the two to sleep. Oberon appears, removes the spell from Titania's eyes. She weeps and is disgusted by her hairy love. Oberon and Titania dance in slow motion as they are reconciled. Puck removes Bottom's ass's head, and the fairies all race off, fleeing day.

10. (4.1) *The Duke's Oak, Day*. Yelping hounds rush at the camera. Theseus, Hippolyta, Egeus, and the foresters discover the lovers asleep by the oak. Wakened by the horns, the lovers embrace, kneel to the Duke. He ratifies their new-found harmony, and they speak in wonder of their dreams.

11. (4.1) *The Forest*. Bottom wakes from his dream. Bright lights wash out his face as he unsuccessfully tries to relate it.

12. (5.1) *"Athens"/English Country House.* In a door with the wood and night sky in the distance, Theseus speaks ambiguously about the visionary power of the lunatic, lover, and poet. Hippolyta argues for mysterious harmony and truth in the lovers' dreams.

13. (4.2) *A Shed near "Athens," Night.* Quince and the other rustics mourn the loss of Bottom and sixpence a day. Bottom appears and joyful preparations begin.

14. (5.1) *"Athens"/English Country House: Main Hall.* Over the objections of snobbish, effete Philostrate, Theseus chooses the tragical mirth of "Pyramus and Thisby." Quince reads the prologue hesitantly as the players present the story in dumb show. Awkward silence, applause. Wall picks his way through his lines as through a minefield, breaks a brick, is pleased at Pyramus's praise and hurt by his curses, has his hand tickled as the lovers kiss the wall's hole (bawdy guffaws from Theseus's manservants). Enter Lion who roars inaudibly, apologizes to the ladies, who split with laughter. Moon's candle is out at the crucial moment, but Bottom generates his own light with dazzling alliterations. He dies a spectacular death, moaning, gurgling, falling, then is mauled by mournful Thisby in a mop wig who falls on him with a thud. Theseus first mocks the play, then congratulates the players and pays them. The audience claps to the burgomask dance, then the lovers retire to bed. Puck appears on the bannister: "Now the hungry Lion roars." Other fairies appear, filling the hall with stars, glitter, and naked green bodies as Oberon and Titania bless the marriage beds.

15. Outside in the dark, Puck circles the camera delivering his epilogue. He claps his hands and day comes. He sits astride the balcony of the house, disappears, leaving the house in sunlight.

## THE TAMING OF THE SHREW

United States, Italy. Royal Films International, F.A.I. 1966. Technicolor. Widescreen.

Director:   Franco Zeffirelli
Script:   Franco Zeffirelli, Paul Dehn, Suso Cecchi D'Amico
Photography:   Oswald Morris, Luciano Trasatti
Design:   John de Cuir, Giuseppe Mariani, Elven Webb, Dario Simoni, Carlo Gervasi, Irene Sharaff, Danilo Donati
Music:   Nino Rota
Sound:   David Hildyard, Aldo De Martino

PETRUCHIO: Richard Burton
KATHERINA: Elizabeth Taylor
BAPTISTA: Michael Hordern
GRUMIO: Cyril Cusack
LUCENTIO: Michael York
TRANIO: Alfred Lynch
BIANCA: Natasha Pyne
GREMIO: Alan Webb
HORTENSIO: Victor Spinetti
VINCENTIO: Mark Dignam

PRIEST: Giancarlo Cobelli
PEDANT: Vernon Dobtcheff
BIONDELLO: Roy Holder
CURTIS: Gianni Magni
NATHANIEL: Alberto Bonucci
GREGORY: Lino Capolicchio
PHILIP: Roberto Antonelli
HABERDASHER: Anthony Garner
TAILOR: Ken Parry
WIDOW: Bice Valori

1. (1.1) *Padua*. Lucentio and Tranio ride through lush countryside, arrive in busy Renaissance city. Occupied with a huge blonde whore, Tranio loses his master in the crowd. Titles over university choir singing somber music, students being blessed in a cathedral. Festive music as students run wild in streets in masks, waving banners, conducting mock funeral, mimicking bishops, kings, and queens. Tranio finds Lucentio falling in love with pretty blonde Bianca as she is bawdily serenaded by gallants: "... give me leave, to do for thee all that Adam did for Eve." Bianca, summoned home, is chased by Lucentio and Tranio, Gremio and Hortensio.

2. (1.1) *Baptista's House*. Kate peers down at Bianca. Baptista tells Gremio and Hortensio Bianca cannot marry until the elder Kate weds. Kate rages, smashes windows, hurls stool. Bianca's temper flares, then she becomes meek and obedient as she sees Lucentio watching. Tranio and Lucentio exchange identities so that the master can woo while the servant "suitor" busies Baptista.

3. (1.2) *Outside Hortensio's House*. Wandering among the celebrants at night, Hortensio and Gremio wonder whom they can get to marry Kate. Enter Petruchio who hurls his taunting servant Grumio against Hortensio's door, tells Hortensio he seeks a wealthy wife.

4. (1.2) *Hortensio's House*. As Petruchio drinks and picks ticks from his dog, Hortensio tells him of Kate the ferocious. Petruchio vows to woo her, staggers to bed with the aid of the others.

5. (1.2) *Hortensio's Guest Room*. Servants bring ruffian Petruchio a pan of water and rose petals. He scares them away, wets his ears. Hortensio enters bearded and luted to be introduced to Baptista as a music teacher for Bianca.

6. (1.2, 2.1) *Baptista's House*. Suitors swarm to woo the two daughters, despite Kate's destroying of property and beating of Bianca. Petruchio bargains with Baptista. Lucentio the "Latin teacher" woos Bianca. Hor-

tensio is crowned with a lute by Katherine, and armed for "some unhappy words," Petruchio prepares to woo Kate.

7. (2.1, 3.1) *Baptista's House and Barn*. Petruchio maps out his strategy of reverse psychology, woos Kate who is destroying a room, chases her past Baptista's study where disguised Tranio is outbidding Gremio for Bianca and the garden where disguised Lucentio dismisses disguised Hortensio and woos Bianca. Petruchio comes up through a trap door interrupting Kate's frolic in raw wool, swings by a rope to an upper landing, crashes through a wall, follows her out onto a rooftop giving Baptista and others panic, and falls with her through the roof into the raw wool where he pins her down and vows to marry her. By holding her in a hammerlock and locking her in a room, Petruchio persuades the others he has won. She protests, peers through window at him, and smiles. Baptista promises Bianca to Tranio since his price is highest.

8. (3.2) *Baptista's House; Cathedral*. Choirboys play in fountain, run in church. While wedding guests watch, Baptista coaxes his daughter to come out. She greets them, looks at rich wedding gifts. Crowd outside Cathedral cheers as they arrive. Sundial shows 10:00 A.M.

9. (3.2) *Cathedral*. Sundial shows 12:30. Weary crowd waits, mocks Kate. Drunken Petruchio arrives in preposterous dress. Angry Kate races down the aisle followed by guests. Petruchio drinks off holy wine, shoves priest, falls asleep, has a coughing fit, cannot find the ring, stops Kate's mouth with a kiss when she is about to say "I will not." Relief and celebration.

10. (3.2) *Baptista's House*. Kate sees Grumio carrying off her price in gold. Petruchio announces he and Kate must leave before the wedding feast, carries her out to delight of guests and makes her choose between ride in rain or mockery.

11. *Countryside in Rain*. Kate drives her donkey over a hill to head off Petruchio and Grumio. She is thrown in a stream. The men ride on laughing.

12. (4.1) *Petruchio's House*. Petruchio showers his mangey servants with gold coins, sings "where is the life that late I led," scolds his men for lack of preparation as cold, bedraggled Kate arrives, cries for food. Cleavers fall and chickens spin on the spit in the kitchen. Petruchio trips and beats the man with the water, says a prolonged grace while Kate sniffs the food, overturns the table over Kate's protests, beats the servants, and takes Kate upstairs.

13. (4.1) *Petruchio's Bedroom*. They embarrassedly undress. She invites him, crowns him with warming pan. He demolishes the bed, fakes rage at his servants. She weeps, then smiles.

14. *Petruchio's House*. Hung over Petruchio wakes from sleeping on

wooden bench, finds Kate and servants cleaning his filthy gothic house, is rebuffed as he offers to make peace.

15. (4.2) *Baptista's House*. Biondello is weary of watching while Lucentio and Bianca neck in the bushes. He spies an old pedant from Mantua who is frightened into disguising himself as Tranio's father, Vincentio.

16. (4.4) *Baptista's Study*. Baptista tells disguised Tranio he may marry if his father (disguised pedant) will provide money.

17. (4.3) *Petruchio's House*. In transformed house with well-groomed servants, Petruchio tells Kate of Baptista's invitation to Bianca's wedding, invites her to a room with waiting tailors, jewelers, etc. He bisects hat, rips gown, leaves Kate in gloom while secretly instructing the craftsmen to repair the clothes.

18. (4.3) *Petruchio's Bedroom*. Petruchio wakes Kate in the middle of the night, says they will go richly clad if she will agree it is 7:00. She does.

19. (4.5) *Road to Padua*. Petruchio gives Kate water, gets her to agree the sun is the moon, and an old man a budding virgin. The man merrily joins them, says he is Vincentio, Lucentio's father.

20. (4.4) *A Paduan Church*. Biondello parts embracing Lucentio and Bianca and urges them to church to be secretly married.

21. (5.1) *Lucentio's House*. Vincentio knocks, is confronted by the pedant disguised as Vincentio, Tranio in his son's finery, and Biondello who disclaims him. Chaos. Lucentio and Bianca arrive, kneel and ask pardon of surprised Vincentio and Baptista.

22. (5.2) *Baptista's House*. Music and festivities. Petruchio and Kate arrive, he asks for a kiss in public, gets a peck on the nose. Children feed dogs. Whore and crowd laugh in balcony. Sour looks between Petruchio and Kate. Watching children, she softens. Verbal squabble over the widow's shrewishness versus Kate's. The ladies withdraw. Petruchio provokes Lucentio and Hortensio to wager 4,000 crowns on whose wife will obediently come when called for. Biondello reports Bianca will not. The widow bids *Hortensio* come to *her*. Grumio goes for Kate. Kate comes in bringing unwilling Bianca and widow, delivers a speech against unkindness and ingratitude to husbands, kisses Petruchio, runs off to renew their chase. Laughter as Grumio closes the door.

23. Credits over stills from the film.


ROMEO AND JULIET


Great Britain, Italy. BHE Verona Productions; Dino De Laurentiis. 1968. Color. Widescreen.

Producers: Anthony Havelock-Allan, John Brabourne
Director: Franco Zeffirelli
Script: Franco Brusati, Masolino D'Amico.
Photography: Pasquale De Santis
Design: Renzo Mongiardino, Danilo Donati
Editor: Reginald Mills
Music: Nino Rota
Sound: Sash Fisher

PROLOGUE AND EPILOGUE: Laurence Olivier

ROMEO: Leonard Whiting
JULIET: Olivia Hussey
FRIAR LAURENCE: Milo O'Shea
TYBALT: Michael York
MERCUTIO: John McEnery
NURSE: Pat Heywood
LADY CAPULET: Natasha Parry
CAPULET: Paul Hardwick
PRINCE OF VERONA: Robert Stephens

BALTHAZAR: Keith Skinner
GREGORY: Richard Warwick
PARIS: Robert Bisacco
BENVOLIO: Bruce Robinson
MONTAGUE: Antonio Pierfederici
LADY MONTAGUE: Esmeralda Ruspoli
PETER: Roy Holder
FRIAR JOHN: Aldo Miranda

1. (Prologue) Titles. Chorus speaks over hazy dawn, quiet city square.

2. (1.1) *Verona.* Square crowded with buyers and sellers. Capulet servants in red and yellow confront Montagues in blue and green. Their squabble escalates into a riot as Benvolio and Tybalt are drawn in. Alarm bell. Capulet and Montague arm and rush toward the square. People of the town hurl furniture and bag of flour on combatants. Several men stabbed. Trumpets. Angry Prince with troops halts fighting, threatens death if it is renewed. In a street Lady Montague tends the wounded, asks for Romeo. Benvolio says he saw him in a wood. The Montagues withdraw seeing Romeo coming, leaving Benvolio to discover what troubles him. Romeo, flower in hand, speaks in riddles about love, throws down flowers in disgust seeing wounded carried by.

3. (1.2) *Capulet's House.* Festive music. Servants pass with food and decorations. Capulet urges Paris to be patient in his quest for Juliet's hand, indicates that his wife was marred by an early marriage, takes Paris to his study and shows him the guest list for the feast.

4. (1.3) *Capulet's House.* Lady Capulet being made up, sends Nurse to call for Juliet. Juliet runs to Nurse, primps, comes before her mother. Lady Capulet impatiently listens to Nurse babble about bygone days, urges Juliet to receive suit of Paris. Juliet says she will "look to like."

5. (1.4) *Square*. Maskers carry torches through night. Mercutio cavorts with death mask, mocks Romeo's ominous dream with tales of Queen Mab, runs crazily into eerie empty square. Romeo quiets him: "thou talk'st of nothing." Others take Mercutio off to the ball, leaving Romeo to worry alone in the square.

6. (1.5) *Capulet's House, Night*. Buoyant Capulet greets guests. Entering with the maskers, Romeo watches dark-haired beauty, then catches Juliet's eye. Tybalt dances with Lady Capulet, sees Romeo exchanging glances with Juliet, angrily tells Capulet. Capulet shouts down Tybalt. Lady Capulet scolds them. Dance accelerates, reaches climax. Youth sings: "What is a youth? Impetuous fire. What is a maid? Ice and desire. The world waxes on. A rose will bloom, it then will fade, so does a youth, so does the fairest maid. Comes a time when one sweet smile, has its season for a while. Then love's in love with me. Some they think only to marry. Others will tease and tarry. Mine is the very best parry. Cupid he rules us all. Caper the caper. Sing me the song. Death will come soon to hush us along. Sweeter than honey and bitter as gall. Love is a pastime that never will fall. Sweeter than honey, bitter as gall. Cupid he rules us all." During the song Romeo finds Juliet. They speak in sonnet, kiss, part as Nurse summons her. Romeo learns from Nurse that Juliet is a Capulet. Capulet bids farewell to his guests, Paris to Juliet. Juliet learns from Nurse that Romeo is a Montague, sighs. Tybalt looks angrily, leaves.

7. (2.1) *Outside Capulet's House*. Juliet passes through eerie blue courtyard. Cries of "Juliet" from within, "Romeo" from without. Romeo climbs wall to escape calling friends, sees Juliet on balcony, interrupts her reverie and says he loves her. They embrace, part, embrace, part, embrace once more before he leaves, runs whooping happily down a hill.

8. (2.3) *Outside Verona Walls*. Friar Laurence gathers herbs at sunrise. Romeo tells him of his love for Juliet. Entering the church, the Friar looks at crucifix, decides to help.

9. (2.4) *Square*. Mercutio asks after love-sick Romeo whom Benvolio reports has been challenged by Tybalt. Enter Romeo. Mercutio mimes sour-faced old man, provokes Romeo into a contest of wordplay. Enter Peter and Nurse trailing long white veil. Mercutio cries out "a sail! a sail!"; mimes a gossip stitching his ever-present white handkerchief. When Nurse asks for Romeo, Mercutio cries "a bawd," lifts her skirts, spins her around. She angrily kicks Peter down steps, goes in church, tells Romeo to meet Juliet and marry her at Friar Laurence's cell.

10. (2.5) *Capulet's Garden*. Impatient Juliet pricks her finger doing needlework, pleads with groaning Nurse to give her news. Nurse dismisses Peter, leads her into the kitchen, munches on apple, tells her to meet Romeo at Friar Laurence's cell.

11. (2.6) *Friar Laurence's Cell.* Friar lectures Romeo against haste and immoderation. Juliet runs to Romeo and they kiss. Friar parts them, marries them at altar. Crescendo of organ and soprano.

12. (3.1) *Square.* Out-of-focus white blob on screen. Mercutio with handkerchief over face: "blah, blah, blah" to Benvolio's advice to withdraw from the heat and the Capulets. Miming washing his linen in the fountain, Mercutio provokes Tybalt. Tybalt spies Romeo, insults him, mocks disgust as Romeo shakes his hand and refuses to fight. Mercutio draws. Circle of spectators forms. Mercutio is disarmed, falls on his bum, is backed against the fountain with sword at his throat, has a piece of his hair cut off, runs up wagon in mock cowardice. He disarms Tybalt with a pitchfork, humiliates Tybalt. Enraged, Tybalt attacks and, as Romeo grabs Mercutio, accidentally stabs Mercutio in the heart. Close-up of bloody swordpoint. Tybalt and Capulets flee. Montagues raise Mercutio on their shoulders cheering, take Mercutio's cries of pain as a joke. He asks Romeo why he came between them, staggers up cathedral steps, curses both houses, falls dead. All mockingly sing "amen." Romeo lifts handkerchief to find blood, runs crazily unarmed to find Tybalt, rubs the bloody rag in his face, and scrambles for weapons. Spectators and supporters encircle them, shout advice. Tybalt disarms Romeo, chases him back into square, rolls in the dust with him, runs up against Romeo's desperate thrust as he is about to finish him off, falls dead on top of him. At Montagues' bidding, Romeo flees screaming "I am fortune's fool!"

13. (3.2) *Juliet's Room.* Nurse weeps for Tybalt. Juliet curses Romeo, then Nurse for doing same. Both weep.

14. (3.1) *Outside Prince's Palace.* Capulets and Montagues set the bodies of Tybalt and Mercutio before the Prince. Lady Capulet and others cry down Benvolio and demand Romeo's life in revenge. The Prince recites the chain of killings, hears Montague's plea, exiles Romeo, grieves for kinsman Mercutio.

15. (3.3) *Friar Laurence's Cell.* Nurse arrives to find Romeo weeping like her mistress at home. Romeo attempts suicide but is disarmed by the Friar who sends him to Juliet and then to Mantua until the marriage can be announced and peace made.

16. (3.5) *Juliet's Bedroom.* The lark wakes the lovers, and they linger in parting despite warnings from Nurse.

17. *Outside Montague's House.* Romeo mounts, rides for Mantua.

18. (3.5) *Juliet's Bedroom.* Lady Capulet in black vows revenge against Romeo, tells Juliet she is to marry Paris. Juliet refuses. As Capulet parts from Paris promising the wedding will be soon, Lady Capulet informs him Juliet says no. He rushes up in a rage, threatens and bullies, exits. Juliet turns to her mother for help but Lady Capulet leaves. She appeals to

Nurse, but gets pragmatic advice to marry Paris. Juliet coldly dismisses her.

19. (4.1) *Friar Laurence's Cell.* Friar protests Paris's suggestion of marriage without courtship. Juliet arrives, brushes away Paris's attempts to conciliate her, and when alone with the Friar begs his help. He looks at his herbs and vials, explains the effects of the drug, gives it to her, stares uncomfortably at extinguished candle.

20. (4.2) *Capulet's Study.* Juliet promises him she will obey.

21. (4.2) *Lady Capulet's Room.* Juliet embraces her and exits.

22. (4.3 *Juliet's Room.* Juliet pulls shut the white gauze bedcurtain, drinks the potion.

23. *Outside Friar Laurence's Cell, Morning.* Friar Laurence sends a brother on a donkey with the letter to Romeo.

24. (4.5) *Capulet's House.* Birds sing. Nurse's cry pierces the quiet: "Juliet is dead!" The Capulets rush to find it is so.

25. *The Road to Mantua.* The Brother proceeds slowly.

26. (4.5) *Capulet's Tomb.* Romeo's man watches Juliet's funeral, rides down tree-lined road.

27. *Road to Mantua.* Romeo's man races past the Brother.

28. *Mantua.* Romeo's man arrives, tells him Juliet is dead.

29. *Road to Verona.* Romeo rides past Brother, through sheep.

30. (5.3) *Verona Churchyard, Night.* Romeo dismisses his man, breaks open the doors of the crypt, passes by rows of rotting corpses to find Juliet. He takes off her shroud, kisses her. Seeing Tybalt's body, he walks to it and asks forgiveness. He holds Juliet once again, weeps, drinks poison. The Friar arrives too late. As Juliet wakes he hears the Prince's trumpet, urges her to flee, goes out. She finds Romeo, kisses him, weeps, stabs herself.

31. (5.3) *Verona Square.* Two families united in a funeral procession. Prince angrily: "all are punished!" Chorus: "A glooming peace this morning with it brings. / The sun for sorrow will not show its head. / For never was a story of more woe / than this of Juliet and her Romeo." Members of the two families make gestures of reconciliation, pass by leaving shot of castellated tower and walls of Verona.


JULIUS CAESAR


United States. M.G.M. 1953. Black and white. 35 mm.

Producer:  John Houseman
Director:  Joseph L. Mankiewicz

Script:  Joseph L. Mankiewicz
Photography:  Joseph Ruttenberg
Design:  Cedric Gibbons, Edward Carfagno
Editors:  Herschel MacCoy, John Dunning
Music:  Miklos Rozsa

Julius Caesar:  Louis Calhern
Antony:  Marlon Brando
Cicero:  Alan Napier
Brutus:  James Mason/
Cassius:  John Gielgud
Casca:  Edmond O'Brien
Flavius:  Michael Pate
Marullus:  George Macready
Soothsayer:  Richard Hale
Decius Brutus:  John Hoyt
Metellus Cimber:  Tom Powers
Cinna:  William Cottrell
Trebonius:  Jack Raine
Ligarius:  Ian Wolfe

Artemidorus:  Morgan Farley
Octavius Caesar:  Douglas Watson
Lepidus:  Douglas Dumbrille
Lucilius:  Rhys Williams
Pindarus:  Michael Ansara
Messala:  Dayton Lummis
Strato:  Edmund Purdom
Calpurnia:  Greer Garson
Portia:  Deborah Kerr
Citizens:  Paul Guilfoyle
John Doucette
Lawrence Dobkin
Jo Gilbert

1. Titles against Roman Eagle. Caesar and Brutus themes. From Plutarch: "Upon Caesar's return to Rome, after defeating Pompey in the civil war, his countrymen chose him a fourth time consul and then dictator for life. ... Thus he became odious to moderate men through the extravagance of the title and powers that were heaped upon him."

2. (1.1) *A Square*. Music and laughter as people celebrate. A fountain with Caesar's image decked with flowers. Angry Flavius and Marullus scold fickle people. Caesar theme rises as people turn sullen and scatter. The tribunes strip flowers from bust. Soldiers arrest them. Cheering and music become very loud.

3. (1.2) *Entrance to Colosseum*. Enter Caesar in procession, reminds Antony to touch sterile Calpurnia during the race. Shrill voice of Soothsayer stops Caesar. "Beware the Ides of March." Caesar passes on. Soothsayer refuses help from Brutus.

4. (1.2) *Entrance to Colosseum*. Cassius follows Brutus up stairs to gallery, urges him more and more openly to help overthrow Caesar as crowd shouts to Caesar within, bitterly looks up at massive statue of Caesar.

5. (1.2) *Entrance to Colosseum*. Shouts and flourish. Caesar enters weakly

on Antony's arm, describes envious Cassius, exits. Sardonic Casca relates the "foolery" by Antony and Caesar inside, reports that Flavius and Marullus are "put to silence." Brutus agrees to see Cassius later, exits. Wind rises and threatening music grows as Cassius strides toward camera noting Brutus's vulnerability, Caesar's dislike, and vows to shake Caesar.

6. (1.3) *A Square, Night.* Storm rages as terrified Casca encounters cool Cicero, and then Cassius who draws him into the conspiracy. Cassius sends Cinna to plant appeals to Brutus. Thunder.

7. (2.1) *Brutus's Garden, Night.* Grotesque shadows, somber music as Brutus resolves Caesar must die. Conspirators arrive. They plan who to include, who is to fetch Caesar, whether Antony should die. They leave. Portia wakes and persuades Brutus to tell her all. Sick Caius Ligarius enters and joins conspiracy.

8. (2.2) *Caesar's Chamber.* Eerie music. Calpurnia screams "they murder Caesar!" Caesar sends to have priests do sacrifice. Their ominous reports and frightened Calpurnia persuade him not to go to the Senate. Decius plays on Caesar's vanity and fear until he decides to go. Other conspirators arrive and join Caesar for wine while resigned Calpurnia retires to her bedroom.

9. (2.3, 3.1) *Capitol Steps.* Artemidorus reads the warning for Caesar, waits. Caesar enters, chides Soothsayer that the Ides of March are come. "Ay Caesar, but not gone." Popilius wishes nervous Cassius well in his enterprise. Caesar refuses Artemidorus's letter.

10. (3.1) *Inside the Capitol.* Caesar ringed about with conspirators pleading for Metellus Cimber's brother. Casca strikes first blow, others follow. Brutus backs away. Caesar staggers toward him, is stabbed by his friend, and falls at the foot of Pompey. Confusion. They wash their hands in Caesar's blood. Antony's frightened servant and then cool Antony enter. He declares love for Caesar, solidarity with conspirators if they have proceeded justly. Brutus lets him live and speak over Caesar's body. They go leaving Antony to lament and predict civil war.

11. (3.2) *Capitol Steps.* Brutus wins the crowd declaring the conspirators killed Caesar for the good of Rome. Antony shocks them by entering with Caesar's body, plays on their emotions, incites them to riot, exits smiling.

12. *Capitol Steps, Night.* Title over Caesar's burning funeral pyre tell of war of Octavius and Antony with Brutus and Cassius.

13. (4.1) *Caesar's Chamber.* Octavius, Lepidus, and Antony determine which enemies are to die. Antony sends Lepidus after Caesar's will, denounces Lepidus's weakness and proposes removing him. Octavius reluctantly agrees. Antony walks to balcony, stretches, studies statue of Caesar, sits in eagle-crested chair. Music rises.

14. (4.2, 4.3) *Brutus's Camp.* Lucilius and Pindarus ride in. Brutus fears

Cassius's love is cooling. Cassius arrives furious that Brutus has rejected his pleas for a wrongdoer. They quarrel in Brutus's tent, make up. Brutus reveals Portia is dead. Stunned Cassius fatally gives in to Brutus's plan to come down from hills and fight on the plain.

15. (4.3) *Brutus's Tent, Night.* Lucius sings sleepy tune to his harp: "Now, oh now, I needs must part. Joy once fled cannot return." Brutus places sleeping boy on bed, reads, falls asleep. Eerie music and moaning wind. Caesar's ghost appears, vows to see Brutus at Philippi. Brutus draws, rouses men, but they saw nothing.

16. (5.1) *Brutus's Camp, Morning.* Cassius says farewell to Brutus, notes to Messala the irony that it is his birthday, swears he never approved plan to risk all in one battle.

17. *Philippi.* Cassius's soldiers march through a pass. Above, Antony signals troops to attack. Cassius's troops decimated. Antony smiles. Caesar theme up.

18. (5.2) *Hillside.* Cassius remains behind his fleeing troops, commands Pindarus to kill him. Pindarus does, runs off in fear.

19. (5.4) *Battlefield.* Octavius's troops mopping up after defeating Brutus. Soldier finds smashed harp of Lucius. Harp over Caesar music. Wounded Lucilius refuses to reveal where Brutus is.

20. (5.5) *Hillside.* Brutus remains behind fleeing troops, finds Cassius's body. "Oh Julius Caesar, thou art mighty yet!" Clitus and Volumnius refuse to hold sword while Brutus runs on it. Caesar theme slowly drowns out Brutus theme. Strato holds sword. Brutus: "Caesar, now be still; I killed not thee with half so good a will." Strato straddles Brutus's body, turns to face enemy.

21. (5.5) *Brutus's Tent, Night.* Funeral drums. Antony and Octavius walk past troops and heap of spoils into tent where dead Brutus lies. Octavius remains at door and declares Brutus will have rites. Antony walks to side of body, says only Brutus did not strike Caesar out of envy. Drums louder. Lamp at Brutus's head goes out at last beat. Titles and theme music.

## CHIMES AT MIDNIGHT
### (FALSTAFF)

Spain, Switzerland. Internacional Films Espagnol; Alpine, Basel. 1965. Black and white. Widescreen. United States title: *Falstaff*

Producer and Director:   Orson Welles
Script:   Orson Welles
Photography:   Edmond Richard

Design:  Jose Antonio de la Guerra, Mariano Erdorza, Orson Welles
Editor:  Fritz Mueller
Music:  Aneglo Francesco Lavagnino
Sound:  Peter Parasheles

NARRATOR:  Ralph Richardson

FALSTAFF:  Orson Welles
HAL:  Keith Baxter
HENRY IV:  John Gielgud
DOLL TEARSHEET:  Jeanne Moreau
MISTRESS QUICKLY:
  Margaret Rutherford
HOTSPUR:  Norman Rodway
KATE PERCY:  Marina Vlady
JUSTICE SHALLOW:  Alan Webb

SILENCE:  Walter Chiari
PISTOL:  Michael Aldridge
POINS:  Tony Beckley
WORCESTER:  Fernando Rey
WESTMORELAND:  Andrew Faulds
NORTHUMBERLAND:  Jose Nietro
PRINCE JOHN:  Jeremy Rowe
FALSTAFF'S PAGE:  Beatrice Welles
BARDOLPH:  Paddy Bedford

1. (*2H4* 3.2) *Shallow's Barn*. Falstaff and Shallow walk through snow among spikey trees to an empty barn where they warm themselves by the fire and recall the past. "Jesus, the days we have seen." "We have heard the chimes at midnight, Master Robert Shallow."

2. (Holinshed) *Tavern and Court*. Titles and jubilant martial music over shots of tavern, fortress, soldiers on ramparts, bodies hanging from gibbets. Narrator: "King Richard the Second was murdered, some say at the command of the Duke Henry Bolingbroke, in Pomfret Castle on February the fourteenth, 1400. Before this, the Duke Henry had been crowned King, though the true heir to the realm was Edward Mortimer, who was held prisoner by the Welsh rebels. The new King was not hasty to purchase his deliverance, and to prove this, Mortimer's cousins the Percies came to the King unto Windsor. There came Northumberland, his son Henry Percy, called Hotspur, and Worcester, whose purpose was ever to procure malice and set things in a broil."

3. (*1H4* 1.3) *Court*. Henry quarrels with the Percies, orders them to leave. In an adjacent hall, Hotspur raves against the King. Worcester and Northumberland reveal the plot against Henry.

4. (*1H4* 1.2) *Tavern*. Hal drinks and sports with the whores, wakes Falstaff and deflates his claimed losses. They plan the Gadshill robbery. Poins and Hal plot against Falstaff. With Falstaff and the inn behind him, Hal thinks aloud, "I will a while uphold the unyoked humor of your idleness," while gazing on the fortress, and leaves.

5. (*1H4* 2.3) *Hotspur's Castle*. While heralds intermittently sound trumpets from the battlements, Hotspur impatiently reads cowardly letter while bathing, rushes to get dressed while importuned by his neglected wife, and rides off after learning his father is sick.

6. (*1H4* 2.2) *Forest at Gadshill*. Hal arms Falstaff in a monk's robe. The robbery, counter-robbery, and chase through the trees.

7. (*R2* 5.3) *Court*. The King asks "can no man tell me of my unthrifty son?", hears the Percies are in arms, and envies Northumberland his son.

8. (*1H4* 2.4) *Tavern*. Hal and Poins arrive, listen to Falstaff's mock-epic of the fight, try to corner him only to be told he was a "coward upon instinct." After news of the rebellion, Falstaff and Hal take turns playing the King and repentant son. It is interrupted at Hal's somber "I do. I will" by the sheriff, who is sent packing by the prince. After squabbles between Falstaff, Mistress Quickly, and then Falstaff and Doll Tearsheet, Hal leaves for court.

9. (*1H4* 3.2) *Court*. The real scene of the King and his repentant son, who vows to be more himself and defeat Hotspur.

10. (*1H4* 4.2; *2H4* 1.2) *A Village*. Soldiers parade through the streets, Pistol and Bardolph pausing to quarrel over money. Falstaff, asked about his threadbare troops, tells how he has misused the draft. Encountered by a bishop and the Lord Chief Justice, he urges them to take care of their health, asks a loan, and wishes for a better Prince.

11. (*1H4* 5.2) *Rebel Camp*. Worcester tells Hotspur the King and Prince are preparing for battle. Hotspur: "If we live, we live to tread on kings. If die, brave death when princes die with us."

12. (*2H4* 3.2) *Shallow's House*. Falstaff greets Shallow and Silence, drafts the sick and the poor, takes bribes from the rest, and goes off in rain.

13. (*1H4* 5.1) *Shrewsbury*. King offers peace to Worcester. Hal offers to settle the dispute in single combat with Hotspur.

14. (*1H4* 5.2) *Rebel Camp*. Worcester lies to Hotspur telling him the King is resolute for war.

15. (*1H4* 5.1) *King's Camp*. Hal: "Why thou owest God a death." Falstaff is reluctant to pay yet, schools Hal on the hollowness of honor.

16. (*1H4* 5.4) *Shrewsbury*. Hotspur vows to kill Hal or be killed. Armed knights are lowered onto their horses on both sides. Falstaff crashes to earth. Charge and countercharge as Falstaff runs and hides. Triumphant music and enthusiasm give way to clashes of steel, cries of agony, slogging in mud. Chorus and bells sound in grim irony. Hal kills Hotspur, pays tribute to Hotspur and fallen Falstaff. Falstaff riseth up.

17. (*1H4* 5.5, 5.4) *Shrewsbury*. Retreat sounded. Henry IV sends Worcester to his death. Prisoners herded away. Enter Falstaff carrying Hotspur's body. Silent confrontation between Hal and two fathers. Sick

King rides off. Falstaff expounds on the virtue of sack. Hal drops his cup and walks off to join the departing troops.

18. (Holinshed) *Shrewsbury.* Bodies swing from gibbets. Narrator: "From the first, King Henry's reign was troubled with rebellion. In the year of our Lord 1408, the last of his enemies had been vanquished. The King held his Christmas this year at London, being sore vexed with sickness."

19. (*2H4* 3.1) *Court.* Henry IV, grieved to hear his son has rejoined his dissolute companions, falls ill, is laid in bed his crown by him. Courtiers speak of disturbances in nature. The weary anguished King at window speaks of the sleep enjoyed by the common man as music plays.

20. (*2H4* 2.2) *By a Still Pond.* Hal tells cynical Poins he is weary. Bardolph and a page bring a letter from Falstaff.

21. (*2H4* 2.4) *Tavern.* Falstaff is weary, broke, sick, and melancholy. He enrages Doll, emerges from the jordan to chase away swaggering Pistol, lies in bed with Doll lamenting his age, impotence. Poins and Hal spy on them, join them. Angered by Poin's charge of hypocrisy at his grief over his father, Hal answers a summons to court. Falstaff pursues him through festive crowd, says farewell, leaves Doll weeping at the gate and departs for Master Shallow's.

22. (*2H4* 4.5) *Court.* Hal enters joking, finds others in sorrow. Thinking his father dead, Hal puts on the crown and goes into another room to pray.

23. (*2H4* 3.2) *Shallow's Barn.* Falstaff: "We have heard the chimes at midnight, Master Shallow." Shallow: "Jesu, Jesu, the mad days that I have seen." They talk of the dead, the price of livestock.

24. (*2H4* 4.5, 5.2) *Court.* The King awakes, finds and berates Hal for wanting him dead. Hal explains, helps Henry to throne where he reveals his guilt and advises Hal to "busy giddy minds with foreign wars" and then dies. Hal reassures his new subjects. "Now call we our high parliament."

25. (*2H4* 5.3) *Shallow's Barn.* Shallow and Silence dance drunkenly; Falstaff notes what liars old men are. Poins charges in to announce Hal is King. Falstaff: "I am Fortune's steward."

26. (*2H4* 5.5) *Court.* Henry V rides through cheering crowds, walks in procession as Falstaff wagers with Shallow and pushes through to greet his "sweet boy." Hal humiliates and banishes Falstaff, passes on. Shallow demands his thousand pounds. Falstaff slowly exits as page watches.

27. (*2H4* 5.5) *Exterior of Church.* Smug lords like the King's "fair proceeding." Arrested, Doll cries out for Falstaff. The page announces he is sick. Nym: "The King is a good king, but it must be as it may."

28. (*H5* 2.3) *Exterior of Court.* King vows to cheering crowd "No King of England if not King of France," orders Falstaff released.

29. (*H5* 2.3; Holinshed) *Tavern and Fortress*. Poins glances at empty tavern chair, finds glum page and Mistress Quickly by huge coffin. "Falstaff is dead." "The King has killed his heart." Mistress Quickly describes his death. They push the coffin out the gate. Narrator: "The new King even at first appointing determined to put on him the shape of a new man. This Henry was a captain of such prudence and such policy that he never enterprised anything before he had forecast the main chances that it might happen. So humane withal that he left no offense unpunished, nor friendship unrewarded. For conclusion, a majesty was he that both lived and died in princehood, a lodestar in honor, and famous to the world alway.'"

30. Credits to funeral drums over slow motion film loop of crowd and soldiers at the coronation.

## HENRY V

Great Britain. Two Cities Film. 1944. Technicolor. 35mm.

Producer and Director:   Laurence Olivier
Script:   Laurence Olivier, Alan Dent, Dallas Bower
Photography:   Robert Krasker, Jack Hildyard
Design:   Paul Sheriff, Carmen Dillon, Roger Furse
Editor:   Reginald Beck
Music:   William Walton
Sound:   John Dennis, Desmond Dew

HENRY V:   Laurence Olivier
GLOUCESTER:   Michael Warre
EXETER:   Nicholas Hannen
SALISBURY:   Griffith Jones
WESTMORELAND:   Gerald Case
ARCHBISHOP OF CANTERBURY:
  Felix Aylmer
BISHOP OF ELY:   Robert Helpman
ERPINGHAM:   Morland Graham
GOWER:   Michael Shepley
FLUELLEN:   Esmond Knight
MACMORRIS:   Niall MacGinnis
JAMY:   John Laurie
BATES:   Arthur Hambling

COURT:   Brian Nissen
WILLIAMS:   Jimmy Hanley
NYM:   Frederick Cooper
BARDOLPH:   Roy Emerson
PISTOL:   Robert Newton
BOY:   George Cole
KING CHARLES VI:
  Harcourt Williams
DAUPHIN LEWIS:   Max Adrian
BURGUNDY:   Valentine Dyall
ORLEANS:   Francis Lister
BOURBON:   Russell Thorndike
CONSTABLE:   Leo Genn
HARFLEUR:   Frank Tickle

MONTJOY:   Jonathan Field
FRENCH AMBASSADOR:
  Ernest Thesiger
CHORUS:   Leslie Banks
PRIEST:   Ernest Hare

SIR JOHN FALSTAFF:   George Robey
QUEEN ISABEL:   Janet Burnell
KATHERINE:   Renee Asherson
ALICE:   Ivy St. Helier
MISTRESS QUICKLY:   Freda Jackson

1. (Prologue) *Elizabethan London: Globe Theatre.* The camera pans over a model of Elizabethan London and moves down into the theatre where the Chorus addresses an energetic audience.

2. (1.1) *Globe Balcony.* Comic Ely and Canterbury worry about royal seizure of church lands, praise the King's reformation (rousing a cheer when they mention Falstaff and a boo when they mention his banishment), and plan to raise money and urge Henry to war on France.

3. *Backstage at the Globe.* Frantic preparations by actors and boy actresses amidst a confusion of costumes and props.

4. (1.2) *Globe Stage.* Henry impatiently hears Canterbury's historical argument that Henry is the true king of France while Ely amuses the audience by bumbling the scrolls. Urged on by his Lords, Henry greets the Dauphin's insult with a declaration of war.

5. (2 Chorus) *Globe Stage.* Chorus: "Now all the youth of England are on fire."

6. (2.1) *Globe Stage: Boar's Head.* Thunder and rain. Nym climbs down from a tryst with Mistress Quickly in the balcony. He is greeted by Bardolph who urges him to make peace with Pistol. Enter bombastic Pistol and Mistress Quickly who are greeted with wild cheers, laughter, and applause. The quarrel of Pistol and Nym is interrupted by news of Falstaff's sickness. Mistress Quickly: "The king has killed his heart." Nym: "The king is a good king, but it must be as it may."

7. (2 Chorus, 2.2) *Southampton.* Dissolve from painted curtain to stylized set with ships. Religious chant. Henry pardons a slanderer, rouses his men with a speech. Cheers. Music crescendos.

8. (3 Chorus, *2H4* 5.5, 2.3) *Boar's Head, Night.* Somber passacaglia. Camera moves through window to view sick Falstaff recalling his rejection by the King. He falls back and Mistress Quickly tends him. Bardolph, Nym, Boy, Pistol, and she sorrow at his death which she describes. The men go, melancholy Pistol quoting Tamberlaine: "Farewell, farewell divine Zenocrate—is it not passing brave to be a King and ride in triumph through Persepolis!"

9. (3 Chorus) *English Channel.* Chorus disappears into fog. Fleet of ships appears.

10. (2.4) *Interior, French Palace*. Weak King Charles urges preoccupied lords to prepare for war. Henry's bold ambassador, Exeter, demands French crown, threatens "bloody constraint," insults Dauphin.

11. (3 Chorus, 3.1) *French Coast*. Dissolve through waves to Henry on spirited charger. He urges his men "once more into the breach." Fluellen forces cowardly Pistol, Nym, and Boy to join charge.

12. (3.2) *English Camp*. Gower, Fluellen, Jamy, and MacMorris discuss tactics, Fluellen being hard on MacMorris.

13. (3.3) *Gates of Harfleur*. The Mayor surrenders to Henry.

14. (3.4) *Garden in French Palace*. Princess Katherine gets a bawdy English lesson from her woman Alice.

15. (3.5) *Interior, French Court*. The ladies join the sullen French lords at a cramped banquet. King Charles orders Montjoy to greet Henry with defiance, keeps his son at home.

16. (3.6) *A Field*. Montjoy offers ransom to doomed Henry. Henry admits they are weak but refuses ransom and offers to fight. The English army wearily marches on.

17. (4 Chorus, 3.7) *The Two Camps, Night*. Dissolve to Constable's armor in French tent. Uneasy lords await morning, try to cheer selves up. Sardonic Constable deflates windbag Dauphin.

18. (4 Chorus, 4.1) *English Camp*. Chorus on "poor condemned English." "A little touch of Harry in the night." Disguised King encounters Pistol, overhears Fluellen and Gower, joins Bates, Court, and Williams who wonder about the responsibility for the dead tomorrow, doubt that Henry will refuse ransom. Henry defends self, but when alone thinks on his responsibility. Called, he prays, goes to join his soldiers.

19. (4.2) *French Camp, Morning*. The jubilant French arm, mount.

20. (4.3) *English Camp*. Henry cheers his somber men with St. Crispin's Day speech of honor, "we happy few."

21. *French Camp*. French lowered onto horses, drink wine.

22. *English Front Lines*. Men sharpen stakes, test bows.

23. (4.3) *English Camp*. Henry refuses Montjoy's last offer of ransom.

24. (4.6, 4.5, 4.7, 4.8) *Field of Agincourt*. Music builds as the French knights accelerate toward the English. Intercuts of archers firing and French in confusion, stopped cold. French pursue English into wood. English leap from trees and knock them from their horses. Two infantries fight. Henry urges his men on. Hot with shame, the French lords gather on a hill. Some return to the battle. Others overrun English Camp and slaughter boys. Henry finds Fluellen in burning camp with dead boy in his arms, takes field in anger and defeats Constable in single combat. Montjoy kneels to Henry acknowledging defeat, begging permission to bury French dead. Henry names the battle Agincourt. Dissolve to dead soldiers on field. The

English give thanks as they learn few of their numbers have been killed. "Te Deum" sung as English file toward village.

25. (5.1) *Snowy Village of Agincourt.* Boys sing carols. Fluellen makes Pistol eat a leek before Gower. Alone, Pistol reveals Mistress Quickly is dead of the "malady of France," determines to turn bawd and thief, steals a chicken and exits to jovial music.

26. (5.2) *Great Hall, French Palace.* Choir sings. English and French royalty greet, are told of ruined France by Burgundy who looks out window on untended vineyards and beggared children. Henry woos and wins Katherine in blunt but charming fashion. Lords watch French king join their hands. They form a tableau under arch.

27. *Globe Stage.* Henry once again in crude stage makeup and boy made up as Katherine bow. Applause. Chorus delivers Epilogue. Actor of Ely leads chorus on balcony. Flag taken down. Pan over London. Playbill with credits floats into frame. Agincourt hymn.


# RICHARD III

Great Britain. London Films. 1955. Vistavision-Technicolor.

Producers:  Alexander Korda, Laurence Olivier
Director:  Laurence Olivier
Script:  Laurence Olivier, Alan Dent
Photography:  Otto Heller
Design:  Carmen Dillon, Roger Furse
Editor:  Helga Cranston
Music:  William Walton
Sound:  Bert Rule

EDWARD IV:  Cedric Hardwicke
PRINCE OF WALES:  Paul Hudson
YOUNG DUKE OF YORK:
  Andy Shine
CLARENCE:  John Gielgud
RICHARD III:  Laurence Olivier
RICHMOND:  Stanley Baker
ARCHBISHOP:  Nicholas Hannen
BUCKINGHAM:  Ralph Richardson

NORFOLK:  John Phillips
RIVERS:  Clive Morton
DORSET:  Douglas Wilmer
LORD GREY:  Dan Cunningham
HASTINGS:  Alec Clunes
STANLEY:  Laurence Naismith
LOVEL:  John Laurie
RATCLIFFE:  Esmond Knight
CATESBY:  Norman Wooland

TYRREL:  Patrick Troughton
BRAKENBURY:  Andrew Cruikshank
FIRST PRIEST:  Russell Thorndike
SECOND PRIEST:  Willoughby Gray
LORD MAYOR:  George Woodbridge
QUEEN ELIZABETH:  Mary Kerridge
DUCHESS OF YORK:  Helen Haye
ANNE:  Claire Bloom
JANE SHORE:  Pamela Brown
PAGE:  Stewart Allen
FIRST MONK:  Wally Bascoe
SECOND MONK:  Norman Fisher
DIGHTON THE MURDERER:
    Michael Gough

FORREST THE MURDERER:
    Michael Ripper
ABBOT:  Roy Russell
MESSENGER:  Peter Williams
OSTLER:  Timothy Bateson
SCRUBWOMAN:  Anne Wilton
BEADLE:  Bill Shine
CLERGYMEN:  Derek Prentice
    Deering Wells
MESSENGERS:  Brian Nissen
    Alexander Davion
    Lane Meddick
    Robert Bishop

1. Ornate Titles: "The story of England like that of many another land is an interwoven pattern of history and legend. The history of the world, like letters without poetry, flowers without perfume, or thought without imagination, would be a dry matter indeed without its legends, and many of these thought scorned by proof a hundred times seem worth preserving for their own sakes. The following begins in the latter half of the 15th century in England, at the end of a long period of strife set about by rival factions for the English crown known as the Wars of the Roses. The Red Rose being the emblem for the House of Lancaster. The White for the House of York. This White Rose of York was in its final flowering at the beginning of the story as it inspired William Shakespeare. [List of principal characters.] Here now begins one of the most famous and at the same time the most infamous of the legends that are attached to THE CROWN OF ENGLAND."

2. (*3H6* 5.7) *Westminster Abbey*. The coronation of Edward IV and procession, conspicuously watched by Richard, Buckingham, and Jane Shore. Procession moves out into street before cheering crowd.

3. (1.1, *3H6* 3.2) *Westminster Abbey*. Alone in the throne room, Richard vents his disgust at peace, celebrations, his own misshapen body, reveals his plan to murder his way to the throne, spies Anne out the window following the coffin of her husband.

4. (1.2) *Westminster Abbey*. Anne laments her husband, curses Richard. Richard halts the funeral procession, woos Anne, and, alone, plots against his brother Clarence.

5. (1.1) *The Palace*. Richard whispers lies about Clarence to the King, watches the King have him arrested, hypocritically comforts Clarence.

6. (1.2) *Tomb Adjacent to Palace*. Richard woos and wins Anne with weeping, flattery, power, sexual attraction. He laughs at her weakness, enters her bedroom.

7. (1.3) *The Palace*. The Queen frets. Richard in his new finery has the King sign Clarence's death warrant, hopes the King will follow soon, and bustles off. The Queen leaves the King in the capable hands of Jane Shore.

8. (1.4) *The Tower*. Clarence wakes from a nightmare, relates it to his jailor, falls asleep once more as Richard watches.

9. (1.1) *The Tower*. Richard takes the King's revocation of Clarence's death warrant from Buckingham. They comment satirically as Mistress Shore brings Hastings's release. Richard assures Hastings his own enemies are also Hastings's.

10. (1.3) *The Palace*. Richard storms against the Queen and her kin for plotting against him and his brother. Catesby brings the sick King's summons.

11. (1.3, 1.4) *The Tower*. Richard gives the murderers the order to kill Clarence, warns them against his pleas, and prevents the jailor from reporting to the King. The murderers cut short Clarence's pleas, club him and stuff him in a barrel of wine.

12. (2.1, 2.2) *Royal Bedroom*. Edward makes the opposing nobles vow amity. Richard announces Clarence's death. The guilty King dies as Hastings and Shore eye each other. Richard and Buckingham arrange for the Prince's entry into London, scheme to keep him from the Queen.

13. *Snowy Countryside*. Nobles ride to Ludlow to fetch Prince.

14. (2.4) *The Palace*. Domestic scene with Archbishop, Queen, her Queen Mother, and son Richard is interrupted by news that Richard has imprisoned Rivers and Grey. The two Queens lament, plan to seek sanctuary.

15. *Sanctuary*. Bell rings. Queen and followers welcomed.

16. *Snowy Landscape*. Prince, choking back tears, rides flanked by Richard and Buckingham.

17. (3.1) *London: Snowy Courtyard, Throne Room*. The Prince receives sparse greeting, asks for his kin, is startled like the others to learn they have taken sanctuary. Wily Buckingham shames the Cardinal into fetching Prince Richard. While young Prince Edward plays in the throne room, Richard and Buckingham plot against him. Prince Edward greets his brother, asks playfully for Richard's dagger and sword, evokes terrifying stare by mocking his hump. Richard conducts them to the Tower and sends Catesby to sound out Hastings.

18. (3.2) *Hastings's Lodging*. As Catesby watches, a messenger interrupts Hastings's lovemaking with Jane Shore to tell him of Stanley's fearful dream of a boar and urges him to flee. Confident, he refuses. Catesby sounds

him out, finds him opposed to Richard's kingship, smiles knowingly as Hastings exults in the coming deaths of his enemies and joins Buckingham to ride toward London.

19. (3.4) *The Tower, Meeting Room.* Hastings ventures to speak for absent Richard about coronation. Richard enters, sends Archbishop to fetch strawberries, takes Buckingham aside and learns Hastings is against him, promises Buckingham earldom and riches, stuns the group by charging Queen and Jane Shore with witchcraft and ordering Hastings executed for his hesitation to agree. Hastings bemoans own follies, England's woes, is beheaded.

20. (3.5) *A carriage.* Richard's henchmen listen in disbelief as Buckingham dupes the Lord Mayor into accepting Hastings's execution.

21. (3.7) *Baynard's Castle.* Buckingham eats, tells disturbed Richard how coldly the people received the idea of his kingship, sends Richard to prepare for his performance, goes outside to set up the audience. Richard refuses, then accepts crown, slides down bell rope and forces Buckingham and others to kneel.

22. (4.1) *The Queen's Apartment.* She removes the crown and places it on remorseful Anne's head. Anne sorrows at giving in to Richard. The Queen worries about the Princes in the Tower.

23. (4.2) *Westminster.* Richard is crowned, drags faint Anne to the foot of the throne, leaves her and ascends alone, sits in a trance. When Buckingham hesitates to have Princes killed, angry Richard sends Catesby to find a killer, orders Stanley to leave his son as hostage, pushes Buckingham away denying him promised wealth. Buckingham flees. Tyrrel agrees to kill Princes.

24. (4.3) *The Tower.* Voice-over narration as the sleeping Princes are smothered.

25. *A Street.* Stanley gives fleeing Buckingham letter for Richmond.

26. (4.3, 4.4) *The Palace.* Tyrrel reports to Richard the deed is done. Richard, noting Anne is dead, intends to marry Elizabeth who might marry Richmond. Messengers report Buckingham has fled, Richmond has landed and claims the crown, rebels are up in arms, Buckingham is taken. "Off with his head. So much for Buckingham." Richard bustles off to prepare to fight.

27. (5.2) *Bosworth Field.* Richard orders his tent pitched, sends message to Stanley to be ready at dawn. Stanley rides to Richmond and promises aid.

28. (5.3) *Richard's Camp, Night.* Melancholy Richard gives final orders, sits alone.

29. (5.3) *Richmond's Camp, Night.* Richmond bids his followers good night, prays for victory over the usurper.

30. (5.3) *Richard's Tent, Night.* Sweating Richard has a nightmare in which the ghosts of Clarence, the Princes, Hastings, and Anne bid him "despair and die!" Buckingham's roaring spirit wakes him. He shakes off fear, arms, draws battle plan on grass with his sword.

31. (5.3, 5.4, 5.5) *Bosworth Field, Day.* The armies clash. Stanley holds off his troops and Richmond's reserve troops turn the tide. Richard has two horses killed under him, fights like a demon. Norfolk is killed on a bridge as Catesby summons him to rescue Richard. Richard: "A horse! A horse! My kingdom for a horse!" Catesby is slain. Soldiers circle Richard, strip off his armor and butcher him, stand back in horror at his death throes and final defiant flourishing of his sword. Stanley recovers the crown from a bush and walks toward Richmond. Crown remains above credits.

## MACBETH

United States. Mercury Productions, Republic. 1948. Black and white. 35mm.

Producer and Director:   Orson Welles
Script:   Orson Welles
Photography:   John L. Russell
Design:   Fred Ritter, John McCarthy, Jr., James Redd, Adele Palmer
Editor:   Louis Lindsay
Music:   Jacques Ibert
Sound:   John Stransky, Jr., Garry Harris

NARRATOR AND MACBETH:
  Orson Welles
LADY MACBETH:   Jeanette Nolan
MACDUFF:   Dan O'Herlihy
BANQUO:   Edgar Barrier
MALCOLM:   Roddy McDowall
DUNCAN:   Erskine Sanford
HOLY FATHER:   Alan Napier
ROSS:   John Dierkes
LENNOX:   Keene Curtis
LADY MACDUFF AND WITCH:
  Peggy Webber
SIWARD:   Lionel Braham

YOUNG SIWARD:   Archie Heugley
MACDUFF'S CHILD:
  Christopher Welles
FIRST MURDERER AND WITCH:
  Brainerd Duffield
SECOND MURDERER:   William Alland
SEYTON:   George Chirello
PORTER:   Gus Schilling
FLEANCE:   Jerry Farber
GENTLEWOMAN AND WITCH:
  Lurene Tuttle
WITCH:   Charles Lederer
THIRD MURDERER:   Robert Alan
DOCTOR:   Morgan Farley

There are different versions of Welles's *Macbeth* in circulation. This outline is based on the final version.

1. (1.1) *The Heath*. Shots of rolling fog, a stone Celtic cross, three witches on a rock peak, their bubbling brew, as Welles narrates: "Our story is laid in Scotland, ancient Scotland, savage, halflost in the mist that hangs between recorded history and the time of legends. The cross itself is newly arrived here. Plotting against Christian law and order are the agents of chaos, priests of hell and magic, sorcerers, and witches. Their tools are ambitious men. This is the story of such a man and his wife. A brave soldier, he hears from witches a prophecy of future greatness, and on this cue murders his way up to a tyrant's throne, only to go down hated and in blood at the end of all. Now riding homeward from victorious battle in defense of his true king, here on the blasted heath, the witches hail him king. Here the spell is laid upon him and the story begins." The witches take a lump of clay from their boiling cauldron and shape it into an image of Macbeth.

2. Titles over eerie music, then a military march.

3. (1.3) *The Heath*. The witches hail Macbeth as Glamis, Cawdor, King, crown clay idol, hail Banquo father of kings. The Holy Father banishes witches. Macbeth named Thane of Cawdor.

4. (1.5) *Cave*. Macbeth tells Holy Father of witches' prophecy.

5. (1.5) *Lady Macbeth's Bedroom*. Aroused Lady Macbeth reads Macbeth's letter, strokes fur sensuously, goes to barred window to call upon spirits to unsex her.

6. (1.4, 1.5) *Macbeth's Castle*. Cawdor is brought in and taken to the the executioner's block. Macbeth arrives and embraces Lady Macbeth as Cawdor is beheaded. She urges him to "provide" for Duncan.

7. (1.6, 1.7) *Castle*. Procession as Duncan and his men enter. Holy Father conducts a service in which all renounce Satan, while Lady Macbeth persuades Macbeth to kill Duncan. Juxtaposition of Duncan learning Cawdor is dead and his thanking Macbeth. Lady Macbeth drugs the wine and precedes Duncan to his room.

8. (2.1, 2.2) *Castle*. Macbeth has doubts, is persuaded once more by his wife. He meets sardonic Banquo. Lady Macbeth takes daggers from drugged guards. Macbeth voice-over soliloquy. Lady Macbeth's shadow passes over sleeping Duncan. A zoom-dissolve from Macbeth's face to the idol with a sword passing before its eyes. Lady Macbeth challenges his manhood and he ascends, his shadow passing over Duncan as he moves toward his bed. She waits in fear. He descends, disgusted with his hangman's hands, weary. She seizes the daggers and ascends as knocking at the

gate begins. Both are shaken by blood as knocking gets louder and they go to wash.

9. (2.3) *Castle*. Porter admits MacDuff and Lennox who talks with shaken Macbeth while MacDuff goes up to arouse Duncan. Cries of murder, treason. Bell rings. Holy Father finds Macbeth cutting the throats of the grooms, tells Malcolm of the murder, eyes Macbeth suspiciously with others as he tries to explain his act. Macbeth is saved only by Lady Macbeth's fainting. Malcolm and MacDuff flee. Banquo accuses Macbeth of the crime, reminds him of the rest of the prophecy, promises to support Macbeth if it costs nothing.

10. *Cavelike Interior*. Macbeth wanders, berates Lady Macbeth for her sterility, finds himself damned to make Banquo's issue kings, pushes his seductive wife away, wanders in watery caves, screams and cries out he has murdered sleep.

11. *Castle Exterior*. Three witches damn Macbeth to no sleep, pour water over the clay image and crown it.

12. (3.1) *Castle Interior*. Macbeth looks at the distorted images of his crowned head in a shield, curses his insecurity, drunkenly walks past his horned troops to comic tuba theme, sits in his throne looking over sparse courtiers, asking Banquo about his ride, urging "fail not our feast."

13. (3.3) *Heath*. Two murderers perch in a craggy tree, kill Banquo. Fleance escapes.

14. (3.4) *Castle Interior*. Murderers report to Macbeth. He backs in a corner "cabined, cribbed, confined," wanders through labyrinthine caves hearing Banquo's voice accuse him. He bathes his face, joins his guests, stares in shock as guests disappear and Banquo's bloody figure sits at the end of the table. He calms himself, sees the image again, rushes to the end of the table, overturns it, babbles of murder. Lady Macbeth dismisses suspicious guests, leaves.

15. (4.1) *Heath*. With grotesque shadows flashing in the sky behind him, exultant Macbeth learns from witches of danger of MacDuff, that none of woman born can harm him, that forest must come to his castle if he is to be defeated.

16. (4.2) *Castle Interior*. Lady MacDuff and children warned by Holy Father. Macbeth enters with armed soldiers and slaughters them. Macbeth and Lady Macbeth wearily speak of fear, wading in blood, longing for death.

17. (4.3) *English Plain*. Celtic cross. Birds sing. MacDuff, Malcolm, and Ross speak of horrors in Scotland. Holy Father tells MacDuff of the slaughter. MacDuff's grief turns to anger, and they resolve to attack Macbeth.

18. *Scottish Heath*. Triumphant march music as Malcolm's followers fill the sky with crosses, exult over Macbeth's weakness.

19. (5.3) *Castle*. Servants, courtiers, soldiers flee. Scorning news of 10,000 enemy troops, Macbeth boasts he cannot be defeated. Voice-over: "I have lived long enough. . . ." Weary Macbeth bids his sparse followers arm, observes doctor tending sleepless staring Lady Macbeth on her bed ("Canst though not minister to a mind diseased?"), arms as more of his followers flee.

20. (5.4) *Heath*. Malcolm's hoards of soldiers march toward Dunsinane. MacDuff orders trees cut. Branches move eerily through fog.

21. (5.1) *Castle*. Doctor and woman watch Lady Macbeth leave scene of murder, drop candle and rub hands. She relives the crime, embraces Macbeth, backs away from him in horror.

22. *Heath*. Branches advance through fog. Eerie music.

23. *Castle*. Lady Macbeth plunges screaming off rocky cliff.

24. (5.5, 5.6, 5.7, 5.8) *Castle*. Macbeth with spiked crown, Stonehenge-like rocks in distance, told by dwarf Seyton that Lady Macbeth is dead. His voice over shifting fog: "tomorrow, and tomorrow, and tomorrow." Wood reported moving. Macbeth cries to arm, finds Seyton hung from bellrope, rushes to wall to find thousands of roaring men invading his undefended castle. He hurls spiked spear and kills Holy Father. Macbeth slays young Siward, sees dark figure of MacDuff as shadow on walls and obscure vision in fog. Macbeth tells of prophecy about no man of woman born. MacDuff was from his mother's womb untimely ripped (witches echo the phrase). Macbeth flees, turns and fights at prospect of being displayed like a monster. They fight. Cut at the moment of beheading to clay doll whose head topples off. The crown falls at Malcolm's feet. MacDuff tosses Macbeth's head down to the cheering troops. All raise torches and crosses, hailing Malcolm king of Scotland.

25. Dissolve to *foggy exterior* of castle. Three witches watch and wait. Shot of rolling fog with three dim figures superimposed on it. "Peace, the charm's wound up."

KUMONOSU-DJO
(THE CASTLE OF THE SPIDER'S WEB)
THRONE OF BLOOD

Japan. Toho. 1957. Black and white. 35mm. United States title: *Throne of Blood*

Producers:   Shojiro Motoki, Akira Kurosawa
Director:   Akira Kurosawa

Script: Shinobu Hashimoto, Ryuzo Kikushima, Hideo Oguni, Akira
   Kurosawa (in Japanese, subtitled)
Photography: Asakazu Nakai
Design: Yoshiro Muraki, Kohei Ezaki
Editor: Akira Kurosawa
Music: Masaru Sato
Sound: Fumio Yanoguchi

TAKETOKI WASHIZU (MACBETH):
   Toshiro Mifune
ASAJI (LADY MACBETH):
   Isuzu Yamada
KUNIHARU TSUZUKI (DUNCAN):
   Takamaru Sasaki
NORIYASU ODAGURA:
   Takashi Shimura

HOSHIAKI MIKI (BANQUO):
   Minoru Chiaki
YOSHITERU (FLEANCE):   Akira Kubo
KUNIMARU (MALCOLM):
   Yoichi Tachikawa
WITCH:   Chieko Naniwa

1. Titles over still of tangled forest.

2. (1.1) *Foggy Hills, Ruins of the Castle*. Chorus sings of mighty fortress, warrior murdered by ambition.

3. (1.2) *Forest Castle*. Wounded soldier reports to Kuniharu (Duncan) that Miki (Banquo) and Washizu (Macbeth) are fighting off the rebels. More messengers report the enemy is defeated. Kuniharu orders the traitor executed and Washizu and Miki to come to him.

4. (1.3) *Forest*. Washizu and Miki become lost in labyrinthine forest which blends sun and rain. They ride and do battle against mocking evil spirit. They come upon a ghostly white figure spinning thread in a house of sticks who sings of men's vanity and death, the attraction of ambition, the futures of Washizu who will rule the Forest Castle and Miki whose son will rule it. The figure blows away and the soldiers find themselves among heaps of skulls and bones. They ride back and forth in the fog, find their way out, laugh off their dream.

5. (1.4) *Forest Castle*. Washizu and Miki appear before Kuniharu. Washizu is made master of First Fort, realizes what may lie ahead.

6. (1.6) *First Fort*. Peaceful scene as soldiers call their master's new home a paradise, speak of Lord and Lady's happiness.

7. (1.7) *First Fort, Interior*. Asaji (Lady Macbeth) urges Washizu to decide, notes Kuniharu killed his Lord and seized the castle.

8. (1.6) *First Fort*. Messengers announce unexpected visit of Kuniharu.

283

Washizu calls men to arm, suspects sneak attack, rushes out to see peaceful group laughing, returning from a hunt.

9. *First Fort*. Kuniharu announces the hunt is a ruse, Washizu will lead the attack against unpunished rebel Inui.

10. (1.7) *First Fort*. Immobile Asaji persuades Washizu he will be shot down from behind while the favorite Miki guards the Forest Castle. He kneels beside her disturbed.

11. *First Fort*. Servants pass Kuniharu's guards, fearfully enter forbidden room with blood-stained walls where a traitor had killed himself, to prepare it for Washizu and Asaji.

12. (1.7) *First Fort, Interior*. Asaji urges Washizu to make the prophecy come true, says she will drug the guards, leads him to the mat on which Kuniharu knelt, challenges his manhood. Lights appear through opaque screens as servants announce forbidden room is ready. Asaji disappears in dark doorway, returns with wine.

13. (2.1, 2.2) *Courtyard and Forbidden Room*. Asaji finds guards drugged. Brings Washizu one of their spears and silently forces him to go in and kill. She stares at the blood-stained wall, does a formal dance. Enter Washizu backing away from his deed. She wrests the bloody spear from his hands, places it by guards, returns to wash hands, opens gate and cries murder. Washizu, jarred into action, stabs one of the groggy guards.

14. *Battlefield*. Horses pull down flower-emblazoned banner. Noriyasu and Kuniharu's son, Kunimaru (Malcolm), flee Washizu's troops and ride to Forest Castle to tell Miki of Washizu's treachery. Miki fires on them and they flee. Washizu intends to test Miki.

15. *Outside Forest Castle*. Washizu shouts before gate that he is bringing in Kuniharu's body, rides ahead of slow procession. Tension breaks as Miki opens gates, rides in with Washizu past mourning women. Miki says he will recommend the strongest man, Washizu, to be Lord.

16. *Forest Castle Tower*. Soldiers looking on their former castle note how far they have come, wish luck would continue and Washizu and Asaji would produce an heir.

17. *Forest Castle Interior*. Washizu intends to proclaim Miki's son heir, but Asaji dissuades him by declaring she is pregnant.

18. (3.1) *Miki's Castle Courtyard*. Miki's soldiers try to saddle his panicked white stallion. Yoshiteru (Fleance) urges him not to go, not to believe the spirit's prophecy. Miki insists. The horse is saddled but still runs wild.

19. *Miki's Castle Courtyard, Night*. Men see Miki's masterless horse enter.

20. (3.4) *Forest Castle Banquet Room*. Nervous Washizu cuts off an actor's sung narrative of an ambitious man punished, drinks in silence, shrieks in terror as he sees the chalk-white figure of Miki's ghost. It disap-

pears and Asaji laughs and covers for him. He sees it again, draws his sword and slashes at the air. Asaji asks the guests to leave. A soldier brings Miki's head in a cloth, says the son escaped. Scornful Asaji exits. Enraged Washizu stabs the man in the neck, backs away in horror as man crawls toward him, dies.

21. *Forest Castle in Fog.* Soldiers gossip about rotting foundations, Washizu's followers falling away. Yoshiteru's troops preparing attack.

22. (5.2, 5.3) *Forest Castle Interior.* Old woman reports Washizu's child was stillborn, begs him to spare Asaji. He returns to room and cries "Fool!" Messengers bring news of attacks. Soldiers prepare.

23. *Forest Castle Interior.* Washizu berates counsellors for failing to have a plan. Storm coming up. He calls for horse.

24. (4.1) *Forest.* Washizu rides furiously through the forest calling for the spirit. It appears among heaps of bones, predicts he will never lose a battle until the forest approaches the castle. Laughing spirit urges him to make mountain of dead, river of blood.

25. (5.4) *Forest.* Noriyasu, Yoshiteru, and Kunimaru lead thousands of men to edge of wood. Noriyasu commands them to ignore the maze of paths and ride straight through. They do.

26. (5.3) *Forest Castle Yard.* Washizu chastizes his troops for giving up their stations in the forest, rushes up on ramparts to see enemy lining up after coming through forest, rouses the courage of his troops by telling them of the spirit's prophecy.

27. *Ramparts.* Soldier looks out in dark, hears chopping of wood.

28. *Forest Castle Interior.* Washizu boasts to his council that the fortress is too strong to be captured. All rise in terror as birds from forest invade the room. Washizu says it is a fortunate omen.

29. (5.1) *Foggy Exterior of Castle, Night.* Inside, council sleeps. Women cry "My Lady!" Washizu rushes through panicked women, sees Asaji with insane mask compulsively washing her hands, shouts but is unable to stop her.

30. (5.5, 5.6, 5.7, 5.8) *Forest Castle Courtyard.* Washizu's troops flee the walls. He climbs up, sees forest moving eerily through the fog, backs away in fear, looks again, backs away again, looks, addresses men commanding them to their posts. First one arrow then scores of them stick all around him as his troops fire at him. Showers of arrows strike all around him as he runs one way, then another. An arrow pierces him in the neck. He struggles down the stairs. They back away in fear. He attempts to draw, and falls dead, the fog swirling around his body. Outside the troops behind the branches are urged on by Noriyasu.

31. *Hills.* Forest Castle disappears in fog. Chorus sings once more of the proud warrior murdered by ambition. "Still his spirit walks, his fame is

known, for what once was so now is still true. Murderous ambition will pursue beyond the grave to give its due." Fog-shrouded hills.

## MACBETH

Great Britain. Playboy, Columbia-Warner. 1971. Color. Todd-a-o 35.

Producer: Andrew Braunsberg
Director: Roman Polanski
Script: Roman Polanski, Kenneth Tynan
Photography: Gilbert Taylor
Design: Wilfred Shingleton, Fred Carter
Editor: Alastair McIntyre
Music: Third Ear Band

MACBETH: Jon Finch
LADY MACBETH: Francesca Annis
ROSS: John Stride
BANQUO: Martin Shaw
DUNCAN: Nicholas Selby
MALCOLM: Stephen Chase
DONALBAIN: Paul Shelley
MACDUFF: Terence Bayler

YOUNG WITCH: Noelle Rimmington
BLIND WITCH: Maisie MacFarquhar
FIRST WITCH: Elsie Taylor
LADY MACDUFF: Diane Fletcher
DOCTOR: Richard Pearson
PORTER: Sidney Bromley
FIRST MURDERER: Michael Balfour
SECOND MURDERER: Andrew McCulloch

1. (1.1) *Tidal Flat, Sunrise.* Three witches dig a hole, bury a hangman's noose, severed hand, and dagger, pour on baboon's blood, and walk slowly into a bank of fog. Titles over fog and brutal sounds of warfare.

2. (1.2) *Tidal Flat.* The fog clears. Victorious soldiers kill the survivors. Duncan arrives, hears bloody soldier report Macbeth's victory, greets Ross, removes chain of office from doomed Cawdor's neck and bids the lords give it to Macbeth.

3. (1.3) *Battlefield.* Macbeth and Banquo watch rebel soldiers being hung, and as slow, sour bagpipe plays, they take shelter in the witches' ruin and watch refugees. Singing leads them to the witches where they hear the prophecies, and they ride away laughing.

4. (1.3) *Macbeth's Camp.* Macbeth wakes in his tent, wonders about prophecies. Ross and others greet him as Cawdor. Banquo warns him of the instruments of darkness. He is "rapt" thinking on ill and good before joining the observant thanes.

5. (1.4) *Duncan's Castle, Forres.* Disturbed Duncan and sons watch

chained Cawdor sardonically mouth "long live the King" and leap to his death.

6. (1.5) *Macbeth's Castle, Inverness.* Lady Macbeth receives Macbeth's letter among peasants and animals in courtyard, ascends the stairs thinking on Macbeth's lack of "ill" to match his ambition.

7. (1.4) *Duncan's Castle.* Duncan thanks Macbeth and Banquo, names Malcolm Prince of Cumberland (drawing disturbed looks from Donalbain and Macbeth), announces his intention to visit Inverness. Macbeth hides his anger, looks at swaying body of Cawdor, leaves.

8. (1.5) *Inverness.* Macbeth's cheerful homecoming. In bed Lady Macbeth flushed with excitement, urges him to murder, kisses him.

9. (1.6, 1.5) *Inverness.* Lady Macbeth, servants prepare for Duncan. As the King rides toward the castle, Lady Macbeth watches from the battlements, calls on spirits to unsex her and fill her with cruelty. Clouds darken sky and sour bagpipe music plays as Duncan approaches. "Come thick night" as Lady Macbeth descends. Macbeth watches the arrival as rain shower begins.

10. (1.7) *Main Hall.* Seated by feasting Duncan, Macbeth thinks "if twere done when tis done." Shutter blows open and horses panic. Proud Banquo watches Fleance sing "O your two eyes will slay me suddenly" as Macbeth thinks on the horror of the crime. Lady Macbeth weeps in shame and disappointment at his decision not to proceed, as Duncan's grooms dance sword dance. Malcolm's insolence and Lady Macbeth's urging persuade Macbeth to do it.

11. (2.1) *Inverness, Night.* Macbeth and Lady Macbeth watch Duncan retire. She goes to drug the grooms. He goes to engage Banquo in conversation, offer him "honor." Alone, Macbeth sees silver dagger, looks over quiet courtyard, backs away from Duncan's door until Lady Macbeth softly rings bell. He enters, drags grooms out of the way, approaches Duncan, can't bring himself to kill. Duncan awakes and sees Macbeth with the dagger. Macbeth leaps astride him, stabs again and again. Crown rolls onto floor, stops moving as Macbeth cuts the King's throat.

12. (2.2) *Courtyard.* Lady Macbeth starts at each sound, stares at the blood on Macbeth's hands and robe, seizes the daggers from him and goes up to smear the grooms with blood. Macbeth goes to the well, drops the bucket at the loud knock at the gate. She returns and they wash and go in. Hook on rope swings. Roosters crow.

13. (2.3) *Courtyard.* Porter relieves himself against wall, opens the gate to let in MacDuff and Lennox and the dawn. Macbeth greets them. MacDuff goes in to discover the murder. Shouts, alarm bell. Macbeth rushes up. Grooms wake and stare at blood. Macbeth draws a sword on them. Confusion. Courtyard fills, terror as all learn. They stare in disbelief

as they hear that Macbeth killed the grooms. People file in to see Duncan. Lady Macbeth faints on seeing minced bodies of grooms. Women wash Duncan's body. Malcolm and Donalbain stay by body as other dress to meet. The brothers resolve to flee. Camera holds on open doors.

14. (2.4) *Exterior*. Funeral procession. Ross looks at the body, learns from MacDuff that the sons are accused and Macbeth will be named king, resolves, unlike MacDuff, to attend coronation.

15. (3.1) *Exterior, Dawn*. Banquo thinks "thou hast it now," as Macbeth in white robe is given sword and scepter and raised on shield.

16. (3.1) *Forres, Courtyard*. Dogs bark at caged bear Macbeth calls his "chief guest." Macbeth asks Banquo where he will ride, complains Duncan's sons have not confessed, ascends stairs part way with Lady Macbeth, then leaves her.

17. (3.1) *Macbeth's Bedchamber*. Macbeth watches Banquo and son ride out, lets in father and son (murderers) and persuades them Banquo is their enemy, drinks with them, sends them out, and retires. In a dream Fleance appears, then Banquo, and they set about to kill Macbeth. He grabs at the hand that is at his throat but it is Lady Macbeth's and he wakes. They embrace wearily. He washes and looks out window ("come seeling night") at rider in distance against orange sky.

18. (3.3) *Forest*. Ross rides to find murderers felling trees across path. They trap Banquo and Fleance, Banquo shoots Ross's horse from under him as he tries to stop fleeing boy, and murderer axes Banquo in the spine and pushes him into water.

19. (3.4) *Forres*. Dogs are set loose on chained bear as Lady Macbeth watches terrified and disgusted, but fascinated. Seyton brings Macbeth to the murderers where he learns Fleance has escaped. Seyton leads murderers to their "reward"—they are pushed into a flooded dungeon. Servants drag dead dogs and bear, wipe up blood.

20. (3.4) *Banquet Hall*. Macbeth washes, welcomes his guests, drinks toast to absent Banquo. He is puzzled to be invited to full table, drops his goblet as he sees bloody Banquo's ghost. Guests rise, Lady Macbeth re-assures. Macbeth backs to the post where the bear was chained as the ghost, with a falcon, strides toward him. Lady Macbeth dismisses thanes. The camera holds on the empty banquet table.

21. *The Macbeths' Bedroom*. As they lie sleepless in bed, the red light of dawn falls on them.

22. (4.1) *Witches' Ruin*. On the ramparts Lady Macbeth watches Macbeth ride along horizon. A witch pulls Macbeth into a room full of naked hags, offers him a goblet of brew. He drinks, drops the goblet and stares into the cauldron where his own reflection tells him beware MacDuff, he sees a womb split open and a child removed, a boy urges him to be bloody and

bold, an armored knight offers him a sword, and as he stabs the armor falls in a heap and a serpent crawls out. Applauding, mocking Malcolm and Donalbain in white robes declare Macbeth cannot be defeated until Birnam Wood comes to Dunsinane Hill. Superimposition of moving forest as Macbeth asks who can recruit the forest. When he asks if Banquo's issue shall reign, he sees one king holding a mirror, another in the mirror, etc. Macbeth smashes the mirror, finds himself in empty ruin, door banging in the wind, cauldron overturned. He goes out in rain and sunshine.

23. (3.6, 5.1) *Great Hall.* Lady Macbeth asleep over her sewing. Lords sitting at table learn MacDuff is fled. She starts to see drops of blood on her hands. Ironic lords chuckle over Macbeth's false accusations. Macbeth enters, learns MacDuff is gone, approaches Lady Macbeth who retreats. He thinks on slaughter of MacDuff's family.

24. (4.2) *MacDuff's Castle.* Outside, soldiers wait. Children play blind-man's buff. Ross reassures angry Lady MacDuff, bids warm farewell, leaves gates open and soldiers ride in. She washes witty boy in tub. A scream. Cutthroats enter, destroy, kill boy. She runs past men raping servant girl to stare in horror at butchered babes in nursery. Flames engulf screen.

25. (5.1) *Lady Macbeth's Bedchamber.* Doctor and Nurse observe nude Lady Macbeth sleepwalking, washing her hands in an imaginary bucket. He makes notes, they cover her, and he reports to Macbeth on the ramparts.

26. (5.2, 5.3) *Forres.* Thanes leave letters and chains of office and ride out. Ross seizes them from Seyton and delivers them to Macbeth, who to the delight of his henchmen tears and burns them. He goes out to the battlements leaving doubtful lords behind, places chain of office on Seyton, leaves Ross smiling bitterly.

27. (4.3) *Exterior.* Malcolm and MacDuff lament Scotland's woe. Ross arrives. They walk past tents, troops, old Siward practice-duelling with his son. Ross tells MacDuff of the slaughter of his family. Malcolm urges anger. MacDuff vows to kill Macbeth.

28. *Exterior.* Lords who have abandoned Macbeth join his cheering enemies.

29. (5.3) *Great Hall.* Macbeth mocks frightened messenger, drinks, thinks to himself "I have lived long enough." Seyton confirms enemy numbers. Macbeth mocks fleeing Doctor about Scotland's sickness.

30. (5.4) *Birnam Wood.* Troops of Macbeth's enemies meet and cheer. Soldiers but boughs.

31. (1.5) *Forres.* Camera booms in on window revealing Lady Macbeth weeping, compulsively reading over Macbeth's letter about the witches.

32. (5.5) *Forres, Night.* Macbeth boasts his castle's strength, hears scream, notices he has lost the taste of fear. Seyton reports Lady Macbeth is dead. Macbeth comes down into courtyard thinking "Tomorrow, and tomorrow,

and tomorrow," sees her contorted body. A soldier cries out. Macbeth goes to see the wood move as dawn comes, is "weary of the sun." Fleeing soldiers kill Seyton, leave gates open, Lady Macbeth's body lying in courtyard. Fog obscures the castle.

33. (5.7, 5.8) *Forres*. Fog lifts to reveal troops advancing. They find the gates open, hunt for Macbeth, find him on the throne. Macbeth kills young Siward and two soldiers, walks out and challenges whole army. Macbeth fights Banquo, knocks him down but refuses to kill him. Banquo reveals he was from the womb untimely ripped, attackes Macbeth, skewers and beheads him. Banquo cries "Hail, King" and Ross wipes blood from crown and gives it to Malcolm. Surreal silent shots of mocking soldiers as Macbeth's head is carried up to the ramparts. Army outside cheers.

34. *Witches' Ruin*. Rain. Slow, sour bagpipe music. Donalbain takes shelter, hears singing, goes to investigate. Horse by the ruins. Credits over sound loop of drum and guitar.


## OTHELLO


Morocco. Mogador Films, Mercury Productions. 1951. Black and white. 35mm.

Producer and Director:  Orson Welles
Script:  Orson Welles, Jean Sacha
Photography:  Anchise Brizzi, George Fanto, Obadan Troania, Roberto Fusi, G. Araldo
Design:  Alexander Trauner, Luigi Schiaccianoce, Maria de Matteis
Editors:  Jean Sacha, Renzo Lucidi, John Shepridge
Music:  Francesco Lavagnino, Alberto Barberis
Sound:  Piscatrelli

NARRATOR:  Orson Welles
OTHELLO:  Orson Welles
IAGO:  Michael MacLiammoir
DESDEMONA:  Suzanne Cloutier
RODERIGO:  Robert Coote
CASSIO:  Michael Lawrence
BRABANTIO:  Hilton Edwards

EMELIA:  Fay Compton
LODOVICO:  Nicholas Bruce
MONTANO:  Jean Davis
BIANCA:  Doris Dowling
SENATOR:  Joseph Cotten
PAGE:  Joan Fontaine

Note: Many of the voices of the minor parts, including Roderigo, were dubbed in by Welles himself.

1. (Cinthio; 1.1, 1.3) *Cyprus*. Mourning chorus, bells, drums as the bodies of Othello and Desdemona are carried in processions silhouetted against the sky. Iago dragged by chain and suspended in iron cage where he looks down on procession. Welles narrates from Cinthio: "There was once in Venice a Moor, Othello, who for his merits in the affairs of war was held in great esteem. It happened that he fell in love with a young and noble lady called Desdemona, who, drawn by his virtue, became equally en-amoured of Othello. So it was that since her father was much opposed to the union of Desdemona with a Moor, she fled her house at night and in secret haste they were married." (Shots of gondola, she rushing out of house to meet him.) "Now there was in Othello's company an Ensign named Iago of a very amiable outward appearance but whose character was extremely treacherous." (Shadow of Iago watching marriage, and glimmering water superimposed.) Iago reveals his hatred of the Moor to Roderigo as they watch Othello and Desdemona pass by in the gondola.

2. (1.1, 1.2) *Brabantio's House*. Barking dogs, bells, cries of "thieves" wake Brabantio. Below his balcony Iago and Roderigo tell of Desdemona's flight. Brabantio and followers descend, travel to Othello's dwelling, threaten to take him to prison.

3. (1.3) *Venice*. Welles narrates: "Now at the same hour there came messengers in haste to the Senate. For there was news that the Turkish fleet was moving against the Venetian garrison in Cyprus. The senators, already raised and met, had selected the Moor to the command of their troops, and officers were searching the town to apprise Othello of this new honor, when lo, Desdemona's old father himself brings the Moor at sword's point to the council chamber upon the charge of working upon Desdemona with unlawful enchantment." (People rushing toward Doge's palace, milling on balcony, rushing past statues, up stairs, Desdemona hurrying along arcade.) Othello arrives before senators, and, accused by Brabantio, tells of his wooing. Desdemona confirms her love, Brabantio leaves in misery, warns Othello outside "look to her, Moor...," collapses and is helped away.

4. (1.1, 1.3) *Venetian Arcade*. Iago assures Roderigo this love cannot last, greets Cassio, tells Roderigo of his envy. Othello calls up from St. Mark's Square ordering Iago to bring Desdemona to Cyprus. Iago scorns Othello's free and open nature, moves toward the camera: "I am not what I am."

5. *St. Mark's Square; Othello's Lodging*. Dissolve from mechanical figures striking clock above square to curtains. Othello parts them, bends to kiss Desdemona.

6. (2.1, 2.2) *Cyprus*. Thunder, lightning, clanking alarm bell as sea pounds the shore. Shouts and trumpets as wind-blown figures look out to sea, hear from ship the Turks are drowned. Envious Iago watches Cassio greet Desdemona. Othello's ship arrives. He climbs swirling stairs, embraces

Desdemona before fluttering pennants. Trumpets sound. Crier announces revels.

7. (2.1, 2.3) *Battlements*. Seeing Cassio above, Iago tells Roderigo Desdemona loves him, urges him to provoke Cassio to fight. Cassio comes down and Iago makes him drink. Revels.

8. (2.1) *Othello's Bedchamber*. Their shadows meet on the wall: "if I were to die...."

9. (2.3) *Cyprus*. Streets and cavernous vaults. Music and shouts. Cassio drinks with Bianca. Iago walks among celebrants. Twice Roderigo provokes Cassio and takes blows for it. Cassio nasty drunk. Taunted by Roderigo, he chases him down in the vaults, engages Montano in fight. Shouts, alarm bell. An officer brings them before Othello, leaving Roderigo in pool below. Othello appears, Desdemona behind him, dismisses Cassio.

10. (2.3) *Archway, Stairs*. Cock crows signalling day. Iago urges Cassio to appeal to Desdemona to be reinstated.

11. (2.3) *Ramparts*. Roderigo complains to Iago of pains and cost. Iago notes Cassio is ruined, Desdemona's virtue will ensnare her. He walks off under suspended cage.

12. (3.3, 3.4) *Ramparts, Fortress*. Troops and banners on walls. Soldiers look up at Desdemona. As Desdemona promises Cassio she will help, Iago and Othello see them: "I like not that." Desdemona comes down, teases and begs Othello to forgive Cassio. As Iago and Othello walk along battlements, Iago plants suspicion. Inside the fortress, Iago works on him more, removing Othello's armor, prodding him as he looks in a mirror. Desdemona arrives, tries to bind Othello's head with the handkerchief. He pushes her away, peers at her in a mirror, stares into her eyes. Emelia finds the handkerchief. Othello rushes past, looks at shadowed bed. Desdemona follows through vaulted room.

13. (3.3) *Steps*. Emelia gives the handkerchief to Iago.

14. (3.3) *Fortress*. Othello peers at Desdemona through pillars, flees her. Iago promises her to ask what troubles Othello. Iago follows Othello up on battlements, is backed to the edge and, as the sea roars below, is threatened if he does not provide proof of Desdemona's guilt. Told of Cassio's supposed revelations in a dream, Othello vows revenge, makes Iago his lieutenant.

15. *Cassio's Dwelling*. Iago walks past soldiers, whores, Arabs, drops the handkerchief through a window onto Cassio's bed.

16. (3.4) *Fortress Armory*. Desdemona interrupts Othello's work. He puts down his maps and reads her hand, demands the handkerchief. Answered by pleas for Cassio, he orders her away.

17. (3.4) *Cassio's Lodging*. Bianca finds the handkerchief on Cassio's bed. Cassio asks her to copy it, agrees to see her that night, is advised by Iago to see Desdemona again.

18. (3.4) *Fortress*. Emelia advises Desdemona cynically about men. Iago presents Cassio, who greets Desdemona on an arcade.

19. (4.1) *Fortress*. Othello and Iago hear trumpets announcing the arrival of ships from Venice. People rush to ramparts. On the wall, Iago says he will urge Cassio to talk of Desdemona while Othello overhears. As Othello listens through portal, Cassio boasts of Bianca's love, angry Bianca arrives and refuses to copy handkerchief, they go off. Iago follows wounded Othello as he wanders among shadows and grillwork.

20. (4.1, 3.3) *Fortress*. Othello sees Desdemona in distance, praises her. Cannonfire, soldiers on battlements. As they walk among sheep and goats beneath mesh of sticks, Iago taunts Othello with visions of the handkerchief and of Cassio and Desdemona in bed. Othello passes out on the beach, looks up at wall. Laughter of whores and soldiers blends with cries of gulls. Iago helps him. Soldiers with spears and banners on ramparts. Solitary Othello above them: "Oh now forever farewell the tranquil mind..." as ship moves near wall and strikes sail.

21. (4.1) *Port*. Othello greets Venetians, reads his orders, strikes Desdemona, humiliates her, exits. Iago won't explain.

22. (4.2) *Chapel*. Othello finds Desdemona praying, sits in shadows, runs his hand down her body, "the fountain from which my current runs," accuses her of being a strumpet, exits.

23. *Inside Fortress*. Iago looks down at stunned Desdemona. Emelia comforts her. Desdemona walks across scallop-patterned piazza.

24. (4.1) *Fortress*. Camera rushes toward troubled Othello. Iago urges him to strangle Desdemona, vows to kill Cassio, walks off in rain.

25. (4.2) *Desdemona's Bedchamber*. Iago finds suspicious Emelia comforting Desdemona. Othello orders her to prepare for bed.

26. (4.2) *Turkish Bath*. Mandolins play. Roderigo wrapped in towel complains to Iago, asks for his jewels back. Iago urges him to kill Cassio, gives him a dagger. Roderigo is betrayed by his dog. Cassio fends him off, is cut down from behind by Iago. Roderigo is trapped under board floor, stabbed by Iago.

27. (4.3) *Desdemona's Bedchamber*. Othello closes door. Desdemona hums willow song, hears Emelia say she would prostitute herself if the price were high enough, retires. Othello's shadow on the wall.

28. (5.2) *Desdemona's Bedchamber*. Othello stalks Desdemona in the darkness, puts out candles, urges her to pray. Accused, she protests her innocence, struggles. He smothers her with the sheet and a kiss. Chorus moans, alarm bell rings, soldiers run through the streets. On the bed, Othello: "roast me in sulpher...." Emelia discovers Desdemona dead, cries out bringing Iago and others, refutes Iago, is stabbed. Iago flees. She dies protesting Desdemona was chaste. Othello takes off his robe, stabs himself

in an archway: "here is my journey's end." Iago refuses to speak. Othello staggers, picks up Desdemona's body, looks up to Venetians from darkness, falls. Venetians slowly close the hatch on the vault.

29. Dissolve to the silhouetted funeral procession from the beginning. Credits over watery reflections of the Cyprus fortress and cage, Venetian buildings, ships.

## OTHELLO

Great Britain. BHE. 1965. Technicolor. Widescreen.

Producers: Anthony Havelock-Allan, John Brabourne
Director: Stuart Burge (Based on National Theatre production directed by John Dexter)
Photography: Geoffrey Unsworth
Design: William Kellner, Jocelyn Herbert
Editor: Richard Marden
Sound: John Cox, Dickie Bird

OTHELLO: Laurence Olivier
DESDEMONA: Maggie Smith
IAGO: Frank Finlay
EMELIA: Joyce Redman
CASSIO: Derek Jacobi
RODERIGO: Robert Lang
LODOVICO: Kenneth Mackintosh

BRABANTIO: Anthony Nicholls
BIANCA: Sheila Reid
GRATIANO: Michael Turner
MONTANO: Edward Hardwicke
DOGE: Harry Lomax
CLOWN: Roy Holder

1. (1.1) *Outside Brabantio's House, Night.* Credits over reddish brown arcade. Iago promises to aid Roderigo in his suit to Desdemona out of hatred for the Moor. They shout images of his daughter coupling with a black ram up at white-haired Brabantio on his balcony.

2. (1.2) *Outside Othello's Lodging, Night.* Othello toys with a rose, hums unconcerned at Iago's warning about Brabantio. Cassio brings a summons from the Duke about Cyprus. Brabantio and armed followers take Othello, who shuns violence, to the council.

3. (1.3) *Council Chamber, Night.* Brabantio charges Othello with witchcraft, flames with anger and loathing. Othello sends for Desdemona, tells

of his wooing. She arrives and confirms her love for Othello, asks to go to Cyprus with him. Brabantio bitterly warns Othello, "She has betrayed her father, and may thee."

4. (1.3) *Council Chamber, Night.* Iago cheers up despairing Roderigo, bids him "put money in thy purse" and follow Desdemona to Cyprus.

5. (2.1) *The Harbor at Cyprus.* Cassio arrives safely in a storm. Iago watches with interest Cassio's amorous greeting to Desdemona as the storm magically abates. Othello arrives and blissfully greets his "fair warrior," announces the Turks are drowned.

6. (2.1) *The Harbor at Cyprus.* Iago tells Roderigo Desdemona is in love with Cassio, asks him to provoke Cassio to fight. Alone, Iago confides his plan to discredit Cassio and be rewarded for it.

7. (2.3) *In Cyprus, Night.* Othello instructs Cassio to see to the watch, takes Desdemona to bed. Drums, shouts, revels. Iago sings, Cassio gets ugly drunk and fights with Roderigo and Montano, wounding the latter. Othello angrily stops the riot, dismisses Cassio, takes frightened Desdemona to bed. Iago urges Cassio to seek forgiveness through Desdemona, tells Roderigo to be patient, plans to have Othello "find Cassio soliciting his wife."

8. (3.1, 3.2, 3.3) *Outside Othello's Lodging.* Cassio has two musicians play. Iago has Emelia arrange for him to speak with Desdemona. Othello passes by. Cassio kneels to Desdemona for help and she agrees. Iago punctuates Othello's glimpse of Cassio hurrying away: "I like not that." Desdemona presses Cassio's suit. Othello resists, gives in. Desdemona exits. Iago takes Othello's robe and sword, works on his suspicion and jealousy, leaves and returns to beg that he not suspect Desdemona. She enters, tries to bind his aching head with her handkerchief, which drops as he tenderly leads her inside. Emelia picks up the handkerchief, reluctantly gives it to Iago, and is pushed away by disgusted Iago. Tortured Othello enters and Iago prods him until he threatens Iago's life, rips off his cross and vows revenge to pagan gods, makes Iago his lieutenant.

9. (3.4) *Desdemona's Room.* Othello notices Desdemona's hand is "hot and moist," demands the handkerchief, exits in a rage when she cannot produce it and presses Cassio's suit. Iago urges Cassio to press his suit. Hurt and puzzled Desdemona can do little.

10. (3.4) *Cyprus.* Accosted by Bianca, Cassio gives her Desdemona's handkerchief to copy.

11. (4.1) *Cyprus.* Iago torments Othello with visions of Cassio and Desdemona naked in bed until Othello has an epileptic fit. Concerned Cassio enters, exits. Iago revives Othello, and sets him behind a column to listen. As Othello mishears, Cassio boasts of Bianca's doting on him. Bianca enters in a jealous rage, throws Othello's handkerchief at him. Cassio fol-

lows her off. Grieved Othello thinks on Desdemona's beauty and accomplishments. Iago notes they make her the worse, urges him to strangle her in her bed.

12. (4.1) *Cyprus*. Lodovico and other Venetians arrive with orders putting Cassio in command, are shocked to see Othello strike his wife and exit bellowing "goats and monkeys."

13. (4.2) *Desdemona's Bedroom*. Othello refuses to believe Emelia's defense of Desdemona, is distraught as Desdemona cannot look him in the face, throws her to the floor, exits showering Emelia with coins as if he had visited a brothel. Iago and suspecting Emelia comfort Desdemona.

14. (4.2) *Cyprus, Night*. Roderigo feels cheated, intends to reveal himself to Desdemona, stabs at Iago. Iago shakes his hand, flatters him, sets him to murder Cassio so Othello and Desdemona will not leave Cyprus.

15. (4.3) *Desdemona's Bedroom, Night*. Othello commands Desdemona to go to bed and dismiss Emelia. He exits with the Venetians. Emelia helps Desdemona undress. Desdemona sings a willow song, has a premonition of death, sings a line out of place ("let nobody blame him, his scorn I approve"), thinks on the meaning of the lines "I called my love false love; but what said he then? / Sing all a green willow. / If I court more women, you'll couch with more men."

16. (5.1) *Cyprus, Night*. Urged to murderous assault by Iago, Roderigo is wounded by Cassio. Iago cuts down Cassio from behind, stabs Roderigo as crowd comes to Cassio's aid, accuses weeping Bianca, and bluffs suspicious crowd with a bold command to go.

17. (5.2) *Desdemona's Bedroom, Night*. Othello wakes sleeping Desdemona, urges her to pray. Her pleas of innocence only enrage him the more, and he smothers and strangles her. Emelia enters, mourns as Desdemona dies protesting Othello did not kill her. Emelia accuses Iago. Othello attacks him but is disarmed. Iago stabs Emelia and flees. She dies protesting Desdemona was innocent. Othello prepares to fight his way out, drops his sword, and laments by Desdemona's body. Iago is brought in, is wounded by Othello, refuses to speak. Othello embraces Desdemona, commits suicide. Cassio is made viceroy. Iago is taken off howling to be tortured. Camera holds on darkening image of the two bodies embracing on the bed.


HAMLET


Great Britain. Two Cities Film. 1948. Black and white. 35mm.

Producer and Director: Laurence Olivier
Script: Laurence Olivier, Alan Dent

Photography: Desmond Dickinson
Design: Carmen Dillon, Roger Furse
Editor: Helga Cranston
Music: William Walton
Sound: John Mitchell, L. E. Overton

Hamlet: Laurence Olivier
Claudius: Basil Sydney
Gertrude: Eileen Herlie
Ophelia: Jean Simmons
Polonius: Felix Aylmer
Laertes: Terence Morgan
Horatio: Norman Wooland
Osric: Peter Cushing
Priest: Russell Thorndike

Marcellus: Anthony Quayle
Bernardo: Esmond Knight
Francisco: John Laurie
Captain: Niall MacGinnis
First Player: Harcourt Williams
Second Player: Patrick Troughton
Third Player: Tony Tarver
Gravedigger: Stanley Holloway

1. Titles over waves pounding rocky shore at the foot of the castle in swirling mist. Boom slowly in toward castle from dizzying height. Olivier (voice-over): "So oft it chances in particular men / That through some vicious mole of nature in them, / By the o'ergrowth of some complexion / Of breaking down the pales and forts of reason, / Or by some habit grown too much: that these men— / Carrying, I say, the stamp of one defect, / Their virtues else—be they as pure as grace, / Shall in the general censure take corruption / From that particular fault." Boom in on soldiers bearing Hamlet's body. Olivier (voice-over): "This is the tragedy of a man who could not make up his mind." The men on the tower disappear into the mist.

2. (1.1) *The Ramparts.* Bernardo climbs spiralling stairs, is challenged by Francisco. Horatio and Marcellus arrive, and they sit to talk of the ghost. Loud heartbeat. They whirl to see crowned, bearded ghost in mist with visor half covering his face. Cock crows, ghost vanishes. Guards search, resolve to tell Hamlet.

3. (1.2) *Great Hall.* Camera travels down stairs, past two empty thrones in dark hall, up and rapidly in on Gertrude's bed. Dissolve to Claudius drinking from goblet as courtiers laugh. Claudius addresses courtiers, Laertes, Hamlet. Gertrude tries to rouse Hamlet from his sorrows and melancholy. Claudius scolds him, announces he is next in succession. All leave but Hamlet, who wanders to empty thrones thinking (voice-over) "Oh that this too too solid flesh...."

4. (1.3) *Polonius's Apartment.* Camera glides through archway to Ophelia reading letter from Hamlet. Laertes advises "best safety lies in fear," and in turn receives advice from his doddering father as Ophelia playfully toys with him. Laertes gone, Polonius reinforces Laertes' advice. Ophelia looks at Hamlet through archway, is called in.

5. (1.2) *Great Hall.* Hamlet watches Ophelia go in. The shadows of Horatio and guards appear; they tell him of the ghost. Hamlet walks to empty thrones: "foul deeds will rise...."

6. (1.4) *Ramparts.* Hamlet peers over the edge to the sea. Guards pace. Sounds of Claudius's revels below provoke Hamlet to speak against drunkenness. Heartbeat as shot of Hamlet goes in and out of focus. Ghost appears, Hamlet follows to the top of the tower where it tells him of murder, adultery, incest (inset of masked dumb show of poisoning of King Hamlet). Ghost disappears and Hamlet passes out. He wakes, vows revenge, makes others swear secrecy.

7. (2.1) *Ophelia's Room.* Ophelia narrates voice-over disturbed Hamlet's entrance to her room, peering into her eyes, exit.

8. (2.2) *Great Hall.* Polonius interrupts Claudius kissing Gertrude to reveal Hamlet's love for Ophelia. Hamlet above overhears plan to loose Ophelia to him, enters more obviously and mocks senile Polonius, exits. Polonius and King spy as Ophelia prays. Hamlet abuses her, hurls angry threats at arras, pauses to kiss hair of weeping Ophelia, exits. Worried spies come out.

9. (3.1) *Ramparts.* Camera sweeps up stairs. Orchestral and visual flourishes during "To be or not to be." Exit into fog.

10. (2.2) *Great Hall.* Hamlet in dark. Polonius announces the actors, reads the genres they have mastered off their playbill. Jovial players enter, Hamlet greets them, sends them with Polonius, asks First Player for "Murder of Gonzago," stares at tableau of instruments, props, costumes, then runs and pirouettes: "The play's the thing."

11. (3.2) *Great Hall with Stage.* Hamlet instructs chief actor, puts blonde wig on boy, dismisses them and urges Horatio to watch Claudius. Enter courtiers. Hamlet conducts Queen to throne, sits at Ophelia's feet and makes bawdy jokes. Camera wanders behind specators as the play (all in dumb show) is mimed. Claudius rises, puts his gnarled hands to his eyes, cries "Give me light!" Hamlet thrusts torch near his face, forcing him to flee. Fear and chaos. Wild Hamlet sings standing on throne, tells Horatio ghost was right. Polonius summons Hamlet to Queen. Hamlet alone speaks "Now is the very witching time of night" in dark, prays he will not kill his mother, ascends stairs.

12. (3.3) *King's Chamber.* Polonius announces to king he will spy on Hamlet and Gertrude, exits. Tormented Claudius prays. Hamlet comes

upon him, draws his sword, pauses, thinks (voice-over) of doing his enemy good, departs. Claudius finds prayer useless.

13. (3.4) *Gertrude's Bedchamber.* Polonius urges firmness, hides. Hamlet enters, hurls angry Queen on bed, hears Polonius's cry and thinking it is the King stabs through the arras. He discovers his mistake, pierces his mother's heart with dagger-words, compares portraits of her two husbands, becomes angry and is prevented from violence by presence of ghost (heart-beat, moan). The (to Gertrude) invisible ghost leaves Hamlet to plead once more, kiss and embrace her, and drag Polonius's body away.

14. (4.3) *Great Hall.* Claudius questions mocking Hamlet about Polonius's body, sends him under guard to England (for execution).

15. (4.5) *By Stream; Castle Interior.* Ophelia peers at her face in the stream, screams, rushes through her room to the Queen in the Great Hall where she raves. Claudius comes in to hear more ramblings. Horatio follows her off. Gertrude refuses to comfort troubled Claudius. Osric enters with two sailors and Hamlet's letters. King and Queen slowly ascend diverging staircases.

16. (4.6) *Ophelia's Room.* Horatio watches Ophelia outside, receives Hamlet's letters from sailors. As he reads Hamlet's voice-over description, dissolve to smoke, two ships grappling and parting, Hamlet taken, then back to Horatio reading.

17. (4.5) *Great Hall.* Ophelia walks through arches to where Laertes, sword drawn, demands to know of his father from the King and Queen. He is shocked as mad Ophelia imagines her father in his empty chair, distributes flowers, kneels at foot of arch, thinks, and exits.

18. (4.7) *Ophelia's Room; The Stream.* Camera travels into her room. Dissolve to stream. Gertrude's voice-over account as we see Ophelia float by, trailing flowers. The stream with Ophelia gone.

19. (5.1) *Graveyard.* Gravedigger sings and tosses out skull. With Horatio, Hamlet amused picks up skull, learns it was Yorick's, and philosophizes. A bell rings and they hide as a court funeral procession appears. Grieving Laertes jumps in grave and embraces Ophelia. Hamlet enters, they fight. Hamlet declares he loved Ophelia, and exits. All leave but Laertes and Claudius, who leads Laertes out.

20. (4.7) *Great Hall.* Claudius and Laertes drink and plot against Hamlet, the camera moving up and away three times.

21. (5.2) *Gallery above Great Hall; Great Hall.* Hamlet praises Horatio's justness and courage. Flighty Osric delivers challenge, falls down stairs. Hamlet speaks of ill about heart. Trumpets and torches as courtiers enter. Hamlet asks Laertes' forgiveness, kisses his mother while Osric gives Laertes an unbated sword. The king promises pearl to Hamlet if victorious. Hamlet wins first pass. Gertrude suspicious of pearl King puts in Hamlet's

drink. Hamlet wins second bout. Gertrude seizes cup and drinks despite King's objections. Third bout a draw. Laertes wounds Hamlet from behind. Hamlet attacks, seizes unbated sword, wounds Laertes in the wrist. Queen falls, reveals poison. Hamlet rushes up ramp and orders the doors locked. Laertes reveals he and Hamlet are dead and the King is to blame. Hamlet dives off ramp to Claudius, stabs him repeatedly. Claudius struggles to pick up crown. Soldiers with spears ring him in. He dies by Gertrude. Laertes dies. Hamlet stands before the throne and all kneel. He sits, asks Horatio to live and tell his story, dies. Horatio orders soldiers to bear Hamlet like a soldier. The camera follows the procession past an archway opening out on the graveyard and showing a firing cannon, past the empty chair with a flower on the arm associated with Hamlet and Polonius, up the stairs past the altar where Claudius prayed, past Gertrude's canopied bed, to the tower where the bearers are silhouetted against the sky.

## HAMLET

Russia. Lenfilm. 1964. Black and white. 70 mm Sovscope.

Director:   Grigori Kozintsev
Script:   Grigori Kozintsev, based on the translation by Boris Pasternak. In Russian, subtitled.
Photography:   I. Gritsyus
Design:   E. Ene, G. Kropachev, S. Virsaladze
Editor:   E. Makhankova
Music:   Dmitri Shostakovich
Sound:   B. Khutoryanski

| | | | |
|---|---|---|---|
| HAMLET: | Innokenti Smoktunovski | ROSENCRANTZ: | I. Dmitriev |
| CLAUDIUS: | Michail Nazwanov | GUILDENSTERN: | V. Medvedev |
| GERTRUDE: | Eliza Radzin-Szolkonis | HORATIO: | V. Erenberg |
| OPHELIA: | Anastasia Vertinskaya | GRAVEDIGGER: | V. Kolpakor |
| POLONIUS: | Yuri Tolubeyev | ACTORS: | A. Chekaerskii, R. Aren, |
| LAERTES: | S. Oleksenko | | Y. Berkun |
| FORTINBRAS: | A. Krevald | PRIEST: | A. Lauter |

1. *Elsinore.* Waves wash through the shadow of Elsinore as a bell tolls. Titles over rock with a blazing torch to the right. Billowing banners of

mourning. Hamlet rides toward the castle, ascends stairs, embraces his mother. The drawbridge is raised.

2. (1.2) *Courtyard; Chambers of State.* A soldier bluntly reads the beginning of Claudius's speech to peasants. Inside, courtiers repeat it and Claudius addresses his council, dealing with Fortinbras, Laertes, and Hamlet, who has left. Primping in a mirror, Gertrude urges Hamlet to cast off his mourning. Claudius names him next in line. Hamlet wanders among courtiers thinking "How weary, stale, flat, and unprofitable / Seem to me all the uses of this world." By a blazing fire Horatio tells Hamlet of the ghost. Hamlet broods sitting at the council table staring at the empty thrones.

3. (1.3) *Polonius's Apartment.* Ophelia dances awkwardly to broken music played by a crone in black. Laertes advises her to hold Hamlet's love "a toy in blood." Polonius gives departing Laertes advice, lectures Ophelia about Hamlet. The dance lesson continues.

4. *Courtyard.* Clock strikes twelve as figures of Bishop, King, Queen, Knight, and Death appear and disappear. Hamlet, Horatio, and soldiers search in dark.

5. *Great Hall.* Festive music as King and Queen appear, satyrs dance. Claudius, with carnal intent, rushes Gertrude into a room.

6. (1.4, 1.5) *Fortress Exterior.* Hamlet and his followers walk in windy dark courtyard. Horses in stable start. Burst of music as ghost appears above with cape flowing in slow motion. Horses panic and break loose. Hamlet follows the ghost to the edge of the sea and is told of the murder. The ghost disappears into the horizon as day comes. Hamlet lies unconscious on the rocks.

7. (2.1) *Ophelia's Bedroom.* Ophelia looks at a portrait of Hamlet. He enters, presses her against the bed and peers into her eyes, leaves. As Polonius instructs Reynaldo to spy on Laertes, weeping Ophelia enters and reports Hamlet's strange behavior.

8. *Great Hall.* Frightened courtiers back away from Hamlet who sits in shirtsleeves on the floor by a dead fireplace.

9. (2.2) *Gertrude's Bedroom.* Claudius paces as Gertrude sits in bed brushing her hair. Enter Polonius, who reports Hamlet's love for Ophelia. Gertrude is anxious to believe he is right. Polonius plans to "loose" his daughter to Hamlet and spy on them.

10. (2.2) *Exterior.* Polonius approaches Hamlet, who leans against the rocks, follows Hamlet along the gallery as Hamlet reads, insults the old man, leaves.

11. (2.2) *Courtyard; Hamlet's Room.* Rosencrantz and Guildensten ride in, greet Hamlet, go with him to his room where he questions why they have come, muses "what a piece of work is man," and learns the actors are coming.

12. (2.2) *Courtyard*. Enter players with their wagon, tumbling, shouting, playing music. Hamlet leaves Rosencrantz and Guildenstern, greets the actors warmly, hears the Priam speech to a background of clucking chickens. He sits on the prop wagon thinking "O what a rogue and peasant slave am I," asks the players to perform "The Murder of Gonzago," beats drum against rising music, shrieks, and leaps from wagon.

13. (3.1) *The Shore*. Waves crash against the rocks. Hamlet wanders among boulders thinking "To be or not to be," ascends the worn steps toward the castle.

14. (3.1) *Great Hall*. As Polonius and Claudius listen, Hamlet verbally abuses Ophelia, suspects she is a spy, pins her against a railing showing desire and anger, hunts for spies, exits. Polonius brushes aside his weeping daughter, tells the King he will spy on Hamlet and Gertrude.

15. *Elsinore Exterior*. Hamlet leans against massive buttresses blazoned with weathered coats of arms.

16. (3.2) *Stage in Courtyard*. Hamlet instructs the players, tells Horatio to observe Claudius, sets himself to watch and play the madman. Smiling King, Queen, and courtiers arrive. Hamlet makes bawdy remarks to Ophelia, bellows against his mother for forgetting his father. Trumpet. Hobbling player in fool's motley with a bladder on a stick rasps out the brief prologue. Claudius and nervous Gertrude watch the stylized melodrama against an ominous sky as Hamlet interjects comments. Hamlet and Horatio watch as the King slowly rises, applauds faintly, runs. Frantic music, chaos. Hamlet rushes in hall, instructs musicians to play flutes. Rosencrantz and Guildenstern are befuddled by Hamlet's antics climaxed by his comparison of himself to a recorder.

17. (3.3) *Claudius's Bedroom*. The King tells Rosencrantz and Guildenstern that Hamlet will be sent to England with them. Polonius leaves saying he will overhear Hamlet and Gertrude. Guilty Claudius looks at the distorted image of his face in the mirror, bows his head.

18. (3.4) *Gertrude's Bedroom*. Hamlet proceeds past spies and attendants toward Gertrude's room. Polonius hides behind a tapestry. Hamlet enters, closes the door threateningly. When Polonius echoes her cry for help, Hamlet stabs through the curtain with his dagger, discovers it is Polonius. He shows the portraits of Gertrude's two husbands, becomes angry as she becomes more hysterical. Music announces presence of ghost. She vows not to sleep with Claudius or reveal Hamlet is mad in craft. He drags the body off, his crazy laugh echoing through the fortress.

19. (4.2) *Exterior; Council Chambers*. Clouds pass over massive towers of Elsinore. Rosencrantz and Guildenstern hunt for laughing Hamlet and find him reclining on the back of a gilded lion. He goes with them, stops

to remove a stone from his shoe, grabs a torch and enters the royal council chamber. "Where is Polonius?" "At supper." Hamlet peers at the faces of the councellors while tracing the progress of a king through the guts of a begger, reveals where the body is to furious Claudius, is ordered to England, peers again at puzzled council members and leaves. Outside he mounts a white horse, sees Ophelia's shadow on a window, rides out.

20. *Polonius's Apartment.* Ophelia is smothered in iron corsets, a black dress and veil by attendant crones as rites are performed for Polonius.

21. (4.4) *Shore of Denmark.* Hamlet rides all night, dismounts and watches Fortinbras's troops marching along shore. Fortinbras orders a soldier to request passage from Claudius. Hamlet learns from the soldier that they go to fight for a worthless patch of ground in Poland. Hamlet thinks "How all occasions do inform against me."

22. *Ship.* Hamlet on deck as sailors set sails and a guard paces. Rosencrantz and Guildenstern sleep, Hamlet burns his death warrant which was locked in a little chest and places in it new orders for Rosencrantz and Guildenstern to die.

23. (4.5) *Claudius's Apartment.* Guards and dog watch outside. Within Claudius catalogues his misfortunes, but Gertrude shrinks from him.

24. *Polonius's Apartment.* Laertes sneaks past guards, raises his family sword and kisses it.

25. (4.5) *Hall.* Ophelia drifts in followed by attendants, sings and speaks distractedly to Gertrude, wanders, suddenly begins her mechanical dance upon seeing her music teacher, unpins her dress and exits in her white shift.

26. (4.5) *Claudius's Apartment.* Laertes and his men smash through doors and overpower Claudius's guards. Claudius backs him down. Laertes goes to see singing barefoot Ophelia wandering among the soldiers, grieves. Claudius comforts him and takes him into another room to explain why he could not act against Hamlet. Letters from Hamlet arrive.

27. (4.7) *Ophelia's Room; Exterior.* Camera passes over decorative tapestries and empty bed, pans past a willow to her body lying still in a stream. A bird flies out to sea. Standing on a cliff, Hamlet in a monastic robe watches the bird, journeys along a heavily travelled road, meets Horatio by a wartorn village.

28. (5.1) *Graveyard outside Elsinore.* Hamlet exchanges witticisms with the gravedigger who eats and drinks, digs. Hamlet studies a handful of dust, Yorick's skull. Soldiers push back the people as the courtiers come to bury Ophelia. Laertes leaps in the grave, Hamlet arrives, they grapple, Hamlet declares his love, goes into castle as gravedigger nails coffin shut.

29. (4.7) *Exterior; State Apartments.* Soldiers pace the ramparts at night.

The clock strikes and figures pass in their round. Claudius plots with Laertes to kill Hamlet, throws goblet of wine to obscure his image in it.

30. (5.2) *Elsinore Exterior*. Horatio and Hamlet look up at a bird. Hamlet regrets anger at Laertes, accepts challenge delivered by Osric.

31. (5.2) *Hall*. Courtiers gather. Hamlet asks Laertes' pardon. Claudius comes between them. They duel and Hamlet makes first hit. The cannon attracts Gertrude who sees Hamlet win second hit. Against Claudius's warning, she drinks to Hamlet. Laertes makes a hit, cuts Hamlet's arm. Hamlet disarms him, exchanges weapons, runs Laertes through. Gertrude swoons, reveals drink was poisoned and she is seconded by Laertes. Ghost theme sounds as Hamlet runs Claudius through and he runs bellowing like a dying bull through an empty hall. Hamlet holds the locket portrait of his father, turns and walks out to the rocks overlooking the sea, and dies. Pan over rock. Fortinbras arrives and takes command ordering Hamlet's body borne in procession. Cannon shoot. Music. Shadow of Elsinore on the sea. The rock and the torch.

## KING LEAR

Great Britain. Athena-Laterna Films. 1971. Black and white. Widescreen.

Producer:   Michael Birkett
Director:   Peter Brook
Script:   Peter Brook
Photography:   Henning Kristiansen
Design:   George Wakhevitch, Adele Anggard
Editor:   Albert Jurgenson
Sound:   Robert Allen

| | |
|---|---|
| KING LEAR:   Paul Scofield | KENT:   Tom Fleming |
| GONERIL:   Irene Worth | GLOUCESTER:   Alan Webb |
| REGAN:   Susan Engel | EDMUND:   Ian Hogg |
| CORDELIA:   Anne-lise Gabold | EDGAR:   Robert Lloyd |
| CORNWALL:   Patrick Magee | FOOL:   Jack MacGowran |
| ALBANY:   Cyril Cusack | OSWALD:   Barry Stanton |

1. *Castle Courtyard*. Titles in absolute silence as the camera slowly pans over a still crowd of men.

2. (1.1) *Throne Room*. Seated in a tomblike throne, Lear informs his

motionless courtiers of his intent to divide the kingdom. Goneril and Regan speak. Cordelia says "nothing" and Lear disowns her. Kent calls Lear mad and is banished. France claims Cordelia for his wife. Enraged Lear exits through the crowd.

3. (1.1) *Wintery Exterior*. Soldiers escort Kent to banishment. Two wooden carriages take separate roads. In one, Goneril and Regan worry about Lear's rashness.

4. (1.2) *Carriage*. Seated between Edgar and Edmund, Gloucester is disturbed by "these late eclipses" and "the bond crack'd 'twixt child and father." Beside the fire in his castle, he worries over Kent's banishment.

5. (1.4) *The Heath*. Kent cuts his beard, begrimes his face: "I do profess to be no less than I seem. . . ."

6. (1.4) Title: "Goneril's Castle. The banished Duke of Kent is now disguised as a servant. He seeks employment with the King, who is now living with his daughter Goneril." Goneril and Albany eat in the dark by the fire, she worrying about Lear's dangerous followers.

7. *The Heath*. Lear and his knights ride over frozen tundra.

8. (1.4) *Goneril's Castle*. Goneril instructs her servants to slight Lear and his knights. They arrive. Lear calls for his dinner and his fool, accepts disguised Kent into his service. Inside Goneril again urges cold looks among her servants. Oswald ignores Lear's calls for service. Kent trips him and others pelt him with bread as Lear howls with laughter. Enter Fool who prods Lear about nothing, egg and crowns, lying. Threatened by Goneril if he does not decrease his following, Lear demands "does any here know me?" He calls for his horses, sets his knights to overturning tables, brushes aside shocked Albany, and delivers a blistering curse of sterility on childless Goneril. Albany is helpless to prevent the rift. Goneril sends Oswald with a letter warning Regan.

9. (1.5) *Lear's Carriage on the Road*. Fool prods. Lear: "I did her wrong . . . let me not be mad."

10. (1.2) Title: "Gloucester's Castle. Edmund, bastard son of the Duke of Gloucester, plots against his brother Edgar." *The Heath*. As they ride, Edmund tells Edgar about astrological predictions of evil.

11. (1.2, 2.1) *Gloucester's Castle*. The two sons put Gloucester to bed, Edgar commenting that when sons mature fathers should be put in their care, and Edmund jokingly adding "and the sons manage the revenue." Edgar says Regan and Cornwall are coming, sleeps. Edmund wakes Gloucester and says Edgar plots against his father's life. With Gloucester listening, Edmund has Edgar read an incriminating letter. Gloucester raises the house with cries of murder. Edmund helps Edgar escape through the roof, wounds himself, cries for help. Inside, Gloucester binds Edmund's wounds and makes him his heir.

12. (2.4, 1.5) *Regan's Castle*. Lear arrives with his train to find them gone to Gloucester's, sends Kent ahead with letters.

13. (2.1) Title: "Gloucester's Castle. Well ahead of the King, the Duke of Cornwall and his wife Regan arrive in Gloucester's courtyard. At the same time, Edgar escapes his pursuers by pretending to be a beggar." Cornwall and Regan arrive, comfort Gloucester, and praise Edmund.

14. (2.3) *The Heath*. Fleeing Edgar evades soldiers, strips and disfigures himself. Found by the soldiers, Edgar as "Poor Tom" howls, hisses, asks for charity, is struck on the head by laughing soldiers. He puts snow to his chest: "Edgar I nothing am."

15. (2.2) *Gloucester's Castle*. Oswald arrives. Kent insults him, chases him, and dunks his head in a barrel. For insulting Cornwall and Regan, Kent is set outside in the stocks. Smiling Oswald removes Kent's boots.

16. (2.4) *The Heath*. Lear's carriage travels through the frozen wasteland with the Fool singing and knights following. Seeing snow-covered Kent in the stocks upon arriving at Gloucester's castle, Fool jokes, Lear asks in disbelief, fights his rage when they refuse to come out to greet him. Fool sits in the stocks by Kent and calls him fool. Regan and Cornwall appear, free Kent, ask Lear to return to Goneril. Humiliated Lear kneels mockingly before Regan and begs for "raiment, bed, and food." Lear curses Goneril and assures Regan he will never do so with her. Regan greets Goneril and by pressuring their father to give up his followers they drive him to desperation, rage, madness. Storm begins. Inside by a fire the sisters agree to let in Lear but not one follower. Outside, chaos as Lear and his men leave. Inside Regan asks for Gloucester. At the gate Gloucester watches Lear and his train ride out. The sisters command him to shut up his doors.

17. (3.2, 3.4) *The Heath*. Lear drives his carriage until a wheel breaks, unharnesses a horse, is pelted by rain as he bellows to the skies. Flashes of white and shattering thunderbolts alternate with close-ups of the faces of Lear and Fool. Watery out-of-focus images and black frames. Wind and whining musical tones. Lear rages and Fool hides his head in an animal hole until Kent finds them and leads them toward a hovel. "Poor naked wretches" spoken over watery images. Poor Tom appears—naked, crowned with thorns.

18. (3.3) *Gloucester's Castle*. Gloucester sends Edmund to busy Cornwall and Regan with talk and to say that Gloucester is sick while he goes to aid his master.

19. (3.4) *The Heath*. Asked by Lear to recount his life, "Poor Tom" reports himself a servant expert in sinning. Electronic sounds and roars accompany brief shots of Edgar in Christ-like agony. Lear's query "is man no more than this" as the camera passes over Edgar's naked, shivering

body. Edgar takes Gloucester for the devil. Lear brings his Fool and philosopher to Gloucester's hovel.

20. (3.5, 3.7) *Gloucester's Castle*. Cornwall thirsts for revenge, names Edmund earl for betraying his father.

21. (3.6) *The Hovel*. Lear holds a trial with Fool, Edgar, and Kent as judges, the three sisters appearing in brief hallucinatory shots. Lear sleeps, and is lifted into a carriage by Kent as Gloucester tells him Cordelia's troops will meet him at Dover. Oswald and servants pinion Gloucester as he returns to his house.

22. (3.7) *Gloucester's Castle*. Cornwall sends Goneril and Edmund to prepare for war. They ride in a carriage.

23. (3.7) *Gloucester's Castle*. Servants bind Gloucester to a chair where Cornwall and Regan question him. Cornwall gouges out one of his eyes with a spoon. Scream. Screen goes black. Servants look on indifferently. Suddenly one stabs Cornwall as he puts out the second eye and servant is clubbed to death by Regan.

24. *Carriage*. Goneril weeps. Edmund stares at her.

25. (3.7) *Gloucester's Castle*. Moaning Gloucester calls for Edmund. Weeping Regan reveals it was Edmund who betrayed him, and aids bleeding Cornwall. Outside, a servant cracks an egg and applies it to Gloucester's bleeding sockets as Edgar watches in horror. Edgar: "World, world, O world! But that thy strange mutations make us hate thee, life would not yield to age" as Gloucester stumbles out onto the swampy wasteland littered with dead horses. Edgar joins him, they hide from horsemen, and set out on their journey. Gloucester (voice-over): "As flies to wanton boys are we to the gods. They kill us for their sport."

26. (4.2) *Goneril's War Camp*. Edmund rides in and is kissed by Goneril. She taunts angry, disgusted Albany in their tent: "Marry, your manhood—mew!"

27. (5.3) *Gloucester's Castle*. Edmund wanders through the deserted house until he finds Regan beside the dying Cornwall, who says "the gods are just, and of our present vices make instruments to plague us. The dark and vicious place where he thee got cost him his eyes."

28. (3.6) *Cliffs of Dover*. Lear wakes in the carriage, tells the Fool to be quiet, and sneaks out.

29. (4.6) *Dover Beach*. Gloucester asks "Poor Tom" to lead him to the edge of the cliffs, rewards him and asks him to leave, falls forward into the sand. Edgar disguises his voice, wakes Gloucester, and says the gods have saved him from a devil. Enter Lear, his hair full of weeds and flowers. He rails against flatterers and injustice as Gloucester weeps. "When we are born, we cry that we are come to this great stage of fools." Surrounded by

Cordelia's soldiers, Lear takes them for enemies, flees into the sea, is captured.

30. (5.1, 4.6) *Goneril's War Camp*. Edmund and Regan ride in, and they put aside differences to fight against Cordelia and the French. In her tent with Edmund, Regan asks if he loves Goneril and he denies it. In her tent, Goneril sends Edmund a letter by Oswald which Edmund reads aloud to Regan. Goneril: "I had rather lose the battle than that sister should loosen him and me."

31. (4.6) *Dover Beach*. Oswald finds Edgar and the hunted traitor Gloucester, but is killed by Edgar.

32. (4.7) *Cordelia's Tent*. Lear wakes and asks Cordelia's forgiveness as Kent watches.

33. (5.2) *Dover Beach*. Sounds of fire and battle over out-of-focus close-up of Gloucester's face. Edgar: "Away old man. King Lear has lost," leads him away.

34. (5.3) *Cordelia's Camp*. With ships burning in the background, Lear and Cordelia come out of their tent to meet the victors. Lear dreams of imprisonment as escape. Edmund commands "take them away" and sends a captain after with orders. Albany and Goneril meet with Edmund and Regan. Albany demands Lear and Cordelia but Edmund refuses. Edgar, as anonymous challenger, appears, fights Edmund, and wounds him mortally. Faced with her letter to Edmund, Goneril kills Regan and then herself by smashing their heads on the rocks. Cut to Cordelia being hung. Lear on the beach howling, carrying Cordelia's body. He swoons, thinking Cordelia lives. Edgar tries to revive him but Kent tosses him aside. Intercut closeups of Edgar and Kent watching as Lear falls back in slow motion.

# KING LEAR

Russia. Lenfilm. 1970. Black and White. 70mm Sovscope.
Director: Grigori Kozintsev
Script: Grigori Kozintsev, from translation by Boris Pasternak (in Russian, subtitled)
Photography: Jonas Gritsyus
Design: Evgeni Enei, Ulitka, S. Virsaladze
Music: Dmitri Shostakovich
Sound: E. Vanuts

KING LEAR: Yuri Jarvet      REGAN: Galina Volchek
GONERIL: Elza Radzin      CORDELIA: Valentina Shandrikova

KENT: Vladimir Emelianov

GLOUCESTER: Karl Sebris

EDGAR: Leonard Marzin

EDMUND: Regimentas Adomaitis

ALBANY: Donata Banionis

FOOL: Oleg Dal

OSWALD: A. Patrenko

1. Titles over rough cloth to Fool's melancholy flute and song. Peasants journey on rocky road toward Lear's castle.

2. (1.1) *Lear's Castle*. Gloucester and Kent wonder who the king favors, meet Edmund and Edgar. Albany, Cornwall, Lear's three daughters, attendants gather, wait. Enter Lear who plays with the Fool by the fire while his intent to step down is read. Goneril and Regan speak and are rewarded, but Cordelia says "nothing." Lear tears the map, disowns Cordelia, banishes Kent. Burgundy refuses Cordelia. France takes her. Lear rushes out, selects men, horses, dogs, hawks to serve him, and as music crescendos climbs the walls and proclaims Cordelia's banishment to the kneeling people.

3. *By the Sea*. France and Cordelia are married. Lear's carriage passes by, Goneril tending the sleeping king inside.

4. (1.2) *Gloucester's Castle*. Camera passes over family tree. Edmund: "Why bastard?" As Gloucester walks his dog outside, he worries about Cordelia, Kent. Inside Edmund enrages him with the forged letter, urges patience.

5. (1.2) *Gloucester's Courtyard*. Edmund warns Edgar of danger, rushes him inside, defies heavenly compulsion, hurls stone at the rumbling clouds.

6. (1.4) *Goneril's Castle*. Lear and train hunt. Kent disguises himself, observes Lear's arrival, trips Oswald when he slights the king. Fool taunts Lear, Goneril lectures him at a polite dinner. Humiliated, Lear rages, calls for his horses, brushes aside Albany, curses Goneril and leaves. Angry Goneril justifies her act inside. Albany is silent.

7. (1.5) *Carriage on the Road*. Fool taunts Lear. Lear sends Kent with letters to Goneril. "O let me not be mad."

8. (2.1, 2.2) *Gloucester's Castle, Night*. Wolves howl. Shadowy bars pass over engravings showing death as Gloucester dreams, clutches his throat. Grim Edmund rouses Edgar, tells him to flee, wounds himself, and rouses the house with cries. Hunted Edgar flees. Regan and Cornwall arrive and comfort Gloucester. Kent pursues Oswald and is put in the stocks by Cornwall.

9. (2.4) *Desolate Plain*. Lear's train passes in the distance. Lear learns Regan is not home.

10. *Plain*. Desperate Edgar tears off his clothes, joins wandering beggars.

11. (2.4, 3.3) *Gloucester's Castle*. Lear's train arrives. Finding Kent in the stocks, Lear rages, quells his passion. Regan, Edmund, and Cornwall listen inside as Gloucester tells Lear they are not well. His anger brings them out. As Lear sits in a large throne, Regan urges him to return to Goneril. Lear curses Goneril, she arrives, and the two daughters agree to strip him of his train. The storm rises as Lear fights tears and madness. The sky darkens. Followed by the Fool, he rushes out the gates which shut behind him. Inside Gloucester tells Edmund they must side with Lear. Edgar finds the incriminating letter.

12. (3.1, 3.4, 3.6) *Heath in the Storm*. Wolves, bears, boars roam woods. Horses panic on plain. Lear runs across windswept wasteland, accusing the heavens, being answered by thunder and rain. Kent brings them to the hovel where disguised Edgar and other wretches have taken shelter. Edgar raves as Poor Tom. Lear sees and understands suffering. "Is man no more than this?" "Off you lendings." He holds a trial for his daughters. Gloucester warns Kent of danger to Lear.

13. (3.7) *Gloucester's Castle*. Cornwall makes Edmund earl, has Gloucester bound and gouges out his eye with a spur. A servant pleads for Gloucester, stabs Cornwall and is in turn stabbed by Regan. As Cornwall puts out Gloucester's other eye, in another room Goneril laces her boots, Edgar buckles on his sword, both ignoring his cries. Cornwall staggers toward Regan. She backs away, watches him fall, seeks out Edmund, rips off his coat and embraces him. Cornwall's corpse is laid out. Regan enters, kisses corpse open-mouthed. Outside Goneril and Edgar ride off together.

14. (4.1) *The Heath*. Taking clothes from a scarecrow, Edgar takes comfort that there is no falling from the lowest. He sees his blinded father, grieves, leads him away.

15. (4.2) *Goneril's Castle*. Aroused by Edmund, Goneril scorns cowardly Albany and is in turn rejected by him. A messenger brings news of the landing of Cordelia and the French.

16. (4.4) *By the Sea*. French powers land. Cordelia bids them seek for Lear.

17. (4.6) *Hills near the Sea*. Lear crawls through the grass picking flowers. Among beggars, he gnaws roots and laughs at how he was flattered, sees Gloucester, and rails against hypocritical justices. Sobbing refugees flee the wars as Lear comforts Gloucester: "We came crying hither." Cordelia's soldiers find him.

18. (4.6) *Plain*. Edgar kills Oswald, reads the letters incriminating Edmund and Goneril.

19. (4.7) *By the Sea*. Half-conscious Lear is borne on a litter as Cordelia's army marches toward battle.

20. (4.7) *Hills, Ruined Castle*. Lear borne as Cordelia's troops retreat. He wakes as Fool plays flute, begs Cordelia's forgiveness. Masses flee Edmund's troops.

21. *Plain*. Recognizing Edgar, Gloucester dies in his arms. Edgar buries him, prays.

22. (5.3) *Besieged Castle*. As thundering choral score sounds, Edmund rejects Regan and embraces Goneril. Fighting. Edgar strides toward the battle. People flee with Lear and Cordelia caught among them. They are captured and brought before Edmund. Their joy provokes Edgar to order their execution. He urges his men to be swords.

23. (5.3) *Albany's Tent*. Goneril prepares poisoned wine. Albany accuses Edmund of treason. The herald announces the challenge. Edgar's trumpet answers, and he defeats Edmund in a duel. Albany accuses Goneril, and she exits. Confronted with his wronged brother and the deaths of Goneril and Regan, Edmund tries to save Lear and Cordelia's lives. All run up toward battlements. Lear: "Howl! Howl! Howl!" Cordelia hangs from an arch. They carry her down, Lear despairs, dies over her body. The bodies are borne on a litter, one of the bearers kicking aside the weeping Fool who sits amidst burning ruins playing his flute. Peasants begin to clear rubble. Edgar stares at the camera, walks out of the frame.

# Notes

## CHAPTER 1: REALIZING SHAKESPEARE ON FILM

1. See Robert Hamilton Ball, *Shakespeare on Silent Film* (New York: Theatre Arts, 1968), which takes a more sympathetic view.

2. For fuller listings, see Charles W. Eckert, ed., *Focus on Shakespearean Films* (Englewood Cliffs: Prentice Hall, 1972); Max Lippman, ed., *Shakespeare Im Film*, Deutsches Institut fur Filmkunde (Wiesbaden: Saaten-Verlag, 1964); Meredith Lillich, "Shakespeare on the Screen," *Films in Review* 16 (June/July 1955), pp. 247-60; Peter Morris, "Shakespeare on Film," *Films in Review* 24 (March 1973), pp. 132-63.

3. See Lawrence Kitchin, "Shakepeare on the Screen," *Shakespeare Survey* 18 (1965), pp. 70-74.

4. John Reddington, "Film, Play, and Idea," *Literature/Film Quarterly* 1 (Fall, 1973), p. 368.

5. John Fuegi, "Explorations in No Man's Land," *Shakespeare Quarterly* 23 (1972), p. 48.

6. John Russell Brown, "The Study and Practice of Shakespeare Production," *Shakespeare Survey* 18 (1965), p. 59.

7. Aristotle, *Poetics*, VI, 19.

8. R. A. Foakes, "Suggestions for a New Approach to Shakespeare's Imagery," *Shakespeare Survey* 5 (1952), pp. 85–86.

9. James Agee, *Agee on Film*, Vol. I (New York: Grosset and Dunlap, 1958), p. 209.

10. James Clay and Daniel Krempel, *The Theatrical Image* (New York: McGraw-Hill, 1967), pp. 231–32.

11. Some useful models of theatrical criticism: J. L. Styan, *Shakespeare's Stagecraft* (Cambridge: Cambridge University Press, 1967); John Russell Brown, *Shakespeare's Plays in Performance* (New York: St. Martin's, 1967); Marvin Rosenberg, *The Masks of King Lear* (Berkeley: University of California Press, 1972).

12. André Bazin, *What is Cinema?* (Berkeley: University of California Press, 1967); John Howard Lawson, *Films: The Creative Process*, 2nd ed. (New York: Hill and Wang, 1967); Robert Gessner, *The Moving Image*

(New York: Dutton, 1968); Susan Sontag, "Film and Theatre," *Film Theory and Criticism*, ed. Gerald Mast and Marshall Cohen (New York: Oxford University Press, 1974), pp. 249–67; Stanley Kauffmann, "Notes on Theatre-and-Film," *Living Images* (New York: Harper and Row, 1975), pp. 353–62.

13. Andrew Sarris, "Film: The Illusion of Naturalism," *The Drama Review* T42 (Winter, 1968), pp. 108–09.

14. Rudolf Arnheim, "Foreword," *Film as Art* (Berkeley: University of California Press, 1957).

15. Siegfried Kracauer, *Theory of Film* (New York: Oxford University Press, 1965), pp. x–xi.

16. George Bluestone, *Novels Into Film* (Berkeley: University of California Press, 1971), p. 1.

17. Roy Armes, *Film and Reality* (Baltimore: Penguin, 1974), p. 120.

18. *The Portable Henry James*, ed. M. D. Zabel (New York: Viking, 1951), p. 151.

19. Wolf Rilla, *The Writer and the Screen* (New York: Morrow, 1974), p. 23.

20. Lawson, *Film: The Creative Process*, p. 196.

21. Alexander Knox, "Acting and Behaving," in *Film: A Montage of Theories*, ed. Richard Dyer MacCann (New York: Dutton, 1966), p. 62. For a sampling of actors' views on film versus theatre, see James Hurt, ed. *Focus on Film and Theatre* (Englewood Cliffs: Prentice Hall, 1974).

22. Bazin, *What is Cinema?*, p. 69.

23. See Roger Manvell, *Shakespeare and the Film* (New York: Praeger, 1971), p. 153; Donald Skoller, "Problems of Transformation in the Adaptation of Shakespeare's Tragedies, From Play-Script to Cinema," Ph.D. dissertation, New York University, 1968; Peter Wollen, *Signs and Meaning in the Cinema* (Bloomington: Indiana University Press, 1969), p. 137.

24. Sontag, in Mast and Cohen, *Film Theory and Criticism*, p. 250.

25. Peter Brook, *The Empty Space* (New York: Avon, 1969), p. 10.

26. Arthur Knight, "Three Problems in Film Adaptation," *Saturday Review* (Dec. 18, 1954), p. 26.

27. Roy Walker, "Look Upon Caesar," *Twentieth Century* 154 (1953), pp. 470–71.

28. Fuegi, "Explorations . . .," p. 40.

29. *Shakespeare, 1971*, ed. Clifford Leech and J. M. R. Margeson (Toronto: Toronto University Press, 1972), p. 191.

30. Kauffmann, *Living Images*, p. 358.

31. Fuegi, "Explorations . . .," p. 41.

32. Hugo Munsterberg, *The Film: A Psychological Study* (New York: Dover, 1970), p. 74.

33. Quoted in Brown, *Shakespeare's Plays in Performance*, p. 53.

34. "Finding Shakespeare on Film," *Tulane Drama Review* T33, 11 (Fall, 1966), p. 118.

35. These categories resemble those used by Stanley Wells, "Shakespeare's Text on the Modern Stage," *Shakespeare Jahrbuch* (West) (1967), pp. 180–81, and Thomas Clayton, "Aristotle on the Shakespearean Film, or, Damn Thee, William, Thou Art Translated," *Literature/Film Quarterly* 2 (1974), pp. 185–86.

36. John Russell Brown, *Free Shakespeare* (London: Heinemann, 1974).

37. Roger Gross, *Understanding Playscripts* (Bowling Green: Bowling Green University Press, 1974), pp. 17–18.

38. Susan Sontag, *Against Interpretation* (New York: Dell, 1969), p. 17.

39. Quoted in Grigori Kozintsev, *Shakespeare: Time and Conscience* (New York: Hill and Wang, 1966), p. 215.

40. Eckert, *Focus on Shakespearean Films*, lists many of these which have wound up on film.

41. Quoted by Joseph McBride, *Orson Welles* (London: Secker and Warburg, 1972), p. 109.

42. Quoted by Hugh Kenner, *The Pound Era* (Berkeley: University of California Press, 1971), p. 150.

43. Bluestone, *Novels Into Film*, pp. 110–11.

44. Paul Dehn, "The Filming of Shakespeare," *Talking of Shakespeare*, ed. John Garrett (London: Hodder and Stoughton, 1954), p. 49.

45. Maya Deren, "Poetry and the Film: A Symposium," *Film Culture Reader*, ed. P. Adams Sitney (New York: Praeger, 1970), p. 174.

46. Stanley J. Solomon, *The Film Idea* (New York: Harcourt, Brace, 1972), p. 341.

47. Kracauer, *Theory of Film*, p. 106.

48. Eckert, *Focus on Shakespearean Films*, p. 17.

49. David Robinson, "Majestic Lear," *Financial Times* (London), July 7, 1972.

50. "*Macbeth* Into *Throne of Blood*," *Film and the Liberal Arts*, ed. T. J. Ross (New York: Holt, Rinehart, and Winston, 1970), p. 133.

51. Lawson, *Film: The Creative Process*, pp. 201–02.

52. Brown, *Shakespeare's Plays in Performance*, p. 41.

53. See Arthur Colby Sprague's *Shakespeare and the Actors* (Cambridge, Mass.: Harvard University Press, 1944) and subsequent books for much interesting information on the stage business of Shakespeare's plays, much of which carries over into films.

54. Quoted in Lawson, *Film: The Creative Process*, p. xxii.

55. See James Naremore, "The Walking Shadow: Welles' Expressionist *Macbeth*," *Literature/Film Quarterly* 1 (1973), p. 361.

56. See Paul A. Jorgensen, "Castellani's *Romeo and Juliet:* Intention and Response," and Roy Walker, "In Fair Verona," both reprinted in Eckert, *Focus on Shakespearean Films.*

57. Skoller, "Problems of Transformation . . .," p. 429.

58. Introduction, Peter Weiss, *Marat/Sade* (New York: Pocket Books, 1966), pp. 5–6.

59. Charles Hurtgen, "The Operatic Character of Background Music in Film Adaptations of Shakespeare," *Shakespeare Quarterly* 20 (1969), p. 53.

60. Ibid., p. 57.

61. See Frances Shirley, *Shakespeare's Use of Off-Stage Sounds* (Lincoln: University of Nebraska Press, 1963), though of course all his nonverbal sounds were not off-stage.

62. Peter Brook, "Finding Shakespeare on Film," in Eckert, *Focus on Shakespearean Films,* p. 37.

63. Jaun Cobos and Miguel Rubio, "Welles and Falstaff," *Sight and Sound* 35 (Autumn, 1966), p. 160.

CHAPTER 2: REINHARDT AND DIETERLE'S
*Midsummer Night's Dream*

1. Two perceptive studies of the play to which I am indebted are Stephen Fender, *Shakespeare: A Midsummer Night's Dream* (London: Arnold, 1968) and David P. Young, *Something of Great Constancy* (New Haven: Yale University Press, 1966).

2. K. M. Abenheimer, "Shakespeare's 'Tempest': A Psychological Analysis," *Psychoanalytical Review,* 33 (1946), p. 402n. For an eccentric, bizarre, but interesting Freudian view of the *Dream* see Weston Gui, "Bottom's Dream," *American Imago,* 9 (1952), pp. 251–305.

3. Roger Moore, *Henry Purcell and the Restoration Theatre* (London: Heinemann, 1961), p. 5

4. *The Fairy Queen: An Opera* (London, 1692), pp. 29–30.

5. *A Midsummer Night's Dream, with Alterations, Additions, and New Songs; As it is Performed at the Theatre-Royal Convent-Garden* (London, 1816).

6. William Hazlitt, *The Examiner* (London), January 21, 1816.

7. Quoted in George C. D. Odell, *Shakespeare From Betterton to Irving,* 2 vols. (New York: Dover, 1966), II, p. 344.

8. Ibid., II, p. 454.

9. Max Reinhardt, "Foreword," *A Midsummer Night's Dream* (New York: Grosset and Dunlap, 1935), p. v.

10. James Clay and Daniel Krempel, *The Theatrical Image* (New York: McGraw-Hill, 1967), p. 233.

11. See Michael Taylor, "The Darker Purpose of *A Midsummer Night's Dream*," *Studies in English Literature*, 9 (1969), pp. 259–73; Alan Lewis, "*A Midsummer Night's Dream*—Fairy Fantasy or Erotic Nightmare?" *Educational Theatre Journal*, 21 (1969), pp. 251–58; Jan Kott, *Shakespeare Our Contemporary* (Garden City: Doubleday, 1966).

12. See William M. Merchant, "*A Midsummer Night's Dream*: A Visual Re-creation," *Early Shakespeare*, ed. John Russell Brown and Bernard Harris (New York: Schocken, 1966), pp. 164–85.

13. G. Wilson Knight, *The Shakespearean Tempest* (London: Methuen, 1963), p. 142. Unaltered from 1932 edition.

14. John Baxter, *Hollywood in the Thirties* (New York: Paperback Library, 1970), p. 92.

15. Otis Ferguson, *The New Republic*, Oct. 16, 1935.

16. Clay and Krempel, *The Theatrical Image*, p. 237.

17. G. Wilson Knight, *The Shakespearean Tempest*, p. 269.

18. Kate Cameron, *New York Daily News*, Oct. 10, 1935.

19. *Shakespeare: A Celebration*, ed. T. J. B. Spencer (Baltimore: Pelican, 1964), pp. 109–10.

20. Pauline Kael, *I Lost It at the Movies* (New York: Bantam, 1966), p. 259.

21. The reference is in Edward Sharpham's *The Fleire* (1607): "Faith like Thisbe in the play, a' has almost kil'd himself with the scabberd," *Shakspere Allusion Book*, ed. J. J. Munro and E. K. Chambers, 2 vols. (London: Oxford University Press, 1932), I. p. 174.

22. *Sunday Times* (London), Oct. 13, 1935.

CHAPTER 3: HALL'S *Midsummer Night's Dream*

1. Peter Hall, quoted in Roger Manvell, *Shakespeare and the Film* (New York: Praeger, 1971), pp. 121–23.

2. Ibid.

3. Discussed in Charles Eidsvik's forthcoming book tentatively entitled *Cineliteracy*.

4. Quoted in Peter Morris, "Shakespeare on Film," *Films in Review* (March, 1973), p. 159.

5. Using the Signet Classic edition by Wolfgang Clemen as a control text, the following are the cuts made by Hall: 1.1.28–38, 48–58, 60–61, 83–90,

96–98, 101–02, 173–75, 193–201, 218, 219, 236–39; 2.1.36–39, 195–202, 230–34; 2.2.98–100, 115–23, 125–28; 3.1.135–37; 3.2.19–32, 52–55, 68–74, 84–87, 90–93, 141–42, 147–50, 179–80, 227–31, 247–50; 4.1.161–66; 5.1.28–31, 40–41, 48–55, 66–70, 77–81, 88–105, 108–26, 231–37, 241–42, 308–11, 318, 320–22, 325. There is one transposition of part of a scene: Theseus and Hippolyta's discussion of imagination (5.1.1–27) is placed immediately after Bottom's awakening at the end of 4.1, so that the discussion seems to apply directly to Bottom's experience.

6. See Hall's statement in Manvell, *Shakespeare and the Film*, pp. 124–25.

7. Ibid., p. 121.

8. It was shown by C.B.S. on February 9, 1969, and received mixed reviews from a rather bewildered set of T.V. reviewers. For a recent discussion, see Michael Mullin, "Peter Hall's *A Midsummer Night's Dream*," *Educational Theatre Journal* 28 (1976).


CHAPTER 4: ZEFFIRELLI'S *Taming of the Shrew*

1. *Shaw on Shakespeare*, ed. Edwin Wilson (New York: 1961), pp. 186–87.

2. D. A. Traversi, *An Approach to Shakespeare*, 2 vols. (Garden City: Doubleday, 1969), I, p. 75.

3. C. L. Barber, *Shakespeare's Festive Comedy* (New York: Meridian, 1963; Princeton: Princeton University Press, 1972). The standard work on saturnalia in England is Volume I of E. K. Chambers, *The Medieval Stage* (Oxford: Oxford University Press, 1903).

4. Quoted by A. P. Rossiter, *English Drama From Early Times to the Elizabethans* (New York: Barnes and Noble, 1967), pp. 64–65.

5. See Northrop Frye, *Anatomy of Criticism* (New York: Atheneum, 1966).

6. Barber, *Shakespeare's Festive Comedy*, p. 6

7. Frye, *Anatomy of Criticism*, p. 163.

8. For representative views of Zeffirelli's *Shrew*, see: Stephen Farber, *Film Quarterly* 21 (1968), p. 61; John Simon, *Movies into Film* (New York: Dell, 1972), pp. 28–30; Judith Christ, *The Private Eye, the Cowboy, and the Very Naked Girl* (New York: Paperback Library, 1970), pp. 248–49; Carey Harrison, *Sight and Sound* 36 (Spring, 1967), pp. 97–98; Wilifred Sheed, ed., *Film 67-68* (New York: Simon and Schuster, 1968), pp. 168–69; Penelope Houston, *Spectator*, March 10, 1967; John Russell Taylor, *Times* (London), Feb. 28, 1967; Patrick Gibbs, *Daily Telegraph* (London) Feb. 28, 1967; David Robinson, *Financial Times* (London), Mar. 3, 1967; Robert

Robinson, *Sunday Telegraph* (London) Mar. 5, 1967; Gerald Kaufman, *The Listener* (London), Mar. 9, 1967; Hollis Alpert, *Saturday Review*, repr. *Film 67/68*, pp. 166–68; Roger Manvell, *Shakespeare and the Film* (New York: Praeger, 1971), pp. 99–100.


CHAPTER 5: ZEFFIRELLI'S *Romeo and Juliet*

1. John Simon, *Movies into Film* (New York, 1970), p. 107.
2. "Shakespeare on the Screen," *Times Literary Supplement* (London), Sept. 26, 1968, p. 1082.
3. Franco Zeffirelli in *Directors on Directing*, ed. Toby Cole and Helen Crich Chinoy (Indianapolis: Bobbs-Merrill, 1963), p. 440.
4. Ibid., p. 439.
5. Louis Gianetti, *Understanding Movies* (Englewood Cliffs: Prentice Hall, 1972), p. 154.
6. Albert R. Cirillo, "The Art of Franco Zeffirelli and Shakespeare's *Romeo and Juliet*," *TriQuarterly* 16 (Fall, 1969/70), p. 81.
7. Zeffirelli, in *Directors on Directing*, p. 440.
8. Cirillo, "The Art . . .," p. 82.
9. Ibid., p. 87.
10. Pauline Kael, *Going Steady* (New York: Bantam, 1971), p. 189.
11. John Russell Brown, *Shakespeare's Plays in Performance* (New York: St. Martins, 1967), p. 168.
12. Paul Jorgensen, "Castellani's *Romeo and Juliet:* Intention and Response," *Film Quarterly* 10 (1955), p. 1.
13. Brown, *Shakespeare's Plays . . .*," p. 176.
14. *Shaw on Shakespeare*, ed. Edwin Wilson (New York: Dutton, 1961), p. 179.


CHAPTER 6: MANKIEWICZ'S *Julius Caesar*

1. Leonard F. Dean, ed., *Twentieth Century Interpretations of Julius Caesar* (Englewood Cliffs: Prentice Hall, 1968), p. 7.
2. Mark Rose, *Shakespearean Design* (Cambridge: Harvard University Press, 1972), p. 152.
3. John Gielgud, *Stage Directions* (New York: Capricorn, 1966), p. 48.
4. Roy Walker, "Look Upon Caesar," *Twentieth Century* 154 (1953), p. 472.

5. John Dover Wilson, ed. *Julius Caesar*, New (Cambridge) Shakespeare (Cambridge: Cambridge University Press, 1968), pp. xxi–xxii.

6. John Houseman, quoted in Roger Manvell, *Shakespeare and the Film* (New York: Praeger, 1971), p. 89.

7. James E. Phillips, "*Julius Caesar*: Shakespeare as a Screen Writer," *Film Quarterly* 8 (1953), p. 128.

8. Quoted in Walker, "Look Upon Caesar," p. 472.

9. Roger Manvell, *Shakespeare and the Film* (New York: Praeger, 1971), pp. 86–87.

10. Eric Bentley, *New Republic* (Aug. 3, 1953), p. 20.

11. Paul Dehn, "The Filming of Shakespeare," *Talking of Shakespeare*, ed. John Garrett (London: Hodder and Stoughton, 1954), p. 68.

12. John Houseman, *Run-Through* (New York: Curtis, 1972), p. 308n.

13. Peter Morris, "Shakespeare on Film," *Films in Review* (March, 1973), p. 153.

14. John Fuegi, "Explorations in No Man's Land: Shakespeare's Poetry as Theatrical Film," *Shakespeare Quarterly* 23 (1972), p. 44.

15. Donald Skoller, "Problems of Transformation in the Adaptation of Shakespeare's Tragedies from Play-Script to Cinema" (Ph.D. dissertation, New York University, 1968), p. 255ff, stresses the lack of "cineplasticity" in the film.

16. P. M. Passinetti, "*Julius Caesar*: The Role of Technical Advisor," *Film Quarterly* 8 (1953), p. 138.

17. Ibid., pp. 134–35.

18. Quoted Ronald Hayman, *John Gielgud* (London, 1971), p. 181.

19. John Gielgud, *Stage Directions*, pp. 49–50.

20. Robert Hapgood, "Shakespeare and the Included Spectator," *Reinterpretations of Elizabethan Drama*, ed. Norman Rabkin (New York: Columbia University Press, 1969), p. 123.

21. The characters are recognizable types from the gangster film: the tough punk who is soft inside (Casca), the cool ironic Bogart-like Cicero, the weak-kneed big-boy (Calhern as Caesar), the scared moll (Calpurnia), and the straight wife of the good guy (Portia).

22. P. M. Pasinetti, "Julius Caesar: The Role ...," p. 137.

23. John Gielgud, *Stage Directions*, p. 49.

24. Portions of the script dealing with the killing of Caesar and the Forum speeches are reprinted in John Houseman, "*Julius Caesar*: Mr. Mankiewicz' Shooting Script," *Film Quarterly* 8 (1953), pp. 109–24. The edition of the play edited by John M. Culkin (New York: Scholastic Library, 1963) reprints the assassination of Caesar, Antony's funeral oration, the battle, and the final scenes. On Miklos Rozsa's score, see John Huntley

and Roger Manvell, *The Technique of Film Music* (New York: Hastings House, 1957), pp. 113–22; Charles Hurtgen, "The Operatic Character of Background Music in Film Adaptations of Shakespeare," *Shakespeare Quarterly* 20 (1969), pp. 53–64.

CHAPTER 7: WELLES'S *Chimes at Midnight*

1. Mike Prokosch, *Film Comment* (Summer, 1971), p. 35.

2. Juan Cobos and Miguel Rubio, "Welles and Falstaff," *Sight and Sound* 35 (Autumn, 1966), pp. 159–60.

3. Ibid., p. 159.

4. Daniel Seltzer, "Shakespeare's Texts and Modern Productions," *Reinterpretations of Elizabethan Drama*, ed. Norman Rabkin (New York: Columbia University Press, 1969), p. 109.

5. William Johnson, "Orson Welles: Of Time and Loss," *Film Quarterly* 21 (1968), p. 16.

6. Cobos and Rubio, "Welles and Falstaff," p. 160.

7. Ibid., p. 159.

8. Joseph Morgenstern, *Newsweek*, Mar. 27, 1967; repr. *Film 67/68* (New York: Simon and Schuster, 1968), pp. 70–71.

9. Cobos and Rubio, "Welles and Falstaff," p. 159.

10. Pauline Kael, *Kiss Kiss, Bang Bang* (New York: Bantam, 1969), p. 241.

11. Peter Cowie, *A Ribbon of Dreams* (New York: A. S. Barnes, 1973), p. 185. He also stresses the ambivalence of the film.

12. Cobos and Rubio, "Welles and Falstaff," p. 159.

13. Pauline Kael, *Kiss Kiss, Bang Bang*, p. 240

14. Cobos and Rubio, "Welles and Falstaff," pp. 160–61.

15. Penelope Houston, *Spectator* (London), Mar. 31, 1967.

16. Charles Higham, *The Films of Orson Welles* (Berkeley: University of California Press, 1971), pp. 170, 125.

17. Johnson, "Orson Welles: Of Time and Loss," p. 17.

18. Peter Bogdanovitch, "Period Piece," *New York Magazine*, Feb. 25, 1974, p. 65.

19. Cobos and Rubio, "Welles and Falstaff," p. 161.

20. Johnson, "Orson Welles: Of Time and Loss," p. 14.

21. Grigori Kozintsev, *Shakespeare: Time and Conscience* (New York: Hill and Wang, 1966), p. 203.

22. Joseph McBride, *Orson Welles* (London: Secker and Warburg, 1972), p. 153.

CHAPTER 8: OLIVIER'S *Henry V*

1. C. A. Lejeune, "Two English Films," *Theatre Arts Anthology*, ed. Rosamund Gilder (New York: Theatre Arts, 1950), pp. 564–65.

2. Harry Geduld, *Filmguide to Henry V* (Bloomington: Indiana University Press, 1973), p. 35. This is the fullest treatment of the film and has a good bibliography.

3. The script is available for study in *Film Scripts One*, ed. George P. Garrett, et. al. (New York: Appleton Century Crofts, 1971), pp. 37–136. Geduld provides a detailed list of the cuts and comments on them.

4. Peter Whitehead and Robin Bean, *Olivier—Shakespeare* (London: Lorrimer, 1966), p. 8.

5. James Phillips, "Adapted From a Play by W. Shakespeare," *Hollywood Quarterly* 2 (Oct., 1946); quoted Geduld, *Filmguide to Henry V*, p. 80.

6. *Films and Feelings* (Cambridge, Mass.: M.I.T. Press, 1971), p. 262.

7. Harry Geduld, *Filmguide to Henry V*, p. 33.

8. Suggested by Roy M. Prendergast in a paper delivered at the 1974 MLA Seminar, "Shakespeare on Film."

9. James Agee, *Agee on Film*, Vol. I (New York: Grosset and Dunlap, 1969), p. 208.

10. Sigfried Kracauer, *Theory of Film* (New York: Oxford University Press, 1960), p. 227.

11. Geduld, *Filmguide to Henry V*, p. 66.

12. Agee, *Agee on Film*, pp. 211–12.

13. Ibid., p. 211.

14. André Bazin, *What is Cinema?* (Berkeley: University of California Press, 1967), p. 88.

15. See Roger Manvell, *Shakespeare and the Film* (New York: Praeger, 1971), p. 39, and Geduld, *Filmguide to Henry V*. pp. 18–19, for the paintings which influenced Olivier.

16. On Walton's coordination of music and images, see John Huntley and Roger Manvell, *The Technique of Film Music* (New York: Hastings House, 1957), pp. 72, 78–92; 110–11, 149; Geduld, *Filmguide to Henry V*, pp. 63–65; Charles Hurtgen, "The Operatic Character of Background Music in Film Adaptations of Shakespeare," *Shakespeare Quarterly* 20 (1969), pp. 56–58, 60.

17. Harry Geduld, *Filmguide to Henry V*, pp. 27, 65.

18. Agee, *Agee on Film*, p. 208.

19. Bazin, *What is Cinema?*, p. 116.

20. Raymond Durgnat, *A Mirror For England* (London: Faber and Faber, 1970), pp. 110–11; quoted Geduld, p. 77.

CHAPTER 9:   OLIVIER'S *Richard III*

1. *A Mirror For Magistrates,* ed. Lilly B. Campbell (London, 1938), p. 62.

2. Constance Brown, "Olivier's *Richard III*—A Reevaluation," *Film Quarterly* 20 (1967), p. 24. She contradicts this historical emphasis on the same page: "The removal of Margaret and the reduction of the other parts forces particular attention on the psychology of Richard—who in any case dominates the play."

3. Quoted Roger Manvell, *Shakespeare and the Film* (New York: Praeger, 1971), p. 48.

4. Alice Griffin, "Shakespeare Through the Camera's Eye," *Shakespeare Quarterly* 7 (1956), pp. 235–36.

5. C. L. Barber, *Shakespeare's Festive Comedy* (New York: Meridian, 1963), p. 193.

6. See Sir James G. Frazer, *The Golden Bough,* 1 vol. abridged ed. (New York: Macmillan, 1960), chaps. 24–26, 43, 57–58.

7. Virginia Graham, *Spectator* (London) Dec. 16, 1955.

8. Harry Schein, "A Magnificent Fiasco?" *Film Quarterly* 10 (1955–56), pp. 409–10.

9. Manvell notes it is rendered in one six-minute take, *Shakespeare and the Film,* p. 49.

10. Brown, "Olivier's *Richard III* . . .," p. 31.

11. James E. Phillips, "Richard III: Some Glories and Some Discontents," *Film Quarterly* 10 (1955–56), pp. 401–02.

12. Schein, "A Magnificent Fiasco?" p. 410.

13. Brown, "Olivier's *Richard III* . . .," p. 25.


CHAPTER 10:   DEFINING *Macbeth*

1. "Introduction to *Macbeth,*" *William Shakespeare: The Complete Works,* ed. Alfred Harbage (Baltimore: Penguin, 1969), p. 1107.

2. Joseph McBride, *Orson Welles* (London: Secker and Warburg, 1972), p. 113.

3. Donald Richie, *The Films of Akira Kurosawa* (Berkeley: University of California Press, 1970), p. 115.

4. Samuel Johnson, *Samuel Johnson on Shakespeare,* ed. W. K. Wimsatt, Jr. (New York: Hill and Wang, 1960), p. 105.

5. Donald Skoller, "Problems of Transformation in the Adaptation of Shakespeare's Tragedies From Play-Script to Cinema," Ph.D. dissertation, New York University, 1968, p. 489.

6. Ibid., p. 500.

7. Roger Manvell, *Shakespeare and the Film* (New York: Praeger, 1971), p. 115.

8. James Naremore, "The Walking Shadow: Welles's Expressionist *Macbeth*," *Literature/Film Quarterly* 1 (1973), pp. 360–66. See also Michael Mullin, "Orson Welles's *Macbeth*," in *Focus on Orson Welles*, ed. Ronald Gottesman (Englewood Cliffs: Prentice Hall, 1976).

9. Welles, quoted in Manvell, *Shakespeare and the Film*, p. 59.

10. Naremore, "The Walking Shadow . . .," p. 363.

11. Kozintsev, *Shakespeare: Time and Conscience* (New York: Hill and Wang, 1966), p. 29; "Finding Shakespeare on Film," *Focus on Shakespearean Films*, ed. Charles W. Eckert (Englewood Cliffs: Prentice Hall, 1972), p. 37.

12. See Skoller, "Problems of Transformation," Manvell, *Shakespeare and the Film*, and Ana Laura Zambrano, "*Throne of Blood:* Kurosawa's *Macbeth*," *Literature/Film Quarterly* 2 (1974), pp. 262–74.

13. Michael Estène, "Le Réalism de *Kumonosu-jo (Le Château de L'Araignée)*," *Études Cinematiques* 30/31 (Autumn, 1964), pp. 71–72. (My translation.)

14. All quotations are from the subtitles for the film by Donald Richie.

15. Zambrano, "*Throne of Blood:* Kurosawa's *Macbeth*," p. 270.

16. Ibid., p. 274.

17. J. Blumenthal, "*Macbeth* into *Throne of Blood*," *Sight and Sound* (Spring, 1965), repr. *Film and the Liberal Arts*, ed. T. J. Ross (New York, 1970), pp. 124–25.

18. Michael Mullin, "*Macbeth* on Film," *Literature/Film Quarterly* 1 (1973), p. 340.

19. Skoller, "Problems of Transformation . . .," p. 455.

20. Blumenthal, "*Macbeth* into *Throne of Blood*," p. 129.

CHAPTER 11: POLANSKI'S *Macbeth*

1. Norman Silverstein's note, "The Opening Shot of Roman Polanski's *Macbeth*," *Literature/Film Quarterly* 2 (Winter, 1974), pp. 88–90, which purports to correct errors made by Kenneth Rothwell, is itself inaccurate. See my note, "The Opening Scene of Polanski's *Macbeth*," *Literature/Film Quarterly* 3 (Summer, 1975), pp. 277–78.

2. See Nigel Andrews, "*Macbeth*," *Sight and Sound* 42 (Spring, 1972), p. 108.

3. Terence St. John Marner, *Film Design* (New York: A. S. Barnes, 1974), p. 32.

4. A point made in Charles Eidsvik's forthcoming book, tentatively entitled *Cineliteracy.*

5. Normand Berlin, "*Macbeth:* Polanski and Shakespeare," *Literature/Film Quarterly* 1 (Fall, 1973), p. 292.

6. Kenneth Rothwell, "Roman Polanski's *Macbeth:* Golgotha Triumphant," *Literature/Film Quarterly* 1 (Jan., 1973), pp. 71–75.

7. Andrews, "*Macbeth,*" p. 108.

8. Frank Kermode objects strongly to the injection of a song "written by Chaucer for the court of Richard II three hundred years later, and in another country." "Shakespeare in the Movies," *Film Theory and Film Criticism,* ed. Gerald Mast and Marshall Cohen (New York: Oxford University Press, 1974), p. 326.

9. Reprinted in the Signet Classic *Macbeth,* ed. Sylvan Barnet (New York: New American Library, 1963).

10. Bernard Weinraub, Interview with Roman Polanski, *New York Times Magazine,* Dec. 12, 1971, p. 68.

11. Roman Polanski, quoted by Francis Wyndham, *Sunday Times Magazine* (London), February 28, 1971.

12. Mark Shivas, "They're Young, They're in Love, They're the Macbeths," *New York Times,* Feb. 28, 1971, Sec. D, p. 13.

13. Weinraub interview with Polanski, *New York Times Magazine,* p. 68.

14. Berlin, "*Macbeth:* Polanski and Shakespeare," pp. 291–93.

15. Pauline Kael, *Deeper Into Movies* (Boston: Little, Brown, 1972), p. 400.

16. William Johnson, *Film Quarterly* 25 (Spring, 1972), p. 45.

17. Michael Mullin, "*Macbeth* on Film," "*Literature/Film Quarterly* 1 (Fall, 1973), p. 337.

18. Weinraub interview with Polanski , *New York Times Magazine,* p. 36.

19. Interview with Polanski, *Playboy,* Dec., 1971, p. 96.


Chapter 12: Welles's *Othello*

1. *Time,* June 6, 1955.

2. Jaun Cobos, Miguel Rubio, and J. A. Pruneda, "A Trip to Don Quixoteland: Conversations with Orson Welles," *Focus on Citizen Kane,* ed. Ronald Gottesman (Englewood Cliffs: Prentice Hall, 1971), p. 8.

3. William Johnson mentions this dichotomy of styles in "Orson Welles: Of Time and Loss," *Film Quarterly* 21 (1968), p. 20.

4. Vernon Young, *On Film* (New York: Quadrangle, 1972), p. 410.

5. André Bazin, "A Review of *Othello,*" *Focus on Shakespearean Films,* ed. Charles Eckert (Englewood Cliffs: Prentice Hall, 1972), p. 78.

6. Quoted Joseph McBride, *Orson Welles* (London: Secker and Warburg, 1972), p. 111.

7. Donald Skoller, "Problems of Transformation in the Adaptation of Shakespeare's Tragedies from Play-Script to Cinema," Ph.D. dissertation, New York University, 1968, p. 352.

8. *New York Herald-Tribune,* Sept. 13, 1955.

9. Peter Cowie, *A Ribbon of Dreams* (New York: A. S. Barnes, 1973). p. 125.

10. Parker Tyler, *Sex Psyche Etcetera in the Film* (Baltimore: Penguin, 1971), p. 146.

11. Michael MacLiammoir, *Put Money In Thy Purse* (London: Methuen, 1952), repr. Eckert, *Focus on Shakespearean Films,* pp. 81–82.

12. Emphasized in Alain Marie, "L'Esthetique Tragique D'*Othello,*" *Études Cinematiques* 24–25 (1963), p. 93.

13. MacLiammoir in Eckert, *Focus on Shakespearean Films,* p. 82.

14. McBride, *Orson Welles,* p. 120.

15. "Francis Koval Interviews Welles," *Film-Makers on Filmmaking,* ed. Harry Geduld (Bloomington: Indiana University Press, 1969), p. 262.

16. Eric Bentley, *What is Theatre?* (New York: Atheneum, 1968), p. 236.

17. Young, *On Film,* p. 411.

18. Noel Burch, *Theory of Film Practice* (New York: Praeger, 1973), pp. 45–46, 94.

19. McBride, *Orson Welles,* p. 119.

20. Donald Phelps, "*Othello,*" *Film Culture* 1 (Winter, 1955), p. 32.

21. *New Yorker,* Sept. 17, 1955.

22. Bentley, *What is Theatre?,* p. 236.

23. "Explorations in No Man's Land: Shakespeare's Poetry as Theatrical Film," *Shakespeare Quarterly* 23 (1972), p. 44.

24. McBride, *Orson Welles,* p. 117.

25. Roger Manvell, *Shakespeare and the Film* (New York: Praeger, 1971), p. 63.

26. Cowie, *A Ribbon of Dreams,* p. 121.

27. Charles Higham, *The Films of Orson Welles* (Berkeley: University of California Press, 1971), p. 144.


CHAPTER 13: BURGE AND DEXTER'S *Othello*

1. Using the Signet Classic *Othello,* ed. Alvin Kernan (New York: New American Library, 1963) as a control text, and ignoring omissions

of fragments of lines, the cuts are as follows: 1.1.1–4, 11–13, 21–28, 31–35, 40–55, 68–70, 95–104, 128–34, 139–40, 159–64, 166–71; 1.2.64, 66–67, 71–75; 1.3.1–47, 101.03, 197–216, 263–69, 304–11, 314–21, 339–46; 2.1.1–4, 20–25, 31–34, 35–42, 103–07, 114–59, 178, 213–15, 219–44; 2.2.1–12; 2.3.53–55, 127–28, 178–216, 273–75, 293–307, 315–18, 319–22, 336–62; 3.1.3–24, 28–29; 3.3.63–67, 139–41; 3.4.1–22, 70–72, 103–06, 114–22, 126–31, 180–86, 191–200; 4.1.26–29, 47–49, 103–05, 115–16, 120, 121–28, 137–38, 271–72, 280–81; 4.2.18–19, 43–46, 140–43, 176–81, 206–11; 4.3.62–108; 5.1.3–5, 8–10, 28–36, 41–52, 82–83, 95, 96–98, 121–3; 5.2.43–46, 103–04, 148–49, 183, 187, 200, 235–37, 283, 303–14, 320–25, 353.

2. Alexander Anikst, in *Othello: The National Theatre Production*, ed. Kenneth Tynan (New York: Stein and Day, 1967), p. 109. Hereafter this collection will simply be referred to as "Tynan."

3. Alan Seymour, in Tynan, p. 13.

4. Ronald Bryden, in Tynan, p. 106.

5. Tynan, p. 6.

6. Marvin Rosenberg, *The Masks of Othello* (Berkeley: University of California Press, 1971), p. 13.

7. Seymour, in Tynan, p. 16.

8. Bamber Gascoigne, in Tynan, p. 107.

9. Tynan, p. 1.

10. Bryden, in Tynan, p. 106.

11. Harland Nelson, "Othello," *Film Heritage* 2 (1966) p. 19.

12. Constance Brown, "Othello," *Film Quarterly* 19 (1966), p. 50.

13. Maynard Mack, "The Jacobean Shakespeare," *Jacobean Theatre*, ed. J. R. Brown and B. Harris (New York: Capricorn, 1967), p. 30.

14. Bryden, in Tynan, p. 106.

15. For an indication of the film which might have been made from this production, see the powerful close-ups taken by Roddy McDowall in Tynan.

16. F. R. Leavis, "Diabolic Intellect and the Noble Hero: or, the Sentimentalist's Othello," *Scrutiny* 6 (1937), pp. 259–83; partially reprinted in Tynan. Rosenberg skillfully sums up the limitations of this view in *The Masks of Othello*.

17. Tynan, p. 4.

18. "The Great Sir Laurence," *Life* 56 (May 1, 1964), p. 88; quoted by James Fisher, "Olivier and the Realistic Othello," *Literature/Film Quarterly* 1 (1973), p. 322, the best treatment of the film in print.

19. Fisher, "Olivier and the Realistic Othello," pp. 322, 331.

20. Robert Hapgood, "Shakespeare and the Included Spectator," *Reinterpretations of Elizabethan Drama*, ed. Norman Rabkin (New York: Columbia University Press, 1969), p. 130.

21. Warren Coffey, *Commentary* 41 (April, 1966), p. 79.

CHAPTER 14: OLIVIER'S *Hamlet*

1. I am indebted to three discussions of this play: Maynard Mack, "The World of *Hamlet*," *The Yale Review* 41 (1952), 502–23; Maurice Charney, *Style in Hamlet* (Princeton: Princeton University Press, 1969); and Stephen Booth, "On the Value of *Hamlet*," *Reinterpretations of Elizabethan Drama*, ed. Norman Rabkin (New York: Columbia University Press, 1969), pp. 137–76. *Hamlet* on the stage has yet to find its definitive historian.

2. Harold Child, "Stage History," *Hamlet*, New Cambridge Edition, ed. John Dover Wilson (Cambridge: Cambridge University Press, 1934), p. lxxiv.

3. James Clay and Daniel Krempel, *The Theatrical Image* (New York: McGraw-Hill, 1967), p. 248.

4. Mary McCarthy, *Sights and Spectacles* (New York: Farrar, Straus, and Giroux, 1956); repr. Charles W. Eckert, ed., *Focus on Shakespearean Films* (Englewood Cliffs: Prentice Hall, 1972), p. 66.

5. Paul A. Rathburn, "Tony Richardson's *Hamlet*," Paper delivered at 1974 MLA Seminar, "Shakespeare on Film," to be included in *Dreams and Realities: Explorations in Shakespearean Psychology* (forthcoming), which will treat Peter Hall's *Dream* as well.

6. Raymond Durgnat, *Films and Feelings* (Cambridge, Mass.: M.I.T. Press, 1971), p. 49.

7. *Harper's* 197 (Sept., 1948), p. 117.

8. See Frances Yates, *Theatre of the World* (Chicago: University of Chicago Press, 1969).

9. The classic exposition is Ernest Jones, *Hamlet and Oedipus* (Garden City: Doubleday, 1954). John Ashworth's acid attack "Olivier, Freud, and Hamlet," *Atlantic Monthly* 183 (May, 1949), pp. 30–33, was sensibly answered by Simon O. Lesser, "Freud and *Hamlet* Again," *The American Imago* 12 (1955), pp. 207–20.

10. Sigmund Freud, *Interpretation of Dreams*, Standard Edition, IV, pp. 264–66; repr. M. D. Faber, *The Design Within: Psychoanalytic Approaches to Shakespeare* (New York: Science House, 1970), p. 84.

11. "An Essay in *Hamlet*," *The Film Hamlet: A Record of its Production*, ed. Brenda Cross (London: Saturn, 1948), pp. 11–12, 15.

12. Arthur Colby Sprague and J. C. Trewin, *Shakespeare's Plays Today* (London: Sidgwick and Jackson, 1970), p. 19.

13. Ashworth, "Olivier, Freud, and Hamlet," p. 30.

14. G. Wilson Knight, *The Wheel of Fire*, 5th rev. ed. (New York: Meridian, 1957), pp. 17–46.

15. Felix Barker, *The Oliviers* (London: Hamish Hamilton, 1953), p. 262.

16. Stressed by Donald Skoller, "Problems of Transformation in the Adaptation of Shakespeare's Tragedies from Play-Script to Cinema," Ph.D. dissertation, New York University, 1968, p. 296.

17. Noted by Robert Duffy in a paper delivered at the Modern Language Association Seminar, "Shakespeare on Film" (1974), and to appear in *Literature/Film Quarterly*.

18. On Walton's music, see Roger Manvell and John Huntley, *The Technique of Film Music* (New York: Hastings House, 1957); Charles Hurtgen, "The Operatic Character of Background Music in Film Adaptations of Shakespeare," *Shakespeare Quarterly* 20 (1969), pp. 53–64.

19. For a sampling of the diverse commentary on this film, see: James Agee, *Agee on Film* (New York: Grosset and Dunlap, 1969), pp. 388–96; R. W. Babcock, *College English* 11 (1950), pp. 256–65; J. Baley, *National Review* 137 (1948), pp. 603–06; George Barbarow, *Hudson Review* 2 (1949), pp. 98–104; John Mason Brown, *Saturday Review*, Sept. 2, 1948, pp. 26–28; Richard Flatter, *Shakespeare Jahrbuch* 87–88 (1952), pp. 58–60; Bernard Grebanier, *The Heart of Hamlet* (New York: Apollo, 1967); Jay L. Halio, *Literature/Film Quarterly* 1 (1973), pp. 316–20; R. Herring, *Life and Letters* 57 (1948), pp. 183–92; Arthur Hopkins, *Theatre Arts* 32 (1948), pp. 30–31; Roger Manvell, *Shakespeare and the Film* (New York: Praeger, 1971), pp. 40–47; John McCarten, *New Yorker*, Oct. 2, 1948; James G. McManaway, *Shakespeare Association Bulletin* 24 (1949), pp. 3–11; James Phillips, *Hollywood Quarterly* (Spring, 1951), pp. 224–36; Parker Tyler, *Kenyon Review* 11 (1949), pp. 527–32. Alan Dent's script was published as *Hamlet: The Film and the Play* (London: World Film Pub., 1948).

CHAPTER 15: KOZINTSEV'S *Hamlet*

1. Grigori Kozintsev, *Shakespeare: Time and Conscience* (New York: Hill and Wang, 1966), pp. 163, 108, 140, 232. This key document for study of the film, abbreviated hereafter as *S:T&C*, contains stills, his production diary, and a critical essay on the play. See also Renate Georgi, "*Hamlet* in Filmischer Poesie," *Shakespeare Jahrbuch* (Weimar) 106 (1970), pp. 176–201; Ronald Hayman, "Shakespeare on the Screen," *Times Literary Supplement* (London), Sept. 26, 1968, pp. 1081–82; Grigori Kozintsev, "*Hamlet* and *King Lear*: Stage and Film," *Shakespeare 1971*, ed. Clifford Leech and J. M. R. Margeson (Toronto: Toronto University Press, 1972),

pp. 190–99 and "The *Hamlet* within Me," *Films and Filming* 8 (Sept., 1962), p. 20; Roger Manvell, *Shakespeare and the Film* (New York: Praeger, 1971), pp. 77–85; Donald Skoller, "Problems of Transformation in the Adaptation of Shakespeare's Tragedies from Play-Script to Cinema," Ph.D. dissertation, New York University, 1968. For a selection of reviews, see John Coleman, *New Statesman*, Jan. 8, 1965; Judith Christ, *New York Herald-Tribune*, Sept. 15, 1964; Peter Cowie, *Films and Filming*, Feb., 1965; Bosley Crowther, *New York Times*, Sept. 15, 1964; Penelope Houston, *Monthly Film Bulletin* (1965); Joan Irwin, *Montreal Star*, May 27, 1967; James Kennedy, *Guardian*, May 2, 1964; Michael Kustow, *Sight and Sound* (Summer, 1964); Dwight MacDonald, *Esquire*, Dec., 1964; *Newsweek*, Mar. 14, 1966; Dilys Powell, *Sunday Times* (London), Jan. 10, 1965; Isabel Quigley, *Spectator*, Jan. 15, 1965; Eric Rhode, *Encounter* 23 (Nov., 1964); David Robinson, *Times* (London), May 1, 1964; *Saturday Review*, May 21, 1966; Kenneth Tynan, *Observer* (London), Jan. 10, 1965.

2. Two good discussions of the art of wide-screen, of which Kozintsev's *Hamlet* is a very fine example: Charles Barr, "Cinemascope Before and After," *Film Theory and Criticism*, ed. Gerald Mast and Marshall Cohen (New York: Oxford University Press, 1974), pp. 120–46; Karel Reisz and Gavin Millar, *The Technique of Film Editing*, 2nd ed. (New York: Hastings, 1968), pp. 275–96.

3. *S:T&C*, p. 233.

4. Ibid., p. 258.

5. Ibid., p. 266.

6. Kozintsev, "*Hamlet* and *King Lear* . . . ," p. 193.

7. *S:T&C*, p. 219.

8. Ibid., p. 156.

9. See the suggestive tracing of the theme of "mortality" in Maynard Mack, "The World of *Hamlet*," repr. *Hamlet* (Signet Classic Edition), ed. Edward Hubler (New York, 1963), p. 247.

10. *S:T&C*, p. 225.

11. Ibid., p. 222.

12. "*Hamlet* and *King Lear* . . . ," p. 192.

13. Frederick Turner, *Shakespeare and the Nature of Time* (Oxford: Oxford University Press, 1971), p. 81. The symbolic value of the opening scene was described in Roy Walker's *The Time is Out of Joint* (London: Dakers, 1948), pp. 4–9.

14. Because the film is in Russian, I include the following list of cuts and alterations as a supplement to the outline. Kozintsev omits the entire first scene, mentions of suicide in the first soliloquy, the "vicious mole" speech, all doubts about the authenticity of the ghost, the swearing on the swords, Polonius's comic instructions to Reynaldo (in fact, most of the play's

humor has been omitted), the welcoming of, Rosencrantz and Guildenstern by Claudius and their report about Fortinbras's uncle, the passage
about the child actors, Polonius's announcement of the players, the section
of the Pyrrus speech describing the sword sticking in the air, the last
section of "O what a rogue and peasant slave am I," Rosencrantz and
Guildenstern with the King and Polonius's declaration of his plan to
"loose" his daughter to Hamlet, Ophelia's lament "O what a noble mind
is there overthrown," nearly all of Hamlet's instructions to the players,
Hamlet's praise of Horatio, the dumb-show, much of the Player King's
speech on the weakness of men and their intentions, the prayer scene,
Hamlet's emphasis on sex in the closet scene, Claudius's learning what
happened in the closet scene, "How all occasions do inform against me,"
the Gertrude and Ophelia scene, Horatio and the sailors, the reading of
the letters, the second gravedigger and their jokes including "to act, to do,
to perform," Gertrude's blessing over the grave of Ophelia, Hamlet's
description of the pirate adventure, the scene where Claudius and Laertes
plan Hamlet's death is shifted to after the graveyard scene, much of the
humor in Osric's scene, all the lines between the killing of Claudius and
"the rest is silence," the lines about Fortinbras taking over and Horatio's
declaration that he will tell Hamlet's story. Added are a number of scenes
without lines, such as the opening and closing images, the clock, the
panicked horses, Ophelia's being harnessed into mourning, Hamlet's
journey on the road back to the castle past a war-torn village. Dramatized
in the film but narrated in the play are: Claudius's court revels, Hamlet's
visit to Ophelia's bedroom, her body floating in a pool, Hamlet's switching
of the death warrants aboard ship.

CHAPTER 16: *King Lear:* BROOK AND KOZINTSEV

1. Simone de Beauvoir, *The Coming of Age* (New York, 1973), p. 245.

2. William Johnson, *Film Quarterly* 25 (Spring, 1972), p. 42.

3. Jan Kott, *"King Lear, or Endgame," Shakespeare Our Contemporary*
(Garden City: Doubleday, 1966). Jack MacGowran gives a Beckettian
flavor to the fool just as Patrick Magee lends overtones of Weiss's de Sade
from *Marat/Sade* to Cornwall.

4. Grigori Kozintsev, *"Hamlet* and *King Lear:* Stage and Film," *Shakespeare 1971,* ed. Clifford Leech and J. M. R. Margeson (Toronto: Toronto
University Press, 1972), p. 199.

5. J. C. Trewin, *Peter Brook* (London: Macdonald, 1971), p. 125.

6. Kozintsev, *Shakespeare 1971,* p. 197.

7. Brook, quoted in Roger Manvell, *Shakespeare and the Film* (New

York: Praeger, 1971), p. 137. Several versions of the script are available for study on microfilm at the Folger Shakespeare Library.

8. David Robinson, *Financial Times* (London), July 23, 1971.

9. Antonin Artaud, *The Theater and Its Double* (New York: Grove, 1958), p. 101.

10. Marvin Rosenberg, *The Masks of King Lear* (Berkeley: University of California Press, 1972), p. 24.

11. Vincent Canby, *New York Times* (unidentified clipping).

12. The Stratford-upon-Avon production (1959) was described by Muriel St. Clare Byrne, *Shakespeare Quarterly* 11 (1960), p. 198.

13. William Chaplin, "Our Darker Purpose: Peter Brook's *King Lear*," *Arion* n.s. I (1974), p. 170.

14. Kozintsev, *Shakespeare 1971*, pp. 194–95, 199.

15. Maurice Yacowar, *Take One* 3 (Jan/Feb. 1971), p. 29.

16. Kozintsev, *Shakespeare 1971*, p. 196.

17. A garland of further reviews and articles: for Brook's *King Lear*, Nigel Andrews, *Sight and Sound* 40 (Autumn, 1971), pp. 223–24; Michael Birkett (interview), *Journal of the Society for Film and Television Arts* (Autumn, 1969); Peter Brook (interview), *Evening Standard* (London), Mar. 7, 1969; Eric Braun, *Film and Filming* 18 (Oct., 1971), pp. 54–56; *Cue*, Nov. 27, 1971, p. 76; *Films in Review* 22 (Dec., 1971), pp. 637–38; *Filmmakers Newsletter* 5 (Dec., 1971); Molly Haskell, *Film 1971–72*, ed. David Denby (New York: Simon and Schuster, 1972), pp. 246–49; Pauline Keal, *Deeper Into Movies* (Boston: Little, Brown, 1973), pp. 354–57; Frank Kermode, *Film Theory and Criticism*, ed. Gerald Mast and Marshall Cohen (New York: Oxford University Press, 1972), pp. 327–32; Arthur Knight, *Saturday Review*, Dec. 4, 1974, p. 18; Robert Speaight, *Shakespeare Quarterly* 22 (Autumn, 1971), pp. 359–64.

Kozintsev *King Lear:* Nigel Andrews, *Sight and Sound* 41 (Summer, 1972), pp. 171–72; Alexander Anikst, *Moscow News* 2 (1971) and *Soviet Literature* 6, pp. 176–82; *Audience* 43 (Jan., 1972); *Commonweal* 95 (Jan. 21, 1972); *Film Quarterly* 25 (Spring, 1972); *Films and Filming* 18 (Aug., 1972); *Film Society Review* 7 (Dec., 1971); *Journal of Popular Film* 1 (Winter, 1972); Grigori Kozintsev, *Shakespeare: Time and Conscience* (New York: Hill and Wang, 1967); Derek Malcolm, *Guardian* (London), June 29, 1972; *Punch* July 5, 1972; David Robinson, *Financial Times* (London), July 7, 1972; *Show* 2 (Feb., 1972); Dilys Powell, *Sunday Times* (London), July 2, 1972; Sergei Yutkevitch, *Sight and Sound* 40 (1971), pp. 192–96.

# Index

Abenheimer, K. M., 36 n2
*Act Without Words,* 240
Adaptation: Shakespeare film as, 14, 15
Agee, James, 4, 127 n9, 129, 129 n12, 133
Aldridge, Michael, 115
*Alexander Nevsky* (Eisenstein), 116
*Amarcord* (Fellini), 74
Anderson, Judith, 149
Anderson, Lindsay, 116
Andrews, Nigel, 162 n2, 166 n7
Anikst, Alexander, 192
Annis, Francesca, 171–2
*Antony and Cleopatra* (Heston), 2
Aristotle, 3
Armes, Roy, 5 n17
Arnheim, Rudolf, 5 n14
Artaud, Antonin, 245
Ashworth, John, 213 n9, 214 n13, 215
*Asphalt Jungle,* 96
*As You Like It,* 34, 77, 138
*As You Like It* (Czinner), 1, 13, 30
Auden, W. H., 224

Bacon, Francis, 107
Ball, Robert Hamilton, ix
Bandello, Matteo, 79
Barber, C. L., 72, 138–9 n5
Barker, Felix, 215 n15
Barr, Charles, 219 n2
Baxter, John, 42
Baxter, Keith, 115
Bazin, Andre, 5, 6, 10, 130 n14, 133, 175, 176 n5, 251
Bean, Robin, 124 n4
Beauvoir, Simone de, 235
Beckett, Samuel, 240, 330 n3
Beckley, Tony, 115
Bentley, Eric, 98, 188 n16, 189–90 n22
Bergman, Ingmar, 23, 104, 184, 251
Bergner, Elizabeth, 1
Berkeley, Busby, 39
Berlin, Normand, 162 n5, 171
Berman, Ronald, 143

Billy Budd, 239
Blake, William, 41
Blocking, 23–4
Bluestone, George, 5 n16, 15 n43
Blumenthal, J., 19, 158 n17 & n20
Bogdanovich, Peter, 116
Bower, Dallas, 124
Bradley, David. See *Julius Caesar*
Brando, Marlon, 99, 100, 250
Brecht, Bertholt, 244
Brook, Peter, 8, 11, 30, 34, 59, 153. See also *King Lear*
Brooke, Arthur, 79
Brown, Constance, 137, 144, 146–7 n13, 199 n12
Brown, Joe E., 23, 46, 49
Brown, John Russell, 3 n6, 6, 12, 21 n52, 87, 90 n13
Brueghel, 224
Bryden, Ronald, 192 n4, 198 n10, 202 n14
Burch, Noel, 189
Burge, Stuart, 191–206. See also *Julius Caesar; Othello*
Burton, Richard, 21, 68, 72, 78
Byrne, Muriel St. Clare, 247 n12

*Cabinet of Dr. Caligari,* 193
Cagney, Jimmy, 39
Calhern, Louis, 96
Cameron, Kate, 43
Canby, Vincent, 246 n11
Carroll, Sidney, 49–50
Castellani, Renato. See *Romeo and Juliet*
*Castle of the Spider's Web* (Kurosawa), 153. See also *Throne of Blood*
Cervantes, 107
Chaplin, William, 247 n13
Child, Harold, 208
*Chimes at Midnight* (Welles), x, 2, 9, 18, 19, 22, 26, 30–32, 106–21, 128, 133–5, 138, 155, 168, 268–72
Cirollo, Albert, 84 n6, 85 n9

Clay, James, 4, 41 n10, 43 n16, 209 n3
Cloutier, Suzanne, 186
Cobos, Juan, 109 n2, 110 n6 & n7, 111 n9, 114 n12 & n14, 116 n19, 176 n3
Coffey, Warren, 204 n21
Coleridge, Samuel Taylor, 148
Composition, Visual, 28–9
Conrad, Joseph, 176
Contre-Machiavel, 142
Corneille, 150
Costume, 22–3
Cowie, Peter, 112 n11, 181
Critics, 3–5, 15–16
Cukor, George, 1. See also Romeo and Juliet
Czinner, Paul, 1. See also As You Like It

Dean, Leonard, 92
Dean of the Faculty of Theology, Paris, 73
de Beauvoir, Simone, 235
de Havilland, Olivia, 39, 43
Dehn, Paul, 15 n44, 99 n11
DeMille, Cecil B., 95
Dench, Judi, 64
Dent, Alan, 124, 208
Deren, Maya, 16 n45
Dexter, John, 175, 191–206. See also Othello (Burge)
Dieterle, William, 36–50. See also Midsummer Night's Dream, A
Disney, Walt, 122
Duffy, Robert, 217 n17
Dunlop, Frank. See Winter's Tale
Durgnat, Raymond, 126, 133 n20, 211 n6

Eckert, Charles, 17 n48
Eidsvik, Charles, 55 n3, 162 n4
Eisenstein, Sergei, 6, 115–16, 131, 169, 175, 185, 193, 226, 251
Eliot, T. S., 163
"Enter Hamlet" (Mogubgub), 19
Estene, Michael, 153 n13
Evans, Maurice, 149–50

Faces, 23
Fairbanks, Douglas, 1
Fairy Queen, 37
Faithfull, Marianne, 21
Falstaff (Welles). See Chimes at Midnight
Fellini, Federico, 74, 184
Fender, Stephen, 36 n1
Ferguson, Otis, 42
Filmic, 10–12

Film Noir, 102
Finch, Jon, 171–2
Finlay, Frank, 193, 205–6, 250
Fisher, James, 203 n19
Flynn, Erroll, 77
Foakes, R. A., 4 n8
Frazer, Sir James, 109
Freud, Sigmund, 14, 126, 151, 213, 214
Fried, Yan. See Twelfth Night
Frye, Northrop, 73, 77
Fuegi, John, 3 n5, 10, 10 n31, 101 n14, 190
Furse, Roger, 210
Fuseli, Henry, 41

Galileo, 107
Gangster films, 102
Gascoigne, Bamber, 195 n8
Geduld, Harry, 124 n2, 126, 128 n11, 131 n15, 133
Gentillet, 142
Gessner, Robert, 5
Gesture, 21–2
Gianetti, Louis, 83
Gielgud, John, 93, 98, 101, 115, 140, 214, 250. See also Hamlet
Golden Bough, 109
Graduate, The (Nichols), 86
Graham, Virginia, 141 n7
Granville-Barker, Harley, 42
Griffin, Alice, 138
Gross, Roger, 13 n37
Gui, Weston, 36 n2

Hall, Peter, 51–65. See also Midsummer Night's Dream, A
Hamlet, 16–17, 19–20, 22, 24, 32, 34, 78, 93, 207–35. See also "Enter Hamlet"
Hamlet (stage, Gielgud, 1936), 214
Hamlet (Gielgud), 8
Hamlet (Kozintsev), x, 2, 13–14, 20, 25, 32–4, 81, 90, 215, 217–34, 246, 248, 251, 300–04
Hamlet (Olivier), x, 1, 8, 13–15, 17, 19, 21, 27–9, 32, 90, 137, 145, 207–19, 225, 228, 231–2, 251, 296–300
Hamlet (Richardson), 2, 8, 12, 20–21, 27, 32–4, 90, 211
Hamlet (Wirth), 2, 8, 13, 19, 27, 211
Hancock, John, 47
Hapgood, Robert, 102, 203–4
Harbage, Alfred, 148
Harvey, Laurence, 21
Havilland, Olivia de, 39, 43
Hayman, Ronald, 81
Hazlitt, William, 37

*Heart of Darkness,* 176
*Henry IV, Parts 1 & 2:* 26, 106–21, 125, 127, 133, 135. See also *Chimes at Midnight*
*Henry V,* 29, 95, 107
*Henry V* (Olivier), x, 1, 8, 10, 12–13, 17–18, 50, 81, 115–16, 122–35, 137, 145, 212, 214, 217, 250, 272–5
*Henry VI, Part 3:* 137
Herbert, Hugh, 49
Heston, Charlton. See *Antony and Cleopatra*
Higham, Charles, 115, 190
History of Shakespeare films, ix, 1–2
Holinshed, 14, 106, 108, 121, 167
Houseman, John, 95–6, 99, 101
Houston, Penelope, 115 n15
Howard, Leslie, 1, 91
Hughes, Ted, 244
Hunter, Ian, 39, 50
Huntley, John, 217 n18
Hurtgen, Charles, 32, 33 n60, 217 n18
Hussey, Olivia, 91

"Icarus," 224
Imagery, 3–4, 11, 16–20
*Immortal Story, The* (Welles), 148
*Importance of Being Earnest, The* (Wilde), 15
Interpretation: Shakespeare film as, 12–13
*Ivan the Terrible* (Eisenstein), 193

James, Henry, 5
Jannings, Emil. See *Othello* (Buchowetzki)
Jarvet, Yuri, 246
Johnson, Samuel, 149 n4
Johnson, William, 110 n5, 115 n17, 119 n20, 172 n16, 176 n3, 237 n2
Jones, Ernest, 14, 213–14
Jonson, Ben, 144
Jorgens, Jack J., xi, 161
Jorgensen, Paul A, 26 n56, 89
Jory, Victor, 39, 42
*Julius Caesar,* 24, 92–105
*Julius Caesar* (stage, Welles, 1937), 94–5, 99
*Julius Caesar* (Bradley), 18, 22, 27, 102–3
*Julius Caesar* (Burge), 2
*Julius Caesar* (Mankiewicz), x, 1, 12, 24, 90, 92–105, 137–8, 265–8

Kael, Pauline, 44, 87, 112, 114, 172
Kafka, Franz, 152, 176, 210, 228

Kauffmann, Stanley, 4, 10 n30
Kean, Charles, 37
Kermode, Frank, 166 n8
*King Lear,* 16, 21–2, 30, 89, 107, 138, 235–51
*King Lear* (stage, 1959), 247 n12
*King Lear* (Brook), x, 2, 9, 14, 17, 18, 23, 26–7, 32, 90, 152, 228, 235–51, 304–8
*King Lear* (Kozintsev), x, 2, 19, 26–7, 29, 138, 235–51, 308–11
Kitchin, Lawrence, 2 n3
Knight, Arthur, 8 n26
Knight, G. Wilson, 41, 43, 215
Knox, Alexander, 6 n21
Kott, Jan, 14, 161, 240, 251
Koval, Francis, 188 n15
Kozintsev, Grigori, 10, 104, 119 n21, 153, 169, 218–51. See also *Hamlet; King Lear*
Kracauer, Siegfried, 5 n15, 17 n47, 127 n10
Krempel, Daniel, 4, 41 n10, 43 n16, 209 n3
Kurosawa, Akira, 153–60. See also *Throne of Blood*

Lawson, John Howard, 5–6, 20
Leavis, F. R., 189, 203
Lejeune, C. A., 122 n1
Lesser, Simon O., 213 n9
Limbourg Brothers, 134
*Little Caesar,* 102
*Long Day's Journey Into Night,* 128
Losey, Joseph, 251
Louise, Anita, 39, 42

*Macbeth,* 16, 21, 27, 30, 93, 148–74
*Macbeth* (stage, Olivier), 160
*Macbeth* (Kurosawa). See *Throne of Blood*
*Macbeth* (Polanski), x, 2, 9, 19–20, 23, 27, 29, 32, 90, 158, 161–74, 250, 286–90
*Macbeth* (Schaefer), x, 2, 18, 20, 27, 30, 148–53, 156, 166
*Macbeth* (Welles), x, 1, 12, 17–18, 20, 26–8, 33, 90, 114–15, 151–3, 158, 162, 166, 185, 210, 228, 245, 250, 279–82
McBride, Joseph, 121 n22, 148, 177 n6, 188 n19, 190
McCarthy, Mary, 209, 214
MacGowran, Jack, 330 n3
Machiavelli, 107
Mack, Maynard, 200, 226 n9
MacLiammoir, Michael, 187 n11, 188 n13

Magee, Patrick, 330 n3
*Magnificent Ambersons, The* (Welles), 110, 175
Mankiewicz, Joseph, 92–105. See also *Julius Caesar*
Manson, Charles, 161
Manvell, Roger, 96, 131 n15, 143 n9, 151 n7, 190, 217 n18
*Marat/Sade* (Weiss), 330 n3
Marie, Alain, 187 n12
Marx Brothers, 75
Mason, James, 97, 250
*Meet Me in St. Louis*, 145
Melville, Herman, 239
Mendelssohn, Felix, 1, 11, 23, 32, 38, 41, 43, 47–8, 57
*Merchant of Venice*, 77
*Merry Wives of Windsor*, 68
*Midsummer Night's Dream, A*, 16, 22, 24, 26, 32, 36–7, 66, 77, 79. See also *Fairy Queen, The*
*Midsummer Night's Dream, A* (stage, Covent Garden, 1816), 37
*Midsummer Night's Dream, A* (stage, Charles Kean, 1856), 37
*Midsummer Night's Dream, A* (stage, Beerbohm Tree, 1900), 38
*Midsummer Night's Dream, A* (stage, Granville-Barker, 1914), 42
*Midsummer Night's Dream, A* (stage, Hancock, 1966), 47
*Midsummer Night's Dream, A* (Hall), x, 2, 11–12, 17, 21, 23–4, 33, 44, 51–65, 84, 250, 255–8
*Midsummer Night's Dream, A* (Reinhardt and Dieterle), x, xi, 1, 10, 13, 19, 21, 32, 36–50, 51, 53–4, 57, 63–4, 251, 252–5
Millar, Gavin, 219 n2
*Mirror For Magistrates*, 136
*Miss Julie* (Sjoberg), 74
Mogubgub, Fred. See "Enter Hamlet"
Montage, 29–30
Montaigne, 107
Moore, Roger, 37
Moreau, Jeanne, 115
Morgenstern, Joseph, 111 n8
Morris, Peter, 101 n13
Movement, 24–5
*Much Ado About Nothing*, 2
Mullin, Michael, 158 n18, 172
Munsterberg, Hugo, 11 n32
Music, 30, 32, 37. See also Mendelssohn; Purcell; Rosza; Rota; Shostakovich; Walton

Naremore, James, 26 n55, 151 n9, 152 n10
National Theatre Company of Great Britain. See *Othello* (Burge)
Nelson, Harland, 199
*Night at the Opera* (Marx Brothers), 75
Nijinska, Bronislava, 39

*Oedipus at Colonus*, 235
Olivier, Laurence, 1, 81, 84, 122–47, 191–217, 244, 250. See *As You Like It* (Czinner); *Hamlet; Henry V; Macbeth* (stage); *Othello* (Burge); *Richard III*
*Othello*, 16, 21–2, 24, 26–7, 32, 67, 138, 175–206
*Othello* (Buchowetzki), 22
*Othello* (Burge and Dexter), x, 2, 7–8, 15, 59, 137, 160, 175, 191–206, 250, 294–6
*Othello* (Welles), x, 1, 11, 22, 24–5, 28–30, 33, 90, 114–15, 175–90, 191–4, 206, 210, 251, 290–94
*Othello* (Yutkevich), 2, 18, 26–7, 32

Pasinetti, P. M., 101 n16, 103
Pasternak, Boris, 13
Peer Gynt, 5
Phelps, Donald, 189 n20
Phillips, James E., 95 n7, 126 n5
Pirandello, Luigi, 231
Plutarch, 14, 95
Polanski, Roman, 147, 161–74. See also *Macbeth*
Popularizing Shakespeare, 2–3, 13
Pound, Ezra, 14
Powell, Dick, 39
Prendergast, Roy M., 126 n8
Presentation: Shakespeare film as, 12
Prokosch, Mike, 109 n1
Props, 27
*Psycho* (Hitchcock), 185
Purcell, Henry, 37. See also *Fairy Queen, The*

Racine, 150
Rackham, Arthur, 39
Rathburn, Paul A., 211 n5
Realism, 5, 8–10
"Real Thing, The" (James), 5
Reddington, John, 3 n4
Rehan, Ada, 67
Reinhardt, Max, 36–50. See also *Midsummer Night's Dream, A*
Reisz, Karel, 219 n2

Renoir, Jean, 211, 251
Renting Shakespeare films, 252
*Richard II*, 107, 120, 133, 138, 142
*Richard III*, 16, 95, 97, 136–47, 158
*Richard III* (Olivier), x, 2, 21, 24, 28, 32, 136–47, 212, 214, 275–9
Richardson, Ralph, 121
Richardson, Tony. See *Hamlet*
Richie, Donald, 148–9, 155 n14, 156
Rigg, Diana, 61
Rilla, Wolf, 5–6
Robey, George, 126
Robinson, David, 19 n49, 244 n8
Rodway, Norman, 115
*Romeo and Juliet*, 16, 17, 21–2, 24, 27, 29, 62, 79–91
*Romeo and Juliet* (stage, Forbes-Robertson, 1895), 90
*Romeo and Juliet* (stage, Zeffirelli), 80, 87
*Romeo and Juliet* (Castellani), 1, 2, 15, 19, 25–6, 32–3, 89–91
*Romeo and Juliet* (Cukor), 1, 10, 90–91
*Romeo and Juliet* (Zeffirelli), x, 2, 18, 19, 23, 27, 29, 79–91, 250, 261–5
*Romeus and Iuliet, The Tragicall Historye of* (Brooke, Bandello), 79
Rooney, Mickey, 23, 39
Rose, Mark, 92 n2
Rosenberg, Marvin, 194, 246 n10
Rossetti, Dante Gabriel, 217
Rosza, Miklos, 32, 96, 105 n24
Rota, Nino, 32
Rothwell, Kenneth, 161 n1, 164 n6
Royal Shakespeare Company, 2, 51. See also *Midsummer Night's Dream, A* (Hall)
Rubio, Miguel, 109 n2, 110 n6 & n7, 111 n9, 114 n12 & n14, 116 n19, 176 n3
Rutherford, Margaret, 115

Salvini, Tomasso, 246
Sarris, Andrew, 5
Saturnalia, 72–8, 80
Schaefer, George, 148–51. See also *Macbeth*
Schein, Harry, 141–2 n8, 145 n12
Schell, Maximilian. See *Hamlet* (Wirth)
Scofield, Paul, 160, 237, 239, 246, 250
Seltzer, Daniel, 110
Seneca, 137
Setting, 25–6
*Seventh Seal* (Bergman), 184
Seymour, Alan, 192 n3, 195 n7

Shaw, George Bernard, 67, 90
Shearer, Norma, 1, 91
Shentall, Susan, 91
Shingleton, Wilfrid, 162
Shirley, Frances, 33 n61
Shivas, Mark, 171 n12
Shostakovich, Dmitri, 32, 239, 246
Silent Shakespeare films, ix, 1
Silverstein, Norman, 161 n1
Simmons, Jean, 21
Simon, John, 4, 81
Sjoberg, Alf, 74
Skoller, Donald, 28, 29 n57, 101 n15, 150 n5, 151 n6, 158 n19, 177–8 n7, 216 n16
Smith, Maggie, 206
Smoktunovsky, Innokenti, 160, 231, 233
Solomon, Stanley J., 16–17
Sontag, Susan, 4–7, 13
Sound effects, 33
Sprague, Arthur Colby, 214 n12
Stanislavsky, Konstantin, 11
Style: Significant, 7, 34–5
Subtext, 11

*Taming of the Shrew, The*, 66–78
*Taming of the Shrew* (stage, 1888), 67
*Taming of the Shrew* (Taylor), 1, 9
*Taming of the Shrew* (Zeffirelli), x, 2, 9, 27, 29, 66–78, 80–81, 85, 111, 155, 250, 258–61
Taylor, Elizabeth, 68, 72
Taylor, John Russell, 43
Taylor, Sam. See *Taming of the Shrew*
Television: Shakespeare on, 1, 12
Thalberg, Irving, 1. See also *Romeo and Juliet* (Cukor)
Theatre and film, 4, 7–8
Theilade, Nini, 39
*This Sporting Life* (Anderson), 116
*Throne of Blood* (Kurosawa), x, 2, 9, 18, 20, 23, 28, 32, 90, 153–60, 166, 173, 210, 250, 282–6
Translation: Shakespeare film as, 14
Traversi, D. A., 69
Tree, Herbert Beerbohm, 38, 101
*Tres Riches Heures du Duc de Berry*, 134
Trewin, J. C., 214 n12, 243 n5
*Trial, The*, 176
*Troilus and Cressida*, 94
Turner, Frederick, 231 n13
*Twelfth Night*, 22, 138
*Twelfth Night* (Freid), 2, 25
Tyler, Parker, 187
Tynan, Kenneth, 161, 171, 192, 198

Van Gogh, Vincent, 191
Verbal performance, 20–21
*Volpone* (Jonson), 144

Walker, Roy, 9 n27, 26 n56, 93 n4
Walton, William, 32, 131 n16, 145, 217
"Wasteland, The," 163
Weinraub, Bernard, 170 n10, 171 n13, 173 n18
Weiss, Peter, 330 n3
Welles, Orson, 10, 14, 15, 23, 35, 60, 94–5, 99, 104–5, 106–21, 151–3, 169, 175–90, 219, 244, 250. See also *Chimes at Midnight; Immortal Story; Julius Caesar* (stage); *Macbeth; Magnificent Ambersons; Othello*
Whitehead, Peter, 124 n4
Whiting, Leonard, 91
Widescreen, 219

Williamson, Nicoll, 21
Wilson, John Dover, 94 n5, 208
*Winter's Tale, The,* 67
*Winter's Tale, The* (Dunlop), 2, 8
Wirth, Franz Peter. See *Hamlet*
Worth, Irene, 250
Wyndham, Francis, 171 n11

Yacowar, Maurice, 249 n15
Yates, Frances, 211 n8
Young, David P., 36 n1
Young, Vernon, 176 n4, 188 n17
Yutkevich, Sergei. See *Othello*

Zambrano, Ana Laura, 156 n15 & n16
Zeffirelli, Franco, 9, 15, 66–91, 110, 171, 244. See also *Romeo and Juliet; Taming of the Shrew, The*

VBee